AFTER THE TRADE IS MADE

PROCESSING SECURITIES TRANSACTIONS

DAVID M. WEISS

PORTFOLIO

PORTFOLIO
Published by the Penguin Group
Penguin Group (USA) Inc., 375 Hudson Street, New York, New York 10014, U.S.A. • Penguin Group (Canada), 90 Eglinton Avenue East, Suite 700, Toronto, Ontario, Canada M4P 2Y3 (a division of Pearson Penguin Canada Inc.) • Penguin Books Ltd, 80 Strand, London WC2R 0RL, England • Penguin Ireland, 25 St. Stephen's Green, Dublin 2, Ireland (a division of Penguin Books Ltd) • Penguin Books Australia Ltd, 250 Camberwell Road, Camberwell, Victoria 3124, Australia (a division of Pearson Australia Group Pty Ltd) • Penguin Books India Pvt Ltd, 11 Community Centre, Panchsheel Park, New Delhi – 110 017, India • Penguin Group (NZ), Cnr Airborne and Rosedale Roads, Albany, Auckland 1310, New Zealand (a division of Pearson New Zealand Ltd) • Penguin Books (South Africa) (Pty) Ltd, 24 Sturdee Avenue, Rosebank, Johannesburg 2196, South Africa

Penguin Books Ltd, Registered Offices:
80 Strand, London WC2R 0RL, England

This second revised edition published in 2006 by
Portfolio, a member of Penguin Group (USA) Inc.

1 3 5 7 9 10 8 6 4 2

PUBLISHER'S NOTE

This publication is designed to provide accurate and authoritative information in regard to the subject matter covered. It is sold with the understanding that the publisher is not engaged in rendering legal, accounting or other professional services. If you require legal advice or other expert assistance, you should seek the services of a competent professional.

LIBRARY OF CONGRESS CATALOGING IN PUBLICATION DATA
Weiss, David M.
After the trade is made : processing securities transactions / David M. Weiss.
p. cm.
Includes index.
ISBN 1-59184-127-5
1. Stock exchanges—United States. 2. Securities—United States. 3. Commodity exchanges—United States. I. Title.

UG4910.W365 2006
332.64'273—dc22 2006045394

Printed in the United States of America
Set in Minion and Requiem
Designed by Amy Hill

To my immediate world:
Marcia, Randi, Craig, Amy, Nicole, Jenna, and Carly

To an industry that I have enjoyed being part of for all these years, I am proud to be one of you. I trust this book is a worthy return on the investment that you made in me.

Thank you.

Preface

I have been fortunate to participate in an exciting and ever-changing industry. The dramatic changes that have occurred are borne out in the major differences that exist between the first and second editons and the second and third editions of this book. One edition, though 80% written, never made it to the publisher because the industry changed directions, necessitating a major rewrite. This edition, like the previous editions, is as up to date as the production schedule would allow.

The industry has changed in many ways since the last edition was published. Technology has played an ever-increasing role in our products and processes. Globalization, a new word then, is now an everyday term. Electronic trading is now a major force in the market. Structured products, once thought to be a strange, one-of-a-kind product, trade alongside other instruments. The efficiencies brought by technology on trade processing, settlement, and finance have permitted these products to be processed in a non-cost-offensive manner.

The growth of the institutional side of the business, which includes new types of entities, has made its own demands on the brokerage business. New trading strategies and complex order and reporting requirements have impacted operations. Their collective demands for more cost-efficient processes, both intrafirm and interfirm, have changed the way we conduct business.

This book captures the products and processes. The products that we trade are explained so that those who must work with them, or are interested to learn, will understand why they are issued and their features, issuance cycles, and trading patterns. These explanations will be valuable, both in business and in personal lives.

The marketplaces where these products trade are examined. The method of trading, who the market participants are and the differences in the types of orders, methods of execution, and methods of trade reporting are all brought out so that the reader better understands these segments of the process.

After the trade is made, the operation process begins. Trade date processes are focused upon. The preparation of trade for the settlement cycle is explored in detail. From trade figuration (monies involved in a transaction) to customer confirmation/affirmation, to the different systems that are used to effect comparison, the workings of the different clearing corporations and clearing banks are examined in detail.

On the clients' side of the process, clients have responsibilities that must be satisfied in the opening and maintaining of their accounts and the ongoing operation of the same. What are DVP accounts? Who can have them? What systems are employed to process the transactions? These areas are covered in step-by-step examples.

Since margin-type accounts are part of the process, the book explains what margin is, how it functions, and what regulations guide it. Different products have different margin requirements. Equity and option margins are used to explain the different ramifications of market activity and client action on their margin accounts.

The various settlement functions and control and uses of securities and funds are the focus of the settlement portion of the book. The settlement of a trade requires the movement of security and money. The methods used by the industry to effect settlement as well as the processes used are a part of those chapters. The workings of Depository Trust and Clearing Corporation (DTCC) and the interaction of two of its divisions, National Securities Clearing Corporation (NSCC) and Depository Trust Company (DTC), are studied in depth. The workings of Fixed Income Clearing Corp (FICC), Option Clearing Corporation (OCC), clearing banks, and the Fedwire are also covered.

The methods used by a firm to finance security positions when it is able to lend securities, and why it does so are also reviewed. The use of repos and reverse repos both as financial tools and security lending vehicles are demonstrated.

Two of the most important records of the firm, the stock record and the general ledger are next explored as to their purpose, content, and use in operations. The types of records produced and methods and importance of balancing are exposed here. A chapter on brokerage accounting introduces the aforementioned section so that the reader can better understand those chapters.

Much of what we must do every day is established by regulation. The results of those actions become part of the firm's financial and regulatory reporting requirements. These subjects are introduced to the reader.

My intention in updating this book is to give the reader an understanding of the many facets that occur after the trade is made. With this foundation the reader can better appreciate and respond to his working environment. I wish you luck.

Contents

CHAPTER II

Products That We Offer 27

CHAPTER III

The Marketplaces and Order Management 135

CHAPTER V

Margin 271

CHAPTER VII

Custodial Services 373

CHAPTER VIII

Role of the Banks 389

AFTER THE TRADE IS MADE

CHAPTER I

Overview of the Industry

The financial industry is complex, as it is comprised of many aspects. While there are general headings, such as securities, brokerage firms, and marketplace, when we look below the surface we see how multifaceted is the world of finance. The industry is changing, of course, but the degree and speed at which it is changing would have been considered impossible a few years ago. The cause for all this change is difficult to focus in on. We are in a chicken-and-egg scenario. Did technology bring about these changes, or did changes in our daily lives bring the need for technological improvements? While we can all agree as to the role technology has played, we may not be able to agree on which aspect has had the greatest impact.

The information highway allows anyone, anywhere to receive up-to-date information about any company as well as any news that may affect their investments. This is not only obtainable on desktop and laptop PCs directly from the Web, but certain television stations have continuous market news throughout the entire day. Included with the market news are interviews with corporate leaders, economists, and industry analysts from broker/dealer firms and other financial entities. From the Web, not only can one obtain a quote, which a few years ago was considered a major breakthrough, but one can also receive a security's price range over a period of months, technical and fundamental research, and the latest news and charts. Recently there has arisen a way for the public to enter buy and sell securities orders via the Web.

Globalization is a force to be reckoned with. Whoever thought a few years ago that Europe would be working toward a single-currency economy? These were countries that, once upon a time, fought each other on a regular basis. Whoever thought that they would give up their precious currencies? Words such as *lira, franc,* and *mark* are aligned with cannon balls, wooden fighting ships, and dinosaurs. Out of the decline of Communism have come new markets and new stock exchanges. Even China, which remains communistic, is modernizing its financial markets.

At first, technological advances were applied to sales and other revenue-producing areas of the firm. Early on, the sales force was equipped with Quotron and similar devices that allowed *registered representatives* (stockbrokers) to obtain the current quote, high and low prices, and the last sale by keying in the security symbol. This was a giant step forward from having to "watch the ticker" (slang for old ticker tape machines that would print last sales of stocks when they occurred) or send a message to the "quote room" asking for a quote on a particular issue. In addition, over-the-counter (OTC) equities (stocks) were listed in a daily report (known as a "pink sheet") that contained the name, phone number, and previous day's quote of the dealers (market makers, traders) in the particular stock. To obtain a current quote, an employee of the inquiring firm would have to call the market maker's firm. Over the years the "information highway" grew first intrafirm, then interfirm. NASDAQ was created, giving participants electronic access to current quotes for most over-the-counter common stock issues.

However, as the operations area of a brokerage firm was not revenue producing, it went along pushing paper. In the 1960s "paper" processing became a major problem as the financial arteries became clogged with paperwork and the U.S. financial market was almost out of control. Out of this near disaster came automation in the form of Depository Trust Company and the partial immobilization of the dreaded stock certificate.

Over the years foreign commerce has grown and, with it, the desire to invest in foreign companies. The growth of cross-border transactions was stifled by differences between countries' methods of clearing transactions. Several attempts were made to address these differences, but little was done. Finally, in the mid 1980s a group of global financial leaders assembled and drew up a list of processes that participating countries would implement. These are known as the G30 recommendations. The United States of America is one of the participating countries and the U.S. financial industry took a hard look at operations, leading to technological advances.

Among the recommendations were:

1. A common security identification numbering system.
2. Comparison effected by T + 1 (one day after trade date).
3. Settlement of corporate issues by T + 3 (three days after trade date).

4. Settlement in same-day funds (funds that are usable immediately upon receipt).
5. The concept of "netting trades" being employed on the street (broker/dealer) side of the trade, thus reducing settling trades to a minimum number of receives and delivers.
6. The rolling forward of unsettled transactions. (Trades that fail to settle on the settlement date are included with the next day's settling transactions.)
7. Pure delivery versus payment for institution and "street side" transactions. (The movement of the security from seller to buyer and the movement of the payment from buyer to seller occur simultaneously through a single control source.)
8. In each country, a central depository for securities for the immobilization of the stock certificates.
9. A common messaging system employed cross-border.

Much of what was recommended has been employed. At the writing of this book, the American financial industry is working to have seamless transaction processing known as *straight-through processing* (*STP*) for order entry to final settlement and recording.

1-A BROKER/DEALERS

I-A-1 What Are Broker/Dealers?

The term *broker/dealer* is bandied about daily without any focus as to its origin. Most of the people who use the term have little, if any, understanding as to what it means and what is involved in becoming a broker/dealer.

A broker/dealer must hold a license that an entity obtains from the Securities and Exchange Commission (SEC). It originates with the completion of a thirty-six-page application to become a broker/dealer. The application asks both business and personal questions, such as:

- Who are the principals?
- Who will be the chief executive officer?

- Who will be the chief financial officer?
- Will the entity be conducting business directly with public?
- Will the entity be a market maker and, if so, of what products?
- Will the entity clear and settle its own trades or use a correspondent-clearing firm?
- Will the entity be accepting checks and securities from its clients?
- Will the entity be issuing checks and sending securities to its clients?
- What is the entity's tax ID number?
- Where will the main office be located?
- What will be the entity's self-regulatory organization (SRO)? An SRO is an industry organization that is empowered to oversee, regulate and, when necessary, take punitive action against broker/dealers or their employees. The New York Stock Exchange (NYSE) and the National Association of Security Dealers (NASD) are examples of SROs.

The completed application is sent to the SEC, where it is reviewed. If it is in order, the license will be issued. After the issuance, should the entity change its business mix, it must change its broker/dealer license accordingly. The term used in the industry is to *amend the BD.*

I-A-2 What Are the Types of Broker/Dealers?

From the largest investment banking firms to individuals trading for their own account on the trading floor of an option exchange, they are all considered broker/dealers. Within the scope of the term *broker/dealer* are:

- *Clearing broker/dealers* are members of a clearing corporation, such as National Securities Clearing Corporation (NSCC, a division of Depository Trust & Clearing Corporation [DTCC]), that compares and settles its clients' and its own trades against those of opposing broker/dealers.

- *Commodity houses* do not deal in securities and do not have to register with the Securities and Exchange Commission. They are regulated by a different federal agency, the Commodity Futures Trading Commission (CFTC). These firms transact business in such products as agricultural produce and lumber. They buy and sell futures on the products as well as deal in the physical products themselves.

FORM BD
PAGE 1
(Execution Page)

UNIFORM APPLICATION FOR BROKER-DEALER REGISTRATION

Date:________________ SEC File No: 8-________________ Firm CRD No.: ____________

OFFICIAL USE

OFFICIAL USE ONLY

WARNING: Failure to keep this form current and to file accurate supplementary information on a timely basis, or the failure to keep accurate books and records or otherwise to comply with the provisions of law applying to the conduct of business as a broker-dealer would violate the Federal securities laws and the laws of the *jurisdictions* and may result in disciplinary, administrative, injunctive or criminal action.

INTENTIONAL MISSTATEMENTS OR OMISSIONS OF FACTS MAY CONSTITUTE CRIMINAL VIOLATIONS.

☐ APPLICATION ☐ AMENDMENT

1. Exact name, principal business address, mailing address, if different, and telephone number of *applicant:*

   A. Full name of *applicant* (if sole proprietor, state last, first and middle name):

   ____

   B. IRS Empl. Ident. No.:

   ____

   C. (1) Name under which broker-dealer business primarily is conducted, if different from Item 1A.

   ____

   (2) List on Schedule D, Page1, Section I any other name by which the firm conducts business and where it is used.

   D. If this filing makes a name change on behalf of the *applicant*, enter the new name and specify whether the name change is of the ☐ *applicant* name (1A) or ☐ business name (1C):

   *Please check above.*____

   E. Firm main address: (Do not use a P.O. Box)

   ____
   (Number and Street) (City) (State/Country) (Zip+4/Postal Code)

   Branch offices or other business locations must be reported on Schedule E.

   F. Mailing address, if different:

   ____

   G. Business Telephone Number:

   ________ ____________________
   (Area Code) (Telephone Number)

   H. Contact Employee:

   ____________________ ________ ____________________
   (Name and Title) (Area Code) (Telephone Number)

EXECUTION:

For the purposes of complying with the laws of the State(s) designated in Item 2 relating to either the offer or sale of securities or commodities, the undersigned and *applicant* hereby certify that the *applicant* is in compliance with applicable state surety bonding requirements and irrevocably appoint the administrator of each of those State(s) or such other person designated by law, and the successors in such office, attorney for the *applicant* in said State(s), upon whom may be served any notice, process, or pleading in any action or *proceeding* against the *applicant* arising out of or in connection with the offer or sale of securities or commodities, or out of the violation or *alleged* violation of the laws of those State(s), and the *applicant* hereby consents that any such action or *proceeding* against the *applicant* may be commenced in any court of competent jurisdiction and proper venue within said State(s) by service of process upon said appointee with the same effect as if *applicant* were a resident in said State(s) and had lawfully been served with process in said State(s).

The *applicant* consents that service of any civil action brought by or notice of any *proceeding* before the Securities and Exchange Commission or any *self-regulatory organization* in connection with the *applicant's* broker-dealer activities, or of any application for a protective decree filed by the Securities Investor Protection Corporation, may be given by registered or certified mail or confirmed telegram to the *applicant's* contact employee at the main address, or mailing address if different, given in Items 1E and IF.

The undersigned, being first duly sworn, deposes and says that he/she has executed this form on behalf of, and with the authority of, said *applicant*. The undersigned and *applicant* represent that the information and statements contained herein, including exhibits attached hereto, and other information filed herewith, all of which are made a part hereof, are current, true and complete. The undersigned and *applicant* further represent that to the extent any information previously submitted is not amended such information is currently accurate and complete.

____________________ ____________________________
Date (MM/DD/YYYY) Name of Applicant

By: ____________________ ____________________________
Signature Print Name and Title

Subscribed and sworn before me this ________ day of ________________, ________ by ____________________
Year Notary Public

My Commision expires ________________ County of ________________ State of ________________

This page must always be completed in full with original, manual signature and notarization.
To amend, circle items being amended. Affix notary stamp or seal where applicable.

DO NOT WRITE BELOW THIS LINE - FOR OFFICIAL USE ONLY

- *Corporate bond dealers* participate in the secondary trading of corporate debt by "making markets" in specific issues. The dealers buy and sell these instruments against their own client and other broker/dealers. They therefore create liquidity in the marketplace, allowing clients to acquire and sell the instruments with ease.

- *Correspondent firms* use the services of another firm to clear and settle trades that they have entered into on behalf of their clients or themselves. If the firm operates on a "fully disclosed" basis, the clearing firm carries and is responsible for the clients' accounts of the correspondent firm. A correspondent firm that maintains the identity of its clients and is responsible for the account is said to be operating on a nondisclosed basis (they are called an *introducing firm* or *nonclearing firm*).

- *Correspondent clearing firms* specialize in servicing nonclearing broker/dealers by comparing and settling the correspondent's contra broker (opposing broker) trades.

- *Dealer's brokers* operate in certain markets where a central place for trading does not exist. These firms act as conduits between broker/dealers, assisting them in locating or selling particular types of securities.

- *Discount brokers* do not offer all of the services and amenities that a full-service firm offers. Therefore, they can offer a lower commission charge than a full-service firm.

- *Equity dealers* are broker/dealers who take positions (make markets) in shares of corporate stock and trade against their own clients and other broker/dealers. They are found primarily in the over-the-counter market.

- *Full-service broker/dealers* offer clients many different products, such as common and preferred stocks; corporate, municipal, and U. S. Treasury debt instruments; derivatives (that is, options, futures and swaps); and research information, new issues (initial public offerings, or IPOs), and different types of account custodial services.

- *Futures trading firms* trade on the floor of a futures exchange. There they trade contracts for a delivery sometime in the future in such products as grains, metals, currencies, indexes, bonds, and, recently, common stocks.

- *Government dealers* must be approved by the Federal Reserve Board (the Fed). Once approved, they buy U.S. Treasury instruments directly from the Fed and sell them to the public. In addition, they maintain positions in government securities, which they buy and sell in trading against the public.

- *Institutional broker/dealers* specialize in offering financial services to institutions, such as corporations, mutual funds, and trust companies.

- *International broker/dealers* have a main office in one country but maintain other offices, both in the home country and in other countries.

- *Investment banking firms* assist corporations, municipalities, and certain other entities in their efforts to raise and manage capital. This includes but is not limited to bringing an entity's securities to the public markets. The term for such an issue is an *IPO*.

- *Market-making firms* risk their capital in trading chosen securities against their own clients and other broker/dealers. These firms are also known as dealers or trading firms.

- *Merchant banking firms* invest, either alone or with a group, in corporations or other perceived opportunities. They become part of the ownership of the entity they are investing in. It is usually not their intention to take control and manage the company. They are primarily interested in the investment aspects of the company.

- *Merger and acquisition specialists* work with their corporate clients in recommending, structuring, and acting as an intermediary in mergers (company A and company B merge to form company C) and acquisitions (company A purchases company B and company A continues to exist). They are also involved in one or the other side of a hostile takeover bid.

- *Mortgage-backed dealers* act as a conduit for issuers that pool loans and issue securities against the pool. The buyers of these issues receive interest and principal payments periodically.

- *Multinational broker/dealers* have several "headquarters" globally; they conduct business in various countries as if they were domiciled there.

- *Municipal bond dealers* specialize in making markets in the secondary trading of municipal debt instruments. Their focus is on the distribution of state and local government debt products.
- *Nonclearing broker/dealers* do not belong to a clearing corporation and therefore use the services of a clearing firm to settle their trades with opposing broker/dealers.
- *Online broker/dealers* are a new entry into the financial markets. Their clients enter orders via the Web through the firm's computer system straight to the marketplace where the particular issue is traded. Once the transaction is executed, a report is sent to the client electronically.
- *Option market-making firms* usually trade on the option exchanges, such as American Stock Exchange (AMEX), Chicago Board Option Exchange, and International Stock Exchange. The market makers trade for their own accounts against other traders and the public. These firms usually do not conduct business directly with public clients. There are also option market makers that write or purchase customized options on a one-to-one basis against their own clients for other broker/dealers' clients. These customized options are basically illiquid and do not use the facility of a clearing corporation to settle their trades.
- *Prime brokers* act as a central custodial facility for institutions that utilize the services of many broker/dealers. Institutions get investment ideas from many broker/dealers that they do business with. They compensate these broker/dealers by executing trades through them. These trades are flipped to the prime broker, who maintains the institution's portfolio. The institution receives one statement at the end of the month from the prime broker detailing all of their activity, which is preferable to receiving statements from many broker/dealers, each with a piece of the monthly activity.
- *Regional broker/dealers* have their headquarters outside of New York and its vicinity. Such a firm probably has sales branch offices near its headquarters office.
- *Retail firms* provide financial services to the public at large. They may have one or several branch offices where sales are conducted.
- *Specialist firms* are member firms of an equity exchange that is charged with making a fair and orderly market in the securities assigned to

them and with executing public orders entrusted to them by other broker/dealers.

- *Third-market broker/dealers* are actually dealers that take positions and trade New York Stock Exchange–listed securities that qualify for "off-board" trading.
- *Wire house* is a general term used to describe a retail firm that has many sales branches that communicate with the main office through telephone wires.

These are only a few of the types of broker/dealers (or firms) that operate in the financial community. In addition, many broker/dealers offer a combination of these specialties. For example, a broker/dealer can be a retail firm as well as an equity market-making firm. A municipal-bond broker/dealer can offer clients access to the equity markets, and so on. Some supersize broker/dealers do all of the above and more.

While the term *broker/dealer* refers to the license, there is an actual difference between a broker and a dealer. A brokerage firm that purchases and sells securities for its clients in the marketplace, but never trades against the client's order, is operating as a broker. A firm that positions a security and trades against the public is operating as a dealer. Therefore, a firm that participates in both functions is truly a broker/dealer. For example, a broker/dealer may execute all of its customers' orders for common stock as a broker (that is, against another broker/dealer that is trying to trade the same security) but will execute its customers' corporate bond orders against its own inventory positions as a dealer.

While there are many firms that concentrate on different aspects of the market, the transactions that they enter into must be processed through a series of industry-standard procedures. These mandatory steps form the *back office*, also known as *operations*. It is the latter topic that this book will focus on.

I-A-3 What Are the Component Parts of a Typical Broker/Dealer?

The typical broker/dealer has three primary components: Front Office, Middle Office, and Back Office. Broker/dealers that are not heavily automated will have only two (front and back offices), with the workings of the middle office being split between the two.

I-A-3-a *Front Office*

The front office is comprised primarily of revenue-producing areas. Here are the retail and the institutional sales forces. This includes the registered representatives (stock brokers), sales managers, and sales office managers. The number of registered representatives and the number of sales offices (branches) vary from firm to firm. Many nonclearing firms use the middle and back office operations of their correspondent clearing firm. Therefore, to the clearing firm the nonclearing firm looks like a branch office.

A front office may also include trading, investment banking, mergers and acquisitions, and research departments.

Trading departments, which handle all of the products that the firm trades for its own accounts as a market maker (trader, dealer), are also part of the front office entourage. The firm could be a market maker in equities, debt, derivatives, currency, and/or commodities, or none of these at all. Which to handle is a strictly business decision that management bases on the goal of the firm, its financial depth, and its available talents.

Investment banking has the responsibility of assisting companies and municipalities in securing funding from a variety of sources for a multitude of needs. This ranges from short-term borrowing to the underwriting and distribution of the entity's securities to the public.

In mergers and acquisitions (M&A) departments, the firm works with the corporate world in locating and setting up consolidations of companies or assisting them in the divestiture of parts of an existing company.

Research employees analyze companies, industries, and or the economy (fundamental research) or study market and/or stock movement patterns, looking for correlations and trends (technical research).

I-A-3-b *Middle Office*

The work performed in the middle office can best be described as "order control." Broker/dealers that are heavily automated employ this function to verify different aspects of a client's order to purchase and sell securities. The order control system verifies the authenticity of the client and the security while keeping track of the order as it goes through the execution process.

Let's envision a firm, Stone, Forrest & Rivers (SF&R). At SF&R, this process includes the employment of a client master database, a security master database, and an order match system.

- The *client database* contains pertinent client information necessary to process transactions as well as data, such as the client's Social Security number, to adhere to legal requirements necessary to operate an account.
- The *security database* contains specific information about the security needed to process the transactions, compute financial requirements, direct the transaction interfirm, set up dividend and interest payments, and more.
- The *order match system* contains the basic requirement that every order must have. The formatted order has specific fields that must be filled in with a choice of preprogrammed data.

While most of the verification occurs before the order is routed to the point of execution, one of the last checks in this process is the execution price itself, which is checked against prices appearing in the security master database for reasonableness. Other tasks include coding, figuration, and trade verification.

- *Coding* is required by rule 10b-10 of the 1934 Securities and Exchange Act. The broker/dealer maintains a list of codes that are used to identify in what marketplace the trade occurred and in what capacity the firm acted. (The capacity in which a firm acts refers to the firm as an agent or principal. This will be further defined in Chapter III.) In addition, a unique number is appended to the particular trade for reference purposes.
- *Figuration* determines the amount of money to be received or paid on a trade. This includes the firm's revenue, accrued interest in the case of certain debt instruments, and fees plus first and net money. First money is what the buying B/D will pay the selling B/D; net money is the sum that the client must address.
- *Trade verification* ensures that every order received from clients that could be executed was executed.

Broker/dealers that are not this automated leave the order verification to the front office and the order control process to the back office.

I-A-3-c *Back Office*

The back office is responsible for taking the executed order from the point of execution to final settlement. This includes both client and "street" sides of the transaction. As you will see later in the book, as every accounting entry must have equal and offsetting entries, so must every trade. Included are:

- *Comparison* (street side trade verification of a transaction between contra broker/dealers). While the fact that a client is told he bought (or sold) a security is important, telling the firm (contra broker) that it was bought from (or sold to) about the trade is equally important. That second step is called comparison.

- *Confirmation* (customer-side trade notification and verification). The confirmation document is official notification to the client as to the terms of the transaction.

- *Margin* (monitoring of client accounts to ensure they are operating within the confines of Regulation T of the 1934 Securities and Exchange Act, self-regulatory organizations' [SROs'] rules, and regulations, as well as the broker/dealer's own "house" rules). Each client account is a cash account and/or a margin account. Margin accounts permit the lending of money to acquire securities, or the lending of securities in the case of a short sale. These accounts must operate under the rules mentioned above. The rules govern the client's responsibilities as well as the firm's.

- *Settlement* (optimizing the firm's security and monetary resources in the settlement of transactions). The efficient use of these resources will minimize expense, thereby maximizing profit.

- *Security control* (1934 Securities and Exchange Act, adhering to procedures set forth in Regulation T and Rule 15C3–3 of the 1934 federal act as to possession or control of Clients' Securities).

- *Financing* (seeking out the minimum expense to the firm for financing day-to-day transaction-related operations).

- *Client account servicing* (making sure that the clients are operating their accounts in accordance with agreed-to processes). This includes following up with clients who are delinquent in performing required actions, such as paying for purchases, delivering negotiable securities against their sales, or meeting maintenance calls for additional collateral. It also involves performing custodial services for clients who maintain security positions at the broker/dealer, which includes proxy (absentee voting privileges), payment of dividends and/or interest to the clients on a timely basis, making sure the clients are notified and their positions operated in accordance with the clients' instructions in the case of certain corporate actions such as tender offers, and accurately maintaining the actual security positions.
- *Books and records* (the backbone of the broker/dealer). There are two main records that in turn are divided into two more records. One of these is known as the Stock Record; the other is the General Ledger.
    - The *Stock Record* has two versions: the Activity Stock Record and the Summary Stock Record. The Activity Stock Record, presented in alphabetic order by security and then by account order within each security, reflects all security movements that occurred on a specific day. The Summary Stock Record, which is also presented in alphabetic security order and then account order within the security, reflects all of the security positions that are the firm's responsibility.
    - The *General Ledger* is also divided into two records. First, the Daily Cash listing, presented in strict account number order, reflects all of the money entries that the firm has processed on a given day. Second, the general ledger, also presented in strict account number order, contains all of the money balances that are the firm's responsibility. The money balances in the general ledger, when totaled, become what is commonly known as the trial balance.

I-A-3-d *Other Key Components*

There are other important parts to a broker/dealer. First and most important is the firm's management. Depending on the broker/dealer, the management could include the chairperson, board of directors, chief executive officer, president, controller, chief financial officer, chief technical officer, chief operations officer, and other officers, such as executive vice presidents, senior vice presidents, vice pesidents, and assistant vice presidents. The firm maintains committees, such as the Executive Committee, Management Committee, and Finance Committee. The purpose for this cadre is to ensure that the firm is optimizing its profit potential. Collectively they form the firm's management team.

There is also a legal staff comprised of the chief counsel and lawyers with various specialties. They review all contracts and agreements that the firm wants to enter into, defend the firm when it is being litigated against as well as proceeding with lawsuits when the firm has been wronged. Part of the legal function is compliance, which monitors and ensures that the firm's policies and procedures are adhered to. They not only oversee operational activity but also review sales and marketing practices.

Internal audit functions in a similar role. They actually perform the same audits as the firm's outside auditors. The difference is the outside auditors, an independent accounting firm, audit the firm once a year. The internal auditors perform their review more often. For example, at SF&R they visit the sales offices (branches) quarterly. They make sure that the stockbrokers' clients' records are up to date and they look for excessive trading and other bad business practices in clients' accounts. They also examine the security custodial areas quarterly, verifying that the firm's records are in balance with the custodian and that the proper quantity of securities is where it is supposed to be. Any discrepancies must be researched and corrected.

As with any other business, there is a personnel function that includes human resources, payroll, and employee benefits. The size of this area is dictated by the size of the firm's overall staff. Employees are compensated differently in the various parts of the firm. Some are salaried, some are paid commission, and others receive compensation based on the profits that they bring into the firm. In addition, the payout is at different rates within the same group. It is the responsibility of the payroll section to make sure that all employees receive their due.

Firms such as SF&R offer their employees medical and life insurance, 401(K) plans, tuition reimbursement, and other benefits. Many of these offerings give the employees choices. The benefits area must keep records of who has selected what benefits. They also process claims and keep track of payments. They must always be on the lookout for better plans and those that are more reasonably priced while offering the same benefits.

Last but by far not least is general services, which oversees the day-to-day servicing of the firm. This includes the office maintenance staff and various technicians that the firm requires to operate.

This book will focus on the middle and back offices.

I-B *THE MARKETS*

I-B-1 What Are Markets?

A security market is the same as any other market. It's a place where people come to buy or sell value. At one time there was a large difference between the listed markets (exchanges) and the over-the-counter market. However, over time advances in technology have blurred the differences in the appearance and operation of these two types of markets. There is still one major difference between the two marketplaces. Security trades on exchanges, such as the New York Stock Exchange or the International Security Exchange for the public, are executed on an agency basis. That means that a broker, who has no financial interest in the trade, executes the public order against another broker and charges a commission for the service. The over-the-counter market is primarily a principal (dealer's) market where public orders are executed against market makers who have a financial commitment to the particular product. For this service, the dealer charges a markup. If we look outside the industry, we see the same use of the terminology. Real estate brokers and insurance brokers act as agents for their clients. They do not own the product that they are selling, and they charge a commission for the service. New car dealers and appliance dealers, on the other hand, own the products that they are selling and add a markup to the price when it is being sold.

In most cases, the nature of the product (security) itself determines in which market it trades. Certain products have enough issue depth and interest to sustain trading without the need of an intermediator (dealer); others do not. Most common stocks trade on an agency basis through a broker. Municipal bonds mostly trade on a principal basis against a market maker. Later on, we'll discuss the various products in detail.

I-B-2 What Is a "Two-Sided" Market?

The markets that we are referring to are known as two-sided markets. That means that there is a *bid* and an *offer*. This is known as the *quote*. The amount of the security comprising the bid and the offer is known as the *size*. Here's an example: Shares of a common stock are quoted 26.50–.70, 40 × 80. Translated, this means the best price that someone is willing to pay for the stock is $26.50 per share, and the best price that anyone wants to sell the security for is $26.70. As we trade in 100-share lots, the last two zeros are dropped when displaying the size. Therefore, the bid is comprised of 4,000 shares; the offer is for 8,000.

I-B-3 The Different Marketplaces

The marketplaces are where financial assets exchange hands. They include the American Stock Exchange (AMEX), Boston Stock Exchange (BSE), Chicago Board Option Exchange (CBOE), Chicago Stock Exchange (CHX), Cincinnati Stock Exchange (CSE), International Security Exchange (ISE), New York Stock Exchange (NYSE), Pacific Exchange (PSX), and Philadelphia Stock Exchange [PHLX]. There are over-the-counter markets, such as the National Association of Security Dealers Automated Quotation (NASDAQ), which was recently approved as an exchange and government bond market, as well as debt markets for corporate, municipal, agency, and money market securities. In addition, there are electronic commerce networks (ECNs), where interests in buying or selling large quantities of securities are posted to solicit interest to trade, and alternate trading systems (ATSs), where securities are traded among participants.

There are futures exchanges, where futures on commodities, currencies, indices, debt and interest rates, and recently, stocks trade. Among these are the Chicago Board of Trade, Chicago Mercantile Exchange, Kansas City Board of Trade, Minneapolis Grain Exchange, New York Mercantile Exchange, and New York Board of Trade.

And these are only the domestic markets.

It is the liquidity in the market that attracts investments. The ease by which securities representing large sums of value exchange hands makes investing, trading, or speculating doable and desirable. The markets are discussed in more detail later in Chapter III.

I-C *INDUSTRY REGULATORS*

I-C-1 Who Are the Regulators?

The brokerage industry is heavily regulated, starting from the federal government, through the state governments, to the industry's own self-regulatory organizations. Each broker/dealer must conform to the regulations and requirements set forth by these different entities.

I-C-1-a *Securities and Exchange Commission*

The primary regulator of the security industry is the Securities and Exchange Commission. Their main headquarters is located at 450 Fifth Street, NW, Washington, DC. There are branch offices in New York, NY; Boston, MA; Philadelphia, PA; Miami, FL; Atlanta, GA; Chicago, IL; Denver, CO; Fort Worth, TX; Salt Lake City, UT; Los Angeles, CA; and San Francisco, CA.

The SEC promulgates and enforces rules that the industry must abide by. Among these are Regulation T, which governs the lending of money by a broker/dealer to the public as well as the control and use of customer securities and funds. There are rules governing how a new corporate issue must be brought to the public market, and the financial requirements that must be satisfied by the broker/dealer.

Broker/dealers have an obligation to notify the SEC and their chosen self-regulatory organization if the firm's capital falls below certain requirements. These requirements are based on the type of business the broker/dealer conducts. There are different capital requirements for market-making broker/dealers, for clearing broker/dealers, and for nonclearing broker/dealers. There are also different capital requirements for broker/dealers that act as underwriters. Each type of business the broker/dealer is engaged in requires that a capital requirement be satisfied.

The rules put forth by the Securities and Exchange Commission are enforced by industry self-regulatory authorities, which we discuss later in this chapter.

I-C-1-b *State Regulators*

State regulators oversee the operation of broker/dealers that conduct business within the state borders. For a firm to be allowed to conduct security business in any state, the broker/dealer must be licensed. In addition, every stockbroker conducting business in that state must be registered with the state's overseeing authority. The state authorities must also approve securities that are not listed on a national exchange before they can be offered for sale within the state. The process of getting the security approved for sale to the public within a state is known as "blue skying" the issue.

It is the home address of the broker/dealer's client that determines eligibility. Therefore, a stockbroker working in Chicago, IL, doing business with a client who also works in Chicago but who lives in Indiana, must be registered to do business in Indiana, as must the broker/dealer, and the securities being offered to the client must be an approved issue. Violation of any one of the three rules could result in serious reprimands, fines, and so on. The compliance department of a broker/dealer monitors the activity of the stockbrokers as it relates to the location of their clients.

I-C-1-c *Self-Regulatory Organizations (SROs)*

Each broker/dealer must select a self-regulatory organization (SRO). The two most dominant ones are the New York Stock Exchange and the National Association of Securities Dealers (NASD). Broker/dealers that are members of the NYSE will select that organization as their regulatory authority. Broker/dealers who conduct business that is under the purview of a particular SRO will choose that regulator. For example, a broker/dealer whose sole business is trading options listed on the Chicago Board Option Exchange would chose the CBOE to be its SRO. A broker/dealer who is not a member of an exchange will choose the NASD.

The rules and regulations of Self Regulatory Organizations encompass the federal rules as well as those imposed by the industry itself. These include but are not limited to:

1. The infrastructure of the SRO itself
2. Days and hours of operation
3. Procedures and policies in the operation of the trading markets

4. Standards for the units of trading
5. Membership requirements
6. Requirements for conducting business with the public
7. Documentation required to operate a client's account
8. Requirements concerning reporting to clients
9. Suitability rules for client investments
10. Requirements concerning reporting to the SRO
11. Procedures for processing customer complaints
12. Rules governing arbitration
13. Settlement cycles of the various instruments
14. Proper application of margin
15. What constitutes security possession and control
16. Procedures for conducting business with other broker/dealers
17. What constitutes "good delivery" of a security
18. Requirements concerning financial reporting to the regulatory authorities
19. What constitutes adequate books and records
20. Ethical rules for advertisements, speaking engagements, and so on

The SROs also perform periodic audits of the broker/dealers. These audits review the firm's controls, procedures, and overall operating proficiency. As part of the audit, clients receive notification, requesting responses should there be any discrepancies in their accounts. The firm's internal books and records are verified for accuracy and the regulatory reports (known as FOCUS and Customer Protection) are confirmed.

I-C-1-d *The Commodities Futures Trading Commission*

Future products come under a separate federal regulatory authority known as Commodity Futures Trading Commission (CFTC). This federal authority maintains its own set of rules and standards that entities doing business in this sector must adhere to. CFTC rules set forth the standards a futures exchange must satisfy to be allowed to conduct business, and state requirements for individuals who want to conduct futures business with the public. These firms and their employees must gain approval by first petitioning the National Futures Association (NFA), an industry self-regulatory organization, before being permitted to file their applications with the CFTC.

The CFTC's rules instruct commodity firms on how clients' accounts must be maintained. For example, the position in a client's account must be revalued every day to its current market value. Customers' funds must also be separated from the firm's funds. Customer margin (the money owed by clients under certain conditions) must be collected within stipulated time frames.

Of course, there are many more rules, regulations, and procedures than outlined here. The purpose of this section is to establish what the back office does on a daily basis. The results of rules and regulations will be explained throughout this book.

As we advance through this book, please keep in mind that many of the procedures outlined are the result of the hard work done by the previously mentioned regulatory authorities. They have the responsibility of making certain that a level playing field exists at all times for dealings among internal participants as well as for internal participants' dealings with external participants of the financial industry.

1-C-1-e *Other Regulators*

Broker/dealers also come under review from governmental entities that we are very familiar with in our everyday lives. The Internal Revenue Service, state and local taxing authorities, and U.S. Department of Justice all play a dominant part in the workings of the industry, as does the Uniform Commercial Code. In this regard, the financial industry is held accountable, as is every other business. Rules governing the illegal use of the mail and fraudulent acts of any kind, so participants of this industry can be penalized as in any other.

1-D *REQUIRED EXAMINATIONS*

Employees of the broker/dealer who conduct business with the public, manage those who do, or influence investment decisions must pass qualifying examinations. Among these are Series 7, the Registered Representative Examination; Series 24, the Principals Examination; and Series 27, the Financial and Operations Principal Examination. In addition, periodic update exams must be passed to keep the various licenses in force. Those who make markets and trade securities against the public must pass a Series 55 examination. The individual states' authorities have their own requirements. To conduct business within a state, the registered representative or broker must pass a Series 63 examination, and so on. In addition, registered employees are expected to participate in continuing education courses that cover new rules and regulations as well as other changes in the industry.

1-E *REGULATORY REPORTING*

Regulatory reporting has many parts. The three major reports are FOCUS (Financial and Operations Combined Uniform Single), Net Capital Rule (15c3–1 of the 1934 Securities and Exchange Act), and Customer Protection (Rule 15c3–3 of the same law).

1-E-1 Net Capital is concerned with the financial strength of the firm. In it, only the liquid assets are applied to the firm's liabilities that represent potential financial exposure. The resulting ratio cannot exceed certain limits. The report is filed with the firm's SRO and the SEC.

1-E-2 Customer Protection 15c3–3 analyzes the firm's exposure to its clients. If the firm owes more money to its clients (credit balances) than the clients owe the firm (debit balances), it must "lock up" the difference in a special bank account for the benefit of the clients. In addition, security differences that have not been reconciled for a period of time are assumed to belong to the client and are added to the client's credit balances.

1-E-3 FOCUS report is a combination of the above two reports as well as items from the broker/dealer's balance sheet, profit and loss statement, and operational control reports. It is comprehensive and gives the regulators and other industry entities a picture of the financial status and operational capabilities of the broker/dealer.

I-F *WHO ARE OUR CLIENTS?*

I-F-1 Clients Who Provide Product

Our clients can be looked at best in terms of the services the particular broker/dealer offers corporations, venture situations, mutual funds, partnerships, and federal, state, and local government agencies, to name but a few. All come to the marketplace to raise funds for their ongoing efforts. The funds are raised through the issuance of financial instruments that are offered into the public market. Firms that assist in the raising of these funds are known as *investment bankers*. Sometimes the firm invests in the entity or effort directly. These firms are known as *merchant bankers*. When a new issue is brought to the market, it is referred to as an initial public offering (IPO).

I-F-2 Types of Clients

On the other side are clients that may be classified as investors, traders, or speculators. The distinction is the intent of the investment.

Investors are generally there for the long term. They buy a security and hold it long-term. Such investors may acquire bonds so that they can collect interest income. They also acquire a particular security because they expect capital appreciation over a long period of time.

Traders, on the other hand, focus on volatility of a security. We are not referring to a broker/dealer that is a market maker in securities and trades against the public or other broker/dealers. We are referring to clients of broker/dealers who actively trade. They are interested in securities whose prices are changing rapidly, either up or down. They buy and sell, trying to outguess the market and thus profit from these short-term transactions. These clients do not hold securities in position for long periods of time.

The last group of investors are known as *speculators*. They anticipate events happening and take market action based on their assessment. One could say they are playing hunches or can "read" certain industry trends. They hold the security position until the event occurs or they realize that something was wrong with their assessment.

I-F-3 Main Categories of Clients

Clients can also be classified as retail or institutional. *Retail accounts* are for the investing public at large. The public has many reasons for investing, such as growth opportunities, generating income, and planning for future needs. *Institutional accounts* belong to legal entities created by law, such as corporate retirement accounts, mutual funds, and trust accounts. People invest large sums of money in securities that they expect will satisfy their respective needs.

I-F-4 Types of Accounts

There are different types of accounts, depending on the needs of the account's principal(s). These include:

- *Individual accounts* owned and operated by one person.
- *Joint accounts* owned and operated by two or at a maximum three people.
- *Power of attorney accounts* operated by persons other than the account owner(s).
- *Custodian accounts* operated for the benefit of a minor or incompetent.
- *Partnership accounts*, which involve a formal agreement among individuals to operate as a unit.
- *Corporate accounts* owned and operated under the charter and bylaws of a corporation.
- *Trust accounts* operated by individual(s) other than the beneficiaries of the trust.

I-G *WHAT ARE THE INDUSTRY ORGANIZATIONS?*

I-G-1 Depositories

Depositories are entities that retain assets for their owners. In the financial industry there is the Depository Trust Company Division of the Depository

Trust and Clearing Corporation, and the Fedwire, a part of the Federal Reserve.

At Depository Trust Company (DTC) settlement movements are accomplished by book entry without the need to physically touch the actual certificates. In addition, DTC offers many services that a broker/dealer's own cashiering area could perform. The Federal Reserve Bank (Fed) also acts as a repository for maintaining security positions in U.S. Treasury, Freddie Mac (Federal Home Loan Mortgage Corp), FNMA (Federal National Mortgage Association) and GNMA (Government National Mortgage Association) instruments for the owners or the owners' nominees.

I-G-2 Clearing Corporations

There are clearing corporations, such as National Securities Clearing Corporation (NSCC), Fixed Income Clearing Corporation (FICC), divisions of DTCC, and Option Clearing Corporation (OCC), where transactions are compared and/or gathered for netting, negating the need to settle each transaction on an individual basis. As you will read later, *netting* is the process by which the individual firm's transactions in a specific issue are reduced to a single net position balance (either receive, deliver, or flat) and that balance is applied industrywide against other participants.

I-G-3 Industry Utilities

Facility managers support these efforts. Among them is Security Industry Automation Corporation (SIAC). The facility manager for many of the NYSE and AMEX systems, it also offers other services to the industry at large. Automatic Data Processing provides processing systems to broker/dealers that do not possess comprehensive computer support. There are pricing and news vendors, such as Bloomberg, Reuters, and Bridge Data, now part of Reuters.

I-G-4 Banks

This discussion of industry organizations would not be complete without mentioning the role played by banks. They provide broker/dealers and other financial institutions with:

- *Collateral loans* used to finance margin and proprietary account loans.
- *Letters of credit* for satisfying daily margin requirements at clearing corporations and other purposes.
- *Unsecured loans*, which are supported only by the good name of the broker/dealer and used in the everyday operation of the broker/dealer.

In addition, banks act as:

- *Transfer agent*, keeping the registered ownership of securities and acting as the servicing agents for the reregistering of securities into another name.
- *Dividend dispersing agent* (DDA), paying dividends, interest, and other corporate distributions authorized by the issuing entity to registered holders appearing on the transfer agent's books.
- *Registrar*, whose function is to verify the accuracy of transfer agents' records.
- *Product issuer*, introducing into the marketplace investment vehicles, such as certificates of deposits (CDs) and asset-backed securities, for the public to invest in.
- *Custodian*, providing custodial services, such as asset servicing for institutions, high-net-worth individuals, and broker/dealers.
- *Underwriter*—along with some broker/dealers, bringing certain types of issues, such as municipal securities, into the public markets.

I-G-5 The Bond Market Association (TBMA)

The Bond Market Association has several functions. It is the regulator of the municipal bond market, promulgating rules known as the G rules. Unlike other SROs, it turns to the NASDR and the NYSE to enforce those rules and take actions against offenders. The Bond Market Association also sets rules governing the mortgage-backed security segment of the financial market as well as setting the delivery dates for the various products trading under that umbrella.

I-G-6 Security Industry Association (SIA)

The SIA is a multipurpose industry organization. It represents industry interests with regulators and lawmakers. It also has several divisions representing different segments of the market—for example, the Data Management Division, Internal Auditors Division, and Security Operations Division. The respective divisions act as an educational hub for their members as well as interpreting the impact of new rules or procedures. The organization also maintains education programs for the public.

All of the above plus many more entities comprise the financial industry in one way or another. Now that we have established the foundation of the industry and where the broker/dealer fits in, we will proceed with an investigative look at the securities that we trade.

CHAPTER II

Products That We Offer

II-A CORPORATE SECURITIES

A corporation is a unique type of business enterprise in that the law recognizes it as a legal individual. As such, it can sue or be sued. Its shares of ownership can be easily transferred. It can amass large amounts of capital in its own name. Generally, its life, as defined by its charter, is perpetual.

The corporate charter describes what the corporation may or may not do. The charter is obtained from one of the 50 states, usually the corporation's home state. In some states, the charters are very strict and precise as to what a corporation may do as a business entity, while in others they are very lenient. Some corporations, therefore, establish their home offices in states with lenient laws, to have as much flexibility as possible in conducting their business. The state that issues the charter becomes the corporation's *state of incorporation*. Naturally, corporations originating in foreign countries must register with their regulatory authorities.

One feature, more than any other, makes a corporation especially important to the financial industry. Shareholders, although they are owners, are liable only for the total amounts of their investment. This protection, which is known as *limited liability*, makes investment in the issues of the corporation very attractive. Individuals can invest—that is, buy shares—in a corporation without fear of being sued and losing all their wealth. This is a major point in choosing to invest in a corporation or partnership, or starting your own business as a single proprietorship.

A corporation can issue shares in two types of stock, *common* or *preferred*, either of which represents ownership in the company. An investor who buys the corporation's stock owns a *share* of the company and is therefore known as a *shareholder*.

A corporation can also arrange long-term borrowing through the issuance of *bonds*. It can issue intermediate-term debt called *notes* and short-term debt known as *commercial paper*. It can also borrow short-term funds from a bank, which is known as a *commercial loan*. Stock is evidence of ownership, while bonds, notes, commercial paper, and commercial loans are evidence of debt. A bondholder has loaned money to the corporation, not invested in it. As lenders, bondholders receive interest on their loan.

This chapter first discusses the three principal types of corporate securities (common stock, preferred stock, and corporate debt) as well as warrants, rights, and commercial paper.

II-A-1 Common Stock

Type:	Ownership
Form:	Registered
Denomination:	Shares
Income payments:	Dividends
Traded:	Stock exchanges, NASDAQ, Bulletin Board, ECNs, ATSs, and Pink Sheets
Duration:	Life of a corporation

The evidence of primary ownership in a corporation is its common stock. Each share of common stock represents one equal part of the entire ownership comprised of the common shares of the company. The remaining portion of the ownership is evidenced by the preferred shares (if they exist).

Example: RAM Corporation has 10,000,000 share of common stock outstanding and no preferred stock. Someone who owns one share owns 1/10,000,000 of the corporation, whereas an owner of 1,000 shares owns 1/10,000 of it (10,000,000 ÷ 1,000).

II-A-1-a *Voting*

Each share of common stock usually entitles its owner to one vote. An owner of 100 shares has 100 votes; an owner of 50 shares has 50 votes. The more shares you own, the more votes you have and, through the votes, control over the board of directors and, through them, the corporation. Common stockholders vote on key issues and on representation on the board of directors. While the vast majority of common shares follow the one-share/one-vote methodology, it is not true for all common shares. Some corporate charters permit a fraction of a vote per share, while others offer no vote at all. Still others permit cumulative voting, which enables a shareholder to spread the cumulative number of votes he has as he sees fit. For example, a holder of 100 shares who is voting for 5 director positions on the board, can take the total 500 votes (100 votes × 5 directors = 500 votes) and apply all of them to one director position. This gives minority shareholders more opportunity to be represented on the board.

There is a form of common stock for which the shareowners surrender their right to vote and in return receive a certificate as proof of ownership. These are known as *voting trust certificates* (*VTCs*). Except for the voting privilege, such shareholders are entitled to all other rights and privileges.

II-A-1-b *Dividends*

Dividends may or may not be paid on shares of common stock. When dividends are paid depends on the policy and status of the corporation. Companies that are young and growing, and companies trying to conserve capital usually do not pay dividends to their common stockholders. When a corporation does pay a dividend, it may pay a cash or stock dividend.

Cash dividends are paid on a per-share basis. Some companies pay annually, while others pay semiannually or quarterly. Rarely are dividends paid more frequently than every quarter.

Stock dividends are paid as a percentage of the shares the shareholder owns. For example, a 10% stock dividend means that for every 100 shares the shareholder owns, she will receive 10 additional shares. Stock dividends are paid when a corporation has good earnings but wants to preserve its cash. They are a nontaxable distribution by the company. While it adds more shares to the holder's position, it has little or no real value initially. This is discussed in more detail later in the book. (The difference between a company worth $1,000,000 that has 100,000 shares outstanding or one with 110,000 shares outstanding is the price of its shares.)

II-A-1-c *Underwriting*

Common stock may be publicly or privately owned. Usually small corporations are *privately owned.* These corporations are either family owned or closely held by a few principals. Because the shares of these companies are not traded on any of the public markets, they are not easily bought or sold. As a corporation grows in size, it needs capital. Once it outgrows the capital raised by the insiders, it must turn to the public.

New issues are brought to public market through underwriting, and the form of underwriting is called "negotiated."

The *Initial Public Offering* (*IPO*) of a corporation's securities takes place through a procedure known as *underwriting.* The corporation wanting to make a public offering will turn to its *investment banker.* The investment banker usually has had a relationship with the company for some time, advising the corporate management on various financial matters. The investment banker, usually a broker/dealer, forms an underwriting syndicate with other underwriters and begins the formal process of publicly issuing the securities.

Corporate underwritings are negotiated. In other words, the corporation usually turns to one investment banker whenever it needs capital. The investment banker advises the corporation on market conditions, the corporation's position in the business environment, and the prospects of a successful issue. The investment banker and the corporation negotiate the type of security to bring to market.

II-A-1-d *Trading of Common Stock*

Once new issues of common stock are brought to market through an underwriting, they may trade in the over-the-counter market and/or on exchanges.

Most newly issued common stocks first trade in the *over-the-counter* (*OTC*) *market.* In this marketplace, broker/dealers *make markets* in the security, that is, the broker/dealer stands ready to buy or sell the security against its inventory in the anticipation of making a profit. When the broker/dealer trades against its own inventory, it is considered to be a *dealer.* A dealer makes a profit (or incurs a loss) by the *spread* (difference) between the prices of the securities the trader buys and sells. This is known as the *trader's quote.* Here's an example: Stone, Forrest & Rivers is a market maker. Its trader Dan DiLyons is quoting 16.10–.30 for shares of ABBAB common stock. Dan is willing to buy the stock at $16.10 per share. That is Dan's bid.

He is willing to sell stock at $16.30 per share. That is Dan's offer. Each time Dan executes a buy-and-sell trade at these quoted prices, he makes $.20 per share or $20.00 per hundred shares on the normal trading unit of 100 shares. Dan can also make a profit by properly maintaining a position in these securities. Let's assume Dan is of the opinion that ABBAB will rise in value. He will maintain a position by buying more shares initially than he is selling. After the desired position is attained, Dan tries to balance his buy-and-sell trades by adjusting his bid and offers.

SF&R is a market maker in ABBAB. So are other broker/dealers. These market makers compete for public business by changing the quotes and staying abreast of the market. If Dan doesn't want to acquire any more shares of ABBAB common stock, he will lower his bid so that other market makers are bidding higher, which makes their prices more attractive to sellers. This is explained in detail elsewhere in this book. However, it should be noted that making a profit isn't as easy as it appears in this text. Dan can just as easily incur a loss if his judgment is wrong.

As the corporation grows and becomes more successful, the stock will trade either on NASDAQ or on an exchange, such as the New York Stock Exchange. Both NASDAQ and the New York Stock Exchange, as well as other exchanges, have *listing requirements*. If a corporation can satisfy various exchanges' listing requirements, then its board of directors will decide on which exchange the security should trade. Securities that are, in fact, listed on an exchange are said to be *listed securities*.

The exchange markets are known as *auction markets*, where brokers meet and exchange or trade securities. Brokers acting as a conduit for their firms' clients are said to be acting as agents. Trades for clients that are executed on an agency basis are charged commission. Trades that are executed in the over-the-counter market on a principal basis, that is, against a dealer's inventory, will be charged a markup.

The unit of trading in common stock is usually 100 shares, which is called a *round lot*. Transactions from 1 to 100 shares are known as *odd lots*. In a very few cases, the unit of trading is 10 shares. *Ten-share traders* are usually high-priced preferred stocks.

Common stock is a *registered issue*, that is, the stock certificates are registered to a party. Securities may be registered in the name of the actual owner. This is known as being registered to the *beneficial owner*. They also may be registered to *a nominee* or *designee* of the actual owner of the securities. This is known as being in *nominee name*. Securities that are maintained by a broker/dealer for a customer are usually maintained in the firm's name or, if they are at a depository, in the depository's name. Most corporate and municipal securities maintained by broker/dealers and banks are kept at Depository Trust Company, a division of Depository Trust and Clearing Corporation (DTCC) and are therefore registered in their nominee name, CEDE. Therefore, stocks owned by the client of a broker/dealer are maintained at Depository Trust and Clearing Corporation, or two steps away from the actual owner. In fact, the Depository Trust and Clearing Corporation does not keep all the securities in their vaults; instead, they keep securities at the transfer agent that maintains them in bookkeeping form.

Here's an example: A client, Sandra Beech, owns 100 shares of the Burr Bon Corporation and maintains the securities at Stone, Forrest & Rivers. SF&R is carrying the position on its books in an account set aside for Sandy Beech. However, SF&R, as we will see later, actually maintains the securities at Depository Trust and Clearing Corporation. Depository Trust and Clearing Corporation has the securities registered in its name, CEDE, but the physical securities are at the actual transfer agent, where the agent is maintaining not only who the registered owners are but also the position itself in electronic form.

Securities registered in nominee name, such as Stone, Forrest & Rivers or Depository Trust and Clearing Corporation's CEDE, are said to be maintained in street name. *Street name* is another way of saying that the stocks are in good deliverable form (negotiable) upon receipt. They do not require any special legal documentation and, in delivering the security in street name, the firm making the delivery is alleged to have the right to represent the owner of the securities. This is important because stock registered in a customer's name might not be good delivery (negotiable) because of missing documentation, or might even be stolen or sold by an impostor.

To keep track of ownership, an issuing entity usually retains the services of one registrar, one or two transfer agents, and one dividend-disbursing agent (DDA). The names and addresses of the registered holders are maintained by the *corporate transfer agent*, which is usually a bank or trust company. When common stock changes hands and there is a need to change the registration, the certificate is sent to its respective transfer agent, which cancels the old certificate and issues a new one in the name of the new owner. We will see later that stocks maintained at DTCC have their ownership adjusted by bookkeeping entry on DTCC books, negating the need to send physical securities to the transfer agent for canceling and issuing new certificates.

It is the function of the registrar to ensure that the quantity of an issue is properly maintained by the transfer agent and that the agent's "books" are up to date. If a corporation is supposed to have 800,000,000 shares of common stock outstanding, it is the registrar's responsibility to see that all of the registrations on the transfer agent's books total 800,000,000 shares.

Dividends are disbursed to registered shareholders by the dividend-disbursing agent, which is also a bank. In the case of securities registered in the nominee name, it is the responsibility of the register's party to see that the beneficial owner receives the payment.

II-A-1-e *Common Stock as an Investment Vehicle*

There are three primary reasons why common stock is attractive over other investments to the investment public. One, a corporation offers limited liability. A corporation is different than a partnership or an individual proprietorship where there is much more at stake than the initial or total investment. Two, ownership can be easily transferred; there is no need to contact lawyers or have all kinds of new agreements made. You simply sell stock to someone else. This brings us to the third very positive reason for investing in common stock—liquidity. There are marketplaces in which the stock trades, thereby enabling the investor to get in or out of security positions with relative ease. Liquidity is a prime factor.

Stock-issuing corporations range from huge multibillion-dollar companies to fledgling concerns offering their shares to the public for the first time. Some fledgling companies even issue stock to the investment public via a conduit known as *private placement*. These stocks are not freely tradable but are given in return for investments by certain types of investors known as *venture capitalists* or *angels*. They invest in these fledgling companies in their very early stages and, of course, they face a high risk of bankruptcy and failure. However, their return, if the company is successful, offsets the risk involved with the transaction.

Some investments in common stock may be considered safe or conservative, while others are very risky or speculative. Some stocks are purchased for their history of dividend payments, while others may be purchased for their growth potential. Some investors are looking toward long-term goals; others are interested in short-term situations. Whatever the investment goal, the investor usually finds something suitable in the common stock arena.

II-A-2 Preferred Stock

Type:	Ownership
Form:	Registered
Denomination:	Shares
Income payments:	Dividends
Traded:	Stock exchanges and NASDAQ
Duration:	Usually perpetual with the company

Like common stock, preferred stock represents ownership in the corporation. Unlike common stock, however, preferred securities usually do not have voting privileges. This type of stock is called "preferred" because:

- Current dividends must be paid to preferred shareholders before they are paid to common stockholders.
- In case of liquidation, preferred owners receive the distribution of assets before common stock owners.

II-A-2-a *Dividends*

Preferred stocks are supposed to pay a stipulated rate of dividend. The rate is expressed in the security's description either as a dollar sum or as a percentage.

The *dollar rate* is the amount to be paid per share per year.

Example: A "$4.36 preferred" is supposed to pay $4.36 per share per year.

The *percentage* is a percentage not of the selling price, but of the *par value* of a security, which is the value assigned to a stock for bookkeeping purposes. It has nothing to do with the market price or current value of a security.

Example: A "4% preferred" with a $100 par value is expected to pay $4 per share per year ($100 × .04). A dividend of 4% on a $50 par value stock is $2 per share per year ($50 × .04).

Most of the preferred stocks have a fixed rate of dividend. Therefore they are included in a group of securities known as *fixed-income securities.*

Included in this group are corporate bonds, municipal bonds, and U.S. government obligations that also have set rates at which interest, in a case of bonds, is paid. The market price of these preferred stocks and bonds is therefore based on the financial strength of the issuer and the current yield for fixed-income investments.

There is another form of preferred stock called an *adjustable-rate preferred*. This adjustable-rate feature, which is also found in some corporate, municipal, and U.S. Treasury instruments, allows the interest rate, or dividend rate in the case of the preferred, to be changed periodically. In other words, as interest rates in the marketplace change, so do the interest rates of these instruments. The benefit of this type of instrument over the fixed-income instrument is that the interest or dividend rate currently being paid by the instrument reflects the current interest rate market in general. Therefore, the price of the instruments should remain close to the issuing price at all times, whereas in a fixed-income instrument as interest rates rise and new instruments are commanding money based on higher interest rates, the older, lower-interest-rate instruments lose value. As for adjustable-rate instruments, since the rate is adjusted periodically, the price of the instrument should stay pretty close to the original value of the instrument. (Conversely, with a fixed-income instrument, as interest rates fall and the new issues are paying less interest—lower dividends in the case of preferred stock—so the older instruments, which are paying higher rates, become more valuable.) With the adjustable-rate instrument, as interest rates fall so will the amount these instruments pay. The major benefit of these types of instruments is that as their interest or dividend rates are adjusted to reflect current values, so should the market price reflect current values of newly issued instruments having the same characteristics.

Investors must ask themselves if they want a steady flow of income over a long period of time or do they want preservation of capital so that, if they have to liquidate the security unexpectedly, they will minimize their risk of loss.

II-A-2-b *Underwriting*

Preferred securities are brought to market through an underwriting, which is usually negotiated. Once the decision is made to issue a preferred security, corporate officials and the investment bankers discuss what features must be included to make the preferred attractive to the public. Among the features discussed are:

- the dividend rate
- cumulative (noncumulative)
- callable (noncallable)
- convertible (nonconvertible)
- participating
- adjustable rate
- reverse floating rate
- putable
- self-liquidating

Each of these features has an effect on the corporation's financial structure.

II-A-2-b-i Dividend Rate

The dividend rate must be competitive not only with those of other issues from similar companies, but also with fixed-income securities. Unlike shareowners of fixed-income securities, who can sue for nonpayment of interest and/or initiate bankruptcy proceedings in the case of nonpayment of interest, the preferred shareowner is an owner of the company and, as such, cannot take that type of action. Such a failure to pay the required dividend also broadcasts the company's financial difficulties to the world. Dividends on preferred stock are usually paid four times a year.

As with fixed-income debt instruments, newly issued preferred stock must carry a dividend payment that is competitive with other fixed-income instruments. In periods of high interest rates they must offer a large dividend payment; in the case of low interest rates, the preferred will offer smaller dividend payments.

II-A-2-b-ii Cumulative and Noncumulative Dividends

One property found in preferred stocks is whether the preferred is a cumulative or noncumulative preferred. In the case of a *noncumulative*, a "missed" (that is, not paid) dividend is lost forever. With *cumulative* preferred stocks, however, all dividends—both past and current—must be paid before the common stockholder can receive any dividends. Therefore, a dividend that is omitted would have to be eventually paid before the common shareholder (the voting shareowners) could receive any dividend payments.

The following example depicts the impact of this feature over a four-year period.

Example: The BAM Company has one share of an $8 preferred stock and one share of common stock outstanding. BAM pays all its earnings in dividends.

Noncumulative Dividends

	Year 1	Year 2	Year 3	Year 4
Earning	$3	0	$10	$20
$8 preferred dividend	$3	0	$ 8	$ 8
Common stock	0	0	$ 2	$12

Note that the preferred should have earned $32 at the end of four years (4 yrs. × $8 = $32), but because of poor earnings in year 1 [received $3 instead of $8] and year 2 [received $0 instead of $8], the missed payments are lost forever.

Cumulative Dividends

	Year 1	Year 2	Year 3	Year 4
Earning	$3	0	$10	$20
$8 preferred dividend	$3	0	$10	$19
Common stock	0	0	$ 0	$ 1

Note that even though years 1 and 2 were poor, the preferred shareholder made up the deficiency in years 3 and 4.

During the four-year period, the preferred shareholder is supposed to receive $8 per share per year. In year 1, the company earned $3, which was paid to the preferred holder. The next year, the company earned nothing, so the noncumulative preferred shareholder lost a total of $13 in dividends: ($8 − $3) + $8 = $5 + $8 = $13.

The cumulative shareholder, however, has the opportunity to recapture the lost dividend, should earnings improve. The preferred stockholder expected to receive $8 per year per share for a $32 total at the end of the four-year period. In the noncumulative example, the preferred owner received only $19, while the common shareowner received $14. In the cumulative example, the cumulative preferred holder eventually received $32, and the common shareowner received only $1. When the accumulated dividend is paid, it is paid to the preferred shareowner of that time. Unlike with bonds and other debt instruments—where interest accrues and is paid to the selling bondholder at the time of trade by the buying bondholder, who in turn is compensated for this when the issuer pays the bond's scheduled interest payment—cumulative preferred dividends are paid to the then existing shareholder, without any recourse by the previous owners.

The common shareholder would prefer the company to issue noncumulative preferred stock, but the company is trying to raise capital through the issuance of the preferred shares, and if it is not an attractive investment, it won't sell.

II-A-2-b-iii Callable

During periods of high interest rates, the corporation may be forced to issue a high-dividend-paying preferred stock. If the corporation and investment bankers believe that interest rates will decrease in the next few years, the corporation will be able to raise the same amount of capital at a much lower dividend cost. The problem is that they need the money now and they are issuing the preferred in the high-interest-rate period, and preferred stock has a lifetime that is as long as the corporation's.

In such cases, the corporation might make the new issue *callable.* The callable feature permits the corporation to "call in," or retire, the issue at its option for a predetermined price. A preferred stock that does not contain the callable feature is referred to as *noncallable.*

It must be remembered that the corporation will call the issue in when it is to its best advantage, which is to the investors' disadvantage. Once the corporation can finance itself at significantly lower cost, it will call the preferred in at the predetermined *call price* and pay the cost from the proceeds of the new issue. The investor must then go into the market and reinvest the proceeds at the current (lower) rate of return. The public will sometimes shy away from a callable issue for fear that the corporation will call the issue quickly should interest rates fall. To avoid this and to assure investors of a return for a given period and yet retain the ability to call the issue, the corporation might offer a noncallable for a period of time—say, ten years, seven years, or five years. Thus, stockholders know that the corporation will not retire the issue early and they are assured of their dividend payout rate for a known period.

II-A-2-b-iv Convertible

If a corporation and its investment bankers believe that the price of the company's common stock is likely to increase over time, they may decide to offer a *convertible* preferred. The convertible feature allows preferred stockholders to convert their shares into common stock. When preferred shareholders actually convert their stock depends largely on the price of the common stock. Convertibility is expressed in terms of the *conversion rate*, that is, how many shares of common stock can be had for each share of preferred. For example, if the rate is four for one, then each share of preferred can be converted into four shares of common.

When the market price of a preferred stock share is equal to that of the converted number of common stock shares, the two types of stock are said to be at *parity*.

Example: A share of WAM preferred stock is convertible into four shares of WAM common stock. The convertible preferred is currently selling at $100 per share, and the common stock is at $25 per share. We have parity—one share of preferred at $100 equals four shares of common at $25 each (4×$25=$100).

As the preferred stock and common stock fluctuate in value, parity is possible whenever the price of the preferred stock and the conversion feature of the common shares are equal. Once parity is reached, if the dividend of the converted shares is greater in total than the dividend on the preferred, the preferred shareholders normally convert.

Example: The preferred WAM above is paying $8 per share per year, while the common WAM is paying $2.25 per share per year. If the two are trading at parity, the preferred holder should convert to the common and receive a larger dividend. So, while one share of preferred is yielding $8, the equivalent number of common shares pays $9 per year ($2.25×4 shares).

If the preferred is worth more than the value of the converted common, it is said to be *above parity.*

Example: A growth company's common stock is trading at $20 per share. The corporation offers a preferred that is convertible into four shares of common. The dividends paid on this preferred and the financial strength of the issuing company cause its market price to be $100. The convertible feature is then computed to be worth $25 ($100/4=$25 per each common share).

If the company continues to prosper, the value of the common stock normally increases. Once it crosses over parity, the common stock pulls the price of the preferred up with it, due to the work of *arbitrageurs,* who buy the preferred, thereby forcing the preferred price upward. Then they convert it and sell the common stock.

Example: The preferred is trading at $96. If the common stock rises in value to $24.50, then arbitrageurs will buy the preferred shares at $96 and convert to common, and sell the common shares at $24½.

Sale of 400 common after conversion @ $24½	$9,800
Cost of 100 preferred	$9,600
Profit	$ 200

Naturally, arbitrageurs perform this conversion practice in greater quantities than 100 preferred shares. In actuality, the arbitrageurs would be entering the market as soon as converted value exceeds the preferred share value. Eventually the demand for the preferred and the supply of common stock in the market neutralize each other, and the stocks go back to parity.

Because of the effect the conversion feature has on the market price, convertible preferred stocks and convertible bonds do not trade on the same trading desk as other fixed-income securities.

II-A-2-b-v Participating

Some companies have radical earning cycles. They can earn zero one year and suddenly earn a huge profit the next year, only to slide back to zero or worse in the third year. This type of company might offer a participating preferred, or the investment banker might strongly recommend it as an inducement in selling the security to the public. A participating preferred offers the following payout structure to the investor: The participating preferred stock earns its set dividend; then the common can earn up to a predetermined amount. Any additional earnings slated for payout as dividends are shared between the participating preferred and the common shareholders.

Example: Let us assume that the Impala Company issues a $6.00 participating preferred that allows the common stock to earn up to $4.00 in dividends, after which any further dividend distribution is shared by paying $.50 to the preferred for every dollar paid to the common. We will assume the company has one share of participating preferred on one share of common.

	Year					
	1	2	3	4	5	6
Paid in dividends	$2	$0	$13	$3	$8	$34
$6 participating pfd.	$2	$0	$6+$1	$3	$6	$6+$8
Common stock	$0	$0	$4+$2	$0	$2	$4+$16

It is important to note that the holder on the *record date* that the dividend is declared receives the dividends. They are not backdated for the benefit of former owners.

II-A-2-b-vi Adjustable-Rate Preferred

A newer form of preferred is *adjustable-rate preferred*, whose dividend rate is reset periodically. The rate is usually "pegged" to the Treasury bills or Treasury bond yields. Barring any other influences, changing the dividend rate by updating the rate to reflect the current rate keeps the value of the issue close to its original issuance price.

While the adjustable-rate preferred offers some protection against market risk (market price fluctuations), it does not offer the steady stream of income that a fixed-dividend preferred does. The acquirer must choose between the two.

II-A-2-b-vii Reverse Floating Rate

This instrument is usually issued in two parts. One is a regular floating rate; the other part is a *reverse floating rate*. As current interest rates fall, the dividend payments on the floating rate preferred will be adjusted down, but the reverse floater will be adjusted upward. The periodic adjustments can be accomplished semiannually or quarterly.

Example: The Concorde Corporation was going to offer preferred shares. Based on the current interest rate and the financial strength of the corporation, it has to pay an $8 per share dividend. The Concorde Corporation's investment banker, Stone, Forrest & Rivers, recommends the use of a reverse floating preferred. Concorde Corporation decides to issue a $6 adjustable preferred and a $2 reverse preferred. The total cost to the Concorde Corporation is the same as if it had issued an $8 straight preferred. The $6 preferred will sell at what a $6 adjustable preferred should be selling at, but the $2 reverse preferred, because of its unique feature, will command a higher price then what a $2 preferred would be trading for. The corporation will raise more capital than if it issued a straight preferred. The regular adjustable preferred will appeal to the traditional preferred stock buyer; the reversible preferred will appeal to other investors, such as those who invest in short-term instruments. They will use this product to enhance their investment performance. As the interest rates fall and investors must replace short-term instruments that mature with new short-term instruments that pay less interest (thereby lowering their average return), the reversible preferred will be paying a higher dividend rate, thereby augmenting the return.

II-A-2-b-viii Putable Preferred

Putable preferred stock usually has a special feature included with the adjustable-rate type of preferred: it permits the shareowners to "put" the shares back to the issuer and receive a predetermined price. Some put features have a fixed life; others are open ended.

Some put features are known as *mandatory put preferred shares.* The company can mandate that the shareholders surrender (put) their shares back to the company. This is just a sleazy way for the issuer to disguise the call feature. Anyone considering acquiring a putable instrument should investigate the terms of the feature before investing in the product.

II-A-2-b-ix Self-Liquidating Preferred

A *self-liquidating preferred* will cease to exist at a specific time. The preferred shareholder will receive some other issue or cash for the preferred shares. Generally, these instruments become common shares.

II-A-2-C *Summary of Preferred*

A preferred may be callable, convertible, cumulative, or participating, or it might have any combination of these features. Investors should know these features to make intelligent investing decisions. Some features of preferred stock benefit the corporation and others benefit the shareholder. The corporation decides what to "give away" to ensure a successful underwriting. All the while, the public is comparing issues and deciding which offer the most attractive opportunity. Somewhere between what the corporation needs and what the public wants lies the compromise. It is here that the successful underwriting occurs.

People working in operations must know the different types of preferred stock to process them correctly and to thereby service the client efficiently.

II-A-3 Rights and Warrants

Type:	Ownership
Form:	Registered (usually)
Denomination:	Rights and warrants
Income payments:	None
Traded:	Stock exchanges and NASDAQ
Duration:	Rights, short-term Warrants, long-term

From time to time, a company may need to raise additional capital by issuing common stock. It may do so either through the usual underwriting methods or through the issuance of rights to current stockholders, or it can issue warrants along with a new issue, which together are called units.

Rights and warrants are similar in that both permit their holders to subscribe to the new shares. They differ in that rights are generally short-term, whereas warrants have much longer lives. Also, a corporation may have several warrant issues outstanding, but it may offer only one rights issue at a time.

II-A-3-a *Rights*

A *right*, or *subscription right*, is a privilege granted under the corporate charter to its stockholders to purchase new securities in proportion to the number of shares they own. The right holders are entitled to purchase at a preset price known as the *subscription price*, which is lower than the stock's current market price.

Rights are offered because the *preemptive rights* clause in the corporate charter or bylaws requires the corporation to offer new issues of common stock to its current common shareholders before offering them to anyone else. Shareholders must be given the chance to maintain their percentage ownership. Therefore, the new shares must be issued to the stockholders in proportion to their percentage of ownership. The easiest way to meet this requirement is to issue one right per share of stock owned. For example, an owner of 100 shares of stock receives 100 rights.

Shareholders who want to subscribe use a number of the rights plus a dollar amount, which is the subscription price.

Example: Angelic Star Rockets, Inc., has 5,000,000 shares of common stock outstanding and wants to raise capital by issuing 1,000,000 additional shares. The common stock is trading at $65, and the subscription value is $60. Since 5,000,000 shares are outstanding, the company issues 5,000,000 rights—one for each share of stock. According to the terms of the rights, a current stockholder, wanting to subscribe to a new share of stock, has to submit five rights and $60 to subscribe to the company's agent to receive one new share.

Shareholders who choose not to subscribe may sell their rights, because they have a market value that is based on their *theoretical value*. To calculate the theoretical value of a right, divide the difference between the subscription price and the market price by the number of rights required to purchase one new share:

$$\frac{\text{Market price} - \text{Subscription price}}{\text{Number of rights for subscription}} = \text{Theoretical value}$$

Example: The market price of Angelic common is $65, and the subscription price of the new stock is $60. If you need 5 rights to subscribe, the theoretical value of each right is calculated as follows:

$$\begin{aligned} \text{Theoretical value} = {} & \$65 \\ & \underline{-\$60} \\ & \$\ 5 \end{aligned}$$

$$\frac{\$5}{5\text{ rights}} = \$1/\text{right}$$

II-A-3-a-i Cum Rights

The value of the right is considered part of the stockowner's principal; if the right is discarded, the owner loses money. Some investors are not aware of this value so they treat rights as junk mail and throw them away. They are throwing away money.

Before the new stock is actually issued, the shareholders of record are informed of the pending rights offering. Before the new stock is actually offered to the public, the current outstanding stock is traded *cum rights*; that is, it trades with the theoretical value of one right included in its market price. (The word *cum* means "with" in Latin.)

To compute the actual value of the issue trading cum rights, one right must be added to the number of rights needed to subscribe as the current price of the stock includes the value of one right (cum rights). Divide the difference between the market price and subscription price by the adjusted number of rights needed to subscribe to one new share. The additional right offsets the value included in the current market value of the old stock.

Example: The subscription price of Angelic is $60, and the market value of the common stock, cum rights, is $66. You need five rights to subscribe.

Value of common stock (cum rights)	$66.00
Subscription value	−60.00
Difference	$ 6.00

Now add one right to the number needed to subscribe to offset the right included in the common stock's market value. Five plus one gives you six rights.

$$\$6.00 \div 6 = \$1.00 \text{ per right}$$

II-A-3-b *Ex-Rights*

Once the rights are issued, the stock and the rights trade separately. As stated earlier, shareholders that do not want to subscribe can sell their rights. Among the potential buyers are holders that want to "round up" their shareholding and traders looking for a large percentage return with a minimum downside risk.

SF&R's client Patty Kaick owns 400 shares of Angelic Star Rockets, Inc. As such she receives 400 rights. The 400 rights will allow her to subscribe to

80 shares (400 rights/5 rights per share = 80 shares). Patty doesn't want an odd lot of stock so she goes into the market and purchases 100 rights. She then takes the 400 she has and the 100 she bought and a check for $6,000 and subscribes for 100 new shares

The trader has a different mission. With the stock at $65, the rights are worth $1. Suppose a trader buys 5,000 rights at $1 each. After the purchase, the stock rises in value to $70 per share, and the rights are worth $2 per share ($70 − $60 = $10; $10/5 = $2). The stock has increased less than 8% but the rights have increased 100%. If the trader is wrong, the most that can be lost is $5,000.

II-A-3-c *Arbitrage*

Arbitrageurs are professional traders who take advantage of price discrepancies in the same or similar issues, watch for price fluctuations, and try to make profit by trading between the rights and new issue.

Example: Angelic Star Rockets, Inc.'s rights are selling at $.75 and the stock is trading ex-rights at $65 per share. An arbitrageur buys 5 rights and then applies the rights plus $60 toward one new share.

Purchase 5 rights at .75	=	$ 3.75
Plus: subscription price	=	60.00
Total cost		$ 63.75
Sell one share of stock		65.00
Profit		$ 1.25

In the real world, the arbitrageur naturally deals in more than one share, but 1,000 shares at $1.25 profit each is $1,250 profit.

Note: Arbitrage situations should be left to the professionals.

II-A-3-d *Warrants*

Initially *warrants* are attached to another security at issuance. The two together are known as a *unit.* The warrant entitles the holder to acquire common stock or some other instrument at a set price during a specified period of time. The acquisition price initially set in the warrant is higher than the current market value of the common stock.

Warrants are longer-term issues than rights. They generally come to the marketplace as part of a unit, which is comprised of two or more issues. For example, a corporation may issue a combination of bonds and warrants. The bonds are in regular form, and the warrants are used to make the offering more attractive. If the issuing company is growth-oriented, with a track record of accomplishing its goals, the warrants will attract investors. In such situations, warrants not only will have conversion value as the underlying security rises and approaches and passes the warrant's conversion price, but due to the attractiveness it permits the issuing company the ability to issue the bonds at a lower interest cost.

Due to the length of time that warrants are outstanding, a corporation can have several different warrants trading at one time. The value of each issue is determined by the relationships among several factors: the conversion price, the time remaining in the warrant, and the value of its underlying stock.

Example: The Malibu Company is a young growth company with a good track record. It wants to raise capital through the issuance of bonds. Its investment banker, SF&R, informs the company that it can issue bonds at a slightly lower interest cost if it issues warrants at the same time as part of a unit. The public will accept the lower interest payment because of the company's growth potential.

Let's make up a case: Malibu's common stock is currently trading at $26 per share. The warrants are issued with an expiration date in 10 years and strike price of $50. Over the 10-year span, Malibu common stock increases in value to $70. The warrant holder can exercise the warrant and buy the stock from the company for $50 a share or sell the warrant in the market for a minimum of $20 per warrant ($70 (market value of the common shares) – $50 (exercise price of the warrant) = $20).

The corporation benefits by issuing stock at a lower issuance cost than a formal underwriting, which is not necessary when the warrant holder subscribes to the common shares.

II-a-3-e *The Certificate*

In the case of either a right or a warrant, the *certificate* itself is referred to as a right or a warrant. Actually, a single right certificate could represent 10 rights,

500 rights, or 1,000 rights; and a single warrant certificate could represent 10 warrants, 50 warrants, 500 warrants, or 1,000 warrants. This term causes confusion and is a constant cause of errors in the brokerage community.

Example: A company issues a unit comprised of a $1,000 bond with a warrant to purchase 10 shares of stock. When the parts of the unit are separated, the bond and the warrant sell separately. At that time, the warrant certificate represents 10 warrants—one per each share of stock.

Operations personnel should *always* make certain of whether the term means the right or warrant certificate *or* the quantity of rights or warrants represented thereupon.

II-A-4 Corporate Bonds and Notes

Type:	Debt
Form:	Registered
Denomination:	Terms established in indenture (usually $1,000)
Income payments:	Interest
Traded:	Electronic stock exchanges or OTC
Duration:	Varies, usually a 30-year maximum

Market conditions, the dilution of ownership, and a host of other factors may lead a corporation to decide against issuing shares of stock to raise capital. Instead, because the corporation is a legal individual, it may borrow money from the public sector in its own name.

- Corporations borrow long-term capital through debt instruments known as *bonds.*
- They borrow intermediate-term financing through *notes.*
- Short-term financing, referred to as *commercial loans,* is arranged through commercial banks. (Some corporations, especially finance corporations, issue a short-term instrument known as *commercial paper.*)

This chapter now focuses on corporate bonds and notes. Bondholders and noteholders are creditors, or lenders, to the corporation. As such, they do not own the company or have any vote in corporate matters. They lend their money to the corporation in return for interest payments as they become due and the repayment of their principal at the conclusion of the loan's term.

Corporate bonds and notes are brought to the public market through underwritings, which are usually negotiated but are sometimes competitive. (See the section "Municipal Bonds and Notes" for an explanation of the competitive underwriting.) In the negotiated underwriting, corporate management and the underwriters meet and decide to issue bonds.

Interest rate as set must be paid or the debtholders can foreclose on the corporation. This set rate of interest must be high enough to compete with other debt instruments but not so high that the corporation cannot pay it. This point, where the two needs meet, is reached with the assistance of an investment banker.

How, then, does the corporation set the interest rate? One factor is the rate of return that the corporation can expect when it invests the borrowed funds.

Example: The issuing company wants to build a new factory. Based on its estimates, the factory will return 10% on money invested to build it. If the corporation must pay 8% on the money it is borrowing, the factory may be worth building. If they have to pay 11% interest, the factory may not.

Another term for using borrowed money to make money is *leverage*. The corporation knows that the income they earn fluctuates while the long-term financing is paid for at a fixed rate. They will therefore be *leveraging* the borrowed funds against the possible income.

Leveraging is a two-edged sword. On one side, the corporation can earn revenue on someone else's money. If the money earned is greater than the cost of money, then the leverage works. On the other side, if the interest cost is greater than the money earned, then leverage isn't a good idea. Remember, the loan has a fixed interest cost. The ability of the corporation to outearn the cost bears some risk. If they don't cover the cost, they still must pay for the loan and will incur a loss.

Example: If a corporation can borrow money at 7% interest, it will earn 2% on the bondholders' money if it can obtain a 9% return on its investment of those funds. (A 9% return on investment less 7% cost of money earns 2%.) On the other hand, if the return on the investment is only 5%, the corporation will lose 2% on the money borrowed, since 7% cost of money minus 5% return on the investment equals 2%.

Another factor is where the issuer stands in relation to other issuers. Remember, these instruments are expected to pay interest on time as well as their principal amount back to the lenders at maturity. The lenders, or debt holders, are selecting from similar instruments and will choose the one that offers the most accommodating terms. No one enjoys paying interest. The lower the amount the issuer has to pay, the better the opportunity for profit and the more willing the issuer is to borrow the funds.

Bonds and notes are issued for periods of time. Bonds are issued with maturity from 10 to 30 years, and notes are issued from 1 to 10 years. When a bond has 10 years or less remaining before maturity, it trades the same as a note with the equivalent time remaining. While the instruments are outstanding, current interest rates change. The fixed-income instrument is going to pay a set amount regardless of the current rate. At times the coupon rate will appear to be attractive in comparison with the current rate. At other times the coupon rate will appear unattractive. As the rate is fixed, the price of the bond has to change to accommodate the current interest changes. The relationship between the coupon rate and price is called *yield*. Here is a simplified explanation of this concept:

First, we look at credit risk. Let us assume that U.S. Treasury 20-year bonds are yielding 6%. Would a 20-year fixed-income instrument of a major corporation, such as IBM or General Electric, be yielding more or less? As the Treasury bond is a safer investment, the corporate bond would have to yield more to attract the investor.

What about Hasenpfeffer Mines Ltd., located somewhere in the West. It hasn't produced anything yet and chances are it won't be in business 20 years from now. Therefore, to attract investors it would have to pay the highest rate of interest, which would give its bonds the highest yield.

Next, we look at market risk.

Say, Marquis Corporation wants to issue a 30-year bond. Based on the prevailing interest rates, it has to issue a bond with a 6% coupon to get par (or dollar for dollar for the loan). It issues the debt instruments.

Ten years later the company comes back to the market to borrow more money. It is as strong financially as it was when the original bonds were issued. It wants to issue 20-year bonds and is told by its investment banker that interest rates have risen over the 10-year period. To be competitive, the corporation must issue a bond with a coupon rate of 10%. It does.

There are now two 20-year Marquis bonds trading in the marketplace:

1. A 30-year bond with a 6% coupon, which is now 10 years old and has 20 years remaining.
2. A new 20-year bond with a 10% coupon.

If both bonds were trading at par (face amount), which one would you buy? Naturally, you would choose the 10% bond as it would yield more of a return to you per dollar invested. To make the 6% bond attractive, the market price would have to fall to a level that would yield a competitive return.

Ten years go by and the Marquis Corporation wants to issue a 10-year bond. Their goal is to have all three bonds mature on the same day. They are in the same healthy financial condition that they were when the previous bonds were issued. Their investment banker tells them that interest rates have eased somewhat and, to be competitive, they must issue a bond with a coupon rate of 8%. They do.

The Marquis corporation now has three bond issues trading, all maturing on the same day:

1. A 6% bond with 10 years remaining.
2. A 10% bond with 10 years remaining.
3. A newly issued 8% bond with 10 years remaining.

If they were all trading at the same price, which bond would you choose? Again, the 10% would give the best return. However, as the 8% bond reflects the current rate requirement, the 10% bond would increase in price until its yield is competitive. And while the 6% bond's market value would have increased in price as the going interest rate fell from 10% to 8%, it still would be priced below the new 8% bond so that its yield would be competitive.

There are two primary yield calculations used in the debt market: *current yield* and *yield to maturity*. We will discuss current yield now and yield to maturity in the municipal bond segment of the book.

Current yield is interest payment divided by market value (IP/MV). An 8% bond will pay $80 per year per $1,000. If the market value of the bond was $1,000, the current yield would be 8% ($80/$1,000 = .08 = 8%). If the market price of the 8% bond was $900, the current yield would be 8.89% (80/900 = .088888 = 8.89%). If the market price was $1,200, the yield would be 6.67% (80/1200 = .066666 = 6.67%). Note that when a bond is trading at a discount (below par), the yield is higher than the coupon rate; when the bond is trading at a premium, the yield is lower than the coupon rate.

Thus we can state that when the current interest rates rise, the prices of outstanding bonds will fall, causing their yields to rise. Conversely, when current interest rates fall, the prices of outstanding bonds will rise, causing their yields to fall.

II-A-4-a *Payment of Interest*

Interest is paid to bondholders, usually on a semiannual basis. The periods are:

- January and July (J&J).
- February and August (F&A).
- March and September (M&S).
- April and October (A&O).
- May and November (M&N).
- June and December (J&D).

The actual payment date can be any day of the month, but it is the same day throughout the life of the instrument. For example, an F&A15 pays interest on February 15 and August 15; an A&O (no date mentioned) pays April 1 and October 1. Because most bonds pay interest on the first day of the interest month, the number "1" is often omitted; such bonds are referred to simply as "A&O," "M&N," and so on.

II-A-4-b *The Marketplace*

Corporate bonds are traded on electronic exchanges as well as over the counter. However, the primary market is the over-the-counter market.

Most bonds trade at the market price plus accrued interest. When a bond is purchased, the buyer pays the agreed-upon price plus whatever interest has accrued from the last interest payment date to the former owner (the seller) of the bond. Let's look at the price of the bond first.

II-A-4-c *Pricing of a Corporate Bond*

The quoted price of the bond represents a percentage of the *face* (*par*) value. The face amount of the bond reflects the indebtedness of the issuer to the lender. A $1,000 bond—that is, a bond with a face amount of $1,000—is supposed to pay $1,000 when the bond matures.

Example: A bond issue of RAM is quoted 96½. In other words, the bond is trading at 96% to 96½% of the par or face amount. For a $1,000 face value bond, a seller with a market order receives $960 ($1,000 × .96). A buyer with a market order pays $965 ($1,000 × .965).

When the bond is trading at 100%, it is said to be trading *at par*. Bonds trading at prices *over par* are said to be *at a premium*, whereas bonds trading *below par* are said to be selling *at a discount*.

The price at which a bond is trading has a direct impact on the investor's return, because interest is paid on the face amount of the bond, not on its market value. A bond pays the same dollar amount of interest regardless of its current market price. If the bond is trading at a discount, the investor's rate of return is higher than the stated interest rate on the bond, which is called the *coupon rate*.

II-A-4-c-i Accrued Interest

The trade price, however, is only part of what the buyer will pay the seller. The buyer must also pay any interest that has accrued to the seller since the last interest payment.

Interest on corporate and most municipal bonds is computed on a 360-day basis, with each half-year interest period comprising 180 days. Therefore, for every full month, 30 days' worth of interest is accrued regardless of the actual number of days in that month.

Example: An 8% bond pays $80 per year per $1,000 of face value, or $40 semiannually.

Interest continues to accrue to the bond's seller up to but not including *settlement day* of the trade, the day the buyer pays accrued interest to the seller. The formula for calculating accrued interest is:

$$\text{Accrued interest} = \text{Face amount} \times \text{Interest rate} \times \frac{\text{Number of days}}{360}$$

Example: On settlement date April 11, William Dewitt purchases $1,000 RAM 8% A&O 2030 @ 96. Because the bond pays interest on April 1 and October 1 (A&O), Willie owes the seller interest from April 1 through and including April 10. Counting days from April 1, the first day of the interest period, up through but not including the settlement date of April 11, we get 10 days. Will owes 10 days of interest. Let's calculate the accrued interest:

Face amount × Interest rate × Number of days divided by 360 = Accrued interest

$$\frac{\$1{,}000 \times 8 \times 10}{1 \times 100 \times 360}$$

$$\frac{\$\ 10 \times 8 \times 1}{1 \times 1 \times 36}$$

$$\frac{\$\ 10 \times 8 \times 1}{1 \times 1 \times 36}$$

$$\frac{\$\ 10 \times 2 \times 1}{1 \times 1 \times 39}$$

$$\frac{20}{9} = \$2.23$$

Willie Dewitt pays the seller $960 (.96 × $1,000 face value) plus accrued interest of $2.23.

On settlement date, September 5, Willie Dewitt sells the bonds at a price of $96. Now let's see the calculations on the sale of the bond. Will owned the bonds from April 11 through September 4. Therefore, Willie has interest owed to him. Counting from April 11 through but not including the settlement date of September 5, we get 144 days during which interest has accrued. Willie Dewitt is entitled to receive 144 days' accrued interest.

	Days
April	20
May	30
June	30
July	30
August	30
September	4
Total	144

Face amount × Interest rate × Number of days divided by 360 = Accrued interest

$$\text{Accrued Interest} = \frac{\$1{,}000}{1} \times \frac{8}{100} \times \frac{144}{360} = \$32.00$$

Because Will paid $2.23 in accrued interest when he first purchased the bonds, representing 10 days of accrued interest, and he earned actual interest of $32, which equals the accrued interest for 144 days, the buyer of the bonds must pay Willie a total of $34.23, which represents a total of 154 days. In other words, the buyer of the bond will pay $34.23 for the 154 days since the last interest payment. Willie has paid $2.23 to the person he bought the bonds from 10 days after that last interest payment. This leaves Willie with $32.

On October 1, the corporation's agents pay $40 to the record holder of the bond. Assuming it's the person who purchased the bonds from Willie, that individual has accumulated 26 days of accrued interest for the sum of $5.77. The new owner, having paid Will $34.23, is left with $5.77 when the $34.23 is subtracted from the $40 received on October 1, the end of the six-month period. In other words, the new bondholder who bought the bonds from Dewitt is going to receive a full six-months' interest even though they only held the bonds for 26 days. However, they paid for 154 days. Therefore, the remainder is theirs: $40, which is the six-month payment, minus $34.23 leaves the new bondholder with $5.77, which is what is earned on that bond for 26 days.

Note that the corporation authorizes its agent to pay the entire six-month interest payment to the holder on record date. The parties who buy or sell bonds during the period simply settle the accrued interest among themselves.

Example:

Original Owner:	Receives accrued interest at time of sale		$ 2.23
William:	Pays at time of purchase	$ 2.23	
	Receive at time of sale	$34.23	
	Accrues to William		$32.00
Last owner:	Pays William at time of purchase	$34.23	
	Accrues to the last owner		$ 5.77
	Total		$40.00
	Receives from corporation	$40.00	

II-A-4-d *Bond Ratings*

Most fixed-income issues are reviewed and rated by various rating services, the two best known being Standard & Poor's and Moody's. Such companies use many criteria to evaluate the financial strength of issuers. With easy access to these reports, the public may use these ratings in choosing the appropriate investment.

When the corporation and its investment banker negotiate the terms of the bond to be issued, the company's rating plays an important part. The higher the rating, the more willing the investing public is to purchase the security. On the other hand, the more willing investors are to buy the bond because of its rating, the less interest the issuer has to pay to attract investors.

II-A-4-e *Indenture*

Other considerations enter into the negotiations. Bonds, like preferred stock, can contain features that make one more attractive than another. Among these features are callable, convertible, floating rate, and zero coupon. The terms of a corporate bond are found in the *indenture* (also known as the *deed of trust*), which is printed on the back of the certificates. The description of a newly issued bond is found in the offering prospectus, whereas the terms of bonds trading in the secondary market can be found in various publications or through the broker/dealer offering them.

II-A-4-f *Retiring Bonds*

Like a preferred stock, a bond can be callable or convertible (into common stock, not preferred). Sometimes a corporation expects to retire an issue of bonds by buying them on the open market with money it has earned. In such a case, the corporation sets up a *sinking fund*; that is, it periodically places money in a fund for the purpose of buying back the bonds.

A sinking fund differs from a callable feature in that the callable price is predetermined and appears in the indenture. With the sinking fund, the corporation acquires the bonds at the current market price. Generally, a corporation is not permitted to acquire or purchase bonds if they are trading at a premium.

Bonds may be retired by three payment methods:

1. In a *redemption*, the bonds are retired by the company paying cash from its reserve accounts.
2. In a *conversion*, the bondholders exchange their bonds for shares of common stock.
3. In a *refunding*, the corporation retires one bond issue by issuing another. Sometimes this is accomplished with the existing bondholders. The bondholders "roll" their investment into the new debt. Another form of refunding occurs when the corporation issues a new bond into the marketplace and uses the proceeds to pay off their maturing debt. To the corporation they are refunding (refinancing the loan) by substituting the new bond for the old. To the existing holders of the maturing bonds, it is a redemption as they are getting cash.

II-A-4-g *Bond Security*

By buying bonds, members of the public are, in fact, risking their capital. Should the company default, what assurance do bondholders have of getting any of their money returned? That depends on what security the corporation has pledged to assure the public of the safety of the investment. Bond issues are commonly supported by mortgages, collateral, equipment, or just the good name of the company. (In the latter case, the bond is known as a *debenture.*)

II-A-4-g-i Mortgage Bonds

Mortgage bonds are supported by a lien on the corporation's property, usually a plant or office building. The mortgage issue may be *open ended*, which means that the subsequent issues are equal in all respects to the original issue. In a *closed-end* mortgage issue, subsequent issues are junior to the original issue in any claims against the corporation. Each subsequent issue is junior to the previous one in the payment of interest and the coverage that supports the issue.

The corporation could also issue several open-ended bond offerings over time and then make the last issue closed ended. All of these bonds would be equal in the claim of assets in case of default, but all subsequent issues would be junior.

II-A-4-g-ii Collateral Trust Bonds

Collateral trust bonds are secured by the collateral of another corporation. A company secures the issue with stock in another company that it owns or is donated by existing shareholders. The strength of another company's securities supports the issue. Shareholders who have sizable investments in the company will pledge securities they own of other companies to secure the new debt. The fact that the new bonds are secured by more financially sound instruments permits the new debt to be issued at a lower interest rate, thereby saving the company much needed funds over the long term.

II-A-4-g-iii Equipment Trust Bonds

Equipment trust bonds are secured by a corporation's equipment, usually its rolling stock. This type of bond is common in the railroad, trucking, and airline industries. For example, an airline pledges its planes and other vehicles as security for the bond.

II-A-4-g-iv Debenture Bonds

The *debenture bond*, issued by only the strongest of companies, is secured by the good faith and name of the issuing company. Nothing tangible secures the issue, but the possibility of the company's defaulting on the issue is generally believed to be nil.

II-A-4-h *Registration*

Corporate bond certificates are fully registered. Until the late 1950s or early 1960s, two other forms existed:

1. *Bearer certificates*, in which the holders are the assumed owners.
2. *Registered-to-principal bonds*, which had the actual owners' names or nominees' names maintained by a corporate transfer agent.

Both forms necessitated the "clipping" of coupons to receive interest payments. As of July 1, 1983, no new bonds can be issued in coupon form.

The *fully registered bond* form has superseded these other forms. For a fully registered bond, the owner's or the nominee's name is maintained by a transfer agent. The semiannual interest payments are mailed to the registered holders by the corporation's interest-paying agent. This type of registration has made transfer of bonds much easier than it was in the past, and it safeguards against theft.

II-A-4-i *Default*

When a company gets into financial trouble, it may turn to two types of debt instruments: a receiver's certificate or an income bond.

A *receiver's certificate* is a short-term note, issued by the *receiver*, that is, the person handling the company's bankruptcy proceedings. It is usually employed to enable the company to complete the production cycle. Bond owners purchase the receiver certificate, thereby giving the company additional cash, in anticipation of getting a better adjustment in the bankruptcy than if the company stopped production immediately. For example, let's say a company fails at the beginning of a production cycle, with most of its capital tied up in inventory. If the company *liquidates*, that is, sells off all its assets, bond owners would receive only pennies on each dollar they invested in the company's bonds. If the bondholders advance funds by buying receiver's certificates, so that the company is able to finish the cycle, they may receive a higher payoff on each dollar invested.

Income bonds are longer-term debt issued by the company with an extremely high interest rate because they are extremely risky. When a company cannot pay interest on its outstanding debt, income bonds are issued on a pay-when-earned basis. The purchaser of these bonds is "trading" the possibility of receiving a very good return against the possibility of losing part, or all, of the principal.

II-A-4-j *Other Bond Features*

Bonds may have several other features that we have not yet discussed.

II-A-4-j-i Callable Bonds

As with preferred stocks, bonds may be callable. The callable feature exists not only in corporate issues, but also in municipal issues and government issues. Issuers have the ability to retire the issue before maturity, if they want to, under predetermined set conditions. Generally, callable bonds are callable at a premium over par. In other words, the bonds will state at what price they can be called in. Generally the corporation is willing to pay a slight premium over face value to retire the bonds. Callable bonds may have a feature that prohibits the issuer from calling the bond in for a specific period of time, such as "noncallable for five years." This goes from the point of issuance, not from the point of purchase, so a 20-year bond being issued with a "noncallable for five years" provision can only be callable after the five years have lapsed from issuance. When there is a call feature and there is time between call and maturity, there will be a prorated premium over the remaining life of the bond. This means that in the case of a 20-year bond that is noncallable for the first five years, from five years until maturity, the amount a company will pay over par diminishes until, around maturity, the call price and par are the same.

Example: A $10,000 TIP 7% J&J 2030 is issued with a "noncallable for five years" feature:

6-year callable @ $106

7-year callable @ $105.90

8-year callable @ $105.80 and so on.

30-year callable @ par.

II-A-4-j-ii Convertible Bonds

Again, as with preferred stocks, corporate bonds may be convertible into another issue at the desire of the bondholder. Usually, the convertible feature allows the bond to be converted into equity (stock), thereby reducing corporate debt. This is an attractive feature to both the corporation and the bondholder. If the corporation is successful and grows, the stock becomes more valuable, and at some point it will behoove the convertible bondholder to exchange the bonds for stock. This could be caused by two events.

First event: As the convertible value of the stock exceeds the value of the bond, the arbitrageurs will enter the market, buy the bonds, give conversion instructions, and immediately sell the common stock. Arbitrageurs are professionals working for broker/dealers; therefore, they do not pay commission or other fees. Here's an example: A $1,000 bond is convertible into 40 shares of common stock. Therefore a $1,000 bond trading at par is worth $1,000. Forty shares of common stock at parity, that is, equal to the value of the bonds, would be trading at $25 a share ($25 a share × 40 shares = $1,000). Let's assume the bonds are trading at $1,000 and the stock is trading at $20 a share. At this point, no one will convert a $1,000 bond for $800 worth of stock (40 shares × $20 = $800). However, if the price of the stock rose above 25, it would become attractive to convert. Arbitrageurs would do the conversion, thereby forcing up the price of the bond. The bond's price would be forced up due to the demand put on it by the arbitrageurs; remember, they are buying the bonds, giving conversion instructions to their settlement area, and then selling the stock immediately. Their risk is momentary. The average bondholder is therefore gaining value in principal on the bond as the common stock rises. They could, of course, sell the bonds at a profit, assuming they bought it below the current market price.

Second event: As discussed in this chapter's "Preferred Stock" section, if the payout (dividend) of the common stock is greater than the payout (interest) of the bonds and all else is equal, the bondholders will convert their bonds to stock.

Another benefit of convertible issues is that, as the bonds are converted to stock, debt is removed from the company's balance sheets and replaced by equity or ownership. The less debt a corporation has, the more attractive it looks to investors.

II-A-4-j-iii Zero-Coupon and Floating-Rate Bonds

Corporations issue two other types of bonds. One is called a *floating-rate* or *adjustable-rate bond*, the other a *zero-coupon bond*. The floating- or adjustable-rate corporate bond will have its interest rate reset periodically. Therefore, the same dollar amount of interest is not paid over the life of the bond. This accomplishes several goals. First, depending on the reset schedule, it keeps the interest rate paid by the bonds competitive in the current market. Second, barring any change in the corporation's financial status, the bonds should trade near or at their original cost as the amount of interest paid always reflects the current rate for that class of bonds. This type of issuance is very helpful to a corporation when they need money for a group of short-term projects. And third, going to the market once, paying the cost of underwriting only one time, they are able to maintain funds at the current rate over the life of the bond. Therefore, the cost of the bond versus the income received from these various short-term projects should assist the corporation maintain a profit margin. The interest rates on these types of bonds are generally adjusted twice a year.

Therefore, should a bondholder suddenly have to sell the bonds during the bonds' life, the bondholder is not exposed to that much market risk due to the fact that interest rates have risen over the period of time they owned the bonds. Fixed-income bonds would now command a much lower price, as their coupon rate is below the current rate for similar instruments. Conversely, should interest rates fall during the life of the bonds, fixed-income bonds would be worth more. (On the other hand, the customer owning the adjustable-rate bonds would miss the opportunity of making a profit as the interest rate on the adjustable bonds would be reduced at the time it is reset.) Since the newly issued bonds will carry a lower interest rate than these bonds carried previously, the opportunity to capitalize is lost because the interest rate is adjusted to reflect the lower rate. Like everything else in this industry, it balances out.

Zero-coupon bonds are issued at a deep discount and, as stated in their description, they do not pay interest. Therefore, the bonds accrue interest in their value over the life of the bonds. For example, a $1,000 zero-coupon bond maturing in 20 years could cost $600 today and at maturity be worth $1,000. The difference between what was paid today and what's received is the interest earned over the life of the bond. These types of bonds are very attractive to investors who are putting money away, let's say, for their newborn child's college education. Zero coupons are also attractive to the issuing corporation, as they don't have to go through the process of paying interest periodically. However, they are faced with a large "bill" at the end of a bond's life. This type of instrument is known as a *discounted instrument* as the amount of interest owed is subtracted from the face value at the time of issuance. Therefore, bond investors pay face value minus interest at the time of purchase. If the investors hold the bonds to maturity, they will receive face value. If the bonds are sold during the period of life, it would be the amount of interest accrued to that point versus the current interest rate for a bond of that nature that would determine the price the customer would receive.

Example: A $10,000, 10-year bond is discounted at a rate of 6%. The formula would be:

$$\text{Present value} = \text{principal}\,\frac{1}{(1+\text{rate})^{\text{term}}}$$

$$\text{Present value} = \$10{,}000\,\frac{1}{(1+.06)^{10}}$$

$$\text{Present value} = \$10{,}000\ \frac{1}{1.79085}$$
$$\text{Present value} = \$10{,}000\ (1/1.79085)$$
$$\text{Present value} = 10{,}000 \times .5560189$$
$$\text{Present value} = \$5{,}560.19$$

This is discussed in detail in the municipal bond section that follows.

Corporate notes follow the same pattern as corporate bonds. They are issued for periods of time ranging from 1 to 10 years. Interest is paid twice a year. There are floating- or adjustable-rate notes and zero-coupon notes besides the standard fixed-income type. Notes with convertible or callable features are extremely rare to nonexistent. The instruments trade at dollar prices, as do their longer-term (bond) counterparts.

II-A-4-k *Bonds and Notes Summary*

Corporate bonds and notes represent loans to, not ownership in, the company. When you buy a bond or note, you are buying the interest payments made—usually two payments per year. On settlement date, the buyer pays the purchase price (expressed as a percentage of the face value) and accrued interest. Bonds may be callable or convertible (usually to common stock). Bonds may be secured in various ways. In the event of default, bondholders might be offered either short-term receiver's certificates or longer-term income bonds.

II-A-5 Commercial Paper

Type:	Debt: discount instrument or principal plus interest
Form:	Electronic
Denomination:	From \$25,000 or \$100,000 and larger
Income payments:	Interest
Traded:	Over the counter
Duration:	Usually 270 days or less

Corporations raise long-term capital by issuing stocks and bonds. They raise short-term money by taking out loans from commercial banks and by issuing commercial paper to the investing public.

Commercial paper is a debt instrument that is offered sometimes as a discounted instrument and sometimes as principal plus interest. In the case of a *discounted instrument*, no interest payments are made. Instead, the price paid to buy the instrument is lower than the face value, which is paid to the buyer at maturity. The difference between the price paid and the face value is the interest earned on the investment. For a *plus-interest instrument*, the client pays the full face value to buy the paper and receives the face value plus the interest accrued at maturity.

Neither type of instrument has a fixed interest rate. Instead, the rate is negotiated at the time of purchase and the interest is calculated from face or full value. To receive the full amount of interest, the buyer must, for all practical purposes, hold the instrument until maturity. If the paper is sold during its life, its price is subject to market fluctuations. In the case of commercial paper, the secondary market is thin, almost nonexistent.

II-A-5-a *Issuance*

Commercial paper is sold through two conduits: by direct placement or through dealers. *Direct placement* takes place between a bank and its customers. On behalf of its clients, the bank contacts the issuing corporation and purchases the paper. The transaction is generally custom-tailored to the needs of the bank's clients. *Dealer-sold paper* is purchased by a commercial paper dealer in bulk and sold to its customers.

II-A-5-b *Trading*

Commercial paper trading lots are $1,000,000, but a minimum of $25,000 is possible, depending on the marketplace. Maturities are 30, 60, 90, and seldom more than 270 days. Since commercial paper is not as standardized as, say, Treasury securities or municipals, the terms of agreement—the minimum denomination, the length of maturities, and so on—can change as the needs of the corporation and lenders change.

II-A-5-c *Settlement*

Transactions in commercial paper settle *same day*. Dealers must pay for commercial paper on the day of purchase. When dealers resell the paper to their customers, the new owners must pay on the day of purchase. Usually both transactions—from corporate representative to dealer and from dealer to customer—occur on the same day. Control and accuracy are therefore mandatory due to the large sums of money involved and the limited time for settling all the daily transactions.

Because of the transaction size, most settlement is effected between banks through the use of the Fedwire, a communication network among member banks of the Federal Reserve System. Funds received through this vehicle do not follow the several-day fund clearance cycle experienced with checks. Because a recipient of Fed funds can use the money when received, as if it were a cash deposit, they are considered same-day funds.

II-A-5-d *Handling the Certificates*

The physical piece of commercial paper, the certificate, is no longer issued by the commercial bank representing issuing corporations. Instead, it is electronically issued through the facilities of DTCC. The bank may purchase the paper for its own clients or issue it for purchase by other banks or dealers.

Because commercial paper is an investment instrument, secondary trading in the instrument is virtually nonexistent. The handling of the commercial paper can take several routes. For the *issuing bank's client*, the certificate of deposit is recorded as issued on the issuing bank's books and placed in the account of the client. In a bank other than the issuing bank, it is transmitted from the issuing bank to Depository Trust and Clearing Corporation and into the account of the acquiring bank. It is maintained there until maturity, when it is surrendered on behalf of the beneficial owner to the issuing bank against payment.

II-A-5-e *Financing*

If a dealer buys and resells paper on trade date, the paper does not have to be financed, because the issuing corporation is paid out of the proceeds of the resale. If the dealer does not resell the paper on the same day as purchase, the issuing corporation must still be paid. Financing is therefore needed.

Financing is arranged through either collateralized loans or repos.

For a *collateralized loan*, arranged between the dealer and a bank, the paper becomes the collateral. The lending bank advances the necessary funds upon receipt of paper into its DTC account from the dealer's account. The dealer has lines of credit with various banking institutions and turns to these establishments for financing.

In a *repo* (or *repurchase agreement*), the borrower (dealer) obtains funds by "selling" the collateral to the lender with the agreement that it will be reacquired at a set price on a specific day. The difference between the sale price and the repurchase price is the interest paid to the lender. Repos are arranged with private individuals or with institutions that have funds available for investing but that do not want to expose themselves or are prohibited from exposing the fund to financial or market risk. They therefore lend their funds for a short period, such as overnight or two days, in such an agreement.

In the case of a repo, the instrument actually isn't sold and repurchased, because ownership doesn't really change. The instrument is delivered to the lender in negotiable form and returned unaltered at the end of the commitment. Since most commercial paper is in electronic form, this fact is often overlooked. The process is handled by DTCC electronically.

II-A-5-f *Maturity*

At maturity, the client instructs its agent bank to surrender the position to the issuing corporation, and the paper is paid off.

II-B *MUNICIPAL SECURITIES*

Municipal bonds and *notes* (*munis*) are debt instruments issued by state and local governments to raise capital to finance projects and other needs. Generally, income (that is, interest) earned on most municipal securities is free from federal income tax. For a resident of the issuing municipality, interest from the bonds may also be exempt from state and local income taxes. However, the tax-free status for interest paid by these instruments is not universal. There are taxable as well as tax-free interest-paying municipal securities. (Profit or loss occurring from the trading of these instruments is subject to usual taxation.)

II-B-1 The Competitive Underwriting

Just as a corporation is answerable to its shareholders, the municipality is answerable to its taxpayers. New municipal issues are therefore brought to market through a competitive underwriting. This method ensures that taxpayers are getting the best terms available. With several syndicates competing for the issue, there is no room for manipulation, collusion, or other illegal practices.

Municipalities work with banks and broker/dealer firms, which form syndicates to study the municipality's needs. In charge of each syndicate group is the *manager*. The manager organizes the group, prepares the prospectus (if required), and performs other assignments that are similar to their negotiated underwriting counterparts. When the group is formed, the upcoming underwriting is discussed. Each participant states what they believe would be a fair and competitive bid, which the manager uses in formulating the final bid. The participants meet and review the final bid, and it is submitted to the municipality.

Each group independently develops a proposal and submits it to the municipality. After all the groups have submitted their bids, the participants wait for the municipality's decision.

Officials of the municipality study all the proposals and select the one that best accommodates their goals. When they make a determination, they notify the winning syndicate. The bids of all the syndicates are available to the public if they desire the information.

Once the decision has been made, participants of the losing groups, if they are still interested in the issue, call the winning manager to see if they can participate in the distribution.

II-B-2 Offering of Municipal Bonds

Generally, when a new municipal bond issue is brought to market, it is brought out in serial form. This type of issuance differs from corporate and federal offerings in that their issues come to market with one maturity date (such as $100,000,000 Starfire Power Corp. 8% JJ-20XX), which is known as a *bullet offering*. Municipals, while perhaps borrowing the same sum of financing, will issue their debt with several different maturities. For example, $100,000,000 Delmont County debt is issued as $2,000,000 6½

FA-2023, 2,000,000 6⅜ FA-2024, 3,000,000 6½ FA-2025, and so on. This form of offering is known as *serial.* Each issue is independent and has its own unique ID or CUSIP number. Therefore, a municipal offering can have 10, 15, or more issues coming to market as part of one offering. If the longest-term issue has a substantially larger quantity than the other issues, the offering is said to contain *a balloon maturity.*

By having a serialized issue, the municipality can retire the issue part by part, rather than face an entire maturity requirement, as the federal government and corporations usually do. The serial form of offering results in the individual bond issue being relatively small in size.

II-B-3 The Effect of Income Tax Rates

Municipal debt instruments compete, in the over-the-counter market, for public funds with other fixed-income securities. Investors choose from the many types of issues traded by determining which type of issue best suits their needs. Municipalities can issue their debt securities at interest rates lower than those for other debt securities because the interest payments are not subject to federal taxation, making the tax-free yield especially attractive to investors in high income tax brackets.

Example: Investor Rick Atee is in the 30% income tax bracket and, therefore, realizes only 70 cents on each dollar he earns. He pays the difference to the government in the form of income tax. Rick is considering buying either a 6½% corporate bond or a 5% municipal bond. Per $1,000 of face value, the corporate bond will pay $65 per year in interest, whereas the municipal bond will pay $50. Tax on the corporate bond's interest payment would be $19.50 (30% of $65), so the net return to Rick would be $45.50. Compare this with the tax-free $50 received from the municipal security. For Rick Atee, the municipal security is therefore the better investment of the two.

II-B-4 Municipal Bonds

Type:	Debt
Form:	Registered, some book entry only
Denomination:	$1,000 minimum

Income payments: Interest
Traded: Over the counter
Duration: Set per issue

II-B-4-a *Trading Municipal Bonds*

At the time of the offering, brokerage firms buy the issue from underwriters for resale to their customers. Most of the trading in the particular muni issue occurs at this time, because purchasers usually buy these securities for investment purposes, not for ongoing trading. Muni debt investors generally buy the bonds, hold them to maturity, and look forward to the tax-free interest payments.

Typically, therefore, individual municipal issues are traded infrequently (*thinly*). The distinctive characteristic of these issues is that they come to the marketplace, they are placed in investors' portfolios, and they disappear from the market. Over time, pieces of the original issue find their way to the secondary market, are resold, and disappear again. That is why municipal bonds are more suitable for trading on the OTC market than on exchanges. It is also why they are not quoted on a dollar basis, as are corporate bonds, whose issues trade frequently throughout their lifetimes. Except for a few muni issues, it is therefore difficult to acquire a particular municipal bond in the *secondary market* (the OTC market) in which these securities are resold. Someone who invests in municipal bonds selects their investment from an inventory that is currently being maintained by a municipal bond dealer. The individual is interested in the municipal debt of a certain state and within certain parameters, such as the length of time to maturity and a minimum rating from one of the rating agencies.

II-B-4-b *Basis Pricing*

Suppose your stockbroker were to read you a list of quotes for municipal bonds as follows: Bond A, 5%-2024 @ 94¾; Bond B, 6⅛%-2029 @ 95⅛; Bond C 5¾%-2025 @ 93½, and so on. As they have been issued by different government entities within the same state and they all fit your parameters, the differences between them seem nebulous. You might eventually say, "Hold up! Just tell me the return on my investment per bond." In other words, "What's my yield?" As a result, municipal bonds are quoted at a *basis price* (that is, in terms of yield to maturity).

The computation of yield to maturity or basis price is complex. It is the rate obtained from the present value of all of the instruments' future cash flows. This complex computation is explained later. A simpler though less accurate method, the *rule of thumb formula*, will give you an approximate figure:

$$\text{Yield to maturity} = \frac{\text{Annual interest amount} \; \begin{array}{c} - \\ + \end{array} \; \begin{array}{c} \text{Depleted premium or} \\ \text{amortized discount} \end{array}}{\dfrac{\text{Face amount} + \text{Current value}}{2}}$$

Example: Investor Varga purchases a $1,000 Aurora County KY FA 7% 2028 bond on trade date January 21, 2003. The bond matures in 25 years (2028–2003). The price of $95 translates into $950. At maturity, the bondholder receives $1,000, including $50 in capital gains ($1,000 – $950). The $50 must be amortized over the life of the bond: $50 divided by 25 years equals a $2 annual amortization. In addition, the 8% bond pays $80 in interest per year. Therefore,

$$\text{Yield to maturity} = \frac{\$80 + \$2}{\dfrac{\$1{,}000 + \$950}{2}} = \frac{\$82}{\$975} = .841 = 8.41\%$$

The rule of thumb formula gives you the yield to maturity of 8.41%. Or you could say that the bond was purchased at an "8.41 basis."

Example: An Ebbets Stadium revenue bond 6% FA 2027 is quoted "6.50–5.50 basis." The "6.50" part of the quote means "6½%." This is not the bid price; it is the percentage of the yield associated with the bid price (which is not reflected in the quote). Someone with a market order to sell these bonds would receive a price that equates to a yield to maturity of 6.50%. The "5.50" means that, given the offer price, a buyer will receive a yield to maturity of 5½%.

What is the relationship between price and yield? Because the coupon rate is fixed, only price and yield change. The rule is, *the lower the price, as compared to the coupon rate, the higher the yield.* Since a yield of 6½% is higher than the 6% coupon rate of Ebbets municipals, it reflects a *discounted* price (a price lower than the face value of $1,000). The yield of 5½% reflects a *premium* price (one that is higher than the $1,000 face amount).

Let's look at this relationship from another point of view. Since lowering the price increases the yield, the bid in any quote is always lower than the offer dollarwise. The bid is the price that a buyer is willing to pay; the buyer, naturally, bids as little as possible to get the greatest yield possible. The seller, on the other hand, has an offering price that is higher than the bid, because the seller wants the best sale price possible. If the bid and offer are equal, then the buyer and seller have an agreed-upon price and a transaction takes place.

In a "basis quote," even though the bids are higher numerically, it represents a lower dollar figure, and the reverse is true on the offer side. Therefore, a quote 7.60-7.40 means the bidder is willing to pay less for the interest payments than the seller (offeror) is willing to accept. Using the current yield formula and a $1,000 bond with a 7% coupon, we would receive $70 per year interest ($1,000×.07=$70). If we sold the bond to the bidder for a basis price of 7.60, we would receive approximately $920 per bond ($70/$920=.076 or 7.60%). If we bought the bonds from the seller, we would be paying approximately $945 per bond ($70/$945=.074 or 7.40%]. Therefore, the dollar equivalent of the basis quote 7.60–7.40 would be 92.00–94.50. (In the actual world, the yield to maturity formula is used, not the current yield, which was used here for explanatory purposes.)

Why does a discounted (below-par) price increase yield, or a premium (above-par) price reduce yield? The difference between the purchase price and face value has to be added to (below par) or subtracted from (above par) the interest rate. At maturity, the bondholder is going to be paid the face value. If the holder paid less than the face value, then that difference is a kind of "bonus" payment and should be added to the interest amount. If the holder paid more, the extra amount is gone by maturity and has to be deducted from the overall or total return.

Example: Investor McKenna buys a $1,000 7% 5-year bond for $950. She holds it for 5 years to maturity, receiving $70 in interest each of those years ($1,000×.70), for a total of $350 interest payments (5×$70). (Don't forget, the coupon rate does not change.) At the end of 5 years, however, she is paid the face value of the bond, $1,000; that is $50 more than she paid. So actually, the extra $50 ($1,000 – $950) is like an extra interest payment.

The question is, to which year does it apply? The answer is that it applies to all 5 years. You have to *amortize*, or spread out, the $50 over 5 years.

To amortize the discount or deplete a premium amount, divide it by the number of years to maturity.

Example: To amortize $50 over 5 years, divide $50 by 5 years, for the sum of $10 a year.

A discount price therefore gives the buyer an increased dollar yield to maturity. Had McKenna paid $1,050 for the bond, she would lose the $50 by maturity. This $50 amount must be depleted over the 5 years at $10 per year, thereby reducing the amount of return. A premium price means a reduced yield to maturity.

Quoting at a basis price is also a convenient way to represent a dealer's inventory uniformly. Muni dealers trade with other dealers, with brokers, and with their firm's own customers from inventory positions. Given a customer's request, a firm will check its own positions (if it is a market maker) and shop among other dealers to locate an issue that suits the customer's needs. Quoting on basis puts all the quotes on a comparable basis and in a form that the customer can understand. In summation, yield to maturity is the present value of a cash payment to be made at a later date.

We will now present the actual computation to prove the rule of thumb computation.

The following are all the computations for a $1,000 10-year bond with a 7% coupon, paying interest every six months, which represents the present value of 20 cash flows of $35 each. The last payment includes the present value of the principal amount of $1,000 in addition to the $35 interest payment. Here's the formula:

For a $1,000 7% bond, paying interest twice a year ($35 each payment) and having a life span of 10 years priced to yield 6%:

$$\text{Present value} = \text{Payout} \times \frac{1}{(1+\text{rate})} \times \#\text{ of times}$$

We calculate the first payment due in six months:

$$\text{Present value} = \$35 \times \frac{1}{(1+.03)} \times 1$$

$$\text{Present value} = \$35 \frac{1}{(1.03)}$$

Present value = $35 (1/1.03)
Present value = $35 (.97087370)
Present value = $33.98

The present value of a $35 payment due in 6 months discounted at a rate of 6% is $33.98. Because it is for half a year, half the annual interest rate is used.

For the full 10 years, the present value would be:

# OF PAYMENTS	PAYOUT × FACTOR	=	Present Value
1	$35 × .970874	=	$33.98
2	35 × .942596	=	32.99
3	35 × .915141	=	32.03
4	35 × .888486	=	31.10
5	35 × .862608	=	30.19
6	35 × .837483	=	29.31
7	35 × .813091	=	28.46
8	35 × .789409	=	27.63
9	35 × .766416	=	26.82
10	35 × .744093	=	26.04
11	35 × .722420	=	25.28
12	35 × .701739	=	24.55
13	35 × .680950	=	23.83
14	35 × .661116	=	23.14
15	35 × .641861	=	22.47
16	35 × .623661	=	21.83
17	35 × .605015	=	21.17
18	35 × .587393	=	20.59
19	35 × .570285	=	19.96
20	1,035 × .553674	=	573.05
		Total	$1,074.42

Using the rule of thumb method:

1. Current market value = $1,074.42
   Less: value at maturity = 1,000.00
   Amount to be depleted $ 74.42

2. Divide $74.42 by 10 years = $7.44 per year.
3. Subtract $7.44 from the $70 annual interest payment to get the amortized return, $62.56.
4. Average the current market value and the value at maturity: ($1,074.42 + $1,000.00)/2 = $1,037.21.
5. Divide the adjusted interest by the average value: $62.56/$1,037.21 = 6.03.

Allowing for rounding, a $1,000 bond with a coupon rate of 7% and maturity date of 10 years from now, that is sold at a basis price of 6.00 (6%) would cost approximately $1,074.42.

Let's see if the same holds true for a bond trading at a discount.

Say we have a $1,000 7% bond paying interest twice a year ($35 each payment), having a life span of a full 10 years, and priced to yield 8%. Let's calculate the first payment due in six months.

$$\text{Present value} = \$35 \times \frac{1}{(1+.04)} \times 1$$

$$\text{Present value} = \$35 \frac{1}{(1.04)}$$

$$\text{Present value} = \$35\ (1/1.04)$$

$$\text{Present value} = \$35\ (.961538461)$$

$$\text{Present value} = \$33.65$$

# OF PAYMENTS	PAYOUT × FACTOR	=	Present Value
1	35×.961538	=	$33.65
2	35×.924556	=	32.36
3	35×.888996	=	31.11
4	35×.854804	=	29.92
5	35×.821927	=	28.77
6	35×.790314	=	27.66
7	35×.759918	=	26.60
8	35×.730690	=	25.57
9	35×.702506	=	24.59
10	35×.676564	=	23.64
11	35×.649508	=	22.73
12	35×.624597	=	21.86
13	35×.600574	=	21.02

(continued)

# OF PAYMENTS	PAYOUT × FACTOR	=	Present Value
14	35×.577475	=	20.21
15	35×.555264	=	19.43
16	35×.533908	=	18.68
17	35×.513373	=	17.97
18	35×.493628	=	17.28
19	35×.474642	=	16.61
20	1,035×.456386	=	472.36
		Total	$932.02

Using the rule of thumb method:

1. Value at maturity = $1,000.00
   less: Current market value = 932.02
   Amount to be amortized $ 67.98
2. Divide $67.98 by 10 years: $6.798 or 6.80.
3. Add $6.79 to the $70 annual interest payment to get the amortized return, $76.80.
4. Average the current market value and the value at maturity: ($1,000.00 + $932.02)/2 = $966.01.
5. Divide the amortized return by the average value: $76.80/$966.01 = 7.95. Allowing for rounding, a $1,000 bond, with a coupon rate of 7% and a maturity date of 10 years from now, that is sold at a basis price of 8.00 (8%) would cost approximately $932.13.

Please note that when the effective interest rate is greater than the coupon rate, the bond is selling at a discount. When the effective interest rate is lower than the coupon rate, the bond is selling at premium.

II-B-4-c *Types of Municipal Bonds*

Municipals may be categorized according to the source of the funds that will be used to pay interest and principal.

General Obligation Bonds are secured by the full taxing power of the issuing state or local government. Money to pay interest and principal comes from general tax revenues.

A *limited tax bond* is backed by a particular tax, such as a state sales tax.

Revenue bonds are secured by the revenue from a project built by capital raised in the bond issue. For example, the proceeds of a bond issue might be used to build a toll road. Revenue from the tolls pays the bondholders.

Industrial Revenue Bonds are issued for the development of industrial sites. Tax revenues collected from the businesses that inhabit the complex are used to pay the bondholders.

There are other types of bonds, and their backing naturally affects their marketability. Municipals may also be categorized according to their time of maturity.

II-B-5 Municipal Notes

State and local authorities often issue short-term instruments as a way of providing interim funding. Known as *municipal notes*, they usually exist for six months or less and are discounted instruments. Notes issued for interim funding in anticipation of collecting taxes are called *Tax Anticipation Notes (TANs)*. Those that are issued in the expectation of revenue received from bridges and highway tolls, for example, are called *Revenue Anticipation Notes (RANs)*. Those offered just before a new bond offering has been brought to market are called *Bond Anticipation Notes (BANs)*. Another form of short-term funding is called *project notes (PNs)*. These are issued when money is needed for a major project, such as a hospital complex. Once the project is built, then a bond offering usually follows that retires (pays back) the note holders. Project notes eventually become a bond offering, such as a general obligation bond in the case of a hospital and the like, or a revenue bond in the case of highway construction.

TANs, RANs, BANs, and PNs are usually discounted instruments. Holders receive no periodic interest payments. Instead, buyers pay a price that is lower than (or discounted from) the full face value, which they are paid at maturity. The difference between the price paid at time of purchase and the sum received at maturity is the interest earned. (Discounted instruments are discussed in more detail in II-C-4.)

II-B-6 Municipal Securities Summary

Municipal bonds represent an important part of the debt market. Issued by state and local governments, they compete with other types of debt instruments, but have a unique advantage in that their interest payments are generally free of federal income tax. If the owner of the debt instrument resides within the state of issuance, the interest paid is also free of state and local taxes. This is important insofar as those responsible for paying the interest on this debt are the general public. So a municipal bond can compete with a corporate bond, which is fully taxable, by paying a lower coupon rate or a lesser interest amount. In addition, because of the serial offering, these bonds trade not at dollar prices, but on a yield-to-maturity basis.

II-C *U.S. TREASURY INSTRUMENTS*

A primary participant in the securities marketplace is the U.S. government, which acts as purchaser, seller, and issuer. Each of these roles represents a method by which the government carries out its monetary policy. The government agency responsible for implementing monetary policy is the *Federal Reserve Board* (the Fed). Through different procedures, the Fed can increase or decrease the amount of money in circulation, which in turn affects the availability of funds, interest rates, and the fixed-income-security segment of the marketplace.

The federal government finances many of its operations through the issuance of debt. Securities issued through the Federal Reserve Bank are known as U.S. Treasury instruments. The longest-term issues are known as Treasury bonds, those of intermediate range are known as Treasury notes, and the shortest-term are Treasury bills. These instruments are brought to market by a special group of dealers known as primary dealers, which must qualify with the Fed and maintain certain standards.

All of these instruments are direct obligations of the U.S. government and, as such, are considered to be the safest investment vehicles available.

II-C-1 The Fed Auction

The Fed brings instruments to the market through an auction. Until recently only a special group of dealers known as government dealers could bid for these securities. The auction was a regular auction with the highest bids getting filled first. The dealers would sell the issues to their clients and to other broker/dealers for investment or for their clients. Recently the Fed changed its procedures and now permits qualified entities to bid for the issues directly. They also changed the auction process to a Dutch auction, where all excepted bids are filled at the same price.

Since no one dealer could possibly finance an entire issue—nor are they permitted to—many dealers compete. Given the size of an issue and the high degree of competition, the dealers fine-tune their bids, taking into account current market conditions, receptivity of the public to the new issue, as well as other factors. The dealers' bids are therefore very close to each other.

The Fed offers the new issue on a *dutch auction basis* (the highest-bid-first basis), meaning it sells as much to the dealer with the highest bid as the dealer will accept. Then it continues down the bids until supply equals demand, that is, until the issue is sold out. At that point, if there is more than one dealer at that price, the Fed will apportion the issue among these dealers. All bids are filled at the same price—the price where supply meets demand.

The public can purchase U.S. Treasuries directly from the Fed by submitting requests to it. Their orders are filled at a weighted average price, formulated from the accepted dealers' bids. All eligible public orders are ranked at one price, making the public's participation a dutch auction also.

The dealers sell the acquired issue to their customers and/or to other brokerage firms. The bid submitted by the dealers for the issue must be in line with current market conditions. Entities that bid too low will not receive any of the issue.

II-C-2 U.S. Treasury Bonds and Notes

Type: Debt
Form: Book entry only
Denomination: According to instrument
Income payments: Interest
Traded: Over the counter
Duration: 10 to 20 years for bonds; 1 to 10 years for notes

U.S. Treasury bonds and notes are longer-term instruments. Notes are issued for one to 10 years. Bonds are issued with maturities ranging from 10 to 20 years. Most Treasury (T) bonds and notes have fixed, or coupon, interest rates and pay interest on a semiannual basis. There are variable-rate and zero-coupon Treasuries also. Recently, Treasury bonds have been issued that are indexed to the inflation rate. These are called TIPS.

Inflation-index bonds change their interest rate according to the rate of inflation. A big objection to owning bonds for a long period of time is that the dollar loses value over time. In the late 1930s a person could buy a new car for $700. Ten years later that new car cost $1,700. Today the equivalent car costs around $30,000. While there have been technical improvements that have added to the cost, the majority of the increase was caused by inflation because, along with the increase in car prices, the cost of everything else we buy, or earn, has increased. Anything that has not kept pace with the rise in prices has lost value. Therefore, someone who has purchased a 30-year $1,000 bond that pays 5% interest would have lost purchasing power if the average inflation rate was over 5%. Bonds have tended to fall behind the inflation rate. Inflation-rate bonds take into account the rate of inflation. Therefore, an inflation-rate bond that pays 5% interest for 30 years is supposed to pay its owner face amount, based on the adjusted rate plus 5% interest, so that the owner has actually earned 5% interest on the investment.

A unique feature of Treasury bonds and notes is that they accrue interest on an actual-day basis (365- or 366-day basis), not a 360-day basis (as with T bills and other instruments). Like most corporate and muni bonds, they also pay interest semiannually. However, while the six-month payments are equal, the number of days in each half-year is different. Therefore, that daily interest rate is different from one six-month period to the next. Here's an example: There are 181 days in a January 1–June 30 non-leap-year period. From July 1 to December 31, there are 184 days.

II-C-3 Treasury Strips

Type: Debt
Form: Book entry only
Denomination: According to instrument
Income payments: Discounted—interest accrues in face
Traded: Over the counter

The Treasury also issues long-term discounted Treasury instruments known as *strips*. The interest payments and the principal are separated, with the actual bonds being placed in escrow. The interest payments are sold either as a separate instrument or instruments. The owners receive the appropriate interest payments when due on the original debt instrument. The principal is sold similar to a zero-coupon bond as the instruments do not pay interest periodically. Instead, they pay face value at maturity. The difference between what is paid at the time of purchase and what is received at maturity represents the interest earned.

II-C-4 U.S. Treasury Bills

Type: Debt
Form: Book entry only
Denomination: $1,000
Income payments: Discounted—interest accrues in face
Traded: Over the counter
Duration: Up to one year

U.S. Treasury bills are short-term instruments. Their longest maturity is one year. Bills are discounted instruments. Discounted instruments do not have a coupon, or fixed interest rate. Instead, the bills are bought at a dollar amount and the investor receives a higher amount (the face value) at maturity. The difference between the two amounts is the *discounted interest amount.* The rate of interest earned is built into the discount.

Example: Ms. Minnie Sota is interested in purchasing a 90-day Treasury bill having a $100,000 face amount, or maturity value. If the bill is discounted at a rate of 4%, Minnie will pay $99,000, the discounted price. The difference between the purchase price ($99,000) and the value received at maturity ($100,000) is the interest earned on the instrument. The formula used to compute the purchase price on a discounted money market instrument is:

$$\text{Purchase price} = \text{Face amount} - \left(\frac{\text{Number of days remaining}}{360} \times \frac{\text{Interest rate}}{100} \times \text{Face amount}\right)$$

$$= \$100{,}000 - \left(\frac{90}{360} \times \frac{4}{100} \times \$100{,}000\right)$$

$$= \$100{,}000 - \left(\frac{\$100{,}000}{100}\right)$$

$$= \$100{,}000 - \$1{,}000$$
$$= \$99{,}000$$

The actual return that Minnie will receive is greater than 4%. The 4% calculation was based on a $100,000 face amount. Therefore, we took $1,000 away from the face amount to arrive at the figure Minnie paid. In effect, Minnie is getting $1,000 on an investment of $99,000, not on $100,000. As Minnie is paying less than face for the instrument to get this $1,000, her return would be greater than 4%:

$$\frac{90}{360} = 1/4 \text{ of a year}$$
$$\$1{,}000 = \text{interest for } 1/4 \text{ of a year}$$
$$\$1{,}000 \times 4 = \$4{,}000 \text{ interest for a complete year}$$
$$\$99{,}000 \div \$4{,}000 = 4.04 \text{ (Minnie's return is 4.04\%.)}$$

If Minnie owns the instrument for its entire life, her actual or effective return would be 4.04%. However, if she has to sell the 90-day instrument before maturity, then the price that she will receive will depend on the interest rate at that time. If interest rates have risen, then for her to sell the Treasury bill, she must discount it at a higher rate than she purchased it at, which means she will get less return than she is expecting. On the other hand, if interest rates have fallen, then she must discount the instrument at a lesser rate than she bought it at, so she will receive more money than expected. In either case, Minnie has earned interest at the original discounted rate and must pay ordinary income tax on that amount. If interest rates have risen during the period (so that Minnie must discount the bill at a higher rate, thereby receiving less that she expected), she has earned the anticipated interest but has a loss on the trade.

Example: Minnie sells the bill 45 days later at a discounted rate of 5%.

$$\frac{\$100{,}000}{1} \times \frac{5}{100} \times \frac{45}{360} = \$625$$

$$\frac{1{,}000}{1} \times \frac{5}{1} \times \frac{1}{8} = \frac{5{,}000}{8} = 625$$

$$\$100{,}000 - \$625 = \$99{,}375$$

Minnie Sota would receive $99,375 instead of $99,500 (½ the $1,000 interest plus what she paid). In reality, she earned the $500 interest but has a trading loss of $125.

II-C-5 Settlement

Treasury instruments are no longer prepared in physical form, though there are still some old physical debt instruments outstanding. New treasury instruments come into market in book entry form only. *Book entry form* means that there aren't any certificates and that the record of ownership is retained on a computer file.

Trades in the secondary market are generally cleared through Fixed Income Clearing Corporation (FICC) Division of DTCC. In a similar fashion, as we will see later, while National Securities Clearing Corporation (NSCC) controls the comparison and netting for equities, corporate debt, and muni debt, FICC performs the functions for the instruments of the Fed with its U.S. Treasuries and certain agencies, namely Fannie Mae, Ginnie Mae, and Freddie Mac. After the comparison or trade processing has been completed, the actual instruments settle via clearing banks at the Fed, which maintains the positions in book entry form. The Fed maintains the positions either in nominee name and address or in the name and address of the beneficial owner. The Fed debits or credits the appropriate accounts as transactions are made. This method of settlement eliminates the need for pushing stock certificates around. Entries are made through a computer system that keeps all the accounts current. While there are still a few certificates in existence, the vast majority of treasury transactions are now settled by simply making entries in a computer file at the Fed.

II-C-6 U.S. Treasury Instruments Summary

In the multimillion-dollar government market, the spread between the bid and offer is small (or *tight*) on most issues. The dealers earn their income from the size of the trades. A sixteenth of a point markup on a $1,000,000 trade equals $625. While that sum may be appealing, remember that a 50-basis-point (or ½-point) drop in the market loses $5,000 for each $1,000,000 worth of securities in the dealer's inventory.

II-D MORTGAGE-BACKED AND ASSET-BACKED SECURITIES

Type:	Debt
Form:	Registered
Denomination:	$1,000,000 round lot
Income payments:	Principal and interest (usually monthly)
Principal:	Paid down periodically (usually monthly)
Traded:	Over the counter
Duration:	Variable, depending on underlying loans

A segment of the industry that has grown in leaps and bounds since first introduced in 1970 is the mortgage-backed securities sector. As the original instruments in this segment of the market were backed by home mortgages, the instruments became known as *mortgage-backed securities.* The concept of pooling debt and then securitizing it has spread to other debt vehicles. Banks now take car loans, boat loans, credit card loans, and so on, place them in a pool with other similar instruments, securitize it, and sell it. These are known as *asset-backed securities.* Securitization exists when securities are issued against a pool of debt.

Initially, this type of issue took the form of a passthrough. The first agency to offer this type of debt was the Government National Mortgage Association (GNMA). GNMA, as part of the U.S. Department of Housing and Urban Development (HUD), is responsible for facilitating mortgages in new homes. The potential homebuyers must qualify for mortgages insured or guaranteed by the Veterans Administration (VA), Federal Housing Administration (FHA), or Rural Housing Service (RHS). As such, all mortgages in a GNMA pool carry some form of U.S. government backing.

II-D-1 Role of the Mortgage Banker

The size of the GNMA pool is usually decided by a *mortgage banker*, of which there are approximately 860. It is the function of this individual, or entity, to obtain funds from "money-dense" areas of the country for use in "money-sparse" areas to facilitate the building of homes. The mortgage banker is usually not a bank at all, but some other corporate entity or division of an entity involved in real estate.

As an example of how the mortgage banker works, let's assume the Seament and Sanders Construction Company is going to build a tract of 100 homes. Some of the potential homeowners will qualify for VA, FHA, or RHS loans. Those who do not qualify will obtain conventional mortgages, which will either be sold as whole loans or become part of some other entities, such as Freddie Mac or a bank-issued pool. Those mortgages that qualify under VA, FHA, and RHS will become part of a GNMA mortgage.

As the potential homeowners apply for their mortgages, some are forwarded to VA, FHA, or RHS for approval. Those that get approved become part of the GNMA pool. As long as the homeowners have not moved into their homes, the mortgages are said to be *approved* but *not in force.*

During this period, the mortgage banker is exposed to losses due to interest rate changes. The mortgages that are approved but not in force are not paying any return. Mortgage bankers want to sell the mortgages as soon as possible since their purpose is not to take market risk but to facilitate the development of homes through the issuance of mortgages. Therefore, they take the pending pool of mortgages and solicit bids from GNMA dealers. The dealers are buying a contract that will be delivered months from now and that is, therefore, known as a *TBA (to be announced)*. What is to be announced is the unique pool number that GNMA will assign when the mortgages are actually in force.

II-D-2 TBAs/Forwards

TBAs trade along with another product known as a *forward*. Both of these are delayed delivery products requiring no monies to change hands until the actual settlement, which could be months from the time the trade is originally contracted.

During the period that the TBA/forward is alive, the contract may be bought and sold as well as sold and bought. The profit or loss from such trading is settled at the end of the contract's cycle.

Example: Abode Mortgage sells $5 million worth of 6% mortgages, retiring in 30 years, for a six-month delivery to Stone, Forrest & Rivers, a GNMA dealer. SF&R can, and probably will, sell some or all of it to its clients and to other broker/dealers who are not GNMA dealers. These firms are acquiring the issue for their clients or for their own proprietary accounts. During the interim period these contracts can be bought and sold, sold and bought. As interest rates in the marketplace fluctuate, so does the value of the contracts.

At the end of the TBA/forwards term, when actual delivery is due, those who own the contract will receive the appropriate GNMA security and pay the called for price. Those who are *short* (those who have sold the contract) will deliver the appropriate issue. Finally, those who are *flat* (that is, have bought and sold, or sold and bought the same face amount) will settle the net profit or loss with their respective counterparties. (Note: It is within a broker/dealer's prerogative to secure funds covering part or all of their clients' losses prior to final settlement of the contract.)

As for the mortgage banker, during this period, when the mortgages comprising the pool are in force, the banker will request GNMA to assign a unique number. That number will represent that pool until all principal is paid down. At the assigning of the unique pool number, it is said to be *announced* (hence the prior name, to be announced or TBA).

II-D-3 Modified Passthroughs

One form the mortgage-backed issue may take is that of passthrough, sometimes referred to as *modified passthrough*. The term *modified* refers to the interest paid on the mortgages being higher than the coupon carried on the passthrough itself. The difference, usually 50 basis points, is compensation for the mortgage banker. In the case of a GNMA, 44 basis points is compensation for the mortgage banker and 6 basis points go to GNMA. For example, a pool of mortgages carrying 7% interest will produce a passthrough bearing 6½% interest.

As the homeowners in a passthrough make their periodic payments, the payments (both principal and interest) are passed through to the security owner. Unlike bonds, which pay their principal at the end of the loan, these instruments pay the amounts of the loan over their life; that is, the principal "depletes" over time. It is this continuous cash flow that makes this product appealing.

Besides the normal pay-down principal, the borrowers often prepay their loans. In the case of mortgages, homeowners prepay their mortgages when they refinance their homes or move to other homes. As the mortgages in these pools are not substitutable, the old mortgage is paid off, and the new mortgage becomes part of another pool or is sold as a whole loan.

The rate at which these prepayments take place affects the longevity of an instrument and, therefore, its pricing. Those instruments that tend to pay down slightly faster than others tend to trade at a slight premium. In trading this type of pool, the unique pool number is specified, and the type of trade becomes a *known pool.* The only pool that can be delivered against this type of trade is that particular pool.

The standard type of trading is known as *guaranteed coupon*. Under this type of trade, the seller may deliver any pool(s) as long as the coupon rate on the pool(s) agrees with the specified one.

Example: SF&R sells a guaranteed coupon 8% pool to another broker/dealer. SF&R can deliver any 8% pool(s) to satisfy its obligation.

As outstanding pools are continuously paying down their principal, it is impossible to know the amount of principal outstanding at any particular time without the use of an official guide referred to as the *Factor Tables*. The tables contain the original principal amount of the pool, the current outstanding principal, and the *factor*. By multiplying the factor by the original value, you obtain the current value. By dividing the current value by the factor, you arrive at the original value.

Since the factor tables provide this pool information for all pools, you can easily obtain current principal information on an existing pool. The particular factor becomes important when only part of a specific pool is in question.

Because principal is constantly changing, it is virtually impossible to deliver exact contract amounts. Therefore, the Bond Market Association sets a tolerance level for accepting over- or underdelivery. The level is currently ±.01% per million.

Example: Against a $1,000,000 8% guaranteed coupon trade, SF&R receives from GRC one face amount $1,000,000 certificate and one $100,000 face amount certificate. (The securities always carry their original value.) It would appear that GRC "overdelivered" (delivered more than was contracted for) against the trade. However, upon checking, we find that the $1,000,000 certificate is from Pool #313131X, which has a factor of .912131843, and the

$100,000 certificate is from Pool #246189X, which has a factor of .879661632. By multiplying the original by the factor, we find the current outstanding principal is $912,131.84 for the $1,000,000 certificate and $87,966.16 for the $100,000. Together, they total $1,000,098.00, which is within the acceptable delivery limits set by the Bond Market Association.

II-D-4 Collateralized Mortgage Obligations (CMOs)

Collateralized mortgage obligations (CMOs) are another form of securitized pooled loans, but they are paid down differently than passthroughs. In a passthrough, all of the owners receive their proportionate amount of interest, principal, and prepayments from day 1 until the loans are paid off. CMO purchasers, however, receive payment of principal in predetermined time slots called *tranches*. The owner of a tranche, or part of a tranche, will receive principal payments when the tranches with earlier payment dates have been paid down.

As an analogy, think of a passthrough as an elevator in a shaft and a CMO as a stack of automobile tires. As the elevator goes down the shaft, the amount of space remaining under the elevator decreases proportionally. If the elevator at its highest point was 200 feet above the ground, should it come down 10 feet, there would be only 190 feet left; the 10 feet would be reduced universally. The same is true with a passthrough. If the passthrough had an original principal amount of $20,000,000 and paid down $1,000,000, there would be $19,000,000 of principal remaining; and the $1,000,000 would have been distributed to each of its owners.

On the other hand, the CMO is similar to the stack of automobile tires. If we had interest in a tire in the middle of a five-tire stack, that tire would not be obtainable until the two tires above it were removed. If the tires were removed and used one at a time and the next tire wasn't removed until the tire being used was worn out, the third tire wouldn't come into play until the first two tires ahead of it were worn out.

Similarly, if the stack of tires were a CMO and each tire a tranche, the owners of the third tranche of a five-tranche CMO would not receive principal until the first two tranches ahead of it were paid off.

As with passthroughs, CMO owners are subject to prepayments, and the owner of a certain tranche may start to receive principal payments earlier than expected if the tranches above are paid down ahead of schedule.

The number of tranches in a CMO can range from five to any marketable number. Some tranches pay interest; some do not. The tranches that do not pay interest are of the zero-coupon type and are therefore known as the *Z tranches.*

CMOs were first offered by the Federal Home Loan Mortgage Corporation. They initially appealed to those who wanted better control of their cash flows than was provided by passthroughs. It also made the instrument more appealing to different sectors of the market. For example, an investor looking to acquire an instrument for a few years would not invest in a passthrough, since principal payments would continue for the life of the instrument. The same investor could, however, invest in the first tranche of a CMO because it would be paid off within a short period of time.

Certain clients demand guarantees as to when they begin to receive principal payments. If these guarantees cannot be given, they buy some other instrument. To accommodate this need, the CMO packagers have developed a *planned amortized certificate (PAC)*. The PAC, which is frozen in a particular tranche, will not start to receive principal until a specific time or criterion has been reached, regardless of what else is happening around it. If prepayments are occurring quickly, owners of a PAC could start to receive principal payments after the next tranche in the stack has been paid off.

As the tranches pay down sequentially, the shorter-term tranches usually carry a lower interest rate than do the longer-term versions. The loans in the pool, however, are at a fixed rate. The difference between what is paid by the borrower (the homeowner) and what is paid to the CMO owner is

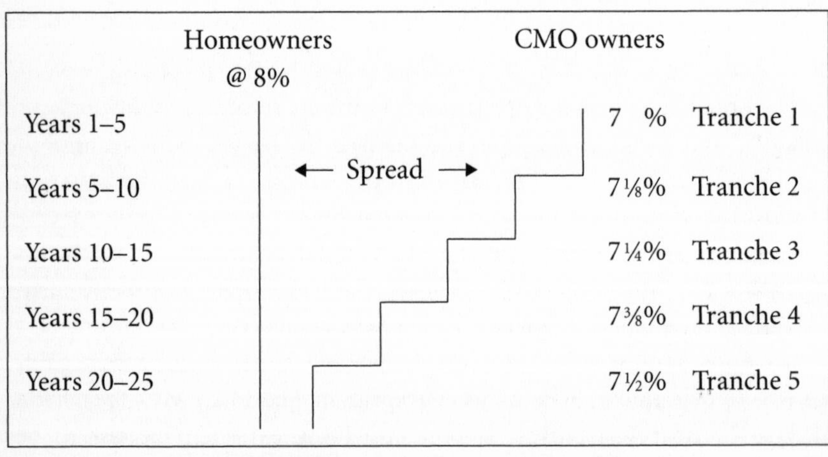

known as the *residual.* The residual can vary from instrument to instrument, and is dependent on how long a period remains to the earlier tranches. The faster they pay down, the smaller the residual will be. These residuals are sometimes sold at a discount to the amount that is expected to accumulate. (This is yet another application of present value that was discussed in the municipal bond section.)

In the chart below, each tranche is expected to last five years. A \$100,000,000 CMO would have a residual of \$18,750,000.

Step 1:

1% of \$100,000,000 = \$1,000,000 × 5 years = \$5,000,000
7⁄8% of \$100,000,000 = \$875,000 × 5 = \$4,375,000
3⁄4% of \$100,000,000 = \$750,000 × 5 = \$3,750,000
5⁄8% of \$100,000,000 = \$625,000 × 5 = \$3,125,000
1⁄2% of \$100,000,000 = \$500,000 × 5 = \$2,500,000

Step 2:

\$5,000,000 + \$4,375,000 + \$3,750,000 + \$3,125,000
+ \$2,500,000 = \$18,750,000

That figure represents the residual spread out in 5-year intervals over 25 years with no prepayments. Traders that deal with the residuals have to contemplate interest rate changes, the degree to which any changes are likely to occur, prepayments, and how much could possibly be prepaid at each tranche level.

II-D-5 Interest Only/Principal Only

Two variations on the previously mentioned themes are called *principal only* and *interest only*. Since the average payment consists of both interest due on the money outstanding and the paydown of principal, it is possible to separate the two and develop two new instruments. One would pay interest on a regular basis, and the other would pay principal when it is time for the principal to be paid down. Where this concept is applied to a CMO, the person buying the interest payment is purchasing the expected interest to be paid on a particular tranche. It's also based on how long the tranche is expected to be in existence.

Remember, these instruments can pay down faster than the supposed maturity date of each tranche. If the tranche pays out faster than expected, then the individual will not receive the amount of interest that he has paid for. If the tranche pays down slower than expected, then the individual will receive more interest than he has paid for. On the other side of the coin, the person purchasing the principal part of the tranche is really purchasing a zero-coupon bond. She will not receive any interest but will start receiving principal when that tranche starts to pay down. In this case, she's buying principal and what she's paying for is based on when the principal is expected to start to pay down. Therefore, the further out the tranche is, the less it is going to cost now.

Present value, discussed previously, will cause the discount to be applied over a longer period of time. If, however, the tranche starts to pay down sooner than expected, then people have paid less for the present value than they should have and, in fact, made a very wise decision. If the tranche pays down later than expected, then they have overpaid for the use of that money.

The present value scenario applies to the purchasing of later principal payments. The longer the time span from today until the expected date of the principal payment, the more the principal will be discounted because the person buying it today does not have use of that money until the principal is actually paid down. So, in our example, if the tranche is supposed to be outstanding for 10 years, the market price would be discounted at an expected rate for 10 years. If that tranche pays down sooner than expected, the amount of money involved in that tranche is discounted at a higher rate than is really necessary—a very good situation for the investor. If the tranche pays down later than expected, that means it wasn't discounted enough to compensate for the time between the purchase of the principal of the tranche and the actual return of the money.

II-D-6 Puts, Calls, and Standbys

Puts are the European form of put options. They give their owners the opportunity of putting (selling) a finite quantity of a specific issuer's pooled debt on a specific date for a specific price. If the owner of the put doesn't want to sell on that date, he doesn't have to. For this opportunity, he pays a premium.

Calls allow their owners to buy a specific quantity of a certain issuer's pools at a specific price on a specific day if they want to. If they don't, they let the call expire. The product is booked by normal processing convention.

Standbys are unique in that the product is usually booked as to what it does, not by its relationship to the principal party. The owner books the standby as a sell trade, because the product allows the owner to "sell" the underlying pool. The person who sold the standby and received the premium books the trade as a buy or debit. This marks the only time a "seller" ever pays a "buyer" in a standby transaction. If the owner of the standby doesn't exercise it at expiration, the instrument dies and the premium is lost. The party on the other side of the transaction keeps the premium and has no further obligation.

All parts of puts, standbys, and calls are negotiable. This includes the exercise ability of the owner. Most puts, standbys, and calls are exercisable only at the end of their life; however, more liberal exercise privileges are possible.

Example: Stone, Forrest & Rivers own $100,000,000 GNMA 8% TBAs at an average price of 97. They are due for delivery in three months. The mortgage market appears to be getting soft, and SF&R is becoming concerned. Rather than reduce the position, SF&R's traders buy puts on $20,000,000 GNMA 8% due in three months at a price of 97 for a premium of ½ point ($5,000 per million × 20 = $100,000). Since puts settle next day, SF&R will pay $100,000 to whoever sold the obligation via the puts. SF&R is comfortable with an "uncovered" position of $80,000,000 in GNMAs. If the market doesn't improve, SF&R may buy more puts. Three months from now, SF&R will make a decision to deliver the GNMAs against the puts and receive a price of 97, or let the puts expire and lose the premium. They will only let the puts expire if they can get higher prices for the GNMAs in the market. The market price of the 8% GNMAs at that time will determine the course of action.

II-D-7 Asset-Backed Securities (ABSs)

Based on the success of mortgage-backed securities, the securitization of other debt instruments soon followed. The pooling of car loans, credit card loans, equity mortgages, collateralized debt obligations (CDOs), and collateralized bond obligations (CBOs) began to be formulated and traded. One of the largest issuers in this market is the Student Loan Marketing Association (Sallie Mae).

These instruments trade in the over-the-counter markets and, as of now, do not settle through a clearing corporation. Trades in these issues settle trade for trade at Depository Trust Company.

These instruments possess certain advantages over MBS products. First, they are generally shorter term and less exposed to market risk. Second, they are less likely to prepay early. On the negative side, they are not, for the most part, guaranteed by the government or an agency thereof.

II-E *BANK-ISSUED SECURITIES*

Banks play a major role in the industry. Besides being the source for collateralized and uncollateralized loans as well as acting as custodian for financial assets, they also provide some of the products that we trade, including banker's acceptances, certificates of deposit, asset-backed securities, and participating certificates.

II-E-1 Bankers' Acceptances (BAs)

Type:	Debt
Form:	Primarily electronic
Denomination:	$100,000
Income payments:	Interest
Traded:	Over the counter
Duration:	30–270 days

Banker's acceptances (*BAs*) are bills of exchange that are issued and guaranteed by a bank for payment within one to six months. The funds raised through their sale provide manufacturers, exporters, and importers with operating capital between the time of production or exporting and the time of payment by purchasers. In effect, the bank accepts evidence of the value of goods being either manufactured or exported. For that evidence, it issues its acceptance in the form of a certificate that can then be bought and sold as security.

II-E-1-a *Use in Importing*

Suppose a U.S. importer wants to acquire goods from a foreign manufacturer. Because the goods must be produced and shipped, the foreign manufacturer needs to be paid as soon as the work is completed and cannot afford to wait until the goods are received in the United States. The importer goes to a U.S. bank with which it has a business relationship, and applies for a letter of credit. The letter of credit is sent to a foreign bank representing the manufacturer. The letter, along with the merchandise invoice (that is, a bill of exchange), is returned to the importer's bank, which stamps "ACCEPTED" on the invoice. The importer's bank pays the foreign manufacturer through the foreign bank. It turns and sells the bill of lading in the U.S. market and the banker's acceptance is thus created.

The procedure can be reversed. A foreign importer can apply to an overseas bank for a letter of credit, and a U.S. manufacturer can be paid before delivery is actually taken. The "paper" is therefore dually guaranteed by two parties: the accepting bank and the importing firm.

BAs can be used by a domestic company to finance merchandise located in one foreign country and awaiting shipment to an importer in another foreign country. Banks in different foreign countries can also enter into an international trade arrangement. If one of the banks has a U.S. bank as a correspondent, the U.S. bank may issue the BA into the U.S. market on behalf of the foreign bank, especially if there isn't a market for BAs where the foreign bank is domiciled.

II-E-1-b *Trading*

BAs are sold to investors as discounted instruments. (They are part of a security group known as *money market instruments.*) Since the instrument is discounted, the difference between what investors pay for the BA and the face value they are paid at maturity is the interest earned.

Interest on BAs is computed on 360 days. Computations are therefore made following the procedures used for U.S. Treasury bills. Trades in BAs settle the same day.

The issuing bank can keep the loan or sell it. If it keeps the loan, it has an account receivable on its books and has used funds representing deposits that were available for loans. Any loan has an effect on the bank's *reserve requirement*, which is the percentage of deposits that, by law, may not be lent out. By selling the BA, however, the bank applies the sales proceeds—the investor's money—to the loan, thereby freeing up bank funds for other loans.

If the bank sells the loan, it endorses it, thereby guaranteeing it, and the loan becomes a banker's acceptance.

II-E-2 Certificates of Deposit (CDs)

Type:	Debt
Form:	Electronic primarily
Denomination:	$100,000 (in secondary market, $1,000,000 round lots)
Income payments:	Interest
Traded:	Over the counter
Duration:	14 days to one year

A *certificate of deposit* is a negotiable security issued by a commercial bank against money deposited over a period of time. The value of CDs varies depending on the amount of the deposit and maturity. Although the maturities of most outstanding issues do not exceed six months, longer-term issues are available.

Included in the category of certificates of deposit are small issues that are not transferable and therefore are nonnegotiable. This form of CD—usually $10,000 in value and sometimes with a duration of two years or more—is advertised by many banks to attract the retail investor. However, because these are not tradable, they are not part of the negotiable CD market.

II-E-2-a *Types of CDs*

There are actually many types of negotiable CDs:

1. *Domestic CDs* are issued by U.S. banks to investors in the United States.
2. *Eurodollar CDs* are issued by U.S. banks to investors abroad.
3. *Yankee CDs* are issued to investors in the United States by U.S. branches of foreign banks.
4. *Saving & loan institutions* also issue CDs.

5. *Bulldogs* are foreign banks issuing CDs in the UK.
6. *Samori* are foreign banks issuing CDs in Japan.
7. *Matadors* are foreign banks issuing CDs in Spain.

II-E-2-b *Trading*

In the secondary market, where these instruments are resold, a round lot has a value of $1,000,000. Issues of lesser amounts are more difficult to sell because market liquidity is not always present.

II-E-2-c *Interest*

The interest on CDs is computed on a 360-day basis. The issue can be either plus interest or discounted. Investors prefer the discounted form because the yield can be understood easily, as in the case of T bills. A novice investor can easily understand, "I pay X today and at maturity I receive Y. The difference is the interest earned." Trades in CDs settle on the same day as the trade.

II-E-3 Asset-Backed Securities and Private Label

Banks also lend money in the form of mortgages. Mortgages that do not qualify for any government enrichment are known as conventional mortgages. The mortgages may be on a single-family home, a multiple dwelling, or commercial real estate. The banks in turn either sell the mortgages as whole loans or else place the mortgages into a pool, securitize them, and then sell the securities into the market. Securitized mortgages are sold as participating certificates, which follow passthrough or CMO formats. Investors in the securitized products receive a higher rate of interest than they would if they had invested in a securitized pool that has government backing, such as Ginnie Mae and Freddie Mac provide. There is also a greater risk involved.

Asset-backed securities are generally shorter term than mortgage-backed securities. These securities are comprised of loans against automobiles, boats, credit card balances, and commercial properties that are pooled and sold as securities by a processor, such as a bank or thrift institution.

Because of the shorter term and the nature of the collateral used to support the loans, these securities usually remain outstanding for the full life of the instrument. As such, prepayment or early payment of loans (which is quite common in mortgage-backed securities, when people refinance their homes or relocate and pay off their former mortgage with their mortgage on their new home) is almost nonexistent.

II-E-3-a

Unlike mortgage-backed securities, the different asset-backed classes have their own processes. For example, asset-backed securities backed by credit-card loans are serviced with a part of the card owners' payments being held in reserve. When the card owners default, the reserves are used to pay the deficit to the asset-backed holder. If the reserve is diminished to a certain level, the asset-backed security is called back by the issuer and paid down, usually from the proceeds of a new ABS. Home-equity loans, as well as some other forms of ABS, are locked into the ABS at a fixed period of time. The loans outstanding at that time are placed in the pool and the pool sold. Should the homeowner borrow additional sums after the pool is formed, the additional loans are part of a new pool. This is unlike a conventional mortgage where the refinancing of a mortgage requires the old mortgage to be paid, usually from the proceeds of the new mortgage.

The advantage to ABS securities is that by pooling loans, the risk of default is spread over many loans, making them an attractive investment.

Private labels are pools of conventional mortgages issued by banks that are pooled together and securitized. The mortgage pools follow the same payout procedures as the MBS products mentioned earlier.

II-F *MUTUAL FUNDS*

Type: Varies according to purpose
Form: Registered in bookkeeping form
Income payments: Dividends, capital gains, interest
Traded: OTC and listed (closed-end type), with fund (open-end type)

A *mutual fund* is any pooling of money by contributors in an attempt to achieve a common goal. In a broad sense, this definition can include a joint venture with a one-time outcome as well as a multibillion-dollar managed company. Nevertheless, in the brokerage industry, the term *mutual fund* means only a managed company.

The purpose of the fund must be clearly set forth in its prospectus and charter, and it may not be changed without the approval of fund shareholders. The fund may be a growth fund, income fund, bond fund, common stock fund, and so on. Each type of fund attempts to acquire securities that best fill its goals, thereby benefiting its shareowners.

II-F-1 Open- and Closed-End Funds

A fund may be open end or closed end.

An *open-end fund* makes a continuous offering of its shares to the public, and it stands ready to buy back (redeem) its shares from fund shareowners who want to liquidate.

Open-end funds can be purchased in several ways:

1. *Outright purchase:* The client invests a fixed sum of money.
2. *Letter of intent:* This is a 13-month commitment stating that the client will purchase *x* amount of the fund over the next 13 months.
3. *Voluntary plan:* Clients are free to purchase shares at such times and in such amounts as they choose, as long as *x* number of dollars will be invested. In this plan, the clients are not penalized for failing to meet their objective.
4. *Contractual plan:* The client contracts to invest so much by a predetermined date. Many investors prefer this method because payments must be made at specific times. Under this plan, the purchasers are penalized if they do not meet their commitment.
5. *Rights of accumulation:* The sales charge is reduced as each amount invested increases the total balance over time. The reduction is not retroactive and is applied to each additional deposit.

A *closed-end fund* issues its shares up to a predetermined number or dollar value. Once all the shares are issued or the dollar target is reached, the fund closes, and its shares are traded among the public. Individuals wishing to buy shares acquire them from shareholders who want to sell.

II-F-2 Net Asset Value versus Market Value

The price of a fund's shares is determined by the method used to buy and sell the shares. Open-end fund shares, because they are sold back to the fund, trade at *net asset value* (NAV). The formula for NAV is as follows:

$$\text{Net asset value} = \frac{\text{Value of fund's portfolio} + \text{Fund's cash awaiting investment} - \text{Expenses}}{\text{Number of shares outstanding}}$$

For open-end funds that have a load, the bid represents the NAV. For no-load or back-load funds, the NAV is the quoted price.

Because closed-end fund shares trade among investors, their prices are determined by supply and demand. If there are more buyers than sellers, the price of the closed-end fund rises. If the reverse occurs, its price falls. Usually these transactions, which are carried out through the services of a broker/dealer or bank, will carry a commission charge.

II-F-3 Load versus No-Load

Open-end funds can be load or no-load. The *load* is the sales charge, which is expressed as a percentage of the purchase price.

II-F-3-a *Load Funds*

Load funds, which charge a sales fee (load), generally reduce the percentage of the fee as the number of shares purchased increases. The point at which the percentage drops is known as the *breakpoint*. Each fund establishes its own breakpoints, and the terms are explained in the fund's prospectus.

Example: Roksollid Growth Fund has the following schedule of breakpoints:

If the customer purchases	*The load is*
\$9,999 or less	6 %
\$10,000–\$24,999	5 7/8%

(*continued*)

If the customer purchases	*The load is*
$25,000–$49,999	5¾%
$50,000–$74,999	5⅝%
$75,000–$100,000	5½%

Breakpoints are an important factor in choosing the method of investment in open-end funds:

1. The *outright purchase* qualifies for the sales charge applicable at the dollar amount of the purchase.
2. The *letter of intent* and *voluntary plan* carry a sales charge based on the total to be invested. The load is adjusted to the applicable higher rate if the investor fails to meet the objective.
3. In the *contractual plan*, the sales charge is based on the total amount contracted for. But a large percentage of the total sales charge is deducted from the deposits over the first few years of the contract's life. (For example, in one form of contractual plan, up to 64% of the total sales charge may be taken out of the client's deposits during the first four years, with no more than 20% permitted to be charged in any one of those years.)
4. Under *rights of accumulation*, the sales charge is reduced (but not retroactively) and periodic investments in the fund increase the amount invested so that the next higher breakpoint is reached. Contributions are completely voluntary, and the rights continue for as long as the client owns the fund.

The sales charge can be applied at the time of purchase or at the time of sale. Those applied at the time of purchase are called *front-end loads*, whereas those charged at the time of sale are called *back-end loads*. In either case, you pay a sales charge on every deposit you make to the fund. In a front-end load, as you put more and more money into the fund, the sales charge percentage will drop. In a back-end load, the money you put in is added to the value that may have accumulated because of investments by the fund (in other words, profit on the investments) and may result in a lower sales charge percentage when the fund is sold. The applicability of the sales charge is important to investors when they determine how many deposits they are going to make into the fund and how long they expect to keep the fund. In some cases, the front-end load and back-end load are the same. In other cases, there could be a substantial difference.

Let's assume you make several deposits into the fund and you reach a level of $100,000. In a front-end loan the fund has a sales charge on each of your deposits. If over a period of time the fund doubles the amount that was invested—so that when the fund is sold, it involves $200,000 worth of the fund—there will be no sales charge when sold. However, in a back-end sales charge fund the sales charge percentage will be based on $200,000, which of course will be at a lower percentage rate than the $100,000 sales charge percentage. The amount of actual dollars charged is dependent on the applicable sales charge. In a front-end load fund, a percentage of every dollar invested is reduced by the sales charge before the investment is made. Using the above rates, $.06 of every dollar invested up to $9,999.99 is never invested. The total amount charged on a $100,000 investment accumulated at the rate of ten $10,000 deposits would be:

$9,999 or less	6%	$ 9,000 × .06	=	$ 540.00
$10,000–$24,999	5⅞%	15,000 × .05875	=	881.25
$25,000–$49,999	5¾%	25,000 × .0575	=	1,437.50
$50,000–$74,999	5⅝%	25,000 × .05625	=	1,406.25
$75,000–$100,000	5½%	26,000 × .055	=	1,430.00
		$100,000		$5,695.00

If the fund's value doubled, then the $5,695 paid in sales charges would have continued with each deposit and cost the investor slightly less than $11,390 (2 × $5,695). The sales charge at the $200,000 level will determine which plan was more beneficial. If the sales charge dropped 0.5% for every $100,000, then a back-end load fund from which $200,000 is being liquidated would be charged $10,000 ($200,000 × (.06 − .005 − .005) = $10,000). While the sales charge is higher, the fund's management did double the investment. However, the opportunity cost states that front-end load fund sales charges here equate to a missed opportunity of $11,390. The back-end sales charge of $10,000 would have left the investor $1,390 richer.

II-F-3-b *No-Load Funds*

No-load funds can be purchased without paying a load, or sales charge. These funds are usually sold directly by the fund to the public. However, a few broker/dealers offer no-load funds as well as load funds to the public.

To maintain a client's assets at the broker/dealer, money funds are connected to the client's security accounts. As funds become available in the client's account, the broker/dealer moves cash between the securities account and the fund at no charge. When the client purchases a security, the firm takes money from the client's money fund and deposits it into the security account.

II-F-3-c *ABC Funds*

Because of the intense competition between mutual fund companies, a variation on the above may be offered to a fund's public by some mutuals. The fund gives the investor a choice on how the charge will be levied. For example, RokSollid Growth Fund offers the following choices to its potential investors:

> Growth Fund A shares: Front-end sales charge, in which the applicable sales charge percentage is based on the amount invested.
>
> Growth Fund B shares: No sales charge if the fund is held for more that six years. Any liquidation before completion of the six-year period will involve a back-end sales charge. The sales charge percentage decreases the longer the shares are held.
>
> Growth Fund C shares: No sales charge if the fund is held for more than 12 months. If liquidated before the 12-month period, a 1% sales charge will be imposed. As C shares are basically no-loads, they customarily have higher operational costs than funds that have sales charges.

II-F-3-d *Quotes*

No-load fund quotes are easily spotted in newspapers. First, their bid and offering prices are equal. Second, the initials *NL* (no-load) appear next to the quote.

For load funds, the offer is higher than the bid. The bid represents the net asset value, and the offer is the net asset value plus the maximum sales charge.

Closed-end funds, because their shares are not continuously offered, can be traded in the over-the-counter market or on a listed exchange. Their bid-and-offer quote follows the usual stock quotation practices.

II-F-4 Rule 12b–1

Rule 12b–1 of Investment Company Act of 1940 allows mutual funds to take money from clients' deposits and use it for advertising and marketing. Therefore, most, if not all, funds use this exception from the rules to do exactly that.

II-F-5 Bond Units

Some brokerage firms *package* (accumulate) a series of bond portfolios. Each series is completed by purchasing bonds in the open market and pooling them in a central account. Then the firm sells what are known as *units* to the public. When one series is sold, a new series is formed and sold, and so on. Corporate and/or municipal bonds are used in these units.

Bond units differ from mutual funds. In a mutual bond fund, the fund managers buy and sell issues in their portfolios as the need arises. Once a bond series is formed, however, the bonds comprising the "trust" are not traded or changed.

II-F-6 Money Market Funds

Money market funds demonstrate how the securities industry adjusts to the needs of the public. With interest rates at a high level in the late 70s and early 80s, the public wanted to invest in short-term, high-yield vehicles. The minimum lot (size) of, say, certificates of deposit or commercial paper was beyond the reach of most investors. Yet the high interest rates available at the time made it unwise to leave credit balances in brokerage firms where, uninvested, they earned little or no interest. So investors faced a problem: How to obtain the high rates of interest that were available, but only for investments of larger amounts than they had in their securities accounts.

In response to this problem, money market funds were developed. Because the money is pooled, the funds can acquire short-term instruments in quantities that pay high rates of interest. At the same time, operation systems were developed so that the brokerage firm can shift money between the customers' accounts and the fund. When a customer sells shares in the security account and does not want to reinvest it immediately, the credit balance can be moved to the fund account, where it earns a high rate of interest. When the client decides to invest in another security, the funds are transferred from the fund back to the security account.

II-F-7 Mutual Funds Summary

The mutual fund sector of our industry is ever changing to meet the public's needs. Demand changed the industry from general funds to growth funds, to bond trust funds, to money market funds, and so on. Whatever the need, a fund is available to fill it.

II-G *EXCHANGE-TRADED FUNDS (ETFs)*

Type:	Exchange-traded funds (ETFs)
Form:	Book entry only
Denomination:	Shares
Income payments:	Dividends/interest
Traded:	On exchanges and NASDAQ
Duration:	By issue

II-G-1 Types of ETFs

Another derivative product is the *exchange-traded fund.* These are either issued as unit investment trusts, depository receipts, or mutual fund shares. The manager acquires the necessary portfolio of securities and deposits the instruments at a custodial facility. ETFs were developed to replicate indexes, such as the Standard and Poor's 500 index (SPX) and NASDAQ 100 index. ETFs can replicate the broad market, business sectors, geographical sectors, and narrowly based indexes.

Exchanges and the NASDAQ list ETF shares. The ETFs track the index they are replicating, giving the investor the opportunity to "buy" shares in an index. Unlike with index options, which are cash settlers, exercise of ETF options results in delivery (though electronic form) of ETFs between participants. The delivery of the underlying shares follows the same procedure used in the exercise of common stock options.

II-G-2 How They Are Named

The shares are known by different names, such as ishares, HOLDERs (*HOL*ding Company *De*pository *R*eceipt*s*), and SPDRs (*S*tandard and *P*oor's *D*epository *R*eceipts). The name used depends on which financial institution is managing the fund. They trade in a similar fashion to common stock, with 100 shares being a round lot and their price interval being

$.01. At the writing of this book, the issuers of HOLDERs are the only ones that do not permit the trading of odd lots (fewer then 100 shares).

II-G-3 Characteristics of ETFs

When stocks or debt instruments contained in an ETF distribute a payout (dividend or interest), the owners of ETFs receive the distribution. ETFs can be bought, sold, and sold short the same as other securities. Because of the nature of the product, they are not bound by short sale (uptick) rules that bind common stock and other instruments. The products are marginable under applicable margin rules.

II-H *HEDGE FUNDS*

Type:	Hedge funds
Form:	Book entry
Denomination:	By contract
Income payments:	Profit distribution, dividends, or interest
Traded:	Over the counter
Duration:	By fund's charter

First and foremost, hedge funds do not hedge. They represent a pooling of money by qualified individuals. Though similar to mutual funds, they differ in several key ways. First, they are partnerships in which the principal(s) of the funds have invested their own money along with other investors'. Second, they are not as severely regulated as mutual funds. Third, as partnerships they are free to trade in a wide range of investment possibilities, including distressed securities, foreign exchange, and risk arbitrage. And fourth, they can use leverage to a much higher degree than is permissible with other forms of investment.

II-H-1 Goals of Hedge Funds

The main purpose of hedge funds is to preserve capital while maximizing profits and minimizing risk. They are not supposed to follow market trends and are considered an alternative investment vehicle.

II-H-2 Pricing Hedge Funds

Similar to mutual funds, hedge fund pricing is based on the value of their portfolios. However, due to the latitude of investment possibilities that hedge funds enjoy, the value of many of their investments are difficult to determine as they can invest in thinly traded and or illiquid markets. They can also invest in receiver certificates, income bonds, and other high-risk vehicles.

II-I *OPTIONS*

Type:	Options
Form:	Book entry
Denomination:	One
Income payments:	None
Traded:	Listed or over the counter
Duration:	By contract

Prior to 1973, a few options traded over the counter, but the public was generally not interested. In 1973, however, options came to the forefront as a trading vehicle when the Chicago Board Option Exchange (CBOE) opened and offered listed option trading to the public for the first time. Options may be used for many reasons. Hedgers use them to protect against a loss in positions they are holding. Conservative investors can use them to generate income. They are also traded by speculators.

An *option* is a contract that entitles its owner to buy or sell a specific product (called the *underlying*) at a certain price (the *strike price*) before a certain date (known as the *expiration date*). If the option owner decides to take advantage of the option, he or she is said to *exercise*, or *assign*, the option. The party who buys an option is the *owner* or *holder*. The holder pays a *premium* to the seller, or *writer*, of the option.

There are basically only two types of options. A *call* option gives the owner the privilege of buying. A *put* gives the owner the privilege of selling.

Example: The owner of a ZAP Apr 50 call has the privilege of buying 100 shares of ZAP common stock at $50 per share between the time the option is purchased and the time the option expires (at expiration date, which in this case is a specific day in April). The seller of the call is obligated to sell or deliver the underlying security (ZAP) should the owner of the option decide to make use of the call (exercise it). While the owner (or holder) of the option has the privilege to exercise (that is, buy), the seller (or the writer) is obligated to perform (that is, sell) the terms of the contract. The owner has paid the writer a premium for this privilege.

Example: A put option on ZAP Apr 50 gives the holder the privilege of selling 100 shares at $50 until a certain date in April, the expiration date. Should the holder exercise the option, the writer of the put must receive and pay for the securities.

II-I-1 Listed versus OTC Options

Since 1973, *listed options* have traded on option exchanges. "Traditional" or "conventional" options, however, have traded over the counter for decades, and they differ from the newer listed options in several aspects.

For OTC options:

1. The premium price is *negotiated* between the buyer and the seller. There isn't any market to turn to, to see what price the option is trading at.
2. The strike price is either the previous day's closing price of the underlying security or what can be negotiated between the contracted parties.
3. The number of days to expiration is not fixed; instead, it is determined at the time the option is written.

Because the strike prices and the days remaining to expiration vary so much, the secondary market for outstanding conventional options is very limited. As a result, most of these options expire. Liquidity is a problem with this type of option and is the main reason that the public has never actively participated in their trading.

In listed options, strike prices are set by the exchanges on which they trade. The exchanges use a formula to establish strike prices. Generally, equity (or stock) options are issued in 2½-point multiples up to a strike price of $25 or $30, then at 5-point intervals after that. There are exceptions to these guidelines.

The expiration dates are also uniform. Equity options are issued in 3-, 6-, and 9-month intervals with the near-two-months expiration dates being continuously offered. Recently, three-year options known as *long-term equity anticipation securities (LEAPs)* have been offered on some popular issues. The expiration date is set as the Saturday after the third Friday of the expiration month.

With such standardization in place, ready markets were established and listed trading began. Today, listed options are traded freely in liquid markets.

The exception to this standardization are flex options. Flex options that trade on option exchanges open a way for institutions and other large positioners to fine-tune the option strategy. The flex option permits strike prices with ⅛-point intervals and different expiration dates than the standard option. Buyer and seller can negotiate any expiration date as long as it doesn't fall one or two business days before or after the expiration date for standard options. This gives users of this form of option the benefits and efficiencies of using Option Clearing Corporation to settle transactions.

Listed equity options may be on listed or NASDAQ securities. Over-the-counter options may be on listed or NASDAQ securities. Where the option trades determines if it is a *listed* or *over-the-counter* option.

II-I-2 American versus European Forms

In the United States we trade two types of options: the American form (which can be exercised anytime during its life) and the European form (which is exercisable only at the end of its life). Listed equity options are usually the American form, whereas listed index options can be either. The method is determined by the majority of the users of the product. For example, there are index futures. Users of that product would want the European form of option to use as a tool in their trading strategies. The future contract and option contact, in this case, would cease to exist at the same time.

II-I-3 Equity Options

When most people think of options, it is equity options that come to mind. The equity option is based on 100 shares of underlying common stock. The owner of a call on RAM has the privilege of calling in (buying) 100 shares of

RAM, whereas the owner of a put on RAM has the privilege of putting out (selling) 100 shares of RAM.

There are many strategies, ranging from relatively conservative to highly speculative, for which this product is used. Covered call writing is considered on the conservative side; uncovered option writing is speculative.

While equity options do not pay dividends, the security underlying the option may. Therefore, an equity option is affected by corporate actions that involve the underlying security. In the case of cash dividends, the premium (market price) of the option could be affected by the closing price adjustment that is made on the underlying security on the night before ex-dividend date. (See the dividend section for an in-depth discussion.)

In the case of a stock dividend, the number of shares underlying the option and the strike price of the option are adjusted to reflect the dividend. The same is true in a stock split. Stock splits affect equity options two ways. If it is a *clean split,* such as 2 for 1 or 3 for 1, the option is split and the strike price adjusted. (For example, ZAP is splitting its common stock 3 for 1. The effect is that 1 ZAP Apr 90 option will become 3 ZAP Apr 30 options. $1 \times 100 \times \$90 = \$9{,}000$; $3 \times 100 \times \$30 = \$9{,}000$.) The other type of split, a *dirty split,* will cause the underlying number of shares and the strike price of the option to change, similar to that of a stock dividend. In a 3 for 2 split (for every 2 shares you will get another share), an option on the standard 100 shares and a strike price of 90 will become an option on 150 shares with a strike price of 60. ($1 \times 100 \times \$90 = \$9{,}000$, $1 \times 150 \times \$60 = \$9{,}000$.)

Exercises of equity options settle in the usual equity trading cycle. At the writing of this book, the settlement cycle is T+3 (three days after trade date). Exercises are against OCC, which assigns the option to a writer on a random basis. The writer is notified of the assignment the next morning and takes the appropriate action. In the case of an uncovered call, where the writer of the option does not have the underlying stock, the writer must go into the market and purchase the shares on the day of notification. Even though that trade will settle one day after the exercise is supposed to settle, the writer is not penalized as they acted in accordance with accepted procedures.

In addition to equity options, clients may trade options on T-bills, T-notes, T-bonds, currency, cash-settling indexes, and exchange-traded funds. These options are intended to fill a need caused by the volatility of interest rates and of the marketplace in general. Like equity options, these options with different underlying instruments may be used as hedging vehicles, for speculation, as well as for other strategies.

As new forms of options are brought to market, they have different exercise and settlement routines. These routines generally follow the usual settlement cycle of the underlying securities.

II-I-4 Debt or Interest Rate Options

II-I-4-a *U.S. Treasury Bill Options*

U.S. Treasury bill options require the delivery of a three-month bill. Because three-month bills are issued on Thursdays, that day of the week becomes the delivery date for exercises. Any exercise from Wednesday of one week to Tuesday of the next week must be delivered on Thursday of the next week.

Six-month T bills are brought to market "in cycle" with three-month issues. So a six-month issue with three months of remaining life is the same as a newly issued three-month bill, and it can be used to satisfy an exercise. A one-year T bill is in the same cycle as a three-month T bill and therefore can be used to satisfy an option exercise when it has three months of life remaining.

II-I-4-b *U.S. Treasury Note and Bond Options*

Options are written on Treasury notes and bonds as they are on stocks. The option has a specific underlying issue of T-bonds or notes. So the particular underlying bond or note must be delivered against exercise. On the exercise of the note or bond, delivery is due two business days after exercise.

II-I-5 Index Options

An *index option* is an option that has as an underlying a common stock index, bond index, or other type of index. An *index* is a weighted average of the prices of the securities chosen to be in the index.

The index may be *share weighted*, that is, the value of all the common stocks contained therein is based on 100-share units. Or it may be *market weighted,* that is, the number of shares outstanding or listed on an exchange is multiplied by the current market price. In both cases, a predetermined formula is applied to arrive at the index value.

Because the mathematical formula is applied against a large basket of stock, delivering an actual security against an exercise of an option is impossible. So, in the case of an index option exercise, cash not securities, is used for settlement. The difference between the exercise (strike) price of the option and the closing index value is settled between the option owner and the option writer on the next business day.

All index options use the value of the given index and a multiplier of 100 or 500 to arrive at the underlying option value.

Example: An option on an index with a current value of 1210.50 has an underlying value of \$121,050 (\$1,210.50 × 100).

Naturally, the premium of an index option cannot be multiplied by 100 shares because there isn't any underlying stock. Instead, an index option uses a multiplier that is applied to an index factor.

Example: If an index option's multiplier is 100 and the premium is \$2, then the cost of the option is \$200 (\$2 × 100).

Example: With the WOW index closing at 1210.50, a client of SF&R who owns a put with a strike price \$1,225.00 decides to exercise. That night Option Clearing Corporation assigns the exercise to one of the broker/dealers who has a written (sold) a position. Assume the written position is that of a client of Giant, Reckor & Crane (GRC). OCC would charge GRC, which in turn would charge their client's account \$1,450 (\$1,225.00 − \$1,210.50 = \$14.50; \$14.50 × 100 = \$1,450) to credit (give to) SF&R, which in turn would credit \$1,450 to the account of the client who owned the put option. These entries would appear in the respective clients' accounts the next morning.

II-I-6 Foreign Currency Options

British pound, Japanese yen, and other foreign currencies are traded against the dollar. Options on these forms of investment sometimes offer better hedging than domestically placed interest instruments. They also can be used to offset dollar fluctuations by those involved in foreign trade.

The different currency options have different contract sizes. The British pound contract is based on 31,250 British pounds (GPB). The Canadian dollar (CD) and Australian dollar (AUD) contracts are for 50,000 of their respective dollars.

II-I-7 Settlement

All exchange-traded options must be compared on the night of trade date and settled on the next business day. Each of the option exchanges has a computer facility that performs the comparison function. For example, the Chicago Board Options Exchange has its own computer facility, and the Philadelphia Stock Exchange uses the facility of Stock Clearing Corporation of Philadelphia. AMEX uses SIAC. The International Security Exchange, an electronic exchange, uses its own facility.

Options not compared by the morning of the next business day must be returned to the exchange for reconcilement. This process on the CBOE is known as *reject option trade notice (ROTN)*. Other option exchanges have their own terms. The notice is sent to the exchange floor the morning after trade date, and the executing broker of the problem trade is responsible for rectifying any discrepancy.

II-I-8 Option Clearing Corporation (OCC)

Trades that are compared are sent to a central clearing facility, *Option Clearing Corporation (OCC)*, for recording. Within this facility, all listed option positions that are being serviced by their member firms are maintained and recorded by segregated positions. These positions are client, firm proprietary, specialist, and market maker. In addition, member firms must settle the net cash differences from their daily activity and deposit the required position margin. This must be done on the morning after trade date.

All compared transactions in a listed option are recorded at OCC. So an investor can purchase an option series on one exchange and, if it is multiply traded, sell the same series on another exchange. The position nets to zero, because the trades are processed through the exchanges' computer facilities to OCC.

Option Clearing Corporation guarantees performance on all compared trades processed through the clearinghouse. Because all trades have been compared and the monies settled, the clearing corporation can stand between the original firms that represented the buyer and seller. A holder (buyer) who exercises options does so against the OCC, which in turn assigns the exercise to a writer on a random basis.

II-I-9 Expiration

Option positions that are not traded out or exercised eventually expire. Upon expiration, the buyer loses the premium paid, and the writer has earned the premium received. OCC has a procedure for expiring options called *ex by ex*. In stock options, any client's option .25 or more that is in the money will automatically be exercised at expiration unless instructions are received to the contrary. For firm proprietary orders, it is .15 or more. Other types of options have different thresholds.

What makes option trading interesting is the relationship between the option and the underlying instrument. As the price of the underlying instrument changes, so does its relationship to the options. For example, by making markets in different series of the same underlying security, a trader can create an artificial position that will react to changes in the underlying security's price as if the option trades actually own the security itself.

An example is a trader who thinks ZAP common stock is going to rise in value. Let's assume that ZAP is trading at $50 per share. The trader believes that something really big may be happening at ZAP. The trader could purchase 10,000 shares and tie up $500,000 (10,000 shares × $50). (Whether the trader paid for the shares in full or purchased them on margin, $500,000 is still at risk.) If the stock increases in value, the trader will profit at the rate of $10,000 per point. If the stock goes down, the trader will lose at the rate of $10,000 per point. On the other hand, the trader could purchase 100 call options and purchase 100 put options for a lower total premium cost than the 10,000 shares would cost. The trader has created the position of being long the ZAP stock with the protection that, should the assumptions be wrong and the stock fall in value, the puts will increase in value, thereby preventing the loss exposure of owning the stock. If the price of ZAP increases as expected, the trader will profit as the calls increase in value and the puts lose value. If ZAP falls in value, the puts will gain in value and the calls will lose value. The trader has the maximum risk of the cost of the options. This is but one of many strategies that option traders employ.

ZAP Stock

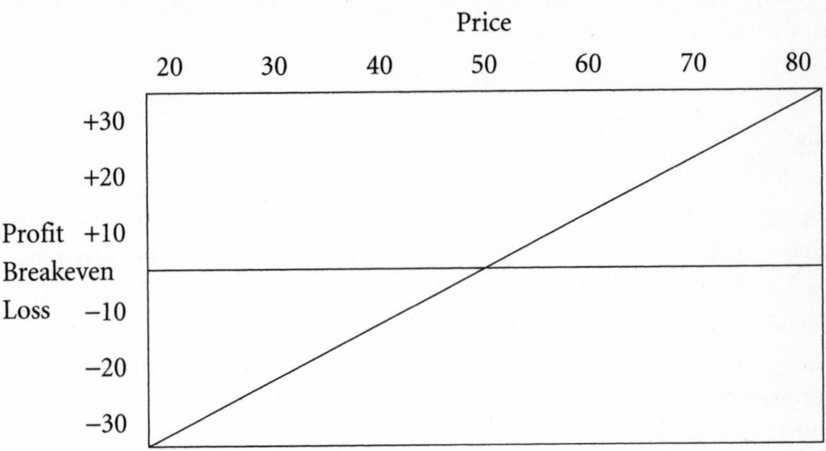

Let's consider the purchase of 100 calls and 100 puts at an assumed premium of $4.

$$\$4 \times 100 \text{ shares per option} = \$400$$
$$\$400 \times 200 \text{ options} = \$80{,}000$$

ZAP Stock Price

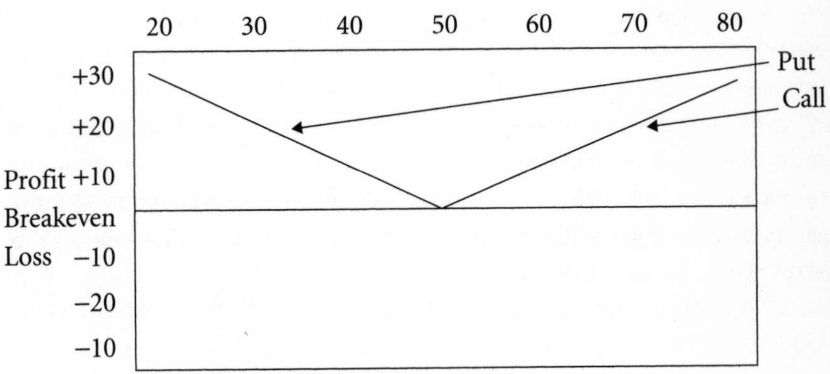

Investors and speculators use options or option combinations to implement many strategies. In the hands of a knowledgeable person, the option is a dynamic vehicle that not only can reduce risk, but also can earn income or maximize profit.

II-J *FUTURES AND FORWARDS*

Type:	Contract
Form:	Book entry
Denomination:	One
Income payments:	None
Traded:	Futures on exchanges; forwards, over the counter
Duration:	By contract

II-J-1 Futures Contracts

Futures are fixed contracts that trade on future or commodity exchanges. Forwards are also contracts, but they are custom made and traded in the over-the-counter market. We will look at futures first.

Futures contracts originally came about to solve an age-old problem: After planting oats, wheat, or soybeans, a farmer waited six months for a crop. How could the farmer be assured of a profitable price when the crop is sold a half-year from planting? If the price is high, the farmer benefits. If it is low, then the buyer of the crop benefits.

Let's say a miller normally buys a farmer's wheat crop. In past years, the miller has either profited or lost depending on price fluctuations. Instead of taking chances on a high or low price, the miller and farmer come to terms on a mutually agreeable price at the time of planting. In so doing, they've arranged a futures contract.

This contract had a value: it ensured a price. A third party who felt that the contract price was too low (that the actual price of the crop would be higher) might be tempted to buy the contract from the miller. Enter the *trader*. If the futures contract trader was right, he could buy the contract at one price, take delivery of the wheat, and then sell it at a higher price. Yet traders have no desire to take or make delivery of the actual wheat (commodity). All they want to do is deal in contracts to make profits. In the futures market, someone who buys a futures contract is said to take a *long position*. Someone who sells it takes a *short position*.

Thus, futures contracts trading was born, and traders—with their willingness to buy and sell contracts—provide liquidity to the futures contracts market.

II-J-1-a *Types of Futures Contracts*

For many years, futures contracts were applied to commodities: wheat, soybeans, pork bellies, and the like. Then they were extended to include oil and precious metals. Today, given the unpredictability of interest rates, they are taken out on debt instruments, such as Treasury securities, and on foreign currencies, such as the South African Krugerrand.

Nowadays, futures are traded on exchange floors by brokers and/or traders. *Brokers* execute orders for the benefit of others, that is, for the customers of firms. *Traders* execute transactions for their own accounts; they are speculators who own seats on the exchange. Also operating in this market is a form of day traders known as *scalpers*. They buy and sell or sell and buy futures and hold the positions for a short period of time. They trade on minimum price movements and thereby add liquidity to the marketplace.

II-J-1-b *Settlement*

Futures trades must be settled by the next business day. On the trade date, selling member firms submit trade data to the clearing corporations of the exchanges. The buying member firm accepts the trade, and the comparison is completed. This concept employs the use of trading zones during the trading day. Trades occurring in one time zone should be compared by a later time zone.

Trades that are not compared by trade date are returned to the floor of execution the next morning. These trades are known as *rejected trade notices (RTNS)* or *out trades*. Corrected trades are resubmitted to the clearing corporation as an *as of*.

Stock futures clear through Option Clearing Corporation and not at the facility of the respective futures exchange.

II-J-1-c *Margin*

Two varieties of margin are involved in futures contracts: margin from the brokerage firm to the clearing corporation and margin from the customer to the brokerage firm.

II-J-1-d *Margin Requirements*

II-J-1-d-i Clearing Corporation Margin Requirements

The margin required by clearing corporations varies. Some require margin on net positions; others require margin on broad. The amount of margin required is calculated on a per-contract basis. The amount per contract is established by the exchange on which the future trades.

II-J-1-d-ii Brokerage Firm Margin Requirements

Customer margin is also computed on a per-contract basis. The amount required on each contract is determined by the exchange, but the firm may ask a higher sum.

II-J-1-e *Types of Margin*

Two types of margin are charged on futures transactions:

1. *Standard margin* is the amount required per contract position.
2. *Variation margin* is an adjustment for market to market.

Market fluctuations affect the values of contracts in both long and short positions. In other words, buyer's money position must equal seller's money position. Because all transactions in margin accounts are compared, there must be a long position (a buyer) for every short position (every seller). If the value of a long position changes, there must be a corresponding change in a short position, somewhere else in another account.

Keeping track of changes in value is important from the point of view of margin. Any adjustment affects the client's standard margin requirements. If credits to the account eventually exceed requirements, they create an *excess*, or profit. *Debits* reduce the amount of equity in the account and can eventually oblige the customer to deposit more money (or equity).

The brokerage firm adjusts the value of contract positions daily, carrying the adjustments through the clearing corporation. Internal adjustments are made by bookkeeping entries, while those netting through the clearing corporation are settled by letters of credit or wire transfers.

Traders and hedgers may maintain large positions in offsetting derivatives. Positions may be offset by different months' contracts on the same product, or by options on the underlying or options on the same future contract that is being carried. The exposure risk can change as the prices for the underlying commodity itself changes. Some of these offsetting positions may negate any risk or exposure to the firm at one time but may pose risk at another. To minimize risk and yet ensure that the firm has proper margin for these complex positions, the exchanges offer their members Standard Portfolio Analysis of Risk (SPAN) margin. SPAN sets risk parameters for each position developing into a risk analysis formula tool. The formula is then applied against the client's portfolio, and then the maximum exposure at that moment in time, based on the positions then present in the portfolio, is established. The firm then charges margin based on the result.

II-J-1-f *Delivery*

Futures trade up to and in the last month of their contract life. During the last month, they cease being futures and become *spot market contracts* or *cash market contracts.* During this month, *delivery notices* are attached to many sales. During this month, traders must close out their positions or be responsible for receiving or delivering the underlying contract. After trading has ceased on the last day, accounts with long positions receive the contracted amount from the short position accounts. Deliveries must conform to the contract's specifications.

What happens if a trader still owns a contract when trading ceases? If a trader is long, say, a potato contract after trading ends, he does not have tons of spuds dumped all over the lawn. All that happens is that the trader *owns* the contents of the contract. Grain is stored in warehouses, U.S. Treasury bills are delivered against payment, and so on. In other words, the holder of a long position owns and must pay for the contracted amount. In the case of commodities, such as wheat or pork bellies, the new owner must pay not only the contracted costs, but also any storage and spoilage costs.

II-J-1-g *Daily Trading Limits*

Due to the relatively low margin necessary for futures trading, exchanges set *daily trading limits* for various contracts. If the price of a future rises above or falls below the limit, trading ceases in the contract until it returns to the allowable limit or until the next day, when new limits are set. The stopping of trading permits member firms to obtain the necessary funds from their affected clients.

II-J-2 Forward Contracts

Forwards trade in the over-the-counter market. What makes them attractive is that they can be custom-made or custom-tailored to the needs of the investor. The primary market in forward contracts is the currency market, also known as foreign exchange (Forex). Due to the need for foreign currency in certain denominations at specific times, a user can buy a forward contract, locking in the rate of exchange at the time of trade. This would guarantee the amount of money the buyer would receive when the forward contract comes due. As with futures, the contract does not truly expire—it becomes deliverable. The usual terminology is *the contract becomes deliverable.* Most foreign currency transactions settle in two days. Therefore, a buyer of a six-month forward contract is locking in the exchange rate that will be used six months from now, and upon expiration the currency will be exchanged two days after the contract expires.

Another product that uses forwards to offset risk or to lock in future prices is mortgage-backed securities. These trade along with such instruments as TBAs, which were discussed in section II-D, "Mortgage-Backed and Asset-Backed Securities."

II-K *SWAPS*

Type:	Swaps (currency, interest rates, or commodity)
Form:	Negotiated contract
Denomination:	Negotiated as part of contract
Income payments:	Depends on contract terms
Traded:	Negotiated, not actively traded
Duration:	Part of contract

A rather old concept, swaps are growing in popularity because they meet a need in international trading, with its proliferation of interest rate products.

Swaps are exactly what the word means. They involve an exchange of assets to better achieve goals.

Example. Marquis Corp. has long-term debt for financing, which goes to support short-term loans that reflect current interest rates. Therefore, its profits or losses are tied to the current interest rate Marquis receives versus the fixed rate they must pay on their debt.

Lincoln Mortgage has the opposite problem. They finance some of their mortgages by short-term money market instruments. Their profits or losses are tied to the difference between the current interest rates paid on short-term money market instruments versus what they receive from the fixed-term mortgages.

II-K-1 Interest Rate Swaps

Enter the first type of swap, an interest rate swap. Marquis would like to pair their short-term income against short-term debt. Lincoln Mortgage would like to finance their fixed-term mortgages with long-term debt.

To accomplish this, each company sets an amount of principal known as the *notional*, on which the swap is based. A rate must be negotiated between the two principals to the swap, and a broker will handle these negotiations.

As the short rates on the loans made by Marquis are tied to some recognizable rate, such as the U.S. Treasury bill rate or the federal fund rate, so are the funds that Marquis wants to obtain in swap. If the short-term money being borrowed by Lincoln Mortgage is at a rate that is attractive to Marquis, or if it can be swapped at such a rate, the first leg of the swap is doable. In the same manner, if the fixed long-term debt of Marquis can be swapped profitably to Lincoln Mortgage, the second leg of the swap will become attractive. The broker negotiates these terms.

As long as both companies maintain their ability to borrow money at the same level (that is, as long as their financial positions do not weaken, causing them to pay a higher interest rate to borrow), the swap will be maintained. The financial strength of each company depends on the ability of both companies to remain viable and to continue their financial composure. This includes their ability to borrow money at the best interest rates. The best interest rates at a moment in time may not be associated with the financing needs of the corporation. Swaps give the corporations another conduit to obtain the best possible terms.

The relationship between long-term and short-term rates changes as the perception of which way interest rates are heading changes. While short-term rates are usually lower than long-term rates, there are times when this is not true. In addition, the difference (or spread) between short- and long-term rates widens and narrows over time. Now add in the actual level of interest rates, and the decision of what and when to borrow becomes even more complex.

Comparison of Marquis Corp.'s and Lincoln Mortgage's borrowing capabilities

	Borrowing Rate	
	Short-Term	**Long-Term**
Marquis Corp.	T bill + 8%	T bond + 4%
Lincoln Mortgage	T bill + 6%	T bond + 6%

The capital structure of a company is one of the main ingredients in determining the company's financial strength; through it, one can estimate the company's future. A company may not want to borrow more long-term funds because of concern over the amount of debt the company may already be carrying. Therefore, it may borrow short-term funds, even though long-term funds may be more attractive as a borrowing vehicle. The company can now enter into swaps of short-term rates for long-term rates and get the desired offsets, without issuing the actual security.

As Marquis Corp.'s primary business is making short-term loans, its ability to finance these loans profitably depends on the debt market and its ability to *carry* loans of differing maturities. Lincoln Mortgage has a similar problem, but its concern focuses on long-term debt. If the long-term borrowing expense of Marquis exceeds the revenue generated from its short-term loans, or if the short-term borrowing of Lincoln Mortgage exceeds the income received from the mortgages, both firms face losses. The use of swaps permits the two organizations to better pair off their expense and revenue streams.

Comparison of Marquis Corp.'s and Lincoln Mortgage's borrowing capabilities

Corporation	Primary Borrowing Rates
Marquis Corp.	U.S. Treasury bond rate + 4%
Lincoln Mortgage	U.S. Treasury bill rate + 6%

The two companies make the following swap:

Swap arrangement between Marquis and Lincoln

	Borrowing at	Lending at
Marquis Corp.	T bill rate + 6%	T bill rate + 8%
Lincoln Mortgage	T bond rate + 4%	T bond rate + 6%

As long as both companies can maintain their financial positions in the industry and continue to borrow money at favorable rates, the 2% spread between each company's borrowing and lending rates will keep the swap viable. As short-term interest rates change, Marquis Corp.'s borrowing and lending will parallel each other; and, as long-term rates change, Lincoln's borrowing and lending will also parallel each other. Both parties benefit.

Interest rate swaps can involve:

- Fixed rates for floating rates.
- Floating rates for floating rates (different reset dates).
- Fixed rates for fixed rates (different payment date).
- Zeros vs. fixed rates (appreciation for payment).
- Zeros vs. floating rates (appreciation for payment).

II-K-2 Currency Swaps

Example: Swaps can also be conducted intercurrency. Stephans International Pte. is a French company. Vargus, Inc., is a U.S. corporation. Each conducts business in the other's country, and both need borrowings to expand their businesses. The problem both companies face is that, while they are well known in their respective home countries, they are little known outside their borders.

Both companies can borrow the money needed to expand their foreign operations from their domestic or local bank at favorable rates. However, in doing so, they would be exposed to currency exchange rate risk. For example, Vargus borrows $500,000 from its local bank for use in France. At the time of the loan, one euro is equal to 88 cents, or $1 equals 1.13 euros. Vargus converts the $500,000 into €565,000 ($500,000 × 1.13 euro = €565,000). A year later, Vargus wants to pay back the loan. At that time, one euro equals 80 cents or $1 equals approximately 1.25 euros. To pay down the $500,000 loan, Vargus would need €625,000 (625,000 × .80 = $500,000). Besides interest, it has cost Vargus 60,000 more euros ($40,000 more) than it originally borrowed to pay back the loan. Of course, at the time the loan comes due, the rates could just as easily have moved in Vargus's favor. However, neither Vargus nor Stephans wants to take the exchange rate risk.

Enter the currency broker, with the swap shown in the following table. Assuming the companies are borrowing equivalent amounts, the swap will occur.

	U.S. Rate	Euro
Stephans International Pte.	10%	7%
Vargus Corp.	7%	10%

Example: Vargus is borrowing from a U.S. bank at 7% U.S. funds, but paying 7% in euro. Stephans is borrowing at 7% euro, but paying 7% U.S. funds. By doing the swap, both companies are able to borrow at the best rates in the countries in which they want to do business. This, plus the fact that neither company is exposed to exchange rate changes, makes the swap attractive. Both firms benefit from each other's good credit rating.

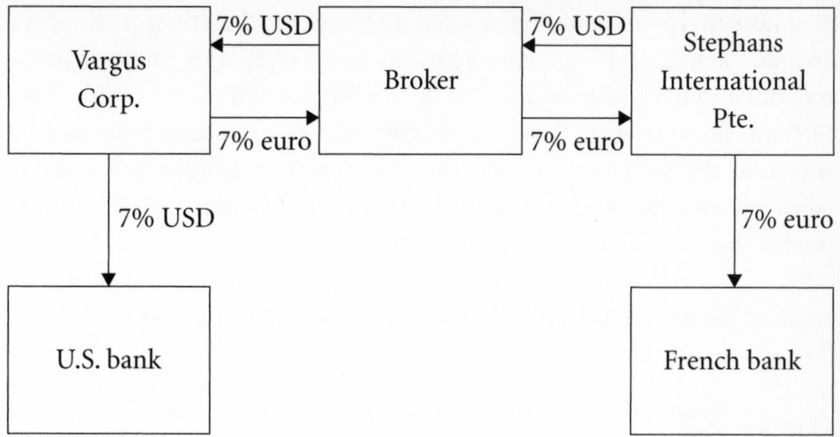

II-K-3 Commodity Swaps

As with most swaps, the purpose is to accomplish mutual goals. In commodity swaps, generally one side is the physical commodity itself. *Exchanges for physicals (EFPs)* are an example. Someone with a future contract is willing to swap it for the actual commodity. It works both ways. Someone who is about to receive a shipment of a commodity (oil) may be willing to swap that oil for a future delivery. This user may have too much physical oil and the storage costs are eroding the company's profits. Therefore, the user swaps the shipment of oil that has not been paid for in exchange for a delivery of oil at a later date. The new owner of the oil that is now being delivered accepts and pays for the delivery.

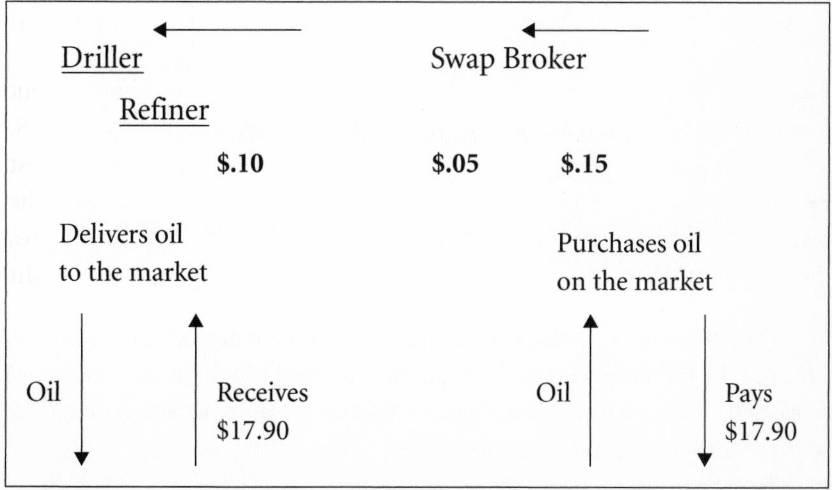

Another type of commodity swap involves the stability of prices. Let's assume oil is fluctuating between $17.80 and $18.20 a barrel. A driller is interested in flattening out the monthly difference. On the other side, a refiner has the same goal. Enter the swap broker. An agreement is reached by which the driller is to receive $18.00 a barrel each month for the oil that is delivered and the refiner is to pay $18.05. In the chart below, the first month shows oil on the market at $17.90 a barrel.

Driller: Received $17.90 for the oil plus $.10 from swap broker = $18.00.

Refiner: Paid $17.90 for the oil plus $.15 to the swap broker = $18.05.

Let's assume the next month oil is $18.20 per barrel.

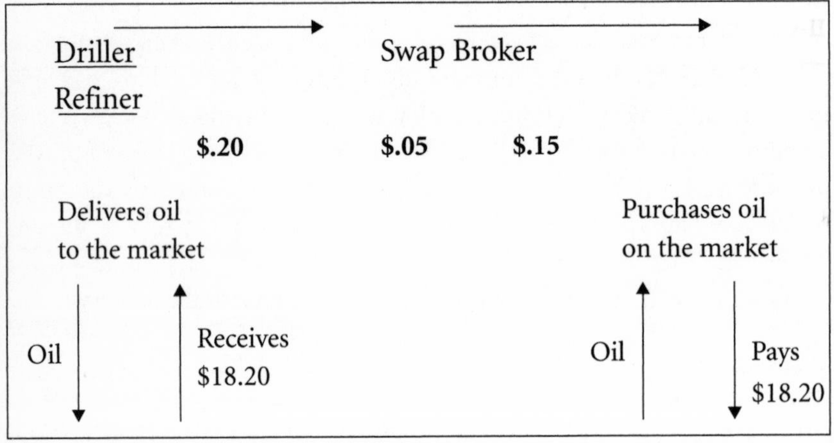

Driller: Received $18.20 and paid $.20 to the swap broker = $18.00.

Refiner: Paid $18.20 and received $.15 from the swap broker = $18.05.

While these are simplistic representations of the real world, the concepts are true. In the above example, negotiations would include the amount of price drift before the contracts would void and the point at which the driller and refiner settle up the adjustments.

These are only a few of the uses for swaps.

II-K-4 Swaps Summary

There is growing concern as to the recording of swaps and other derivative products, since they are *off-balance-sheet* items—that is, no mention of the swap appears in the company's financial report. In the case of Vargus Corp., their records would show a loan that is really supporting Stephans's business, yet no mention is made of Stephans's loan, which is the loan really supporting Vargus's business. The same is true in the first example, showing Marquis and Lincoln Mortgage. What would happen if one of the participants to the swap fell into financial difficulty? Would the lender seek restitution from the other party, claiming that the obligation was actually theirs since they are benefiting from the loan? Would this leave the remaining participant with both obligations? Time will tell what actions regulators will take.

II-L *CURRENCY*

Type:	Cash
Form:	Bearer
Denomination:	By issuing country or group of countries
Income payments:	None
Traded:	Over the counter (FX)
Duration:	Viable economy of issuing country or group of countries

II-L-1 What Is Foreign Exchange, or Forex (FX)?

The U.S. dollar (USD), the British pound sterling (GBP), the Canadian dollar (CAD), the euro (EUR), the Mexican peso (MXN), the Japanese yen (JPY), the Swiss franc (CHF), and the South Korean won (KRW) are just a few of the 100-plus currencies traded on a daily basis and used for settlement of transactions on a worldwide basis. Based on the economies and monetary policies followed by their respective governments, the relationship of one currency to another is forever changing. Individuals involved with the exchanging of currency are involved in the foreign exchange (*FX* or *Forex* market).

Currency relationships are best described in terms of inflation. Under inflation, the dollar will buy less in the next period than in this period; in other words, the dollar can be described as falling against the product purchased. You need more dollars to buy the product later than you need today.

In the case of Forex trading, the "other product" is another currency. Instead of naming inflation as the reason that currency *x* cannot purchase as much of currency *y* as it used to, currency *x* is said to be falling. As currency *x* is *falling* against currency *y*, currency *y* is, by definition, *rising* against currency *x*.

Example: Let's say it cost 2 British pounds to manufacture a widget in the United Kingdom and 4 U.S. dollars to manufacture the same widget in the United States. For simplicity, further assume that 1 British pound sterling is exchangeable for 2 U.S. dollars. (We will also assume that there aren't any transportation charges, tariffs, taxes, or other charges, so that, before currency conversion, it costs the same to manufacture a widget in England and America as well as to sell widgets in each country.) If the dollar were to rise against the British pound, you would need fewer dollars to buy a British-made widget in America than you would need to buy an American-made widget. If the dollar should rise so that $1 equals £1, a British-produced widget would cost 2 U.S. dollars in the United States, where a U.S.-made widget would still cost $4. A U.S.-made widget in England would cost 4 British pounds, or double what a British-made widget costs.

Why? When 1 GBP equals 2 USD, a British-made widget costs 2 GBP and a U.S.-made widget costs 4 USD. As the British–U.S. exchange rate is 1 for 2, then a British-made (2-GBP) widget would cost 4 USD in America and a U.S.-made widget would cost 2 GBP in England. When the dollar is 1 for 1 with the pound (it buys more British pounds), the U.K.-made widget (2 GBP) would cost $2 in the United States versus $4 for a U.S.-made one. Conversely, a U.S.-made widget would cost 4 GBP in England versus 2 GBP for a British-made one.

II-L-2 Users of the Market

Intercountry exchange rates do not affect the price of a product manufactured and sold within a country. Therefore, a $4 widget manufactured and sold in the United States would cost $4 no matter what the exchange rate was. It would change its value only in another country as the exchange rate fluctuated.

Individuals or companies involved in international trade must be concerned with currency fluctuations. As the rate changes, so does the opportunity for profit.

Example: An American investor wishes to purchase 1,000,000 CAD (Canadian dollar) Canadian government bonds, which are trading at 98 CAD. Therefore, the U.S. investor must buy 980,000 CAD to pay for the purchase. At the time of purchase, 1 CAD equals .86 USD. Therefore, the U.S. investor must pay 842,800 USD for the 980,000 CAD needed (980,000 CAD × .86 = $842,800). Let's assume that, when the bonds mature and the Canadian government pays the 1,000,000 CAD owed, 1 CAD equals .81 USD. The U.S. investor would receive 810,000 USD on conversion (1,000,000 CAD × .81 = 810,000 USD) for a loss of 32,800 USD, even though the Canadian bonds increased in value from 980,000 CAD to 1,000,000 CAD.

Let's observe this process on a micro level.

Canadian bonds have a three-business-day settlement cycle. The U.S. investor could buy the Canadian dollars on trade date, T+1, or T+2 (settlement date). Let's assume at the time of the trade, that 1 CAD equals .86 USD; the next day 1 CAD=.84 USD, and by settlement date 1 CAD = .82 USD. On which day should the investor have bought Canadian dollars to best position the transaction for a profit? A look at the three days would point to the settlement date as the one that would require the least amount in U.S. dollars.

As of the writing of this chapter, the exchange rates for some of the major currencies are as follows:

	U.S. Dollars to . . .	*. . . to U.S. Dollars*
Australian dollar	.65	1.52
British pound sterling	1.45	.69
Canadian dollar	.64	1.54
Euro	.91	1.09
Japanese yen	.008	120.00
Mexico	.093	10.73
Swiss franc	.595	1.68

For example, $1.45 will buy 1.00 British pound sterling, or .69 pence will buy 1.00 USD. Check your newspaper for the rates in force on the day you are reading this.

II-L-3 Derivatives

To offset the risk involved with currencies, hedgers can take advantage of options, futures, and forwards. Options on currencies trade on the PHLX (Philadelphia Stock Exchange) or over the counter. Futures trade on IMM (International Monetary Market), a part of the Chicago Mercantile Exchange (CME).

Options on currency are structured like equity options, with strike prices and expiration months. Unlike listed equity contracts, however, currency options have two expiration cycles during their expiration month: the Saturday before the third Wednesday and the last business day of the month. Exercise results in a two-business-day settlement.

Futures and forwards follow traditional product procedures. Futures contracts, which trade on exchanges, have rigid contract specifications, whereas forwards are negotiable and trade OTC.

II-L-4 Settlement

In dealing with FX trading and FX derivatives (forwards, futures, and options), participants must have arrangements not only with domestic banks but also with banks in the country of the foreign currency. Settlement of FX trades is two days after trade date at the bank where the currency is domiciled.

II-M *AMERICAN DEPOSITARY RECEIPTS (ADRs), AMERICAN DEPOSITARY SHARES (ADSs), AND GLOBAL DEPOSITARY RECEIPTS (GDRs)*

Type:	Security
Form:	Registered
Denomination:	Shares
Income payments:	Dividends (at management's discretion)
Traded:	Listed and NASDAQ
Duration:	Discretion of issuer

II-M-1 American Depositary Receipts and Shares

American depositary receipts (ADRs) and American depositary shares (ADSs) represent shares of foreign corporations on deposit at a U.S. bank against which the bank issues the ADRs and ADSs. This process gives foreign corporations access to the U.S. markets. For all intents and purposes, ADRs and ADSs are the same.

The process by which foreign shares are converted to U.S. shares accomplishes several benefits for all. First, the shares of the foreign corporation are escrowed at the U.S. bank and reconstituted as an instrument for the U.S. market. For example, the minimum share quantity in the U.S. market is one. It may take 4.8 shares of the foreign stock to equal one share of ADR. The bank makes the conversion so that the product fits into the U.S. processing stream.

Another advantage is that many countries tax dividends at the point of distribution. Some of these same countries have reciprocal tax agreements with the United States. The bank assures the foreign government that all of the shareholders qualify for the exemption unless otherwise notified. This saves the shareholder from having to file a claim with the foreign government for the incorrectly withheld taxes.

Still another advantage is the transferring or reregistering of ownership. The issuing corporation knows the bank as the owner of the shares. The bank keeps its own records as to who the registered owners are. This makes transferring ownership names easy as it occurs at the bank level and not at a facility located in the issuing country. In this case it is not only a distance problem but also a communication problem, since a shareholder and the personnel with whom he's communicating may not be conversant with each other's languages. Also, required forms may be in an unfamiliar tongue.

The last paragraph also impacts corporate actions that may affect the shareholder. Dividends are paid by the issuer to the bank, which in turn pays the registered holders as they appear on the bank records. The same is true for rights offerings and acquisitions. It is much easier communicating with a domestic bank than hunting down the proper party at an institution located in a foreign country.

II-M-2 Global Depositary Receipts

Global depositary receipts (GDRs) are similar to ADRs. These represent the shares of a corporation domiciled in one country being offered through a bank located and domiciled in another country. The bank is acting as an interface between the issuer of the securities and the shareholder residing outside the issuer's borders.

II-N *RESTRICTED STOCK*

Restricted stock is stock that cannot be readily sold to the public. This could be because the owner is an insider, or the security has not been registered with the Securities and Exchange Commission, or another shortcoming. It usually is acquired as compensation to key officers of the company or as payment by a new company to vendors.

II-N-1 Rule 144 Stock

Type: Stock
Form: Book entry or physical

Denomination: Shares
Income payments: Dividends
Traded: Controlled
Duration: One year from date of ownership

Stocks issued under Rule 144 of the 1933 Truth in Securities Act are restricted stocks and are not publicly traded. These shares are usually common stock. The issuance of such stock cannot be as an underwriting as defined by the 1933 Act. In other words, the purchaser of the shares did not acquire them with the intention of immediately selling them as an underwriter does. The stock is sold as Rule 144 stock where there is insufficient current public information about the issuer available or where it is being sold to an affiliate of the issuer (insider stock).

Stock that is to be sold to the public under Rule 144 exemption has certain restrictions. First, stock must be fully paid for and the owner must have held it in the fully for condition for one year. Second, there must be sufficient public information available about the stock and the company for an individual to be able to make an investment decision. Third, the shares must be sold in quantities equal to or less than an amount obtained by formula.

Here's the formula for the sale of restricted securities: Restricted stock sold by an affiliate of the issuer, together with all sales of nonrestricted securities within the previous three months, cannot exceed the greater of

> 1% of the shares of that class outstanding as shown by the most recent published report of the issuer.
>
> the average weekly reported volume of trading in such securities on all national securities exchanges and/or the average weekly volume reported through the automated quotation system of a registered securities association during four calendar weeks.

II-N-2 Rule 145 Stock

Stock received under Rule 145 is a result of corporate actions (a distribution, acquisition, or spinoff) affecting Rule 144 stock and therefore has the same restrictions as Rule 144 stock. The holding period and all other restraints refer back to the basis applicable to the 144 stock.

II-N-3 Rule 144A Stock

The United States has very strict disclosure requirements for a security to be registered. Many foreign corporations thus have trouble qualifying their securities for registration. In addition, many domestic corporations have institutional following, where these institutions know enough about the issuer not to require the in-depth detail that is required for registration with the Securities and Exchange Commission. In addition, as the reason for the issuance of a security is generally to raise capital, the cost of a formal underwriting must be considered. To satisfy these needs, Rule 144A was adopted. The rule makes the issuance of securities to knowledgeable investors easier.

Securities sold under Rule 144A may be sold to a qualified investment buyer (QIB) or such individual that the sellers believe has the investment experience and expertise to qualify. To qualify as a QIB, the client must own in the aggregate and invest on a discretionary basis at least $100 million in securities of issuers that are not affiliated with the buying organization and that has an audited net worth of at least $25 million in its latest annual financial statement. The audited financial statement cannot date back more than 16 months preceding the date of sale. However, in determining the aggregate amount of securities invested in on a discretionary basis, the following types of securities cannot be included:

- bank deposit notes
- certificates of deposit
- loan participations
- repurchase agreements
- securities owned but subject to a repurchase agreement
- currency, interest rate, and commodity swaps

To qualify as a 144A security, the same class of security cannot be traded on a national exchange or quoted on a national interdealer electronic quote system. In addition, at the time of issuance, any security that is exchangeable or convertible into a fully registered and tradable security that is at a 10% or lower premium will be considered to be a fully tradable security and not qualify for 144A status.

For an issuer to qualify the security under Rule 144A, the organization must provide a balance sheet that is not older than 16 months before the date of sale, a profit and loss statement, and a statement of retained earnings for the 12 months prior to the date of the balance sheet.

If the date of the balance sheet is more than six months before the resale date, additional profit and loss and retained earnings statements are required for the period from the date of the balance sheet to a date that is less than six months before the resale date.

The statement of the nature of the issuer's business and its products and services offered is as of a date within 12 months prior to the date of resale.

With regard to foreign private issuers, the required information must meet the timing requirements of the issuer's home country or principal trading markets.

II-O SUMMARY OF INVESTMENT PRODUCTS

ADR, ADS: Foreign securities issued through a U.S. bank.

Banker's acceptance (BA): Short-term debt issued by banks and used in international trade.

Certificate of deposit (CD): Short-term debt issued by banks.

Commercial paper: Short-term debt of a corporation.

Corporate bond or note: Debt of a corporation. It usually carries a fixed rate of interest and is of long duration.

Currency: The buying and/or selling of currency from different countries to use for multiple purposes.

Exchange-traded fund (ETF): A portfolio of securities designed to replicate an index against which shares are sold.

Future/Forward: Contract for settlement or delivery to occur sometime in the future.

Mortgage-Backed Security: Either GNMA (Government National Mortgage Association), FHLMC (Federal Home Loan Mortgage Corp.), or FNMA (Federal National Mortgage Association) represented by the modified passthrough form of issue.

Municipal bond and note: Long-term debt instrument (bond) or short-term instrument (note) issued by state or local governments.

Mutual fund: Pooling of money to acquire a desired portfolio of securities or investment goal. We most commonly use the term for a managed company that collects funds from the public to invest in predetermined stated goals.

Option: A contract to trade an underlying security at a fixed price over a specified period of time. The owner has the privilege to exercise the option. At the end of the period, the contract will expire if it's not exercised.

Stock: Ownership of a corporation. The ownership is evidenced by shares. Two forms of ownership are common and preferred.

Swap: An exchange of currency for a fixed period of time or the exchange of interest payment terms for a stated period.

U.S. Treasury obligation: Debt issued by the federal government. Short-term instruments are known as *bills*, intermediate-term instruments as *notes*, and long-term instruments as *bonds*. There are other government securities known as *agencies*, which are also backed by the Fed.

Warrant and right: Privilege issued by the corporation that gives the owner the opportunity to acquire stock under prescribed provisions.

CHAPTER III

The Marketplaces and Order Management

Brokerage operations is an overall term that includes trade processing, trade-related entries, security and fund movements, asset servicing, financing, and regulatory-mandated record keeping. Each of these operates under an umbrella referred to as brokerage operations.

III-A *THE MARKET*

Brokerage operations don't begin until there has been an exchange of value between two parties. This exchange of value usually takes the form of a *trade.* The trade begins with an order being entered. Stone, Forrest & Rivers' clients' orders are entered electronically.

A client—let's name him Theodore E. Baer—wants to purchase the common stock (shares) of a company. Let's say the company is Electra Corp. The shares—in this case, the common shares of Electra Corp.—trade in a securities market. Let's assume the market is the New York Stock Exchange. A securities market, like any other market, is where buyers and sellers of value meet to trade. To operate in this market, Theodore, or Ted, must have an account with a firm known as a broker/dealer, which is a member of that particular market or which has access to that market. The member firm has qualified under the rules and conditions of that marketplace and is therefore permitted to conduct business there.

SF&R will transmit Ted's order to the NYSE for execution. At this point, the most important function of a market is *price discovery*. What is this "thing" worth now? Value is based on many factors, and it changes over

Exhibit 1 Electronic Order Entry Form and Explanation

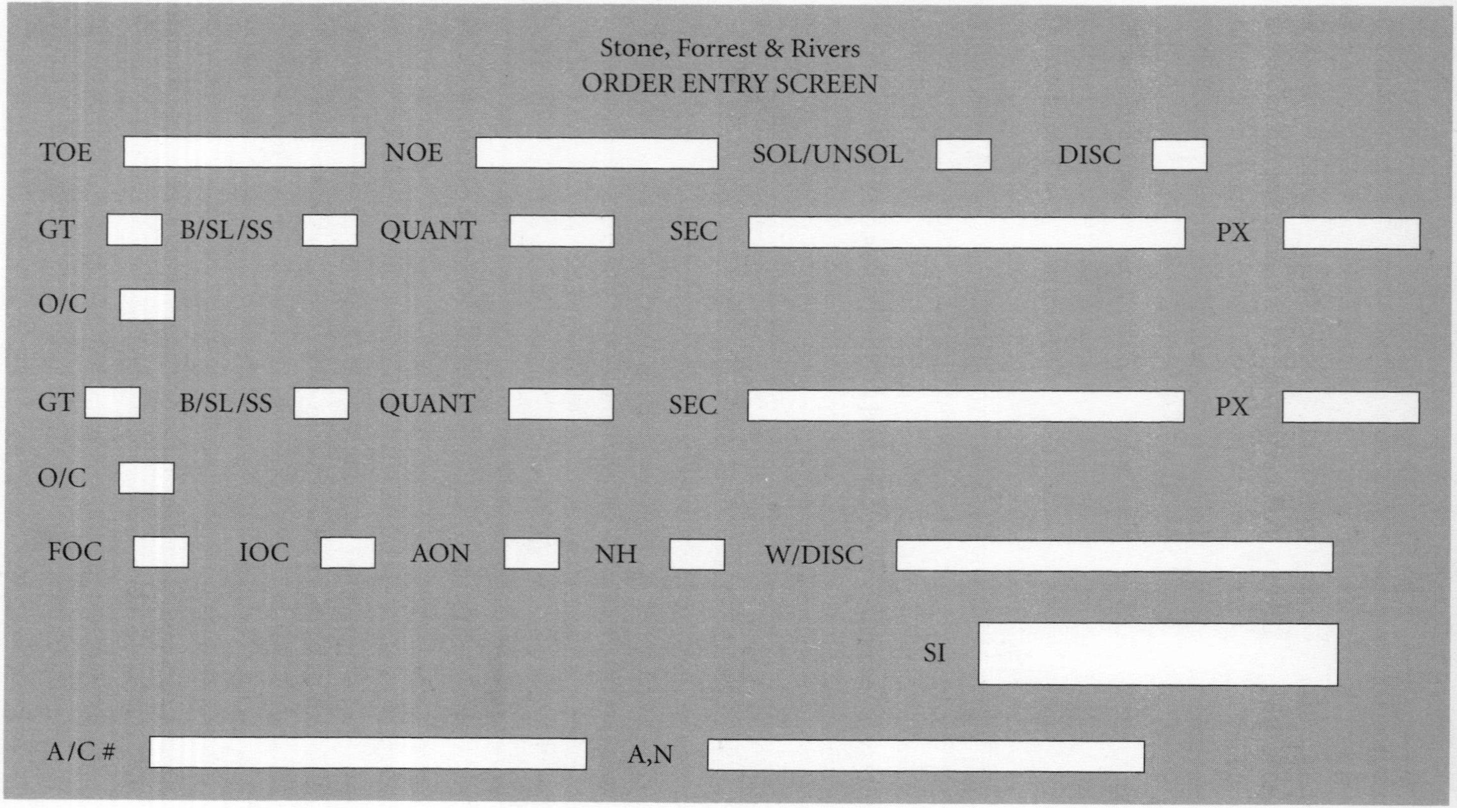

Stone, Forrest & Rivers
ORDER ENTRY SCREEN

TOE NOE SOL/UNSOL DISC

GT B/SL/SS QUANT SEC PX

O/C

GT B/SL/SS QUANT SEC PX

O/C

FOC IOC AON NH W/DISC

SI

A/C # A,N

LINE NUMBER

1—*T*ime *O*f *E*ntry [computer filled]; *N*otice *O*f *E*xecution [computer-filled]; Was the order solicited by the registered representative or unsolicited. Did the registered representative use discretion?

2—Good till = length of time order is in force; buy, sell long, sell short; quantity;

Security, Price

3—For Options—is it an Opening or Closing transaction?

4—and 5—the same as 2 and 3 used for certain option orders and other contingency orders

6—Special execution instructions—see text

7—Special instructions

8—Client account number, type of account and registered rep number time because the factors change. What is important is the concept that a fair and orderly market always displays the "true" value of something at a given moment.

SF&R can purchase 100 shares of Electra Corp. for its client, Theodore E. Baer, at $42 per share. That is what the market is saying a share is worth at a particular time. As instructed by Ted when he gave the order, SF&R executes the order and trade processing begins.

Ted gave the order to buy Electra Corp. to a representative of Stone, Forrest & Rivers known as an *account executive*. This individual—also known as a registered representative, stockbroker, or salesperson, among other titles—has qualified with regulatory authorities to conduct business with the public. Let's call our stockbroker James (Jim) Nasium. Jim works with other account executives in a sales office called a *branch office*.

Another client, Miss Ali Waih, is a participant in SF&R's Web-based trading system. Ali can enter orders over the Web directly to the point of execution by using SF&R's computer networks. Her account has been approved for trading up to $25,000 worth of securities on any given day. SF&R's systems verify every order coming in to make sure that they are within the limits set for the various Web customers. Ali provides the information requested on the screen. She enters the necessary passwords and other verification and puts the order in to buy 100 shares of Ultra Corp. at $62. The order is routed through SF&R's systems to the point where Ultra Corp. trades. Let's assume that Ultra Corp., symbol ULTR, trades in the NASDAQ market. The order will be routed to the point of execution and, if the order is executable, the report will come back to Ali in a matter of seconds.

Ted's order is transmitted from the branch office to an area of Stone, Forrest & Rivers responsible for ensuring that all orders that can be executed are, and that pending orders are attended to. Ali Waih's order is also routed through this area. This entire process is known as the *order management system.*

Orders are routed to the appropriate market for execution. Once received, an order is executed according to the terms of the order and the execution rules of the marketplace. The terms of the order are compared to the current quote and size of the particular stock. In the case of Electra Corp., assume the quote is 41.75–42.00 and the size is 8,000 shares comprising the $41.75 per share *bid* and 5,000 shares comprising the $42.00 per share *offer*. The quote of 41.75–42.00 or 41.75–2 means that the highest price anyone wants to pay for the stock is $41.75 per share, and that the lowest price anyone wants to sell the stock for is $42.00 per share. Ted's order was to buy 100

Exhibit 2

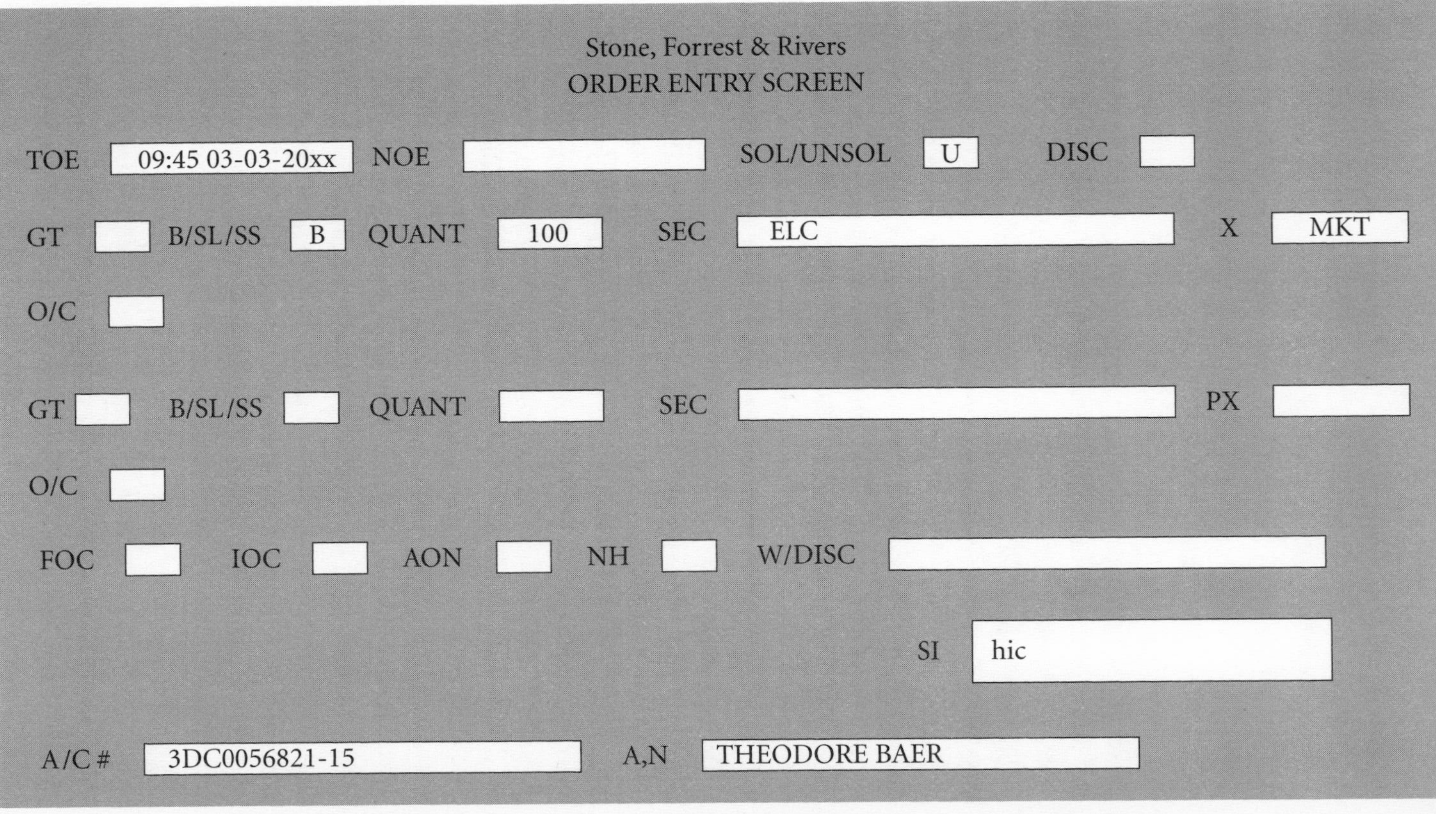

Stone, Forrest & Rivers
ORDER ENTRY SCREEN

TOE 09:45 03-03-20xx NOE SOL/UNSOL U DISC

GT B/SL/SS B QUANT 100 SEC ELC X MKT

O/C

GT B/SL/SS QUANT SEC PX

O/C

FOC IOC AON NH W/DISC

SI hic

A/C # 3DC0056821-15 A,N THEODORE BAER

shares "at the market." It would be *filled* or executed against one of the orders comprising the 5,000 shares to sell at $4 per share.

III-A-1 Agency Transaction

Orders on the NYSE can be executed in two ways. One is via electronic order routing systems such as NYSE's Super DOT system. The other is by a broker on the exchange floor who intervenes and executes the order on behalf of the member firm and its customer. Usually orders of small size are routed electronically.

Shares of stock of a particular company that are listed for trading on the New York Stock Exchange (and on all other stock exchanges that operate through a trading floor that requires member firms to have a physical presence) trade at only one location on the floor. That location on the NYSE is known as a *trading post.* The particular securities are assigned to an exchange member firm known as a *specialist firm.* Working for the specialist firm are individuals, known as *specialists,* who are responsible for maintaining fair and orderly markets in the securities assigned to them. Electra Corp. has been assigned to the specialist firm of Hill & Dale. The member of the firm responsible for Electra Corp. is Hy Hill.

Ted's order has been accepted by SF&R's account executive, Jim, and transmitted electronically to SF&R's central computer facility. Because the order is for one *round lot* (100 shares), the order management system routes the order to the exchange's Super DOT system, which in turn routes the order to the *post* location where Electra Corp. is trading. The order appears on a monitor called the *Display Book,* located at the trading post, where Hy Hill, the specialist, is standing.

Hy executes the order against a sell order at $42 per share as prescribed in the exchange rules. Hy notifies SF&R and the selling firm of the execution. SF&R, through its account executive, Jim, notifies Ted of the purchase. The firm that represented the seller does the same.

III-A-2 Principal Transaction

Ali's order was executed in a similar fashion. However, Ali's order trades in the over-the-counter equity market known as the NASDAQ market. In this market, instead of a specialist or a floor broker executing the trades, market makers (AKA traders) who commit a firm's capital, make two-sided markets. They make a bid and an offer, known as a *quote*. As Ali's order is for 100 shares, it will be routed via SF&R's order management system to NASDAQ's Small Order Execution System (SOES) to one of the market makers that can best fill the order. In this particular case, let's assume that the SF&R over-the-counter equity-trading desk also makes a market in this security. Therefore, Ali's order will be routed to SF&R's trading desk. If they have the best price for Ali, they will execute the order; if not, they will route the order through SOES to the market maker making the best price. Let's assume that SF&R's market makers have the best price. As this will be a principal trade, that is, a trade executed against SF&R's proprietary accounts, the trade will be processed on a markup basis. Therefore, included in the price will be the markup or commission. The SF&R trader is willing to sell the stock to Ali at $61.50 with a ½-point markup, making the price equal to Ali's $62 a share. Ali will not bear commission on top of the markup.

The basic difference between the execution of Ted's order and Ali's order is the fact that Ted's order was executed on the floor of the stock exchange on an agency basis. That means that a broker (or specialist) executed the order against a third party's order and as such they acted as agents. SF&R will charge Ted commission and add the commission to the cost of the Ted's purchase. Ali's order, however, was executed on a principal basis. SF&R is a market maker in Ultra Corp. and, therefore, they executed the order on a principal basis. The price Ali receives will include a markup.

In summation, a client of SF&R has purchased 100 shares of Electra Corp. with the assistance of an exchange floor member—in this case, specialist Hill—from someone or some entity represented by the selling firm that neither the specialist, the specialist firm, SF&R, James Nasium, or Theodore E. Baer knows. The actual seller is known only to the selling member firm with whom Hill transacted business. In addition, a second customer of SF&R purchased stock in the NASDAQ market. This was done between a client and a market maker. The market maker was trading from their inventory. They're managing the firm's money, trying to make a profit from trading. Whether it was an SF&R market maker or a market maker from another firm, they would treat Ali's order the same. Ali's order is getting the best price from all the market makers that is available at that time.

We briefly looked at two marketplaces: the New York Stock Exchange and the NASDAQ market. Later we will examine the exchange and the over-the-counter markets in much more detail. We will discuss the different types of orders, how they are executed, and how they are reflected in the various marketplaces.

III-B *ORDER ROUTING*

The genesis for the entire operations process starts with the entry of an order. How the order enters the processing stream is where we will begin.

III-B-1 Retail Order Entry

Clients of SF&R have several avenues by which they can enter orders to buy or sell securities. Two of the more common ways are the use of a stockbroker or directly over the Web. Clients seeking advice from a stockbroker as to what they should buy or what the firm is currently recommending, or clients not sure of how to manipulate through the Web, will use the advice and services of a stockbroker. They call the stockbroker to discuss their personal situations, and the stockbroker may recommend a course of action for them to take or may recommend a particular security that they might want to trade. Stockbrokers are armed with research material from the firm's own research department and various other sources permitted by the firm.

Another way orders are entered into the system is by people using the Web. They go to their terminals, access their account, put in their personal IDs, and then select the order screen, which allows them to complete the order that they wish to enter. After the Web site verifies that this is what they want to do, the order is sent forward to SF&R's order management system for verification and further processing.

Still another way orders are entered is by individuals who are professional traders called *day traders*. They sit at terminals supplied by SF&R and trade in and out of positions on a daily basis. The orders are entered directly from these terminals into SF&R's order management system in a similar fashion to the way orders are entered over the Web.

III-B-2 Institutional Order Entry

Orders are also entered by institutions such as pension plans and mutual funds. These clients are adjusting their portfolios to reflect current events in the marketplace, the economy, and the world in general. In addition, some people use the services of a professional money manager to handle their finances. These types of clients have institutional order entry systems.

Institutional types of clients usually manage more then one account so when they enter orders to transact securities, there could be more than one account involved in the transaction. At the time of entry, the institution does not know what percentage of the order will be executed and therefore must wait until the the end of the trading day to allocate the resulting transaction. Systems used to accomplish this are known as OASYS, a product of Thomson Financial; Trade Suite, a product of DTCC; and Omgeo, a joint product of Thomson Financial & Depostory Trust Company & Clearing Corporation. Through these systems, the institution wires notification of the allocation to the broker/dealer at the end of the day.

The goal of the industry is to take the error factor out of the process. At the present time, Omgeo is the closest to achieving this. Ideally,

1. The institution transmits the order to a central matching unit (a compute system).
2. The central matching unit stores the order and sends it on to the broker/dealer, which sends it to the marketplace(s) for execution.
3. The broker/dealer reports the executions to the central processing unit as they occur.
4. The central processing unit checks the execution report against the original order, to ensure that all is in order. With each execution, the central matching unit reduces the quantity of the order remaining to be executed and reports the executions to the institution.
5. At the end of the day, the institution allocates the executed quantity among the accounts represented by the original order.
6. The institution reports the allocation to the central processing unit.
7. The central processing unit verifies the quantity of the allocation against the quantity reported as executed. If all is in order, the central processing unit forwards the allocation on to the broker/dealer.
8. The broker/dealer processes the allocation through the individual accounts that the transaction has been allocated.

Working of the Central Matching Unit

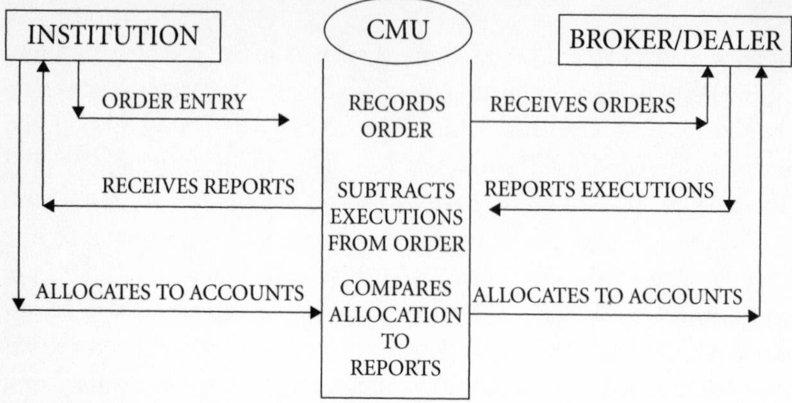

Throughout this process, any discrepancies or other problems are reported from the central processing unit to the submitting party at the time of the occurrence.

III-B-3 Order Requirements

Regardless of where the order originates, it must contain certain information: whether the order is to buy, sell long (meaning the customer owns the stock and wishes to sell it), or sell short (meaning the customer does not own the stock; here the firm will borrow it on the customer's behalf and the customer expects to buy it back at a later date at a lower price), the quantity being transacted, the description of the security, or its symbol (for example, for Zappa Corp., the person would enter the symbol that has been assigned by the marketplace), the ZAP, customer's name and account number, and the order type. (Is it a market order or is it a limit order, which we'll explain later?)

This information enables the employees who are responsible for monitoring and/or executing the order to know which securities are being traded, what quantities are involved, and the terms under which the customer is willing to do this transaction. The customer's name and account number are, of course, necessary for the later processing of the order as well as for satisfying various rules and regulations. In purchasing or selling securities, clients are attempting to attain certain goals: to buy or sell at a certain price, to lock in a profit, to minimize a loss, and so on. To assist them in accomplishing these goals, a myriad of different types of orders is at their disposal. Each type of order entails the use of additional information that custom-tailors it to the needs and wishes of the customer.

Exhibit 3

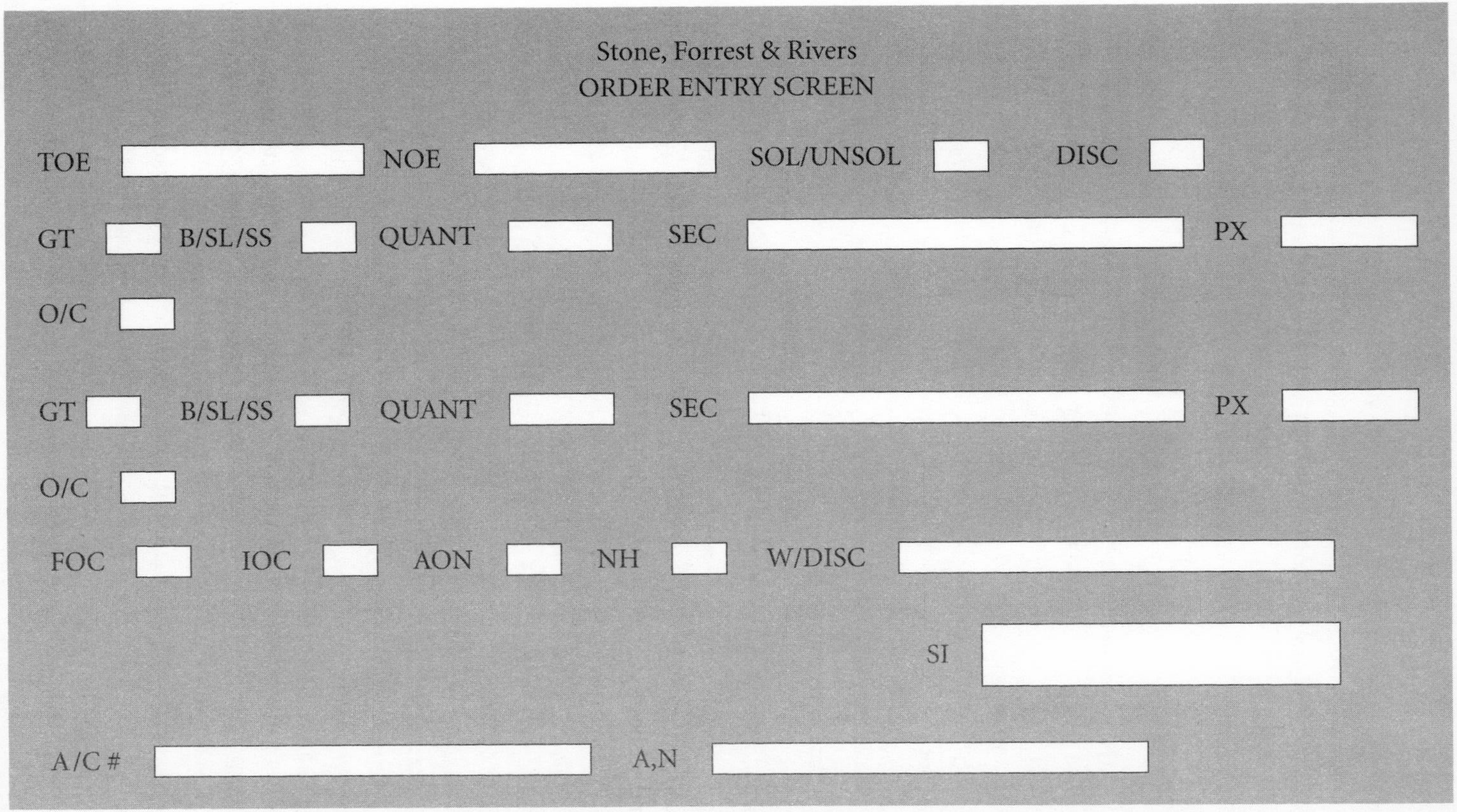

Stone, Forrest & Rivers
ORDER ENTRY SCREEN

TOE NOE SOL/UNSOL DISC

GT B/SL/SS QUANT SEC PX

O/C

GT B/SL/SS QUANT SEC PX

O/C

FOC IOC AON NH W/DISC

SI

A/C # A,N

In addition to the basic order information, traders and floor brokers on the exchange must know if there are any constraints on the price and method of order execution. These constraints are governed by the rules and regulations of the exchange and other self-regulatory organizations, such as the NASD.

III-B-4 The Quote

The market is made up of participants willing to buy a particular issue and those willing to sell. Whenever buyer and seller agree on the price, a trade occurs. This leaves buyers who do not want to pay what the sellers are offering and sellers who do not want to accept what the buyers are bidding. Other participants who have yet to declare their intention may want to know where the market stands: What is the highest price anyone wants to pay (bid) for the stock and what is the lowest price anyone is willing to sell (offer) at? The two together form the quote. The quote is comprised of the highest bid and lowest offer.

Example:

Stock symbol: ZAP

Highest bid: $35.20 per share

Lowest offer: $35.50 per share

Quote: Bid 35.20, offer 35.50 which is displayed as

ZAP 35.20–.50

III-B-5 The Size

Of importance to the potential market participant is the number of shares comprising the bid and the offer. This is referred to as the *depth of market* or the *size.* Let's suppose you want to buy 1,000 shares of PIPP @ $6. SF&R's broker tells you that the quote is 5.50–6.00 1 × 1. As the trading lot is 100 shares, it is known as a round lot. The size of 1 equates to 100 shares. The bid at $5.50 is for only 100 shares and the offer at $6 is also for only 100 shares. In other words, there are only 100 shares offered at $6. Of the 1,000 shares that you wanted to purchase, only 100 shares are known to be for sale at that price. The next lowest price at which anyone wants to sell PIPP is unknown and will be higher. This is known as a very *thin market.* Of concern to you, supposing that you did acquire the 1,000 shares, is whether there would be any market for the stock should you want sell it at a later date and, if there was and it was only for 100 shares, what price would you receive for the entire 1,000-share lot. However, if the broker told you the market was 500 bid × 500 offered, that would translate into 500 lots or 50,000 shares, so you would feel more comfortable knowing that you could buy your 1,000 shares at the offer price and be fairly sure that the market depth would still exist at a later date when you could sell your shares and get a fair price.

Let's put the two together: the *quote* and the *size* for ZAP. Assume the following: The highest price buyers are willing to pay for ZAP at this moment in time is $35.20 per share. The total number of shares comprising this *bid* is 20,000 shares. The lowest price sellers are willing to offer the stock at is $35.50 per share and the total comprising this *offer* is 30,000 shares. Then the quote and size for ZAP common stock are:

ZAP
35.20–50
200 × 300

In industry parlance the term *bid and asked* is often used in place of *bid and offer.*

III-B-6 Time Constraints of Orders

III-B-6-a *Day Order*

A *day order* is one that is entered and, if not executed in part or whole when the market closes, is automatically canceled. The day order can specify a market, or limit, or have any other nontime constraint when it is entered.

III-B-6-b *Good Through (GTC, GTM, GTW, and so on)*

An order may have a time constraint such as *Good till Cancel (GTC), Good thru Week (GTW),* or *Good thru Month (GTM).* Orders with these constraints will remain in force until either they are executed or time runs out. Good till canceled orders remain in force until they are either canceled by the originator or executed. In the marketplace most broker/dealers remind their clients of the pending orders by listing them on the clients' monthly statements. (Beware. If you enter this type of order, it will be executed when the then current market price of the security satisfies the order's limit price, be it in an hour, a day, a week, a month, or later. Whatever may have prompted you to enter the order in the first place may not exist when the order is finally executed. No matter, it is still your trade.) GT X orders remain in force until the X time period ends.

The limit prices that appear on equity good till/through buy limit orders and sell stop orders are affected by dividends. The marketplace in which the stock trades adjusts the closing price to reflect the dividend on the night before the *ex-dividend date.* (See the "Dividend" section for more detail.) For example, RAM closes at $45 per share on the day before the ex-dividend date. The stock is "going ex-dividend" $.20 the next day. The marketplace in which RAM trades will adjust the closing price to $44.80 because the worth of the company will fall by $.20 per share when the dividend is paid. To prevent the execution of "good through/till" pending orders due to nonmarket trading activity, the limit prices on these orders are reduced also. For example, a buy limit order with a price of $44.90 would be reduced to $44.70. Clients may override this process by including the instruction *do not reduce (DNR)* or *do not increase (DNI).* The instruction DNR refers to the limit price on pending orders affected by the payment cycle of cash dividends, whereas DNI refers to the share quantity and resulting lower price on pending orders affected by stock dividends. To best explain this latter concept, think of a pizza pie. The difference between cutting it into six slices or into eight slices is two more slices—but each slice is smaller. The type of pending orders that can be affected by these corporate actions are "buy" and "sell stop" orders. Sell limit orders and buy stop orders are entered above the current market price, so they won't be inadvertently executed by the market price adjustment.

III-B-7 Types of Orders

III-B-7-a *Market Order*

A *market order* is an order to be executed at whatever the market price is when the order is entered. A *buy market order* accepts the current offer of the quote. A *sell market order* accepts the current bid.

Example:

ZAP
35.20–.50

The current quote on ZAP is 35.20 to 35.50. As $35 is the current dollar price for both the bid and offer, it is not displayed again on the offer side. In this particular example, 35.20 represents the highest bid and .50 (meaning $35.50) represents the lowest offer. A customer wanting to buy 100 shares of stock at the market would pay $35.50, that is, $35.50 per share for a total purchase price of $3,550. A person willing to sell stock at the market would receive $35.20 per share, or $3,520 principal for the sale. These are gross dollar amounts and do not include fees and other expenses associated with the transaction.

III-B-7-b *Limit Order*

A *limit order* places limits on the price at which the customer is willing to enter into transactions. A *buy limit order* establishes the highest price that the client is willing to pay for the securities. The order cannot be executed above that price. A *sell limit order* sets the lowest price someone is willing to accept for her securities. The order cannot be executed lower than the limit price.

Using the above quotation of 35.20–.50, a client entering a limit order to buy the stock at $35.30 would not receive an execution as there is no one who is known to be willing to sell the stock at that price. The lowest offer price in the marketplace at this time is $35.50. In a similar fashion, someone entering a sell limit order with a price of $35.30 would not receive an execution because the highest price that anyone would want to buy the stock at this moment in time is $35.20.

In the market, the highest bid and lowest offer comprise the quote. As the quote is currently 35.20–.50, someone entering a buy limit order (bidding) below $35.20 would not have the bid reflected because the higher bid would be filled first. Likewise, someone offering stock for sale above $35.50 would not have their offer reflected in the quote, as the lower offer must be filled first. Let's assume the bid is $35.20 and someone enters a bid of $35. To whom would you rather sell your securities? Would you want to receive $35.20 per share for your shares or $35? Naturally, you would want to receive $35.20 per share. Bids entered below the current bid and offers entered above the current offer are not reflected. However, bids entered above the current bid but below the current offer, and offers entered below the current offer but above the current bid will be reflected. In the previous paragraph, should the order to buy stock at 35.30—say, 1,000 shares—be entered, the quote and size would change to reflect the higher bid:

ZAP
35.30–50
10 × 30

III-B-7-c *Short Sales*

A short sale is a unique type of transaction that permits the person entering the order to earn a profit from falling stock prices. The individual entering into this type of order does not own the stock being sold. Instead, the firm will borrow the stock to be sold on behalf of the client; therefore, the client is said to be *short the stock*. If the client's prediction is correct, the value of the stock will fall, allowing the repurchase of the stock at a lower price at a later date, thereby locking in a profit. If, however, the stock should rise during the period of the short sale, the client will be purchasing the stock at a higher price than it was sold at and will therefore incur a loss. Ellie Fant, a customer of Stone, Forrest & Rivers, wishes to sell short 100 shares of ZOW at the current market price. Fant does not own the security, and therefore goes to SF&R to see if the firm can borrow the stock. In Chapter 6 ("Settlement"), we will examine how this is arranged, but for the sake of this example, Stone, Forrest & Rivers borrows the stock and lends it to Fant for sale. The stock is sold in the open market under the short sale rules, which state that a short sale must occur at an *uptick* or *zero uptick* on an exchange-traded issue or on the bid that is higher than the previous bid for a NASDAQ issue. The purpose of these rules is to prevent the artificial falling of stock prices by excessive short selling. *Ticks* are another term for *trades*.

Here's an example of upticks and zero upticks: Last sale 35.00, the short sale order is entered. Sales occur 35.10, 35.10, 35.20, 35.10. The first trade at 35.10 is an uptick; the next trade at 35.10 is a zero uptick, as are any other 35.10 trades that immediately follow the first 35.10 trade. However, the next trade is at 35.20, which is also an uptick. The trade following the 35.20 trade is at 35.10, which is a downtick. Any subsequent 35.10 trades occurring would be referred to as a zero downtick. Short sales are only permitted on upticks or zero upticks and, therefore, the first, second, and third trades occurring after the short sale order was entered could accommodate a short transaction.

The following trade prices demonstrate upticks, zero upticks, downticks, and zero downticks:

```
                                                   o      o
35.10↑35.10↑35.10↑35.20↑35.20  ↑  35.10↓35.10↓35.10↓35.05↓35.10↑
           o      o              o
```

The acquirer of the stock becomes the new owner. Fant is therefore "short" the stock. Let's assume Fant sold the stock short at $80 a share and is correct in the assessment. The stock drops in price from $80 a share to $60 a share and Fant buys the stock in the open market. When the purchase occurs, the stock is returned to the lender and Fant has locked in a 20-point profit. During the period of the short sale, Fant is responsible for all corporate actions (except for the right to vote) that have occurred during that period. For example, if ZOW paid a cash dividend, Fant's account will be charged the amount of the dividend and the person's account lending the stock credited (paid) the amount of dividend that he would have earned had his security not been lent. Short sales are also covered in Chapter 5, "Margin" and Chapter 6, "Settlement" (see VI-D).

A recent rule change, known as Rule SHO, permits short sales to be made without upticks in certain securities. This change was brought about because of the fragmentation in the marketplace and the difficulty in determining when a true uptick or zero uptick has occurred.

III-B-7-d *Stop Orders*

A *stop order* is a memorandum order that becomes a market order when the price on the order is reached or passed. A *buy stop order* is entered above the current market price; a *sell stop order* is entered below it. Stop orders could be executed immediately if it weren't for the word *stop* in the initial instruction.

Example: Mike Rafoen buys 100 shares of RAM at $55 per share. He does not have access to an ISP that offers quotations and therefore cannot monitor the price movement of the security during the workday. Yet he is willing to risk $500 on this transaction (5 points on 100 shares = $500). This represents the amount Mike is willing to lose and does not want to risk any further loss. Mike could enter an order to "GTC Sell 100 RAM at 50 *stop*." Because the market is now $55, Rafoen's order would be executed immediately if it were not for the stop instruction. With the word *stop* in the instruction, the market has to fall to 50 or below before this order can be executed as a market order. The first time a trade occurs at the price of $50 or lower, that transaction becomes the electing trade as it satisfies the "50 stop" criteria. The trade converts the stop order to a market order that should be executed on the next available bid.

In a similar fashion Ms. Lucille Cannon sells short 1,000 shares of PEW at $75 per share. Luce is afraid the stock may rise instead of fall and wants to protect the $75,000 (1,000 shares × $75 per share) that she has at risk. Luce enters a buy stop order at $78 per share, which represents the $3,000 leeway to which she is willing expose the position. Should the stock rise to $78 per share or go above that price, the buy stop order will be executed, "closing out" the short position.

III-B-7-e *Stop Limit Order*

A *stop limit order*, while similar to a stop order, becomes a limit order instead of a market order when the *stop price* is reached or passed. All stop orders are memorandum orders, which remain in the background until their stop price is reached or passed. Unlike the market order, when the stop price is reached this order becomes a regular limit order.

Here's an example: With the market at $55 per share, the client enters an order to sell 100 shares at $50 stop 49 limit. The market closes above $50 per share but opens the next day at $45 per share. If the stop order were a stop market order (known as a *stop order*), when the stop price was reached or passed, the order would have been executed around $45 per share. Since the order was a stop limit and had a $50 stop price and $49 limit, the order would not be executed because, while the stop price of $50 was satisfied, the stock never traded at or above the limit price. It fell from above $50 per share to $45 per share; the $49 limit price would prevent its execution.

Here's another example: A client enters a sell stop limit order to sell 100 shares of PIP at 30 stop, 29 limit. The market is currently above $35. The market closes and, during the evening, bad news is released about Pipper.

The next day the stock opens at $25 a share. Had the client entered a regular stop order, the order would be executed at around $25 a share. Since the customer chose to enter a stop limit order, the order will not get executed since the customer has stated he will not sell the stock below $29 a share. If, during the day, the bad news is found out to be false or not as detrimental as originally thought and the stock trades back up to $29 per share or above, the stop limit order will be executed since the $30 stop price criterion was satisfied when the price of the stock first fell.

Remember, stop orders become market orders when their stop price is reached or passed. Stop limit orders become limit orders when their stop price is reached or passed. In either case, stop and stop limit orders are memorandum orders that become live orders when the stop price is elected.

III-B-7-f *Fill or Kill (FOK) Order*

Fill or kill (FOK) is an order used by institutions or traders of large quantities of securities that stipulates that the order must be executed in its entirety immediately or it is to be canceled. If the order size cannot be satisfied by the current market, the order is terminated immediately.

Here's an example: The Varga Fund wishes to purchase 100,000 shares of PIP at 35 FOK. The order is routed by SF&R's order management system to the point of execution where the broker or market maker, depending on where the stock is traded, determines whether there are 100,000 shares available. If there is sufficient stock available at that price or better, the order will be filled; if there isn't, the order will be canceled. Even if there was some stock available at $35, the order stipulates that they must purchase 100,000 shares immediately or cancel the order.

III-B-7-g *Immediate or Cancel (IOC) Order*

The *immediate or cancel (IOC)* order is a variation of a fill or kill order, the difference being that it will accept a partial fill and the remaining shares will be canceled.

Had the Varga Fund entered an order to buy 100,000 shares of PIP at $35 IOC and there were 20,000 shares available at that price, the person doing the execution would have accepted the 20,000 shares and canceled the remaining 80,000 shares. Both fill or kill and immediate or cancel orders have a time constraint where the action must occur immediately or the order is terminated.

III-B-7-h *All or None (AON) Order*

There are many variations of the *all or none order (AON)*. The most prominent one gives the individual executing the order a specific period of time in which to complete the order.

Here's an example: Varga Funds enters an order to buy 100,000 shares of PIP at 35 all or none within a given day. During the period of that day, the broker or market maker executing the order acquires 100,000 shares at $35; Varga Funds accepts the execution. If, however, during the course of the day the person doing the execution acquires fewer than 100,000 shares (say, the broker is only able to acquire 80,000 shares), Varga Funds does not have to accept the execution report.

III-B-7-i *Not Held (NH) Order*

A *not held (NH) order* is one that is entered into the marketplace instructing the individual doing the execution that she is not to follow the rules and regulations for executions of a particular marketplace. This may sound confusing; however, there are times when an order being entered for a rather large quantity would upset the market if it maintained its status according to the rules of that marketplace. This order simply states that the client entering the order is aware of the risks involved and is instructing the person doing the execution to use her best judgment in executing the order over a period of time.

Here's an example: Varga Funds enters an order to buy 100,000 shares of PIP at the market. At the current time there are only 8,000 shares available at, let's say, the price of $35. Varga's market order would take the 8,000 shares at $35 and continue to buy stock as it filled the various offers that were available. Naturally, since the market is made up of the highest bid and lowest offer, each of the offers that the order would tick would be at a higher level than the previous sale. Therefore, Varga would wind up overpaying for the stock, and the market would be temporarily upset. The price of the stock would return to its actual value after the order was filled. To avoid upsetting the market, Varga places the market order with a *not held* instruction, and the people doing the execution—the broker or market maker—execute the order in small portions that the market can absorb, thereby getting the best fill for Varga Funds as well as not upsetting the market. They execute the order over a period of time, allowing the market to trade freely and in a normal way.

Another point to remember is that, if the individual trying to execute Varga's order announced the entire order as required by the marketplace, any savvy trader desiring to sell a large quantity of stock would pull their order from the market to see how badly Varga Funds wanted the stock. Is Varga willing to pay more than $35? Any price Varga has to pay above $35 benefits the seller. With a not held order, the Varga Funds representative does not have to reveal the entire order at once, thereby "hiding" the intent from sellers.

The orders mentioned above are applicable for most of the securities that are traded. There are special orders, however, that are used for specific types of products. Examples include at-the-opening orders, on-the-close orders, spread orders, straddle orders, combination orders, one-cancels-the-other orders, and facilitation orders.

III-B-7-j *At-the-Opening Orders*

At-the-opening orders are market or limit orders that are entered before the market opens. The instruction is to execute the order at the opening price or cancel the order.

III-B-7-k *On-the-Close Orders*

On-the-close orders are market orders that are to be executed at the last trade of the day.

III-B-7-l *Spread Orders*

Spread orders are used in the trading of options, futures, and forward instruments. A spread order contains the instructions to buy one product or issue and simultaneously sell the same issue but with slightly different terms. For an example of an option order, SF&R's client Chris Anthemum thinks ZIP is going to rise in value from $39 per share to $45. Chris doesn't want to invest too much in this idea and wants to minimize any loss possibility should she be incorrect in her assessment. Chris is interested in purchasing the April 40 call. However, she discovers that it is trading at 6 (6 × 100 shares = $600). That would put her breakeven for 100 shares at $46 per share ($40 per share for the stock plus $6 per share for the option). To lower the cost of the transaction, Chris checks the $45 strike price call that expires at the same time as the $40 and discovers that it is trading at $3. She enters into a *spread transaction*. She buys 1 Call ZIP Apr 40 and simultaneously sells 1 Call ZIP Apr 45. Translation: Chris owns a call that permits her to call in (buy) 100 shares of ZIP exercisable any time between the day of purchase and the Saturday after the third Friday in April when the option expires. (All listed equity options expire the Saturday after the third Friday of their expiration month.) The stock can be called in (bought) at a price of $40 per share. The other option Chris sold. This permits whoever owns it to purchase 100 shares of ZIP from Chris any time they want between the day of this trade and the Saturday after the third Friday in April and pay $45 per share. For this privilege the buyer paid Chris $3 per underlying share. Naturally, neither party would entertain exercising their option unless the market price of ZIP were above the individual's option strike price. In the case of this spread, the secondary option (sale) is reducing the cost of the position. Let's assume the following premiums:

B 1 Call ZIP Apr 40 with a premium of 6

S 1 Call ZIP Apr 45 with a premium of 3

The net cost (excluding commission) to the buyer of this spread is $300 ($600 paid for the 40 Call less $300 received for the 45 Call = $300). If ZIP does not trade above $40, Chris would lose only the $300 cost. If the stock trades between $40 and $43 per share at the end of the options' life, Chris can reduce the loss. For example, if ZIP is at $42 per share at expiration, the $40 strike price call would be worth $2 and the $45 strike price call would be worth zero. Chris can sell the 40 call and recoup 2 of the 3 points that she paid. On the other hand, if ZIP is trading at $45 at expiration, Chris can earn a $200 profit (less commission cost) as the $40 strike price option would be worth 5 points and the $45 would be worth zero. At over $45, what is earned on the $40 strike price option that is purchased is lost on the $45 strike price option that is sold; therefore, the $200 profit would remain. That would be a $200 profit on a $300 investment or a return of 66⅔%.

With a breakeven of $43 per share, if ZIP reaches $46, there is a 3-point profit on the bought option but a one-point loss on the sold option (+3 − 1 = 2). At $47, it's +4 − 2 = 2, and so on.

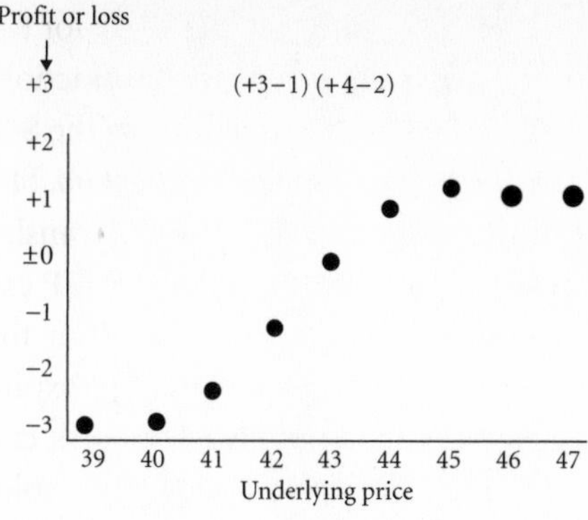

At 46, Long Call w/S.P. 40 worth 6 pts, Sold Call w/S.P. 45 worth 1pt less cost of Spread = 2 pts profit
At 45 Long Call w/40 S.P. worth 5 pts Sold Call w/S.P. 45. worth 0 less 3pt cost = 2pt profit
At 44 Long call/S.P. 40 worth 4 pts. Profit 1pt
Breakeven ($40 strike price + 3 points cost)
At 42 Long Call w/.40 S.P. worth 2 pts: Loss 1 pt
At 41 Long Call w/S.P.> worth 1 pt. Loss = 2 pts
Long Call w/S.P. 40 = 0, Loss 3 pts

This is one type of spread that is used in the option market. Futures use similar types of spreads where they may spread one future contract against a different one, such as May wheat against July wheat. The use of spread orders is either to reduce the cost, limit the risk, or take advantage of a pricing anomaly.

There is a code used to express option expiration months and strike prices. Here's an example:

Expiration month codes	Calls	Puts
January	A	M
February	B	N
March	C	O
April	D	p
Strike price codes		
(same for calls and puts)	5	A
	10	B
	15	C
	20	D

III-B-7-m *Straddle Orders*

Straddle orders are used in options and involve the simultaneous purchase or sale of both a put and a call option with the same underlying stock, with all other details of the contract being the same. Here's an example: "B (buy) 1 Call WIP Jul 60, B (buy) 1 Put WIP Jul 60." As straddles "straddle" both sides of the market, the buyer of the straddle expects the underlying security's

Exhibit 4

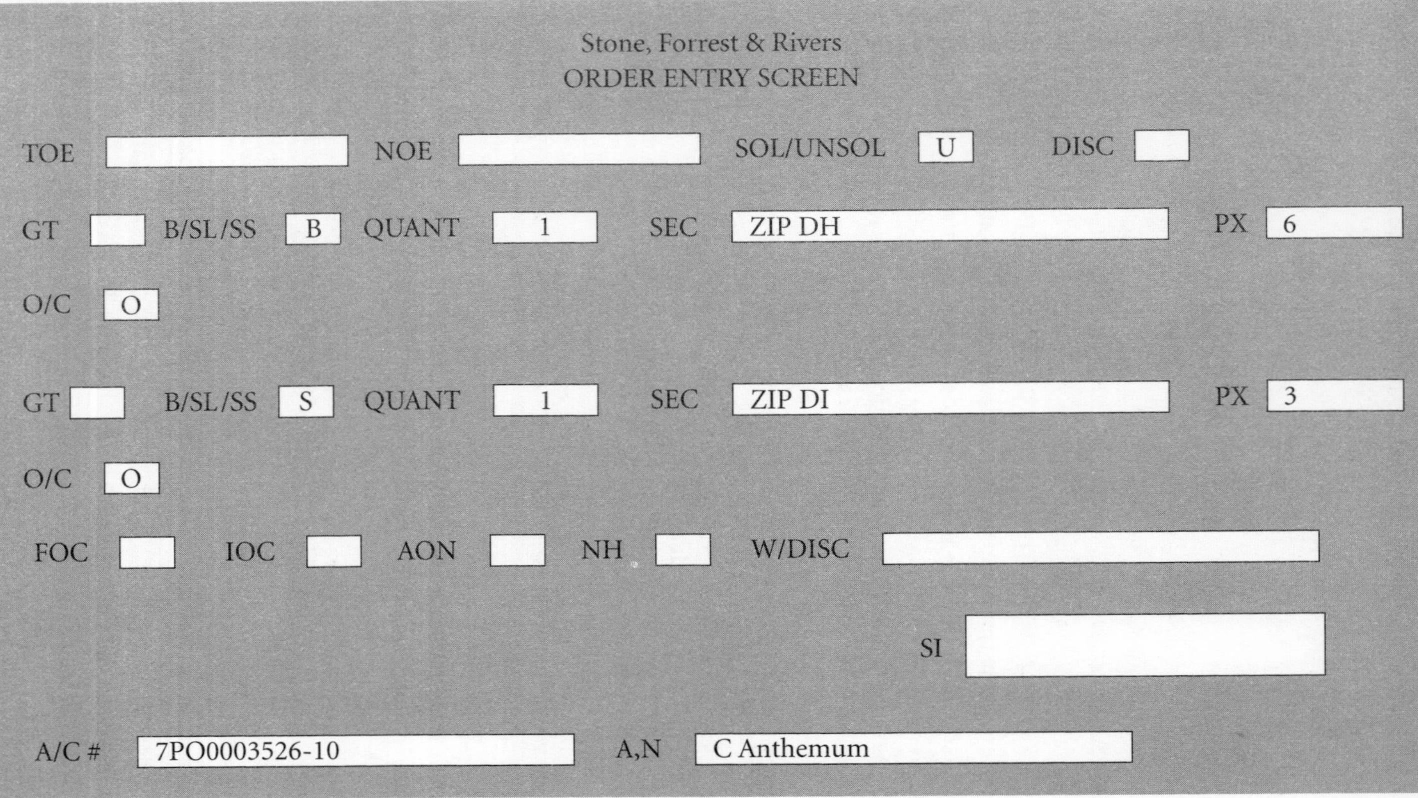

Stone, Forrest & Rivers
ORDER ENTRY SCREEN

TOE [ ] NOE [ ] SOL/UNSOL [U] DISC [ ]

GT [ ] B/SL/SS [B] QUANT [1] SEC [ZIP DH] PX [6]

O/C [O]

GT [ ] B/SL/SS [S] QUANT [1] SEC [ZIP DI] PX [3]

O/C [O]

FOC [ ] IOC [ ] AON [ ] NH [ ] W/DISC [ ]

SI [ ]

A/C # [7PO0003526-10] A,N [C Anthemum]

market price to outperform the cost of the straddle (higher volatility), whereas the seller of a straddle expects the underlying security price to underperform the amount of premium received (lower volatility).

Example: It has been announced that the ZICK Company (ZIK) is making a bid for the shares of Antyred Inc. (ANT). ANT is currently trading at $55 per share and has risen 7 points since the announcement. ZIK's bid for ANT's common stock is at $60 per share. Antyred's management thinks the company is worth more than that and has advised shareholders to turn down the bid. What will happen? Will enough ANT shareholders accept the bid so that ZIK can get voting control? Will ZIK make a higher bid? Will some other company come along and make a higher bid? Or will the attempted takeover situation just die? Each of these outcomes will affect ANT's price. Some will cause the price to rise; others will cause the price to fall. To attempt to profit from either movement, a straddle order would be employed.

B 1 Call ANT X months 55 = Y

B 1 Put ANT X months 55 = Z

If ANT's market price fluctuates more than the cost of the straddle (Y + Z), the straddle's buyer will profit.

III-B-7-n *Combination Orders*

Combination orders are similar to straddle orders, but use different series designations. An example of a combination order is to "B (buy) 1 Call WIP Jul 60 B (buy) 1 Put WIP Jul 65." Generally, combinations are less expensive than straddles as one of the two positions is further out of the money. There are also variations of combination orders that are used to attempt to establish certain trading strategies.

III-B-7-o *One-Cancels-the-Other (OCO) Order*

A *one-cancels-the-other (OCO)* order has two possible executions; the first order to get executed automatically cancels the other. For example, an order is entered to "B (buy) 1 call WIP July 60 at 6," or "B (buy) 1 call PIP Apr 40 at 3." The person doing the execution tries to see which order is executable at that particular moment. The first order to get executed automatically cancels the other; hence the name *one cancels the other*.

III-B-7-p *Facilitation Order*

When a trader is trying to make a market for a block of stock that a client is trying to purchase or sell, the trader may enter a *facilitation order* into the marketplace to offset some of the exposure risk. The amount and price of the facilitation order is disclosed so other participants can react to the request. Any participant willing to trade at a better price will take priority. The quantity responded to is totaled with the entering firm taking any portion not spoken for.

Facilitation orders are announced in option markets as traders try to use options to hedge their market risk in underlying securities.

III-B-8 Conclusion

As there are many types of orders, some of which are not mentioned above, individuals entering orders should be certain that the instruction dictated by an order is exactly what they want to do. For most of us, the basic market order or limit order will accomplish our goals.

III-C *THE EXCHANGES*

- Why should corporations have their securities listed on an exchange?
- Why are exchanges called auction markets?
- Who owns the exchanges?

These questions and many more are answered in this section.

III-C-1 Types of Exchanges

When a security is traded on an exchange, it is said to be *listed.* All stock exchanges have listing requirements, although they differ from one exchange to another. A corporation that seeks the listing of its common and preferred stocks must satisfy the exchange's listing requirements before it may even submit an application. Among the requirements are a:

- minimum number of shares outstanding
- minimum number of shareholders
- wide geographic distribution of its securities
- history of earnings of a certain amount

There are two *national stock exchanges*: the New York Stock Exchange (NYSE) and the American Stock Exchange (AMEX). NASDAQ is about to be approved as a national exchange at the writing of this book.

The requirements of the New York Stock Exchange are the more stringent of the three. On this exchange you find the securities of the major national and international corporations.

While the listing requirements of the American Stock Exchange are not quite as strict as those of the NYSE, the AMEX-listed securities are nevertheless those of well-known corporations. These companies, however, are usually younger or have smaller capitalization than those listed on the New York Stock Exchange.

Regional exchanges trade a few of the securities traded on the NYSE and the AMEX in addition to the securities of local corporations. These exchanges include the Boston Stock Exchange (BSE), Cincinnati Stock Exchange, Chicago Stock Exchange (CSE), Pacific Stock Exchange (PSE), and Philadelphia Stock Exchange (PHLX).

In 1973 a new type of exchange was created in Chicago. It was the first *options exchange* and it was named the Chicago Board Options Exchange (CBOE). Following in the path of this pioneer were a number of stock exchanges that have added options to their product mix to offer more salable products for their members to the public.

More recently, on February 24, 2000, the International Securities Exchange (ISE) became the first new exchange to be approved by the SEC since it approved the CBOE in 1973. This all-electronic option exchange began trading on May 26, 2000. Unlike the exchanges mentioned above (except the Cincinnati), the ISE does not have a trading floor. Instead, trading is conducted electronically from its participants' offices.

Commodity futures, or *commods*, are also traded on specific exchanges, including the Chicago Board of Trade and the Mercantile Exchange. (Commods, as well as listed option and bond trading, are discussed elsewhere in the book.)

Each exchange operates in a slightly different fashion from the rest, to provide an auction market where the public's orders can be executed. The prices on the exchanges represent the highest bid for a purchase and the lowest offer for a sale of a given stock, option, or commodity.

III-C-2 The New York Stock Exchange

The New York Stock Exchange acquired Archipelago and formed the NYSE group. This section is concerned with the NYSE and its methods of trading. The NYSE offers two methods of trading NYSE listed stocks. One is NYSE Direct+℠, an electronic routing and execution service for those who need fast executions and the conventional trading floor, for those orders wanting or needing human judgment or guidance or are looking for price improvement.

NYSE Direct+℠ accepts orders of up to 1,099 shares of NYSE listed securities and applies them against then best bid and offer. At the writing of this book the exchange has filed a rule change to increase the order size. Orders executed through this system are reported back to the point of entry as well as to the trade processing systems of the exchange.

Members of the New York Stock Exchange, as on most other exchanges, are said to own *seats* on the exchange. These seats allow the members access to the trading floor and as well as affording them the privilege of trading there.

Members of the New York Stock Exchange may be categorized as follows:

1. House brokers
2. Independent brokers
3. Specialists

III-C-2-a *House Brokers*

House brokers are individuals who are employed by member firms and who execute orders on the exchange trading floor for their firm's customers and the firm's proprietary trading.

III-C-2-b *Independent Brokers*

The prices of seats (memberships) fluctuate with the activity on the exchange. The busier the market, the more expensive the seats are. Brokerage firms can only afford to have a certain number of house brokers in its employ. Firms try to minimize these expenses by employing only enough house brokers to satisfy their basic needs.

What happens when the house brokers cannot handle a peak load of orders?

Assisting the house brokers when they are busy are the *two-dollar brokers*, who either own or lease their seats. Either way, they act as freelance brokers, working for their own firms, helping the commission house brokers by executing orders for the firm. Formerly, that name was *two-dollar broker*, which originated when such members actually received $2 for each 100-share trade executed. Today the rates charged have changed but the name remains.

III-C-2-c *Specialists*

On the NYSE and the AMEX, *specialists* perform three functions:

1. *Overseeing trading in their assigned securities.* This is to ensure that a fair and orderly market exists.
2. *Making markets.* They buy and sell securities for "their own account and risk" in attempting to maintain fair and orderly markets.
3. *Executing orders.* They are responsible for executing customer orders entrusted to them by the brokerage firms.

III-C-2-c-i Making Markets

Specialists are assigned securities by the exchange in which they are to *make markets*. The stock assignments are made by a member committee comprised of their peers.

As market makers, specialists are responsible for maintaining a *fair and orderly market*, which simply means a logical succession of prices, not controlling the price of an issue. In this capacity, specialists are expected to buy or sell for their own accounts in an attempt to absorb any temporary imbalance of orders being entered. If the market becomes too erratic, the specialists call for a floor governor. They discuss the situation and, if warranted, the exchange temporarily stops trading in this issue. The halt stays in effect until a fair market is reestablished. Depending on how well they facilitate trading in their assigned securities, they may be assigned additional securities or have securities removed from their control.

In recent times, certain derivative products have been used in strategies that have caused major movement of stock prices. The volatility created by these strategies as well as other factors causes prices of securities to take large swings over a short period of time. To offset this effect, the marketplaces—with the approval of the SEC—have installed "circuit breakers." When the governing index has fluctuated to a certain level, the marketplace will stop trading, thereby giving market forces time to regroup and analyze the situation.

III-C-2-c-ii Executing Orders

The specialists receive *limit orders* (orders with a fixed price requirement) that are *away from*, or *off*, the current market. These orders are posted in the *specialist's electronic book* (known as the display book) along with other orders already received. As the market fluctuates, the specialist executes the orders whose prices reflect the new market in the sequence received.

Example: WIP is trading at $50. William Bord, a client of Stone, Forrest & Rivers, enters an order to buy 10,000 shares of WIP at $46. The most Bill is willing to pay is $46 per share. With the market currently trading at $50 per share, prospective sellers are unwilling to trade their securities at $46. The client with the buy order must wait until the market price falls, if it ever does, to $46 before the order can be executed. SF&R's commission house broker, Gerald Mander, receives Bill's order. Gerry cannot stand in the crowd and hold the order until the market price falls, as he has other orders to execute. Instead, the order is turned over to a specialist who posts it "in the book." Should the price of WIP drop to $46, the specialist will try to execute it. If the specialist has already received other orders to buy WIP at $46, those orders will be executed first.

III-C-2-d *The Crowds on the Floor*

The floor of the NYSE is divided into two parts: the telephone booths and the trading posts.

Along the periphery of the floor are *member booths* where the member firms' floor employees work. Here the orders are taken from the firm's order management system and from the firm's upstairs trading desks and assigned to the floor broker. A member firm may have positions at one or more of those booths.

Orders received at the booth are either handed to the broker or sent via pages who run the order to the broker. The broker takes the order to the *trading posts*. Each listed security is assigned to a particular post, which is the only place on the floor that the assigned security may be traded. For instance, WIP common stock might be traded at, say, post 10. Specialists who are assigned to WIP stand in front of the post. (All the securities assigned to a given specialist firm are traded at the same or adjacent posts.) Brokers who want to execute customer orders for WIP or who are interested in trading WIP come to this post. They make up what is known as the WIP *crowd*. Specialists may also be members of the crowd, depending on whether they are holding public orders at the current market price or trying to balance supply or demand.

III-C-2-e *The Auction Market*

To observing visitors, the people on the trading floor appear to be yelling at each other amid wholesale confusion. Actually, the brokers are shouting their respective bids and offers, while others yell out their acceptance, thereby creating the trades.

The special language of trading might also mislead observers. When brokers call out their orders, they use an abbreviated jargon that all members understand. For example, a broker bidding for a security calls "45.25 for 100," meaning, "I am bidding $45.25 per share for 10,000 shares." A broker offering the security might call, "One at 45.25." Or, "I am offering 100 shares for sale at $45.25 per share." If a broker has a sell order that can be filled by one of the shouted bids, the broker calls out, "Sold!", meaning he is accepting the entire bid, or "Sold" plus the quantity (e.g., "Sold 100," which equates to "Sold 10,000 shares!"). A broker with a buy order that can be executed calls, "Take it!" (meaning she is accepting the entire offer) or "Take" plus the quantity being purchased (e.g., "Take 20," which equates to "Purchase 2,000 shares").

III-C-2-f *Priority, Precedence, and Parity*

The brokers and specialists in the crowd on the NYSE execute orders according to a procedure known as *priority, precedence, and parity.*

III-C-2-f-i Priority

One order and one order only can have *priority*, which is determined by the order's time of entry. The first member to call out the highest bid or lowest offer has priority on the floor. Sometimes the first bid or the offer is a mere fraction of a second sooner than the rest.

Example: The current quote on the floor for WIP is 22.20–.50. The highest price that anyone wants to pay for the security is $22.20 per share. The lowest price that anyone wants to sell for is $22.50 per share.

Each bid and offer rendered on the exchange floor must be for at least one *round lot*, or 100 shares. While the *quote* informs an interested party of the current market, it does not reveal the density or number of shares that the quote represents. The interested individual must request the *size*.

The response to "quote and size" will contain the highest bid, lowest offer, and the number of round lots available at each price.

Example: A broker enters the crowd with an order to buy 100 shares. Upon requesting the quote and size, the broker is told "22.20–.50 30 by 50." This translates to "Highest bid is $22.20 per share, lowest offer is $22.50 per share, 30 round lots (3,000 shares) bid at $22.20 and 50 round lots (5,000 shares) offered at $22.50." The broker bids $22.25 for 100. Another broker enters the crowd at that moment with an order to sell at $22.25. The broker calls, "Sold." A trade is consummated.

What if you want to *sell* stock?

Example: Entering the crowd with an order to sell and requesting quote and size, a broker offers the security at $22.25. At that moment, another broker entering the crowd hears the offer and is willing to buy it. The broker calls, "Take it!" A trade is consummated.

III-C-2-f-ii Precedence

The order that can fill or best fill the quote takes *precedence*.

Example: The quote and size is 22.20–.50, 30 x 50. The offer is comprised of orders announced by four floor brokers. (The times are exaggerated for explanatory purposes. In reality, the offers are entered within seconds of each other.) All offers are at $22.50.

- Broker A: 1,000 shares at 10:15 A.M.
- Broker B: 1,000 shares at 10:16 A.M.
- Broker C: 2,000 shares at 10:17 A.M.
- Broker D: 1,000 shares at 10:17 A.M.

If Broker X enters the crowd with a buy order for 1,000 shares *at the market* (that is, at the best possible offer), the trade is executed with Broker A, who has priority.

Let's say, however, that Broker X entered the crowd with an order to buy 3,000 shares. Then, Broker A and Broker C execute: Broker A, who has priority, sells 1,000 shares, and Broker C, who has precedence, sells 2,000 shares. After A's priority, Broker C can "best fill the order" with the 2,000-share order. As B & D have 1,000-share orders, C gets the execution because C's order can fill it.

If Broker X enters the crowd with a buy order of 2,000 shares, then A sells 1,000 shares and B the other 1,000 shares. A has priority, and B has a time advantage over C and D (even though B, C, and D can all fill the order).

Were Broker X to enter the crowd with an order for 4,000 shares, A executes because of priority, C executes because of precedence, and B executes before D because of time advantage.

III-C-2-f-iii Parity

When two brokers can both fill the order and both enter their intentions at the same time, there isn't any logical way of awarding the trade. This is *parity*. In this case, either the brokers agree to an equitable distribution, or they flip a coin and the winner takes the trade.

Example: The quote is 22.20–.50, and the bids are:

Broker M: 1,000 shares, 10:14 A.M.

Broker N: 1,000 shares, 10:15 A.M.

Broker O: 1,000 shares, 10:15 A.M.

If Broker Z enters the crowd with a sell market order for 1,000 shares, Broker M executes. If Broker Z enters the crowd with a sell market order for 2,000 shares, M executes 1,000 shares. Since Brokers N and O can fill or best fill the order and neither has a time advantage, they have parity. So Brokers N and O agree to either one of these two taking the 1,000 shares, each taking 500 shares, or tossing a coin (which is rare), with the winner of the toss executing 1,000 shares.

When an execution takes place, *the floor is cleared*, and all remaining bids or offers at that price must be resubmitted. This procedure keeps quotes updated while reaffirming all orders.

III-C-2-g *The Specialist's Book*

Specialists enter public orders, which are away from the market, in their electronic books by price and in the order they are received.

Specialist Display Book (Mock)

Buy	Price	Sell
	22.00	
	22.01	
	22.02	
	22.03	
	↓	
	22.05	
	↓	
	22.10	
	22.20	
800 RR	22.23	
500 ONP	22.24	
200 GRC	22.25	
300 OU		
	22.30	
	22.35	300 SFR
		600 CSD
	22.36	1,000 HP
	22.37	200 DSH

(continued)

Buy	Price	Sell
	↓	
	22.40	
	22.45	
	22.50	
	22.55	
	22.60	

Example: If this specialist's book represents the highest bid and lowest offer of the crowd, the quote is 22.25–35. The highest bid is $22.25; the lowest offer, $22.35. If these orders are the only shares comprising the quote, the size is 5 by 9. The highest-priced order for a buy at $22.25 is for a total of 500 shares (200 by broker/dealer GRC and 300 by broker/dealer OU). The lowest-priced order for sale at $22.35 is 900 shares (300 by broker/dealer SFR and 600 by broker/dealer CSD).

Specialists execute orders from their books by price on a first-in/first-out (FIFO) basis. The first order in at a particular price is the first order out.

Example: If the broker from Knight & Knoon (KK) enters the crowd with a 200-share buy order at the market, the specialist executes 200 of SF&R's 300-share order at $22.35 per share.

The NYSE specialist's book is maintained on a CRT and referred to as the display book. This electronic book sorts all orders coming to the specialist in time and price sequence; it also keeps track of executed orders, so that inquiries from member firms may be quickly researched.

The display book is part of a larger system, known as *designated order turnaround (DOT* or *Super DOT)*. DOT orders are executed by the specialist either against other DOT orders (orders entered by member firms into the DOT system), or against brokers in the "crowd," or against the specialist's own position.

III-C-3 The American Stock Exchange (AMEX)

Recently, the American Stock Exchange (AMEX) has been acquired by NASDAQ. This shows how the marketplace has changed as the AMEX was predominantly an auction market and NASDAQ was primarily a principal market. The thought, only a few years ago, of NASDAQ acquiring the AMEX would have been laughed at. However, with the growth of institutions and the explosion of financial information over the Web and other sources, the need for market makers (dealers) in certain equity products became suspect as there was enough interest (volume) to permit clients operating through broker/dealers to trade between themselves as they do in an auction market. The Securities and Exchange Commission passed rules that forbade market makers from "standing in front of" customer orders on NASDAQ securities at a set price. This means that if a client (the public) put an order in to buy stock at $13.50 and that was the same price as a market maker bid, the customer's order would be executed first. These rules drastically changed the operations of the over-the-counter, or NASDAQ, market. We will discuss the NASDAQ market in detail later in this chapter.

The AMEX, though heavily option oriented, still offers shares of common stocks to the public. It operates in an auction market consisting of specialists and brokers in a fashion very similar to that used by the New York Stock Exchange. The specialists are allocated the securities that they are to "specialize" in through the use of allocation committees and most of the regulations and procedures used by the AMEX are very similar to those used by the New York Stock Exchange. The major difference, however, is how orders are executed. While the New York Stock Exchange uses the system called priority, precedence, and parity, the AMEX uses a system called priority and pro-rata. In this situation, one bid or one offer can have priority, the same as on the NYSE. After that has been satisfied, or should there be no way of distinguishing who the bidders are and which offers are at given prices, then the trade taking place is allocated among those buyers or those sellers in the market at that time.

Example: The following bids appear on the floor of the AMEX to buy ZAP at $46.00 a share:

Broker A bids 100 shares at 10:52 A.M.

Broker B bids 500 shares at 10:52 A.M.

Broker C bids 1,000 shares at 10:52 A.M.

As all these bids were made simultaneously, it is impossible to take them apart to determine who was truly first. Let's say Broker X enters the crowd to sell 800 shares of stock at $46. The 800 shares will be allocated over Brokers A, B, and C based on the size of their orders. Since Broker C was bidding for 1,000 shares, Broker C would get a lion's share of the selling order. In all likelihood Broker C would get 500 shares, Broker B, who was the next largest bidder, 200 shares, and Broker A, who was the smallest bidder of all, would get 100 shares. Remember that the trading lot is 100 shares; therefore, we cannot break up the round lot into smaller quantities to be fairer in this allocation process. Other than this, major similarities exist between the New York Stock Exchange and AMEX.

The primary market offered by the AMEX is an option market. It is one of the three primary domestically traded option markets. The other two option exchanges are the Chicago Board Option Exchange (CBOE) and the International Securities Exchange. (Both will be discussed soon in this chapter.) The AMEX option market operates under a specialist concept also, except in the AMEX option market, specialists, brokers, and market makers operate on the floor. The specialists on the AMEX option market are responsible, as they are on the equity markets of the NYSE and AMEX, for maintaining a fair and orderly market and trading when necessary for their own account and risk. Most of the trading that occurs on the floor is either between brokers, between market makers, or between brokers and market makers. The market makers on the floor of the AMEX are known as *downstairs traders*, whereas traders that trade off trading desks located at the broker/dealers are known as *upstairs traders*. The market makers from the floor of the AMEX are allocated the securities that they are to make markets in. They are free to trade other options; however, they must maintain the majority of their trading from those options that are assigned to them to add liquidity and to be at the option's location should their presence be required. This mandating of which options market makers can trade is necessary to ensure that all of the options that trade on the floor of the American Stock Exchange have depth of market, known as liquidity, at all times.

Besides equity options, the American Stock Exchange also has the XMI, one of the paramount index options trading in the United States. The XMI is a 20-stock index that resembles in its trading patterns the Dow Jones Industrial average itself. In addition, one of the newer products issued by the AMEX are ETFs of which one of the first is *spiders*, whose symbol is SPY. The product is a trust comprising securities that will replicate the Standard and Poor's (S&P) 500 Index. With this product, traders can hedge against the S&P options and the S&P futures. Other similar products offered by the

AMEX are known as *diamonds*. Whereas Spiders are based on the various S&P indexes, diamonds are based on the Dow Jones averages. Both of these products are trusts with expiration dates. However, within the trusts are the securities that would make the instruments replicate the actual indexes themselves. Other ETFs are also offered post trading.

III-C-4 Chicago Board Option Exchange

Conventional (OTC) options were custom-tailored to fit the needs of clients, and their prices were negotiated with a *put and call dealer*. OTC options offered little liquidity to investors because there was no central point to trade and each option was unique.

Listed option trading began in April 1973, when the Chicago Board Option Exchange (CBOE) was born. The CBOE standardized option contracts with fixed terms, thus allowing the public to buy and sell the exact same instrument.

Example: A listed option notation is POW Jan 50. All the options issued in POW and expiring in January expire the same day. Anyone who is interested in POW at around $50 per share would trade this option. Conventional options on POW might read, "POW Jan 12-48.50," "POW Jan 15-49.25," and "POW Jan 16-50.50," with differing expiration dates and strike prices.

III-C-4-a *Opening Rotation*

CBOE options are open for business at the same time as the markets of the underlying stock. But before a class of options starts trading for the day, the underlying security must open for trading.

Options open for trading by a method known as *rotation*, by which each series is called out in order. Trading in any series cannot begin until it is called. Once all the issues are called, trading can be conducted in all issues at once.

III-C-4-b *The Floor*

There are two types of members on the CBOE: floor brokers and market makers. In addition, an exchange employee known as an *order book official (OBO)* executes customers' limit orders maintained on the limit order book. Some market makers assume additional responsibilities when trading their designated options. They are known as *designated primary market makers (DPMs).*

III-C-4-c *Executing Orders*

All orders entering the floor must be marked as representing a client, firm, or market maker. Order book officials are permitted to execute only client (public) orders. Floor brokers can execute customer or firm orders, and, of course, market makers execute their own orders.

Because the CBOE operates for the public, the order book official's quote has priority at a given price over that of a floor broker or market maker. This rule ensures that the market is attending to the public's interest.

The CBOE assigns option classes to order book officials. OBOs receive customer orders for their assigned classes of options from member firms. The orders are usually limit orders that are *booked* by price and the time of receipt. As the market prices of the options fluctuate, the OBOs execute the orders from their books.

Every order going to the floor of the CBOE and any other option exchange must contain at least seven pieces of information:

1. Time and date entered
2. Buy or sell
3. Open or close
4. Quantity
5. Type, class, and series of option
6. Customer, firm, market maker, and specialist
7. Firm name or designation

Example:

May 11 20XX 10:42

Buy 5	Call	ZOW	Oct 50
(B/S) (quantity)	(type)	(class)	(series)

Open (Open/Close)

Customer
Stone, Forrest & River (firm)

III-C-4-c-i *Time and Date Entered*

These are particularly important because, on most orders, the firm or other participants are held accountable for executions or lack of them.

III-C-4-c-ii *Buy or Sell*

This is self-explanatory.

III-C-4-c-iii *Open or Close*

This entry informs what effect this trade will have on the account's position (that is, on the account entering the order). *Open* either establishes a new position or increases an existing position. *Close* either eliminates or decreases an existing position. For trading purposes, this entry is important because an open order cannot be entered under certain conditions. In operations, the information becomes important in balancing and reconcilement.

III-C-4-c-iv *Quantity, Type, Class, and Series of Option*

"Buy 5 call ZOW Oct 50" gives the instructions to the executing broker. The quantity is 5 contracts, the type is put or call, the class is the underlying security (in this case ZOW common stock), and the series is comprised of the strike price and expiration month. The absence of a premium price tells the executing broker that this is a market order.

III-C-4-c-v *Customer, Firm, Market Maker/Specialist*

The firm must indicate who the principal behind the order is. Whether the order is being entered for a customer, the firm itself, or any market maker/specialist that the firm may be clearing trades for. This designation follows the order through the firm's records as well as the Option Clearing Corporation. The segregation is required to maintain control of positions and not allow for the commingling of the positions. SF&R's internal records must agree with the records maintained by the clearing corporation not only in quantity, option description, and price, but also who the principals behind the positions are.

The number of categories required depends on the type of business the clearing firm conducts. A clearing firm that only executes trades for its customers and its proprietary accounts will only need to use those two categories on its orders, whereas a firm that clears trades for many market maker firms will maintain accounts for each firm.

It is important to note that it is the category and not the identity of the principal that is carried forward.

III-C-4-c-vi *Firm Name or Designation*

Every order entered on the exchange carries the name of the firm or its designation for identification purposes. While the order remains with SF&R's employees, there isn't a problem, but many times orders are given to others to execute and the identification becomes important then.

Market makers are assigned the options that they trade by the CBOE. It is their responsibility to buy and sell for their account and risk, to maintain liquidity in the marketplace.

Floor brokers execute both customer and firm orders, and the order must be so designated. Some member firms, however, use the services of other member firms to have their orders executed on the floor. In this case, although the submitting firm is a "customer" of the executing firm, the floor brokers of the executing firm treat the orders of the other firm as if they were their own. Nevertheless, these orders must identify the principal—that is, who is the principal that entered the order. If entered to the executing firm by the submitting firm for its own trading account, the order must carry the designation "firm." If entered to the executing firm by the submitting firm's customer, the order is marked "customer."

The order must designate whether it is for a customer, firm, or market maker/specialist, but the account number, name, or other actual identifier is optional.

The CBOE has developed a hybrid trading system that combines electronic trading with floor-derived competing *open outcry*. It is called CBOEdirectHYTS. Through this system, electronic orders are routed to the OBO's trading location. It then compares the terms of the orders to the current bid and offer as well as the current size. If the order can be executed, it is executed immediately and reported back to the customer.

Besides equity options and interest rate options, the CBOE trades index options such as the S&P 500 Index (symbol SPX) and the S&P 100 Index (symbol OEX). The exchange offers trading in exchange-traded funds also. Stock futures are traded through the CFE (CBOE Futures Exchange subsidiary).

III-C-5 The International Security Exchange

One of the newest option exchanges is the International Security Exchange (ISE), which is singled out here because of its uniqueness. The ISE doesn't have a trading floor. It is an electronic exchange. There are *primary market makers* that are responsible for maintaining markets in their assigned options and for the execution of limit orders when the option price reaches the limit order specifications. They are augmented by *competing market makers*, who add liquidity to the market but do not have the responsibilities of the primary market makers. Brokers, representing their firms' proprietary and customer orders, trade with these market makers. The ISE's computer programs keep track of orders, quotes, and executions. Executable broker-entered orders are filled by the exchange's system against the then existing quote and the broker/dealer who entered that particular bid or offer, be it a broker or market maker. No executable limit orders are stored electronically until they are canceled, expire, or are executed.

The BOX is another newly introduced electronic option exchange. It is a subsidiary of the Boston Stock Exchange on which equities are traded.

III-C-6 The Future Exchanges

The Chicago Board of Trade, the Chicago Mercantile Exchange, the New York Board of Trade, and the New York Mercantile Exchange are all future exchanges. They trade futures on agricultural, mining, fuel, interest rates, and currency products. Their method of trading is open outcry with brokers, traders, and scalpers trading in an area known as the *pit*.

Generally, the brokers who have to communicate with their phone people stand on the top steps of the pit. Their phone or *booth* personnel are standing near the pit so that the broker and phone personnel can communicate with each other either verbally or by hand signals. At the other end of the phone clerk's line is the firm's order personnel or the customers themselves.

Further into the pits stand the various types of traders that trade for their own accounts or for the accounts of their respective firms. Among these are hedgers, spreaders, and scalpers. Hedgers offset physical positions with futures. Spreaders trade on the price differences between future delivery months. Scalpers trade in and out of their positions, adding the all-important liquidity to the markets.

III-D *THE OVER-THE-COUNTER (OTC) MARKET*

In the previous chapter, we looked at securities that are listed for trading on the various exchanges. These included stocks, options, futures, and other derivative markets. However, by far the largest of all markets is the over-the-counter market. In this market, one will find the trading of stocks, debt instruments, customized options, forwards, and other unique types of products.

III-D-1 NASDAQ

The marketplace that is most popular to the public is the NASDAQ market. In this market, one finds a combination of securities from some of the leading corporations of the world, mainly in the high-tech area, all the way to the startup companies that have just offered their shares to the public and begun to trade. The NASDAQ market has two components: the National Market System and the Small Cap market. Like most of the over-the-counter markets, NASDAQ is known as a dealer or principal market. In this market, unlike the security exchanges, firms commit capital to buy and sell securities against the public. It is said that they make markets in the securities that they want to trade. In this marketplace we find the term dealers. All dealers are market makers; all market makers are traders. However, all traders are not market makers as we will explain later. Stone, Forrest & Rivers is one of these market makers in the NASDAQ market. It also participates in other markets, including the corporate bond market and the municipal and government markets. We will look into these markets as we go along.

In those securities in which Stone, Forrest & Rivers is not a market maker, it employs traders whose job is to seek the best prices possible in those securities for the clients of SF&R. Therefore, SF&R has two types of traders: the ones who make markets, who have the firm's capital and credit lines committed to the trading effort, and those traders who respond to customers' orders to buy or sell securities in which SF&R is not a market maker. In either case, SF&R's clients are assured of the best possible price at the given time.

In the NASDAQ market, Stone, Forrest & Rivers' management committee determines the type of securities that SF&R is going to make markets in.

They allocate the amount to be used for trading purposes based on the performance provided by the various trading desks and the needs of the products. These markets are highly competitive. Therefore, the ability to earn revenue from trading is dependent on the traders' skill and understanding of the markets and the events affecting those markets. This includes not only the traders in the equity, but traders who also trade the debt desk. One of Stone, Forrest & Rivers' traders is William Bord. Bill makes markets in five different equity securities. These securities have been approved for trading by the management committee of the firm, and Bill allocates the capital that he is allowed to trade among the five securities. While Hollywood dramatizes this function, it is really no different than any other inventory maintained by any other type of vendor. Bill will trade the securities based on their daily activity and price movement. He will also determine which securities he wants to maintain in position and which securities he may even want to short in the marketplace. Bill has his perception of the securities' values and their current status; therefore, as he trades in and out of positions, he's keeping an eye on the actual trading spreads and the movement of the securities.

Let's elaborate on the previous paragraph. Bill is making a market in five different stocks. One of those stocks is Ultra Corporation (symbol ULTR). Bill likes the stock because it is actively traded and likes the company because he sees the potential for growth. Therefore, Bill will maintain a position, committing some of the firm's capital as well as their credit lines that it allows him to trade, investing in the security. He will trade all day long, but maintain that particular security level in position. In other words, let's assume that Bill wants to keep 50,000 shares of Ultra Corp. in inventory. At first he aggressively prices his quotes so that he can acquire the securities; he bids higher than the other market makers who are also making markets in Ultra. Once he has reached the 50,000-share level, then he will buy and sell securities against that position but at all times maintain approximately 50,000 shares. If he is correct in his assessment, then as the price of Ultra Corp. rises, he will make money based on the pricing of the position. As he buys new shares and sells from the inventory position, his average pricing for carrying the position is rising. Therefore, as long as the security continues to increase in value, he will earn a profit by having the standard average price be below the market price. Bill also will profit from the spread, which is the difference between his bid and his offer. (The bid is where Bill wants to buy stock; the offer is where he wants to sell.) When Bill makes his quote, he makes a bid and an offer.

In the case of Ultra Corp., let's assume that Bill is willing to bid $26.40 for 5,000 shares and is offering 5,000 shares at $26.80. If he has the highest bid and lowest offer, he will be making .40 per share on every share he trades at those prices. He would buy from the customers or other broker/dealers at $26.40 and sell it to other customers or broker/dealers at $26.80.

However, there are three other market makers in Ultra Corp. besides Stone, Forrest & Rivers. Their traders are also maintaining positions. Whether they maintain positions in all the securities that Bill is maintaining is doubtful. However, in the case of Ultra Corp., all four market makers are competing to get order flow necessary to generate revenue from trading.

Giant, Reckor & Crane	26.20–26.60
Hart, Paine & Co.	26.25–26.65
McKenna & Co.	26.30–26.70
Stone, Forrest & Rivers	26.40–26.80

For simplicity's sake, we will assume that all four market makers are willing to trade 5,000 shares at their prices. With the current quote as presented, any broker/dealer representing a customer, or its own proprietary trading, that wants to sell Ultra Corp. would first contact Stone, Forrest & Rivers, because it has the highest bid. Any broker/dealer representing a customer, or its own investments, that wants to buy the stock would contact Giant Reckor & Crane because it has the lowest offer. Remember, these quotes are only good for 5,000 shares. Anyone wanting to buy or sell more than 5,000 shares would have to contact the various market makers and negotiate the best price possible for the lot they want to do business with. This negotiation between the broker/dealer that has the order and the individual market makers in that security to determine the best price available to trade at gives the over-the-counter market the label *negotiated market.*

This is a subtle difference between the exchange markets and the over-the-counter markets. In the exchange markets, the highest bid or lowest offer must be satisfied before execution can take place at a price below the current bid or below the current offer. What this means is, assume on the New York Stock Exchange there is a bid for 1,000 shares at a price of $50 per share. Let's assume someone wanted to sell 5,000 shares, and those 5,000 shares could be filled at a price of $49.80 per share. In the exchange market, either the 1,000 shares would be sold at $50 and the remainder at $49.80, or the entire lot, including those for the buyer at $50, would "go off" (trade) at

$49.80, thereby saving the buyer $.20 per share. This is not true in the over-the-counter market, as these are dealers' quotes. Using the previous scenario with each dealer making a market of 1,000 shares, someone willing to sell 5,000 shares would contact the various market makers and negotiate the best price possible for the entire lot. It is, therefore, very possible that the trade could be accomplished at a price below the current bid or above the current offer without satisfying the existing bid or offer.

III-D-1-a *NASDAQ Systems*

NASDAQ offers four electronic order routing systems to be used by broker/dealers: SOES, ACES, and CAES.

III-D-1-a-i SOES

In the *small order execution system (SOES)*, the maximum size of an order in the National Market System is 1,000 shares, and in the Small Cap Market issues is normally 500 shares. SOES is used to expedite small round-lot transactions. The market makers in the various stocks set parameters on SOES by which they will be responsible for trades occurring without their knowledge. This sounds risky, but stop and think of the cost involved with a market maker looking at every small order that arrives on the desk and then executing each order manually. SOES works electronically and automatically. The system selects the market makers to each trade by a rotation among the participating market makers. An order arriving in the system is matched against the current quote and, if executable, is executed against one of these market makers.

Stone, Forrest & Rivers participates in the SOES system. It has sent a parameter of 10,000 shares long, or owned, or 10,000 shares short, or not owned. The day starts off neutral and during the course of the day when the system selects SF&R to execute a trade, it does it against the SOES system. The SOES system executes the order coming in and rebalances SF&R's system. The SF&R traders in Ultra Corp. will not be apprised of anything going on in SOES until the 10,000-share limit that they have set is surpassed. This frees them up to focus on larger orders that require their attention to give the best possible service.

Since market orders coming into SOES and executable limit orders are executed immediately, it is imperative that the traders keep their quotes current. Let's assume a trader is actively trading one of the securities that she's making a market in and is not paying attention to another security, which suddenly starts to move. The quotes of the unwatched security will become "stale" and if they're not changed, orders coming into SOES will be executed against their then current quote. For example, let's assume SF&R is bidding $26.40 and offering stock at $26.80, and while the trader is watching a different stock, Ultra Corp. falls in value to where the highest bid is of the other market makers and is now $26.10. As SF&R's trader never changed her bid from $26.40, even though it is overpriced at that bid, sellers will come into the SOES system and sell stock until the quote is corrected or until Stone, Forrest & Rivers' erroneous bid has used up the available securities and the trader is notified that the parameter has been exceeded. At this point, the trader will correct the quote, but it will be too late. The common term for people who watch for this to happen is *SOES bandits.*

III-D-1-a-ii ACES

Some firms are not market-making firms and do not want to go through the expense of maintaining an over-the-counter trading desk. Even firms that are not market makers may have traders who enter the markets representing their customers and negotiate transactions on their clients' behalf. Firms that do not want to go through that expense will contract with a larger market-making firm to represent them in the marketplace. This process is called the *Advanced Computerized Execution System (ACES).* Via this route, the broker/dealer who is using ACES looks to the market-making firm as if it were one of its own branch offices. Whatever rules the market-making firm has in place, as to the types of orders it will accept, apply to this nonmarket-making firm. Orders in the over-the-counter market are routed from the smaller firm to the market-making firm as if it were a branch office of the market-making firm and the market-making firm's traders will execute the orders as if they're from one of their own branches.

III-D-1-a-iii CAES

The final system we will look at is called *Computer Assisted Execution Systems (CAES).* CAES augments the exchange's intermarket trading system (ITS). Securities that trade in the over-the-counter market, as well as being listed on one or more of the exchanges, create a unique problem to public customers. They are entitled to receive the best price regardless of what market they enter; that is the function of the ITS. CAES augments that by bringing into the system over-the-counter securities that are duly traded. A market maker receiving an order for a mutiply traded security will check the listed market to see which market has the best price. The order will be routed to that marketplace or the trader may execute the order at the same best price against their inventory position. That is the price the customer is entitled to and that is the price the customer will get.

III-D-2 Other Over-the-Counter Equity Markets

Other over-the-counter equity markets exist either for stocks not eligible for listing on NASDAQ or traded in large quantities among institutions and market makers. The former are traded on the Over-the-Counter Bulletin Board market (OTCBB), the latter on the Electronic Commerce Networks (ECN) or Alternate Trading Systems (ATS). ECNs and ATSs are discussed later in this chapter.

In an attempt to bring the quotes and other data from the fragmented marketplace to one location, the NASDAQ developed super montage screens for use by its broker/dealers. The quotes, size, and other information on securities traded in several different markets are displayed on one screen.

III-D-2-a *Bulletin Board Securities*

There are many securities that cannot qualify for listing on exchanges or on NASDAQ. They are usually small companies, perhaps new and/or undercapitalized companies. Their securities trade in a special marketplace called *bulletin board*. Most of these securities trade for pennies and very few have any substantial pricing. Market makers of bulletin board securities announce their intentions to buy or sell securities and put up quotes. This market is not governed by the same rules as NASDAQ is so it is quite possible that a bid or an offer will not be accepted. Stop and think of the mathematics involved with this. A stock that has a quote .06–.09 has a spread of 50% of the value of the bid. People will come in and buy large quantities of these securities—thousands and thousands of shares. At a nickel a share, you could buy 10,000 shares for $500. If the stock should rise from .05 a share to .10 a share, the individual has doubled her money. Of course, the reverse is true also: a stock is selling at .05 because that is what the company is worth and there is a good chance that by tomorrow the company will be gone. However, the bulletin board is a very important segment of the market as it's an avenue for small startup companies to raise capital in the open market.

III-D-2-b *Electronic Commerce Network (ECN) and Alternate Trading System (ATS)*

Block trades (orders to buy or sell large numbers of shares) often cannot be entered into one marketplace, as the marketplace for execution cannot handle orders of that size. Therefore, firms representing clients who trade securities in this size will turn to specialized firms that create what is called the *third market*. Firms in this market (called third-market firms) will take the order and execute it among their clients and other firms that may have an interest, using their own inventory as well as the stock exchanges (if the security is listed). These third-market firms will break the order into tradable pieces and then execute the order for the customer.

These firms have a good "feeling" for the market and what it will absorb when and where. They also have contacts with many of the largest institutions and firms that represent them. Therefore, when they are presented with a large block order, they have a general understanding of what a fair price for that security is and where they can unload or acquire it. If the order they are receiving is to buy stocks, they will contact institutions, broker/dealers representing institutions, and their various marketplaces to get a depth-of-market feeling for what quantity can be executed and what will be a fair price to charge. When they receive a large sell order, they contact these firms and the marketplaces and try to determine a fair price to the customers. Quite often they will take securities into position and work the position off over time. This is a function of adding liquidity in the marketplace.

In taking the position into their inventory, they may hedge *poison* with equity or index options or index futures. These products will be used to offset market risk. For example, they may buy *out-of-the-money* put options to offset a long position. An out-of-the-money option is one whose exercise price is away from the market so that the option will not be exercised. In the case of a put option, the exercise price is below the market price. The trader would purchase out-of-the-money put options in case the market price of the stock should fall while the trader is maintaining a position in that stock. If the stock should fall in value, the puts would go *into the money* and could be exercised by the trader. In other words, the put option, which gives its owner the privilege of selling, has a provided a *floor* for the trader should the stock fall in price. It minimizes the potential market risk in carrying the position.

III-D-3 The Debt Market

By far the largest of all markets is the debt market. This market is comprised of the debt securities of corporate, municipal, government, and agency bodies. They range from very short term, known as money market instruments, to long term, known as bonds. The instruments themselves are different and, therefore, trade differently. A corporate bond trader is not looking for the same attributes that a municipal bond trader is looking for, and so on.

III-D-3-a *The Corporate Bond Market*

Corporate debt instruments (bonds and notes) are brought to market through a negotiated underwriting between the investment banker and the issuing corporation. The bonds themselves are issued in what is known as *bullet form*. That means that the entire issue will have a single maturity date. All of the bonds in the issue are identical. Therefore, the corporate bond trader is looking for attributes to the instrument that differentiate it from other instruments. As with all debt instruments, as interest rates rise, the new bonds being offered for the first time will reflect the higher interest rate. Therefore, bonds that are currently outstanding will lose market value because their interest rates are not competitive. The reverse is true when interest rates fall. The newly issued debt will carry the appropriate lower rate, causing the price of the bonds already outstanding to rise.

Corporate debt is rated by agencies such as Standard & Poor and Moody's. However, within these ratings are differences. When most of us went to school, there was a grading system for the pupils: A, B, C, D, F. However, there were A students who scored in the top percentile of the class and there were A students who just barely qualified for the A grade. Likewise, there were B students who qualified in the top percentile of the B group and there were those who were in the opposite end of the B range, and so on. The difference between the lower end of the A group and the highest end of the B group may have been a point or two in the students' averages. A similar situation exists with corporate bond ratings. Not all triple-A (AAA) corporate bonds are equal. Some are truly triple-A, while others just make the grade. Some corporate bonds are really very strong double-A bonds, but because of some weighting criterion used in the analysis have qualified for the basic triple-A rating. Should the single element deteriorate, the bonds will be reclassified as double-A. As rating companies do their ongoing analyses of the issuers of the bonds, criteria used in developing the ratings will change over time, causing the ratings to change. And with that change, so does the price of the bond shift.

To the issuer, the lower the rating, the more expensive it is to borrow money, i.e., the higher will be the rate of interest carried by the bond. After all, the lower the bond's rating, the greater the risk of default to the investor. The higher the bond's rating, the easier it is for the issuer to borrow money as more people will be willing to invest in the bond because of the lower possibility of default. Therefore, the lower will be the interest rate the bond will carry. (Municipal debt, covered later in this chapter, is also rated.)

Preferred stocks also trade on the corporate debt trading desk. This is because their dividend rate is set at issuance, in the same manner that the interest rate on a bond is set at the point of issuance. As their dividend rate is fixed, they are an *interest-rate-sensitive* instrument. They trade in a similar fashion to long-term bonds. A large corporate-bond-trading operation will divide its trading desks into long-term debt, medium-term debt, and short-term debt. Preferred stocks trade alongside the long-term debt instruments.

The corporate debt dealer selects those instruments of issuers that they want to make markets in. As stated above, there are slight differences between the individual bonds. The coupon rate carried on the bond, its maturity date, when it pays its interest, and other special features of the bond will differentiate it from other bonds that look identical. However, those differences affect the price of the bonds.

The time remaining in the life of a bond could affect its price. Generally speaking, people look for bonds that fall into certain categories. For example, they want a bond that will be outstanding for a specific period of time ("out for 5 years," "out for 10 years," etc.). Therefore, a bond that has 7 years and 3 months remaining of life may not be as easy to trade as a bond that has a 10-year life span. A client looking for a bond that has 10 years of life remaining will accept a bond with slightly more or less than 10 years, but the further the maturity date of a bond moves from a new debt instrument maturity date, the harder it is to sell. All other things being equal, any debt instrument that has 10 years remaining before maturity has the same properties as a newly issued 10-year instrument and so will trade alongside a newly issued 10-year bond.

In addition, the general market conditions, the general economic conditions, and, of course, what the Fed may or may not be doing to interest rates affect the trader's decisions as to pricing of these instruments.

The price of any bond is a calculation of the present value of all of the bonds' cash flows. This sounds complicated, but it's really not.

Example: Let's assume Peter Cole is going to get a $10,000 guaranteed bonus six months from now but can use the money immediately. You decide that you will buy Pete's bonus from him today. Would you give Pete $10,000 today? If your answer is yes, then you are willing to forfeit any benefits that you could derive from *you* having the use of the money for the next six months and Pete has received the equivalent of his bonus six months early with no penalty. A fairer approach is to pay less—say, $9,750 to Pete—and six months from now Peter will pay you $10,000. Your compensation for not having the use of the $10,000 for the six months is $250 (which equates to 5% of $10,000 for half a year). It could be said that the present value of $10,000 payable in six months is $9,750.

To compute present value for an instrument that was issued for one year or less, simple interest calculation is used. For the above example it would be:

Principal × Rate × Time	= Interest Amount
$10,000/1 × 5/100 × 180/360	= $250

For debt instruments issued for longer than one year, we use the formula for the present value of cash flow:

$$\text{Present value} = \text{Payout}\left[\frac{1}{1+\text{Rate}}\right] \text{ to the number of times payment is made or}$$

$$\text{PV} = \text{PO}\left[\frac{1}{1+\text{Rate}}\right]^{t}$$

Let's calculate the fourth sixth-month interest payment (end of second year) of a $10,000 20-year bond carrying a 5% coupon and priced to yield 5%. The interest payment will be $250.00.

$$\text{PV} = \$250\left[\frac{1}{1+.025}\right]^{4} =$$

$$\$250\left[\frac{1}{1+.025}\right]^{4} =$$

$$\$250\left[\frac{1}{1+.025}\right]\left[\frac{1}{1+.025}\right]\left[\frac{1}{1+.025}\right]\left[\frac{1}{1+.025}\right] =$$

$$\$250[.975609756]\,[.975609756]\,[.975609756]\,[.975609756] =$$

$250[.905950644] =
$226.49

Thus, we find that the present value of a 5% semiannual (2.5%) interest payment to be paid at the end of the second year using a discounting interest rate of 5% is $226.49.

A 20-year bond pays interest every six months with principal and interest being paid at maturity. Therefore, there are 40 cash flows. After discounting each cash flow based on the current applicable interest rate, the resulting answers are totaled. This total is the value of the bond. Multiply the value by 10% (.10) per $1,000 to get the bond's price. For example, a bond with a face amount of $1,000 is calculated to have a present value of $987.50. The price would be ($987.50 × .10) or $98.75.

But note that "convertible" corporate debt and preferred stocks are not traded on the bond desk. The conversion feature permits its owner to convert the issue to common stock (usually) under fixed terms and preset ratios. Due to this conversion feature, the values of these instruments are affected by the underlying common stock prices and lose their association with interest rates. They do not react to changes in the debt market as do nonconvertible issues and as such are not interest rate sensitive. Therefore, they are not traded along with corporate bonds, notes, and preferred stocks. The conversion feature negates their ability to track interest rates.

Corporate bond market makers post their interests to buy or sell specific bonds on bond trading screens. One of the primary screens is the New York Stock Exchange's Automated Bond System (ABS). Subscribers buy and sell bonds for their own accounts as well as their clients'. Some major corporate bond-trading firms have formed a consortium called Bond.Hub on which they post their positions and trade against. There are other trading screens from which brokers, representing their clients, buy and sell debt instruments.

Over-the-counter corporate bond trades must be reported to NASD's Trade Reporting and Compliance Engine (TRACE). The purpose of TRACE is price dissemination and to be a gateway to comparison.

III-D-3-b *The Municipal Bond Market*

The municipal bond market is different than a corporate bond market in many respects. First of all, municipal bonds are issued under a *competitive underwriting* procedure. Under this procedure, investment bankers compete for the issue, whereas with corporate bonds, the investment banker that represents the corporation is usually the one that brings the bonds to the public. Another major difference with municipal bonds is that they are issued in *serial* form. This means that while the issue itself may be substantial in size, it is comprised of many different bonds maturing sequentially. Each of these bonds will have its own unique CUSIP number and, therefore, they trade as separate instruments. The trading demographics of municipal bonds are also different than corporate bonds'. Because of the typical size of a corporate bond issue, there is an ability to sustain trading in particular issues. In other words, a market maker can select certain corporate bonds in which they make a market. They buy and sell these particular issues on an ongoing basis. In the case of the municipal bonds, because the sizes of the individual issues are usually small, the municipal bond traders generally select a state of issuance and/or a type of bond within the state, such as different general obligation bonds from certain cities in the states in which they specialize. They buy and sell these general categorized issues rather than specific issues. In other words, in the municipal bond environment, bonds come to market, they are placed, they leave the market, and over time pieces return to the market to be resold. Generally speaking, a bond that is available on Monday may not be available Tuesday because the supply of the bond is so "thin."

Due to this unique difference, municipal bonds generally trade at basis prices instead of at dollar prices like corporate bonds do. *Basis price* is short for the term *yield-to-maturity basis*. People familiar with this side of the market understand the relationship between the basis price and the coupon rate that the bond carries. The closer those two are to each other, the closer the bond is to trading at par. Yield to maturity takes into account not only the interest payments, but also the difference between the purchase price and the value at maturity. Here's a simple method of computing this:

1. Subtract the lower of market price or value at maturity from the larger value.
2. Amortize or deplete the answer from step 1 over the life of a bond.
3. If the bond is at a discount, add the annual figure arrived at in step 2 to the annual interest payment. If the bond is trading at a premium, subtract the annual depletion amount from the annual interest payment.
4. As you are accounting for the difference between cost and value at maturity, add the two together and divide by two to arrive at an average value of the instrument over its life. This average value is for computation

purposes only and has nothing to do with the instrument's market value over the same period of time.

Use the following formula:

$$\text{Annual interest payment} \pm \text{Annualized adjustment/Average value} = \text{Yield to maturity}$$

Using this rule-of-thumb method, the yield to maturity of $1,000 NYS Thruway 6% FA maturing in 10 years costing $1,077. 95 is calculated as follows:

Step 1.

$$\begin{array}{rl} \$1{,}077.95 = & \text{Current market value} \\ -\$1{,}000.00 = & \text{Value at maturity} \\ \hline \$\quad 77.95 = & \text{Amount to be amortized over 10 years} \end{array}$$

Step 2.

$77.95 /10 = $7.79—amount to be depleted each year

Step 3.

$1,000 + $1,077.95 = $2,077.95 /2 = $1,038.97 average value

Step 4.

$$\frac{\$60.00-7.79}{\$1{,}038.97} = .0502 = 5.02\% \text{ yield to maturity}$$

The shortcut calculation will always produce a figure close to the actual yield to maturity, which can only be obtained by calculating the present value of cash flows.

Payment	Amount	Factor	Present Value
1	$30.00	0.97560975	$29.2682925
2	$30.00	0.95181439	28.5544317
3	$30.00	0.92859994	27.8579982

(*continued*)

Payment	Amount	Factor	Present Value
4	$30.00	0.90595055	27.1785165
5	$30.00	0.88385445	26.5156335
6	$30.00	0.86229717	25.8689151
7	$30.00	0.84126506	25.2379518
8	$30.00	0.8207465	24.622395
9	$30.00	0.80072898	24.0218694
10	$30.00	0.78119812	23.4359436
11	$30.00	0.76214458	22.8643374
12	$30.00	0.74355634	22.3066902
13	$30.00	0.72542039	21.7626117
14	$30.00	0.7077271	21.231813
15	$30.00	0.69046563	20.7139689
16	$30.00	0.67362521	20.2087563
17	$30.00	0.65719516	19.7158548
18	$30.00	0.6411662	19.234986
19	$30.00	0.6255857	18.767571
20	$1,030.00	0.6102711	628.579233
Total:			$1,077.94777

$1,077.95
−1,000.00
$77.95
7.79
$77.95

$$\frac{\$60-7.80}{\frac{(1{,}078+1{,}000)}{2}} \quad \frac{\$52.20}{1{,}039.00} = 5.02$$

As stated earlier, a bond's price is determined by the present value of all its cash flows. Let's see if the accurate way of calculating a bond's value gets a result that's close to the short method's.

If the bond owner purchases the bond and holds it to maturity, this is the return (yield) the purchaser can expect to receive on the investment. If the yield to maturity is greater than the coupon rate, the bond is selling at a discount (see above). On the other hand, if the yield to maturity is lower than the coupon rate, the bond is trading at a premium. Clients purchasing municipal (muni) bonds are attracted by the fact that the interest paid on most muni bonds is free from federal income tax and, if the purchaser resides in the state of issuance, interest is free of state and local taxes. This feature only appears in municipal securities. Interest paid on corporate bonds is fully taxable, interest paid on U.S. Treasury bonds is taxable by the federal government but not by state and local governments. Because municipal bonds' interest is free from federal tax, a municipality can issue debt instruments at a lower rate than that of comparable corporate bonds, which are fully taxable. After all, it is we, the people, who pay the taxes that go to pay the interest on municipal securities. So the less expensively the municipality can raise money, the better it is for all of us.

If we focus on the above, we start to realize that municipal bond dealers generally trade municipal bonds in those areas in which they maintain a presence. Stone, Forrest & Rivers maintains offices in many states. It will not, however, trade municipal bonds in states where it does not have a presence; that would serve no purpose. If you buy a bond of another state, you are liable to the taxation of that state. Therefore, Stone, Forrest & Rivers will make markets in bonds issued by, let's say, New York, Illinois, California, and Georgia. We will assume that those are some of the states where SF&R has offices and where their customers are, so these will be the debt instruments that those customers will be looking for. If SF&R also has offices in Florida, Maine, and Michigan, then they will be interested in trading bonds of those states too. However, let's assume that Stone, Forrest & Rivers does not have an office in Colorado. Let's also assume that Daniel D. Lyons moves from Colorado to Illinois because of a job promotion. Let's assume again that he owns Colorado municipal bonds and wants to sell them for Illinois municipal bonds, again, for tax reasons. If he lives in Illinois (in legalese, Illinois is his *abode*), then the interest paid on Illinois bonds (since he's a resident of Illinois) is free from federal, state, and local taxes. If he maintains the Colorado bonds, then the interest paid on those bonds will be taxed by the state of Illinois; city taxes too may be applicable. Therefore, Dan wants to exchange the Colorado bonds for Illinois bonds. The municipal bond trader of SF&R, Erik Torr, has a problem. While the trader would like to do the transaction, the trader would be stuck with Colorado bonds and no outlet to release them or to sell them through. SF&R's municipal bond trader, Eric, contacts a dealer's broker, a firm that specializes in representing different municipal bond firms throughout the country as their clients. Eric offers the Colorado bonds through the dealer's broker network. Another firm, Harte, Burns and Payne, Inc., which has offices in Colorado, sees the bonds appear on the dealer's broker network. It either has clients that are interested in acquiring them or wants to purchase them for the firm's inventory for sale at a later date, so Harte, Burns and Payne purchases them. Through the use of dealer's brokers, municipal bond markets are made even more liquid. Firms like dealer's brokers act as conduits between many firms and provide a very valuable service in the distribution of these securities. Eric will buy the Colorado bonds from Dan, sell them through the dealer's broker (not knowing or caring who the actual customer is on the other side), and sell Dan the Illinois municipal bonds from his inventory. Therefore, Dan, Eric, SF&R, the dealer's broker, Harte, Burns and Payne (which bought the Colorado bonds) and a customer of theirs all benefit from this transaction.

III-D-3-c *The Treasury Market*

The government bond trading desk is unique in its own right. In the first place, SF&R had to be approved by the Federal Reserve Board to be a registered *government dealer*. This "privilege" allows SF&R to bid for U.S. Treasury instruments directly from the Federal Reserve Board and resell them in the public market. These are known as *U.S. government dealers*. The Federal Reserve issues U.S. Treasury bonds, notes, and bills in accordance with their fiscal policy. These instruments are brought to market through a Dutch auction process where these government dealers and others bid for the particular issues. Bids are filled in descending order but all who are alloted bonds pay the same price. The government dealers then turn around and offer these products to the public. Other firms buy and sell these government securities for their clients, which include institutions and foreign governments. The Fed institutes its financial policies through these broker/dealers. When they want to place more money into circulation (for example, during holiday periods), they buy back government securities. When they want to take money out of circulation, they sell government securities through these dealers. The open market operation of the Fed deals very closely with these government dealers who, in turn, deal with the rest of the world. In addition to new issues, these government dealers maintain inventory positions of outstanding U.S. bonds, notes, and Treasury bills. The Treasury bills are generally traded separately as they are short-term money market instruments, with the longest maturity going out a year. Bills generally trade as a short-term instrument with other money market instruments. The Treasury bonds and Treasury notes trade on the trading desk based on the time left to maturity.

III-D-3-d *The Mortgage-Backed and Asset-Backed Securities Markets*

The mortgage-backed securities (MBS) market is comprised of dealers who purchase mortgage pools from mortgage bankers and sell them into the market. Mortgage bankers are not true bankers but are the loan-arranging arm of a builder or project manager. They are not in the business to take market risk but to facilitate the issuance of mortgages. Some of the mortgages they arrange will qualify for Veterans Administration (VA) Guarantees of Federal Housing Authority (FHA) Insurance and Rural Housing Authority (RHA). These government-backed mortgages can be sold as Government National Mortgage Association (GNMA) instruments. From the time the mortgages are placed and the homeowners move into their new homes, the mortgage banker is exposed to interest rate changes and, through that, to market risk. Therefore, the mortgage banker sells these approved but not yet enforced mortgages to the GNMA dealer. The trade is known as TBA (the name TBA stands for to be announced and refers to the unique number that will be assigned by GNMA when the security is issued).

The mortgage-backed security dealer trades these TBAs and actual (physical) instruments. However, as these instruments have unique characteristics, such as paying down the principal amount of the loan during the life of the instrument, the traders must know their inventory.

After trading a particular TBA for a couple of months, the actual instrument will be delivered against the TBA by the mortgage banker. The MBS dealer will pay the mortgage banker and then deliver the pool to whomever it had been sold.

However, it is not that simple. The mortgage-backed security dealer may be settling multiple TBAs and other trades at the same time. Because mortgages pay down their principal amount during their life, the chances of the MBS dealer receiving exactly a round lot ($1,000,000 in MBS securities) is remote. The Bond Market Association has set a tolerance level of ±.01% per million as good delivery. Therefore, per million dollars, the dealer may receive from $999,900 to $1,000,100 worth of principal and, if the coupon rate of mortgages is below 11%, there can be up to three pools as long as no lesser number of pools reach the $999,900 level. If the coupon is 11% or more, up to five pools can be delivered per $1,000,000. The dealer can then mix and match the pools in putting the deliveries to clients and/or other dealers together. This process is known as *allocation*.

Due to the successful launch of mortgage-backed securities, banks soon followed by pooling and securitizing various loans. Included in the products are car loans, credit card loans, and home equity loans. This group is known as asset-backed securities. As with mortgage-backed products, these products pay interest and principal periodically and trade in an over-the-counter dealer market. Unlike the MBS product, they are not guaranteed or insured by the federal government or a government-sponsored entity (GSE).

III-D-3-e *Money Market Instruments*

Billions of dollars in money market instruments are exchanged daily and the trades settle on trade date. In the case of commercial paper, the majority is bank placed. The bank, knowing how much money their clients have to invest and for what period of time, shop the money around to their corporate clients who issue commercial paper. Wherever they get the best terms is where they will invest the money. There are also commercial paper dealers who purchase (take down) commercial paper from the issuing corporation and sell it in the marketplace. Certificates of deposit and bankers' acceptances are traded among banks, dealers, and the public.

III-D-3-e-i *Certificates of Deposit Banker Acceptances*

These instruments trade in an over-the-counter environment and settle at Depository Trust Company (a division of DTCC). They operate in a paperless environment with DTC holding the paper in the name of the depositing firm. Due to same-day settlement, and the size of the trades, speed and accuracy are of paramount importance. The instruments are issued through DTC, the trading of them settles at DTC, and the maturity process is handled through DTC. The instruments include commercial paper, bankers' acceptances and certificates of deposits.

III-D-4 The Derivative Market

A *derivative product* is one whose market value is based on the market value of the underlying product. Included in this group are options, forwards, futures, and swaps. Other products that we trade are also derivatives but are not referred to in that manner. For example, the value of an open-end mutual fund's shares is based on the value of the portfolio of securities underlying it. The value of an index such as the S&P 500 is based on an arithmetic value of the securities comprising it.

III-D-4-a *Options*

Options are traded in two ways: over the counter and by listing on an exchange. As stated elsewhere in this book, the listed options are traded more frequently. Over-the-counter options are custom-tailored to the needs of the particular customer and are therefore illiquid. Listed options are structured by the exchange on which they trade so they follow a strict regime. They are therefore liquid, as clients can trade in and out of positions. In addition, listed options are cleared through Option Clearing Corporation (OCC), which guarantees performance of the contract by standing on the other side of all compared trades. Over-the-counter options remain the responsibility of the buyer and seller.

Option traders exist on the trading floor (known as *downstairs traders*) or in the trading rooms (known as *upstairs traders*) of their respective broker/dealers. Upstairs traders trade listed as well as OTC (customized) options.

III-D-4-b *Forwards*

Forwards are over-the-counter futures. Like futures, they set the price today at which a delivery will occur at a later date. Unlike futures' terms, the terms of the forwards are customized to fit the needs of the client, so forwards do not trade in a liquid market. The most active product in the derivative OTC market is currency (also known as *foreign exchange*). Foreign exchange lends itself to the over-the-counter environment as the needs of the individual user change from trade to trade.

Currency traders offset their positions by using such products as listed futures and listed options.

Note that there are other instruments that trade in the OTC market. Most of them are debt instruments.

III-E *THE THIRD MARKET*

With the rise of institutional trading and the concentration of wealth in the hands of professional money managers, a need grew to trade blocks of stocks and bonds. These large-quantity orders (blocks) could possibly be larger than the primary marketplace could support at one time. To accommodate the need, a new market grew in which market-making broker/dealers with contacts in the institutional side of the business would assist in the distribution or acquisition of these blocks.

One of Stone, Forrest & Rivers' institutional clients wants to sell 50,000 shares of Monterey Corp. The order is too large for the specialist at the NYSE to handle at one time as Monterey Corp doesn't usually trade in that great a quantity. Stone, Forrest & Rivers traders contact third-market firms to see if they can be of support. One of these firms, Wrode and Laine, has an interest and makes a bid for the entire block. SF&R traders check with their institutional client, who accepts the bid and the trade occurs. Wrode and Laine begin to contact their clients and other broker/dealers that generally have an interest in Monterey Corp. or companies in the same business line as Monterey Corp. Wrode and Laine are exposed to market risk while they own the stock; therefore, their short-term opinion of the company and the current market conditions will determine how quickly they will want dispose of it. Their short-term assessment of the company and the market in general also were key elements in determining the price that they were willing to pay SF&R for the block.

Wrode and Laine may use derivatives, such as options, while they have the security in position to offset market risk. Naturally, if their assessment were incorrect, they could take a loss on the transaction.

III-F *THE FOURTH MARKET*

The so-called *fourth market* exists between institutions who post their interests and trade among each other. One leader in this field is Instinet. They are registered with the Securities and Exchange Commission as an exchange. This permits them to route listed and over-the-counter securities to the different marketplaces. Orders entered into Instinet will go out to the security's primary market and various electronic commerce networks (ECNs) seeking the best liquidity pool and the best current price. As liquidity pools change, the system will reroute the remaining quantity of the order to the then best or most liquid pool.

All executions occurring in the fourth market must be reported through the normal channels to the public.

III-G *ODD LOTS*

In the United States the standard unit of trading for equities is 100 shares. For bonds, it is 5 bonds or $5,000 face amount of bonds. Trades for lesser amounts are considered *odd lots.* Therefore, individuals can buy 1 to 99 shares of a given stock if they so desire. The 1 to 99 shares are called an *odd lot.* They can also purchase corporate bonds in less than $5,000 denominations. On the New York Stock Exchange, odd lots are traded by the electronix odd lot system. SF&R's order management system directs these orders to the trading location. The programs then monitor the bid and offer, and execute the odd lot order when the client's instruction on the order can be satisfied. If the odd lot order is executable, it will be executed; if not, it will be held in a pending file until it is either canceled or executed. Odd lot orders follow the same rules as round lot orders insofar as there are day orders, good till cancel, and so on.

CHAPTER IV

The Trade-Processing System

IV-A *ORDER MANAGEMENT SYSTEM*

SF&R employs a very sophisticated order management system. When orders enter the system, either from stockbrokers or from clients themselves, they pass through a series of validations before the order is permitted to go to the point of execution. The order first passes through the security master database, which contains information such as the security's symbol and last price. Orders being entered are verified for the symbol accuracy and then, in the case of a limit order, the price is verified against the last sale of the security to ensure that an order for the wrong security is not being entered. This reduces costly errors.

The order then passes up against the customer's name and address file, known as the customer master database, or similar name depending on the individual firm. Here we find all the pertinent information regarding the client, including name, address, account number, and registered rep number. This file is checked to ensure that the entering stockbroker or customer has placed the proper account number and name on the order. Again, if there is any discrepancy between what the client or stockbroker has entered and what the records show, the order will be rejected and sent back to the point of origin. Note that during this verification process, the status of the client is also verified. This means verification of the type of trading that the customer has been approved to conduct. Should the client start to transact business in a particular product or type of trading that was not approved, a notice will be sent to the branch office responsible for the client's account as well as to the compliance department.

Once all these verifications have occurred and the order has satisfied the various criteria, the order management system forwards the order to the point of execution. Directions to the marketplace (or the point of execution) are found in the security master database. The order is also placed in an order pending file, where it can be reviewed by approved personnel.

At the point of execution, the order is executed either electronically or with the assistance of a market maker or broker. In the case of the stock exchange floor, it might be with the assistance of a specialist. Orders executed through the NASDAQ market can be done through SOES or through some of the other systems offered by the NASDAQ marketplace, such as CAES and ACES. Use of these various order-routing and -reporting systems depends on the size of the order and/or business decisions made by Stone, Forrest & Rivers. Orders going to the New York Stock Exchange can be routed by the order management system to either one of the booths that SF&R maintains on the floor of the exchange or directly to the specialist in the given security via a system called *designated order turnaround (DOT)*. The order can also be directed to NYSE Direct+[SM]. Other exchanges and marketplaces have their own order-routing and -reporting system. Some of these systems do executions electronically; some just route the order to the point of execution where a broker, trader, or specialist intercedes on behalf of the customer and executes the order.

When the execution occurs, it is reported back to Stone, Forrest & Rivers. The SF&R order management system locks the execution report to the original order. Included with the execution price is the name of the contra broker with whom the trade was done. Notification of the execution report is routed to the client either through the stockbroker if the order was entered that way or over the wire if it was entered through the Web system. This report contains the execution price but not the name or the contra broker. At the same time the order is forwarded to the trade processing system for further processing, and it's moved from the "Pending" file to the "Executed" file along with the price and the rest of the execution information, to the trade processing system. Except for one more process to be conducted at the end of the day, the order/report movement from the order management system (OMS) to the trade processing system (TPS) and the work of OMS have been completed.

As the order enters the TPS, the trade is completely *figured*. This includes first money, any accrued interest in the case of debt instruments, plus or minus the firm's commission, plus or minus service fees, minus SEC fee, and net (final) money. For buy trades, commission and service fees are added to first money. For sell trades, commission and service fees are subtracted. The computation is then forwarded to the client as part of electronic confirmation or to the stockbroker, who informs the customer as to the

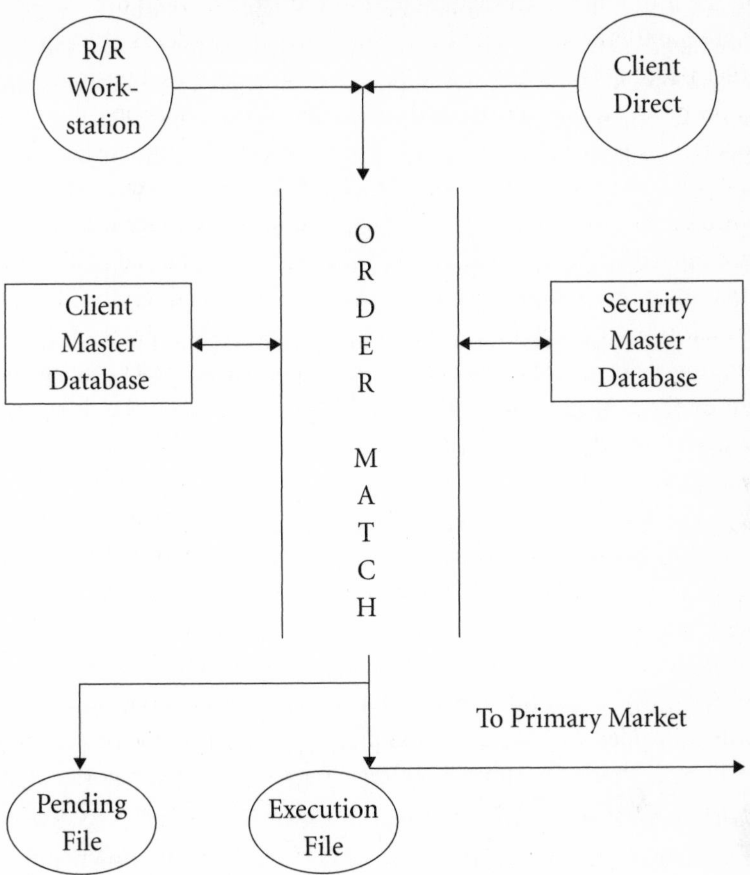

Note: Databases are also referred to as reference files

monies involved with the transaction. By this method, the SF&R client knows the amount of money involved with the transaction immediately after the execution occurs. With the execution now in place, we are ready to proceed to the next area for processing; however, the order management system still has responsibilities to perform before the end of the day.

Orders entered by the clients may be either day orders, which expire at the end of the day should they not be executed, or good-till-cancel (GTC) orders, which remain in force until they are either executed or canceled. Recently SF&R has been offering their clients good-through-month orders (GTMs) and good-through-week orders (GTWs). These orders remain in force until they are either executed or the time established by the client at order entry expires. All pending buy limit and sell stop orders that are good till week, good till month, or good till cancel will be adjusted each evening for dividends and other corporate actions that affect the price of the securities. This process is performed automatically by SF&R's order management system, which receives information from outside vendors. For example, client Ms. Della Kattesin has an order to buy 1,000 shares of POP at $80.20. POP announces a 20¢ per share cash dividend. On the night before ex-dividend date (which is explained in Chapter VII), the system will automatically reduce Della's order from $80.20 to $80.00 to reflect the payment of the dividend. Good-till-cancel and other types of good-till buy orders and sell stops are reduced by the amount of these dividends, but buy stops and sell limit orders are not. Other types of corporate actions also affect the price of the securities. However, in the case of stock splits, stock dividends, and rights offering, all good-till orders are adjusted.

Should a client not wish to have the order price adjusted for cash dividends, rights offerings, or stock dividends, he would enter on the order a *do not reduce (DNR)* and/or *do not increase (DNI)* indicator. These instructions should be entered at the same time as the original order enters Stone, Forrest & Rivers' order management system.

SF&R's order management system then reviews orders that were entered and not executed during the course of the day. It verifies the high and low prices per security per order to determine if the order was eligible for execution. Orders that were eligible for execution are queried into the marketplace the next morning to determine why the order was in fact not executed. There are many reasons for this, such as *stock ahead* (other orders preceded it) and/or the order missed the actual market (arrived later). There could be two causes for this: First, the client might have entered the order after the price that she would have been entitled to occurred and the security did not trade at that price or "better" the rest of the day. Second, someone in SF&R might have delayed entering or attending to the order. This may cause SF&R to execute the order the next day and absorb any loss if it was at fault in the delay.

Note that there are many types of markets operating at one time in our marketplace. For equities we have exchange markets, over-the-counter markets, and NASDAQ markets, bulletin board markets, pink sheet markets, third markets for listed securities being traded over-the-counter, and, most recently, ECNs (electronic commerce networks) and *alternate trading systems (ATSs)*. ECNs operate under the premise that institutions can trade their securities or buy securities in a nonmarket type environment. In other words, the market makers and other brokers are not necessary for them to exchange trades. In the ECN market are institutions as well as market makers and other types of traders who wish to exchange or transact their securities. ATSs will actually trade against the order being presented to them. All trades done in ECNs, ATSs, NASDAQ, bulletin board, or a third market must be reported to the Automated Confirmed Trade system (ACT) operated by the National Association of Security Dealers (NASD).

At the end of the day, the system produces reports for the branch office as well as the customers that highlight those open orders (either good-till-cancel, good-through-week, or good-through-month) that were entered today and are now part of the Pending file. It also reports former open orders that were canceled during the day. As for orders that were entered previously and have been executed during the course of the day, the customer and branch office were notified of the execution at the time the trade actually took place. For customers coming in over the Web or other direct means, the reports were funneled to them as soon as they occurred via the vehicle that the order was entered on.

SF&R is also active in the bond markets, commercial paper, and other money markets, currency markets, derivative markets, over-the-counter options, listed options, and foreign exchange, as well as in several international markets. All such securities trade in their own marketplaces. The industry is ever changing and technology is pushing it to new areas where one never thought it possible to trade before.

With the order entered, executed, and reported to the stockbroker and/or client, the trade must now go through a series of steps leading to settlement, which is handled by the trade processing section. Because each type of issue has its own settlement cycle, the trade processing section must ensure that all of the functions are completed within the instrument's specific time constraints.

The following functions comprise the trade processing system, which is responsible for overseeing that they're completed:

1. Client master database information gathering
2. Security master database information gathering
3. Coding
4. Figuration

5. Comparison
6. Confirmation
7. Reconcilement

IV-B *CLIENT ACCOUNT CONTROL*

IV-B-1 New Accounts/Name and Address

The broker/dealer, through its sales and marketing teams, generates revenue from its clients. As Stone, Forrest & Rivers is a full-service firm, its clients come in all types and sizes. The firm has retail and institutional clients. Some of its retail clients are wealthier than some of its institutional clients and have larger portfolios. Some institutional clients use SF&R as a prime broker. Many clients use the services of a stockbroker located in one of SF&R's offices, yet others conduct their business via the Web or voice recognition. Regardless of who they are or how they conduct business, each client's account requires certain documentation to be completed and on file at SF&R.

In addition, clients relocate, change jobs, change their names, become adults, die, and so on. They maintain individual accounts, joint accounts, trust accounts, and so on. Each type of account requires its own set of documents. Some of these documents restrict the type of business a client can conduct. Based on the information provided, other accounts are restricted from conducting certain types of business by SF&R itself. Daily changes must be captured and maintained so that SF&R records are current.

To reduce the number of different name-and-address–related forms that SF&R employs, the firm has consolidated as many forms as possible into multipurpose forms. It has also tried to keep a basic continuity running through all of its forms so that those responsible for completing them or for verifying their completeness can do so with a minimum of effort.

IV-B-1-a *New Account Form*

The basic form that is used to open most new accounts is the new account form. At SF&R and most other broker/dealers, the form has five components:

1. Terms and conditions
2. Client information
3. Standing instructions
4. Type of account
5. Client's signature block

IV-B-1-a-i Terms and Conditions

The terms and conditions under which the account is to be operated set the operating rules the client is expected to abide by. This includes the timely payment for purchases, the delivering of securities when sales are made, the broker/dealer's right to operate the account should the client not respond in good faith, and the procedure by which client funds, known as credit balances, residing in the client's account above a certain amount will be placed in a money market fund.

Should the client elect to have a margin account, the terms and methodology that will be employed for charging interest on the client's debit balance (loan) are explained. The client's responsibility for answering T calls and maintenance calls is explained as to what they are and how they are to be satisfied. T calls are issued on new trades as required by Regulation T of the Federal Reserve. Maintenance calls are issued when adverse market conditions cause the equity in the client's account to fall below established limits. (This is explained in more detail in Chapter V.) The margin agreement also states the action the firm can and will take should these calls for additional collateral not be satisfied. Also included is the fact that SF&R has the right to assign margin rates based on each individual account as well as to call in loans any time market conditions warrant.

The multipart form also contains what is required for a client to qualify for SF&R's "*S*afe, *F*ast & *R*eliable" check writing and debit card service. The terms under which such privileges are offered, including restrictions on their use, are stated.

A client wanting to trade options must complete the option portion of the form. This sets the limitation and understanding that a client will abide by when employing different option strategies, should she elect to have an option account.

The client agrees to take to arbitration any matters with SF&R that cannot be resolved between the two parties.

The client(s) must sign and date the terms and conditions.

IV-B-1-b-ii Client information

Besides the client's name, address, and telephone number, SF&R must obtain the client's Social Security number (SSN) or tax identification number (TIN) as well as the employer's name, business address, and telephone number, occupation, date of birth (or date of majority), marital status, citizenship, and mailing address if different from the client's previously given name and address. In the case of a joint account, SF&R must obtain this information on all parties. Because there are rules covering accounts of employees of other broker/dealers, banks, insurance companies, and other financial institutions, the occupation of the spouse is also required.

To protect the client and the broker/dealer, the client provides SF&R with financials, which include annual income, net worth, and liquid net worth. In the Investment Objectives section the client states the purpose of the account (e.g., preservation of principal, growth, speculation, income, or growth and income). The client must rank these in order of importance. Finally, the client must complete the section covering the level of market knowledge he claims to have for each product and how long he has traded the different products that SF&R offers.

SF&R's risk management personnel use this financial and experience information to set limits on the client's trading exposure. For example, it will set the maximum amount that a client can have outstanding on a particular trading day. SF&R's margin system monitors the client's financial exposure on a real-time basis. Matthew Adoor is a client who uses SF&R's online order entry system. Based on Matt's financials, as reported in the new account form, SF&R has set a trading exposure limit of $20,000. If Matt enters an order to buy or sell short securities that will involve more that $20,000, the order is routed to Matt's registered representative or a client relationship manager (CRM). However, SF&R's monitoring software has been programmed to include the proceeds of any sales that have occurred that day prior to the questionable order. Therefore, if Matt had sold $10,000 worth of securities that day, prior to entering an order to buy $30,000 worth of securities, the buy order will be accepted.

IV-B-1-c-iii Standing Instructions

The standing instructions convey the clients' instructions as to the handling of distributions, proceeds of sales, disposition of securities, and so on. For example, a retail client who resides in Massachusetts wants all cash dividends, interest received on investments, and proceeds from sales invested in SF&R's Massachusetts Tax Free Money Market Fund. A client who is retired may want all dividend and interest distributions paid out monthly but all proceeds of sales to be housed in SF&R's Taxable Money Market Fund. An institution may want all funds and securities received or delivered against their custodian. SF&R must follow these instructions.

IV-B-1-d-iv Type of account

The type of account to be opened is stated on the new account form. How this question is answered will determine what other forms or external documentation may be required. The more popular types of accounts are:

A. Individual Account

B. Joint Tenants with Rights of Survivorship Account

C. Joint Tenants in Common Account

D. Uniform Gift to Minors Act/Uniform Trust to Minors Act (UGMA/UGTA) Account

E. Power of Attorney Account

F. Discretionary Account

G. Investment Club Account

H. Sole Proprietorship Account

I. Partnership Account

J. Corporation Account

K. Unincorporated Association Account

L. Trust Account

M. Estate Account

N. Transfer on Death Account

O. IRA Account

P. Prime brokerage account

IV-B-1-e-v Client's Signature block

All of SF&R's forms are for naught if the client(s) does (do) not sign and date the necessary document[s]. In addition, any modification to an original document must also be properly signed (off) on. While some clients may get annoyed at the amount of initial paperwork, it is there for the benefit of all parties. Because it is an annoyance, SF&R's staff makes sure that all required documents are given to the client initially, and they verify completeness and reasonableness upon their return. This minimizes the amount of time new clients or clients changing investment habits need to spend in satisfying this requirement.

IV-B-1-b Types of Accounts
Each type of account has its own requirements and limitations. Additional account forms must be completed by the account's principal(s) or may be required before that account is permitted to conduct business.

A. An *individual account* can be operated by the account's principal only. If the principal should die, the account is frozen until the principal's will has gone through probate and an executor is established or, in the absence of a will, the court has appointed an administrator.

B. *Joint tenants with rights of survivorship accounts* are generally opened by married couples. Both principals have access to the account. When one of the two dies, the entire account belongs to the survivor.

C. A *joint tenants in common account* can be opened for no more than three principals, usually only two. The account is assumed to be equally owned. Any other distribution requires a written agreement, dated recently, and signed by all principals. Should one of the principals die, that portion of the account becomes part of the deceased's estate.

D. The *Uniform Gift to Minors Act* and the *Uniform Trust to Minors Act* enable a type of account that cannot include a margin account. When a minor comes of age, a new account is opened and the position transferred from the old account to the new. The minor must furnish a copy of the birth certificate, and the minor's custodian must write a letter approving the movement of assets.

E. A *power of attorney account* may be for full power of attorney or limited power. A person with a full power of attorney can buy and sell securities as well as deposit and withdraw funds and securities. A person with a limited power of attorney can only buy or sell securities. Besides the new account forms required for the principal of the account, a complete set of new account forms are required for the individual having the power of attorney.

F. *Discretionary accounts* permit a stockbroker to operate their clients' accounts without discussing the action with the clients beforehand. Because of the exposure to lawsuits, SF&R has restrictions on which stockbrokers may have discretion over their clients' accounts and under what conditions that discretion may be used.

G. *Investment club accounts* must have a formal written agreement between club members stating clearly the investment objectives of the club and who is authorized to operate the account.

H. A *sole-proprietorship account* is similar to an individual account but is a business account.

I. A *partnership account* requires a formal partnership agreement listing and signed by all the principal partners. The purpose and objective of the account must be established and the individual(s) responsible for operating the account must be identified.

J. Before SF&R will allow corporations to operate a corporation account or even have *margin* or *option accounts*, a copy of the corporate charter and/or bylaws must be presented. They must state what type of business the corporation can conduct. It is conceivable that the corporate charter and/or bylaws prohibit the corporation from conducting business in certain types of securities.

K. An *unincorporated association account* requires legal proof of the association's existence, including the tax ID number and the purpose of the association. The principals, the proof that the association can have an account, the investment objectives, and the individuals responsible for the management of the account must be stated.

L. A *trust account* requires the completion of the trust agreement, a new account form completed by the trustee as well as the usual new account papers.

M. An *estate account* requires copies of the will or documents naming the administrator appointed by a probate court, copies of the death certificate, an affidavit of domicile, and tax waivers.

N. *Transfer on death accounts* are established to bypass the legal proceedings involved with the death of the principal. This type of account is not covered by probate nor is it part of the principal's estate.

O. There are numerous types of *IRA account*:

1. *Traditional.* This is an account or an annuity set up for the individual for whom contributions may be tax deductible, depending on his income level and other plans he may be participating in. All earnings, both capital gains and income, are tax deferred. Contributions can be made to it until the end of the calendar year in which the client reaches 70½. The maximum that can be contributed to the client's total IRAs annually is $3,000 ($3,500 if over age 50) or 100% of the client's income, whichever is less. For a husband and wife, the maximum is $6,000 ($7,000 if over age 50) or 100% of their total income, whichever is less.
2. *Roth.* With the exceptions noted below, a Roth is treated the same as a traditional IRA. The maximum deposit per year is $3,000 ($3,500 if over age 50) or 100% of the individual's annual income, whichever is less. However, unlike with a traditional IRA, contributions to the IRA are not tax deductible. In addition, withdrawals made under certain conditions are not taxed or penalized. Contributions can be made after age 70½ and there isn't any requirement to withdraw money at any time.
3. *Simplified Employee Pension (SEP–IRA).* This can be set up by management for each eligible employee. The company makes the contribution to the plan. The employee controls the plan. Employees are eligible if they meet all of the following conditions: They are at least 21 years old; they have worked for their employer during at least 3 of the 5 years immediately preceding the current year; and they have received from their employer at least $450 in compensation in the current year. The maximum contribution is 15% of the employee's compensation or $30,000, whichever is less.
4. *Elective Deferrals (401(K) Plans).* These are not subject to the deduction limits that apply to qualified plans. Also, elective deferrals are not taken into account when figuring the amount you can deduct for employer contributions that are not elective deferrals. The maximum is $15,000 in the year 2006.

5. *Rollover IRA*. This is used by individuals who want to change IRA trustees without incurring a tax liability or other penalty. An example is when an individual leaves the employment of a company that had a 401(K) plan. The balance in the 401(K) must be moved to a rollover IRA within 60 days to avoid a tax penalty. However, assets involved in a rollover cannot be rolled over again for a year.
6. *Beneficiary distribution account (BDA)*. Here, if a client inherits an IRA from a deceased spouse, he can roll it over to another IRA established for him or he can make it his own. If it is his own, he can make contributions to it but does not have to make required distributions from it.
7. *Savings incentive match plan for employees (SIMPLE)*. This can be set up for a company that has 100 or fewer employees where each earned at least $5,000 per year. Employees can contribute up to $6,000 per year; the employer can match up to 3% of the employees' compensation. If the employer is going to contribute less than 3%, it must inform the employees 60 days in advance of payment.
8. *Educational account*. This can be used for a child's higher education. Contributions of $500 per year are not tax deductible and contributions grow tax free until withdrawn. During the life of the Educational IRA, the beneficiary can be changed as long as it is a member of the same family who is under age 30. Educational IRAs can be rolled over to another educational IRA for the same beneficiary or member of the beneficiary's family and retain its tax status if done within 60 days. Withdrawals are generally tax free if they do not exceed the actual educational expenses.
9. *529 Plan accounts*. These are authorized under state law. The money deposited in the fund account must be professionally managed. As these are authorized by the individual states, the properties differ from one state to another. The earnings on investments are tax free and withdrawals are also tax-free as long as the money is used for the beneficiary's higher education. In addition, the money itself belongs to the depositor and not the beneficiary. The tax status is due to change in the year 2010.
10. *Keogh plans*. Sometimes called *H.R.-10 plans*, Keoghs are maintained by self-employed individuals or a company of fewer than 100 employees. They are primarily funded by the employer. The two types of Keoghs are the *defined-benefit plan* (where the retirement

income is based upon a contribution formula) and the *defined-contribution plan* (in which the current contribution is usually based upon an accrual rate, the employee's length of service, and the employee's rate of pay).

11. *403B plans.* These are qualified plans that involve tax-deferred investment in retirement plans. The plan is operated by the employer for the benefit of the employees and is not transferable between employers. Should an employee leave an employer and decide to or have to move the plan to another custodian, the plan will become a rollover IRA plan.

P. A *prime brokerage account* is more of a custodial type of account than any of the above. Large institutions, such as hedge funds, obtain investment ideas from several sources. To compensate these resources, the institution places trades through the representing broker/dealers. After the trade has been executed and the commission earned by the representing firm, settlement will ultimately reside on the prime broker's books. This places the hedge funds (or other client's) portfolio in one location rather than have it piecemeal at each of the broker/dealers that the client transacts business through.

As you can see, there are many variations. Some accounts are restricted as to the types of trades they may enter into. Some of the restrictions are imposed by the laws covering the particular type of account. Other restrictions are imposed by the SROs and marketplace in which the particular security trades. And, finally, some are imposed by the broker/dealer itself.

IV-B-2 Client Master Database Information Gathering

IV-B-2-a *Data Entry (NAOW)*

The new account information form, which is required for all of the above accounts, has been designed in conjunction with SF&R's workstation screen layout that appears at certain secure locations. This permits the registered representatives or sales assistants to open an account online on a real-time basis with the actual completed and signed paper forms following later. The process of sending the new account information from the point of entry to the client master database is known as *name and address over the wire (NAOW).*

Clients can open accounts online, but there is a strict verification process. The client is restricted from making certain types of purchases in both quantity and quality until the client's identity can be established. Clients who are transferring their accounts from other firms cannot sell any security until the other firm has confirmed the position and signed the Automated Client Account Transfer System (ACATS).

IV-B-2-b *Automated Client Account Transfer System (ACATS)*

The ACATS serves three main purposes. First, it affirms the client's position to the new firm. Second, it freezes the account at the old firm by advising them of the pending transfer. This process keeps the client from selling the same security twice—once at each firm. And third, it creates the document that is used to transfer the securities electronically through the Depository Trust Company.

IV-B-2-c *Account Opening Procedure*

All new accounts must be reviewed and signed off on by two individuals of the firm. One is a registered representative who is responsible for knowing and verifying the essential facts that the client has stated on the new account form. The other is a principal of the firm, who must review the form for reasonableness and completeness. The registered representative is to perform due diligence in learning and/or verifying the essential facts about the client. This is covered by Rule 405 of the NYSE, called the "Know Your Client Rule."

If the client elects to have a margin account, the section of the new account form dealing with the margin account privilege must be signed and dated by the client. This is in addition to the signature required in the signature block section. The signature in this portion of the account form attests that the client has read the portion of the new account form that covers the operation of a margin account. The most important part of this section states that the firm can operate the account without the client's permission should the client not respond quickly enough to a margin call for more collateral. That section also discusses how interest is calculated on debit balances and when interest will be paid on credit balances.

The section on operating an option account must be signed by the client insofar as it states that the client is to receive SF&R's option agreement letter and the booklet "Characteristics and Risks of Options." The client must sign the option agreement letter in which the client agrees to abide by the rules of the Option Clearing Corporation.

As part of this country's USA Patriot Act (Unifying and Supporting America by Providing Appropriate Tools Required to Intercept and Obstruct Terrorism) broker/dealers must have written procedures as to what must be done in the investigation and record keeping parts of opening a new account. In addition, SF&R's compliance personnel perform periodic checks to ensure that the new account personnel are adhering to the requirements.

IV-B-2-d *Account Maintenance*

The name and address function includes the follow-up of missing and/or incomplete documentation. SF&R staff is very diligent in ensuring that the documentation required to operate the account in its current state is complete and on file at SF&R. However, they are limited to known information. In the final analysis, it is the client and the registered representative who know the current status. Moreover, the main source for updated information is the client.

If documentation has been requested but is still missing, it is noted and the client will receive notification requesting that forms be completed and filed. For example, let's suppose a client opened a cash account and has never completed and filed a margin agreement with the firm. Through some mistake, the client has actually entered into trades in their margin-type account. The first notification of the deficiency will appear on SF&R's client support personnel's workstation. They in turn will notify the registered representative (stockbroker) responsible for the account. Broker/dealers that do not have specific representatives assigned to clients' accounts would have a customer relationship manager follow through on rectifying the problem. In addition, on the review conducted by the Compliance Department of Stone, Forrest & Rivers, the fact that the client has margin positions without the proper documentation being filed will appear on a client documentation delinquency report. This report is developed by comparing the type of transactions the client has in position against the client master database. In the case of individual or joint tenants with rights of survivorship accounts, the form requires that the occupation of the spouse be identified. This is important as there are rules governing the operation of a joint account if one of the two parties (or the spouse in the case of a single account) is employed by another broker/dealer, a bank, an insurance company, and so on. The database can also identify the account numbers of related accounts so that if an individual opened up, let's say, a joint account, an individual account, an individual account for the spouse, and custodian accounts for each child, all of these accounts would be cross-referenced in the client master database.

Clients relocate, have changes in their financials, alter their investment objectives, get married, reach the age of maturity, die, and so on. These changes must be recorded on the client master database to keep the client information up to date. This information is transmitted from the point of entry, a branch office, to the client master database via the NAOW system.

In addition, SF&R mails periodic notices to its clients. These contain the client's information as it appears on the client master database. The client is then asked to make any changes that may be required. This updated information is then added to the client master database.

IV-B-2-e *Institutional Accounts/SID/ALERT*

Institutions generally maintain institutional accounts at several broker/dealers—each with its own form of client master files or database. When a corporation makes any change to its client profile, it must notify each broker/dealer of the change. Depository Trust Company (DTC) developed a system called *Standing Instruction Database (SID)* and Thomson Financial developed ALERT. (Currently, these are both under the Omgeo umbrella.) Now the institution makes the change to the ALERT or SID database and the broker/dealers that service the institution update their files directly from these central databases.

IV-C *SECURITY PROPERTIES CONTROL*

Once, the security master database contained only the data most directly related to identifying the security. It now contains a more complete story about the particular issue, which includes its processing routine, settlement cycle, dividend payout policy, and more. It is the second main database used in the processing cycle.

IV-C-1 Security Master Database

The main purpose of the security master database is to allow the system to process each and every transaction in accordance with the requirements for that particular product. Therefore, one will find in the security master such items as the *CUSIP number*. The CUSIP number is a nine-digit figure whose first six digits identify the issuer. The next two digits identify the issue. The final digit is a check digit, which verifies the proper application of the preceding eight digits. Should a transposition or mistake be made in any one of those eight digits, the algorithm that is used to compute the check digit will not arrive at the same answer as what the check digit is supposed to be.

To accommodate securities that are involved in international transactions, the CUSIP numbering system has been modified into 12-digit *International Security Identification Number (ISIN)* codes. ISIN numbers' additional three digits identify the country of origin.

Often a firm will use internal symbols or codes in addition to CUSIP and ISIN numbers that identify the securities that appear in the firm's security master database. These internal codes are generally alphanumeric and minimize the number of characters necessary to identify the particular issue.

Firms that use an internal identification numbering convention utilize internally developed libraries that convert these internal numbers to CUSIP numbers for external usage—for example, in communicating computer to computer with the Depository Trust Company.

Also on the security master database are the name and description of the issue itself. Adventurer Corporation common stock will be listed exactly that way. Adventurer 6% preferred would be listed as Adventurer 6% Pfd., and an Adventurer 8% F&A bond maturing in the year 2030 (F&A standing for February and August interest payment dates) would be listed as Adventurer 8% FA 2030. As some of the products have very long descriptions that use more than the standard allowable fields found in the security master database, the industry has adopted an acceptable list of abbreviations, such as *Rev* for the word *revenue* in a municipal revenue bond's description.

Another important element in the processing stream is the trading lot that the product has. This is important in routing the order to its respective trading location as well as in computing the amount of money involved in the trade. In the United States, the trading unit for common stock is 100 shares. Some preferred shares are also traded in units of 100 shares, but some of the higher-priced preferred stocks trade in 10-share lots. In the United Kingdom, a round lot of ordinary shares (British version of common stock) is 1,000. In Switzerland, it's 20 shares. As the security master database carries the trading lot of the issue, it must also be able to associate the issue with the marketplace in which it is being traded.

Most securities, including common stock and preferred stock, utilize symbols to identify the issue for trading purposes. The symbol for the particular issue would also appear in this location. It is expedient to write or type GM for General Motors Corporation or IBM instead of International Business Machines Corporation. In our example, we will give Adventurer Corporation of America a symbol—AVNT. This symbol will be part of the identifier for all of the issues that the company has.

Options use both a code and abbreviations to identify the expiration month and the strike price (or exercise price). Both of these methods of identifying the particular option series would be found in the security master database. For example, a call option on Adventurer common stock with an April expiration and a strike price of \$40 per share would appear on the master as "C AVNT APR 40" and as "C AVNT DH." Based on industry convention, the letter D in the expiration month field of a call option signifies the month of April and the letter H appearing in the strike or exercise price field signifies the price of \$40 per share.

As different types of securities have different trading lots, the prices shown on execution reports are sometimes representative of different meanings. For example, 1,000 AVNT at \$96 could represent 1,000 shares of Adventurer common stock at \$96 per share, for an initial cost of \$96,000. It could also stand for a bond: 1,000 AVNT 8% F&A of 2030 would at \$96 represent a purchase totaling \$960. For the system to understand and instruct the figuration programs on how to compute the correct amount of first money, or initial money, the security master contains multiplier instructions. For example, the multiplier for common stock is 1 (one), 1,000 shares at \$96 would be $1{,}000 \times 1 \times \$96 = \$96{,}000$. For a bond it is .01 (1%) 1,000 bond @ \$96 would be $1{,}000 \times .01 \times \$96 = \$960$. For an equity option contract, it's 100, 1 call option Oct 40 @ \$6 would compute as $1 \times 100 \times \$6 = \$600$, and so on.

Most corporate and municipal securities are eligible for processing by NSCC and are resident or maintained at the Depository Trust Company (DTC). These two agencies recently merged to form Depository Trust and Clearing Corporation (DTCC). However, their processes as of the writing of this book are still separate and are known as NSCC and DTC processing.

Securities may be eligible for processing by one or both of these entities. A security may be eligible for NSCC comparison processing but not be eligible to be maintained at the Depository and vice versa. Options listed on exchanges use Option Clearing Corp. (OCC) for the maintenance of their members' positions. This information would also be located in the security master database. The security master database contains information as to where trade comparison occurs and where the security is maintained in position.

Most securities traded on the exchanges and NASDAQ can be purchased on margin. However, new issues, for example, have a time limit (90 days) before they can be purchased that way. Besides that, there are other reasons why SF&R may not want to margin a security or even margin it at the "house" rates. Among these reasons could be high volatility, low price, or an extremely "thin" trading market. These notations are made in the security master database.

Different securities have different settlement cycles. Some settle on trade date, some settle on trade date + 1, and some settle on other cycles. For example, commercial paper transactions settle on trade date. Options and future transactions settle the day after trade date (trade date + 1), currency trades settle two days after trade date (T + 2), and equity and corporate bonds settle three days after trade date (T + 3). The normal settlement cycle for a particular transaction in a particular type of issue is located in the security master database and used by the processing systems to prepare data when needed for processing purposes.

Depending on the nature of the security, it may or may not be marginable. Margin is used to permit clients to purchase securities using part of the purchase money in a borrowed form. Equities have their own margin requirements, bonds have theirs. As different products have different margin calculations, pointers to the various calculations are located in the security master database.

The security master database also contains securities related to the one being examined. Let's refer to Adventurer common stock's position in the security master database. Upon examination, one sees what other securities the Adventurer Corporation has outstanding—the different types of preferred, bonds, options, and so on. This reference from a single point, the security master database, is important in reconciling trade or position differences.

Some stocks pay dividends; bonds pay interest. These payments occur on specific dates set by the issuer. This information is located in the security master database. By researching the security information in the database, one can ascertain:

1. If the particular stock that is being researched pays a dividend.
2. If it does pay a dividend, how frequently the dividends are paid or what the dividend payment cycle is.
3. The amount of dividend paid.
4. The date on which the dividend was last paid.

Preferred stocks, for example, generally pay their dividends in a quarterly cycle. The security master database would list that cycle, such as J, A, J, and O, which would stand for January, April, July, and October. It would also give you the amount of the dividend. Let's suppose Adventurer preferred pays a $.15 per share quarterly dividend. This will appear in the security master database. The database will also reflect the last time the dividend was paid and the amount paid at that time. Bonds pay their interest semiannually. There are six such possible payments. While the payment cycle is listed in the bond description, it also appears in another place on the security master database. It will say J&J, F&A, M&S, A&O, M&N, or J&D, which, stand for January and July, February and August, March and September, and you can figure out the remaining ones. If the bonds pay their interest on a different date than the first day of the month, the actual payment date will also appear. The employee may see something like M&S 15, which would tell the employee that the bond pays its interest on the 15th of March and September. The security master database would reflect the last time the bonds paid interest. This is a quick way of determining if they are in default or not and the amount paid at that time.

Let's recap the contents of the security master database. Here one can ascertain:

1. The name of the issuer
2. The symbol used to identify the issue
3. CUSIP, ISIN, and internal identification codes
4. Country of original issue
5. Class of issue—corporate, municipal, derivative, and so on
6. Type of issue—common or preferred stock, type of bond, and so on
7. Trading lot
8. Settlement cycle

9. Primary market
10. Most recent market price
11. End-of-month price
12. Marginablity
13. Multiplier (for money computations)
14. Clearing corporation eligibility
15. Depository or custody arrangement
16. Dividend/interest payer and annual amount
17. Last dividend/interest payment date
18. Last dividend/interest payment amount
19. Description of special features (convertible, callable, etc.)
20. Related security issues
21. Accrued interest methodology (debt instruments)
22. Maturity date (debt instruments) or expiration date (options and trusts)
23. Other product-bound information

As you can see, the security master database houses information about the issue itself, processing requirements, and client support needs.

IV-C-2 Security Master Database Information Gathering

As the order is being entered into the order management system, the security master database verifies the security description, or symbol, the price at which the client requested the order be executed, and several other factors before the order can be executed. Having satisfied these foundation checks, the order is allowed to be entered and an execution takes place. Now the trade processing system looks to the security master database for (1) where the primary market was and was the order executed there, (2) the method by which the monies involved with the trade are calculated, (3) the settlement cycle, (4) the clearing corporation that security is to be processed through, if any, (5) whether the trade was executed as agency or principal, (6) the depository where the issue resides, if any, and (7) the rest of the routing the order will have to go through as it is set up for final settlement.

The trade now carries the CUSIP number obtained from the security master database (and/or the International Security Identifying Number), any internal identifying codes that Stone, Forrest & Rivers may be using, and (depending on the primary market) whether the trade was done on an agency or principal basis. All this information is required in coding.

The information contained in SF&R's security master database is obtained from several vendors. Among these are DTCC, the Bond Market Association, Reuters, and Standard and Poor's. Each vendor provides a different part of the database. SF&R obtains CUSIP numbers from Standard and Poor's, bond rating information from Standard and Poor's, Moody's, Fitch, and Duff and Phelps, pricing information from Reuters, mortgage-backed securities settlement cycles from the Bond Market Association, and new eligible security information from DTCC.

IV-D *CODING*

For processing control purposes, every execution being entered into the system receives a unique number. At SF&R, that number is composed of the date of entry, the sequential number of that order, the place of execution, and the capacity the firm operated in.

IV-D-1 Unique Number

An execution being entered on February 25, if it is the 17th order of the day, would carry 0225000017. That unique number remains with the execution throughout its life. Other information is appended to that unique number. Among the information added is where the trade took place and whether the firm acted as a market maker (principal) or broker (agent). Stone, Forrest & Rivers, like all other firms, has a unique system of coding for this information. For example, at Stone, Forrest & Rivers, any trade that is executed in New York starts off with the code number 1, 2 is for any trade executed in Chicago, 3 is for San Francisco, and so on. Trades executed outside of North America use a letter for the first digit (e.g., L for London, F for Frankfurt, T for Tokyo, H for Hong Kong). As to the capacity the firm operated in, trades consummated for SF&R's clients at the New York Stock Exchange must be done on an agency basis. These are coded 1N. The code 1N therefore signifies an agency trade. For control purposes, SF&R goes even further, using the letter O for option trades. So a trade done on the Chicago Board Option Exchange would carry the code 2O, with the number 2 signifying Chicago and the letter O signifying option. Municipal bonds carry the code M, so a municipal bond executed in the San Francisco office would carry 3M, whereas a municipal bond trade executed on the trading desk in New York would carry the designation 1M.

In addition, as SF&R's operation personnel work on exception reporting, should there be a problem with this trade at any time, the problem trade will appear on a report and they will use this reference number as a research tool.

IV-E *TRADE FIGURATION*

After the execution has occurred, the trade passes through the security master database and the client master database and obtains the information necessary to do the computations, known as *figuration*. From the security master database it obtains the multiplier, in the case of bonds, the method by which accrued interest is calculated, and the interest payment cycle.

Debt instruments accrue interest differently from one another. This accrual is important in trade figuration as it represents the interest owed by the buyer to the seller. That is the sum accrued up to the settlement date of the trade. Bonds accrue interest differently from most money market instruments. Most corporate and municipal securities accrue interest on a 30/360-day basis. Treasury bonds and notes compute interest on an actual/actual-day basis. Treasury bills and most money market instruments are discounted instruments. (Interest is subtracted from the face amount of the loan. The lender pays out the discounted amount and receives face at maturity.) Interest on discounted instruments is computed on an actual/360-day basis. The methodology to be used in computing accrued interest on debt trades is gained from the security master database.

From the client master database, the rate of commission that has been negotiated with the client is obtained and applied to agency and principal trades. This rate is generally set up as a percentage of the actual commission schedule charged by the firm. In doing figuration, first money is simply the quantity of the securities involved in the trade times the price of execution without any deductions.

Example:

Common stock = 100 shares BIL @ $42 = $4,200 first money

Corporate bond = $1,000 ZAP 7% FA 2025 @ $94 = $940 first money

Equity option = 1 call option PIP Oct 40 @ $6 = $600 first money

IV-E-1 Agency versus Principal Transactions

On agency transactions, the commission is added to the first money in the case of buy transactions and subtracted from it in the case of sell transactions. The commission schedule is set by the management of Stone, Forrest & Rivers. The firm may decide to base it on the number of shares, on total money, or on some other term. As we operate in a negotiated commission environment, depending on the amount of business the client gives and the size of those transactions, the firm may negotiate a commission schedule for that client that is less than that charged for the base clients.

IV-E-2 Regulatory Fee

The federal government taxes sell transactions in the form of a .0039 regulatory fee for every $100 of first money or fraction thereof. The tax is applicable only to sales of securities on national securities exchanges and the NASDAQ. The rate of the fee changes periodically. Some firms, at their discretion, add an additional charge for postage and handling. Those charges are not uniform from one firm to another.

IV-E-3 Equity Trade Figuration

Example: SF&R shows the following transactions have occurred on a given day:

In the NASDAQ market, a client bought 100 shares of Regal Corp. at $15, net from SF&R's inventory. SF&R was a market maker in this trade. Because this is a principal transaction, no commission is charged. The markup is in the price, or first money.

100 shares of Regal Corp. @ \$15 = first money	\$1,500
Commission, taxes, and fees	+ 0
Net money	\$1,500

This client owes SF&R \$1,500.

Example: In a listed transaction, a client sold 100 shares of Bonneville, Inc., on the AMEX at \$42 a share. Because this is a listed equity sale, it is subject to commission and fees. The SF&R commission schedule for this client calls for a 2% charge based on first money. Therefore, the client would be charged \$84 commission. As this is a sell trade involving the regulatory fee, which is \$.0039 for every \$100 or fraction thereof, a charge of \$.17 would be imposed on the client.

100 Bonneville, Inc. @ \$42	\$4,200.00
Less: Commission (\$4,200 × .01) =	84.00
Less: SEC fee (\$4,200/100 × .0000307) =	.17
Total deductions	84.17
Net money	\$4,115.83

The client selling the 100 shares receives \$4,115.87 for the security.

IV-E-4 Bond Figuration

In the United States, corporate, municipal, and U.S. Treasury bonds pay interest every six months to the registered holders. In other words, anyone who owns the bond on the record date for the interest payment receives the full six-months' interest. With any transaction occurring between interest payment dates, the buyer and the seller must settle interest accrued to the settlement date. Interest accrues up to, but not including, the settlement date.

Example: A Sable Company 6% FA 20XX is sold for settlement date February 28. As the bond paid interest on February 1, the buyer owes the seller 27 days of accrued interest. However, as corporate bonds compute interest on a

30/360-day basis, every month has 30 days (so if the trade settled on March 1, 30 days of interest would be accrued). If the trade settled on April 16, 75 days of accrued interest would have to be accounted for:

February	30
March	30
April	15
Total	75 days

Special note: Because corporate bonds use the 30/360 convention, a situation arises when the settlement date is the 31st of the month. One method, known as the 30/360 method, counts the 31st as part of the settlement month and accrues interest up to but not including the settlement date (the 31st). Under this method, the 31st and the 1st of the following month have the same accrual. The other method states that if we are computing all months at a maximum of 30 days, there cannot be a 31st. Therefore, the 30th and the 31st are combined into one day. This method is known as 30/360 E. Under this scenario, interest accrues as if the 30th had 48 hours.

Example: Let's assume the Sable FA bond settles on the following dates. The number of accrued interest days would be:

Settlement Date	30/360	30/360E
March 30	59	59
March 31	60	59
April 1	60	60

The difference in application only surfaces when the settlement date is the 31st day of the month. The methodology used is resident in the SF&R security master database as part of the bond's information.

Corporate bond and municipal bond interest is computed on a 360-day basis. Because of the transactions between purchaser and seller, accrued interest belongs to the seller. It is always added to first money. Because commission belongs to the client's firm, it is added to the cost of the purchase, but subtracted from the proceeds of sale.

Example: A client purchased $1,000 Continental 9% FA 20XX @ $92. The purchase transaction occurred for settlement date May 16. The previous time to the trade that the bond paid interest was February 1. The trade settles on May 16. Accrued interest is therefore 105 days:

February	30 days
March	30
April	30
May	15
Total:	105 days

First money:

$1,000 Continental 9% FA 20XX @ 92 = $920.00	
Plus: Accrued interest	
($1,000 × .09 × 105/360)	$ 26.25
Total contract money	$946.25
Plus: Commission ($5/bond, with a minimum of $50)	+ 50.00
Total to the client	$996.25

The number of days of accrued interest was calculated as follows: As this is a corporate bond, every month has 30 days. The settlement date was May 16; the interest accrued up to but not including the 16th, or 15 days from May 1. Therefore, we would have February, 30 days; March, 30 days; April, 30 days; and 15 days in May, for a total of 105 days.

The calculation for accrued interest is:

$$\frac{\text{Principal}}{1} \times \frac{\text{Rate}}{100} \times \frac{\text{Time}}{360}$$

$$\frac{1{,}000}{1} \times \frac{9}{100} \times \frac{105}{360} = \$26.25$$

SF&R must be careful in computing interest. Some bonds, such as income or adjustment bonds, may not carry accrued interest. Neither do bonds that are already in default; they *trade flat* (that is, without accrued interest). This information is carried on the security master database.

In calculating accrued interest, the firm must also be aware of the payment periods on recently issued bonds. Many new bonds are not issued on their interest payment dates, so their first coupon (and only their first coupon), may be less than six months (a short coupon) or more than six months (a long coupon).

Example: An F&A bond pays interest every February 1 and August 1. If the bonds were issued on March 1, the first payment on August 1 is for only five months (a short coupon). If the bonds were issued in January, the issuing organization may not want to go through the expense of paying one month's interest; instead, it may pay seven months' interest on the next payment date, August 1 (a long coupon).

Making a long or short coupon payment on the first payment date is based on the date of issuance, which is commonly known as the *dated date.* After the period has passed, the bond reverts to its six-month cycle.

U.S. Treasury bonds and notes compute interest on an *actual/actual basis.* Therefore, a trade of U.S. Treasury 5% JJ 20XX trading at par and settling on March 1 in a non-leap year would accrue interest for 59 days:

January	31
February	28
Total	59 days

Let's assume the purchase of \$100,000 U.S. Treasury bonds 6% JJ 20XX with a settlement date of March 1 in a non-leap year:

$$\frac{\$100{,}000}{1} \times \frac{6}{100} \times \frac{59}{365} =$$

$$\frac{200}{1} \times \frac{6}{1} \times \frac{59}{73} = \frac{7{,}080}{73} = \$969.86$$

In this case, \$969.86 would be accrued and paid by the purchaser to the seller of the bonds.

IV-E-5 Money Market Instruments

Instruments that trade at discount prices, such as Treasury bills and most money market instruments, have to be computed in a different fashion. The instruments use actual/360 as their method for computing interest. As they are discounted instruments, the price quoted is their yield known as *basis price*, which stands for *yield-to-maturity basis*. To obtain the conversion from the yield to the actual dollar, SF&R has imbedded in its systems a conversion table that converts from yield to dollar as part of the normal process.

A client purchases a $100,000 Le Baron Loan Corp. 90-day commercial paper. This instrument is discounted at a rate of 5%. The purchaser of this discounted instrument receives full face value if it is held to maturity. The difference between the value paid at the time of purchase and value received at maturity is the interest earned on the money that was invested, and it translates into yield:

$$\frac{\$100{,}000}{1} \times \frac{5}{100} \times \frac{90}{360} = \$1{,}250$$

Therefore, this instrument will be discounted at $1,250, which is the discounted rate of 5% on $100,000 for 90 days.

$$\begin{array}{r} \$100{,}000 \\ -\quad 1{,}250 \\ \hline \$\ 98{,}750 \end{array}$$

While crude, this computation satisfies our purposes here. The client will pay $98,750. At maturity, 90 days later, the client will receive $100,000. The difference of $1,250 is the interest earned for 90 days (a quarter of a year) at 5%.

Should the instrument be sold before it matures, the new buyer will pay the seller whatever the then-existing discount rate is. The difference between the two discounted rates, should one exist, less the interest that accrued, would be a profit or loss on the trade.

IV F COMPARISON

IV-F-1 Order Management System

Whether SF&R's clients have transacted business on a principal basis against the firm's trading accounts or as an agent, where SF&R has acted as a broker representing the client in the trade but never taking ownership, there must be an offset for each of these trades. Therefore, every trade will have a client side and a street side. Both sides of the trade must agree as to the quantity of the security, the name of the security being transacted, the price, and what is called first money, which is quantity times price. In a case of trading a bond or other type of debt that carries accrued interest, the amount of interest involved in the transaction must also be agreed on to both sides. Part of SF&R's order management system is an order match system, which locks the report of the execution to the client's order. Therefore, there cannot be a discrepancy between the two.

Long ago, there were actually two separate streams feeding through SF&R's computer systems. One was a client side; the other was a street side. The client side would receive the report from the point of execution—either the trading desk or the floor of an exchange. That price would be copied onto the order ticket and reported to the client, as well as being entered into the processing system. At the same time, the place where the execution occurred would be copying the price and whom the trade was executed against. And those two streams would come together in what was called P&S and would require reconciliation between the client side and SF&R's version of the street side.

With the introduction of the order match system and its eventual perfection, the street side of the trade, the report, is appended to the order, making one data stream going through the processing cycle. Therefore, there cannot be a discrepancy between SF&R's version of the street side and the client's side. However, while SF&R's record is intact, there could possibly be problems with the other side of the transaction.

Say, SF&R purchased 100 shares of Cavalier Corp. at $29 for $2,900 from Giant Reckor & Crane (GR&C). SF&R acted as a broker. The Cavalier Corp. was purchased for their client, Stephan Nee. As far as SF&R's records are concerned, its client side and its version of the street side agree. However, what does Giant Reckor & Crane's record show? Does Giant Reckor & Crane's record show that they sold the 100 shares of Cavalier Corp. at $29 for $2,900 to Stone, Forrest & Rivers? This part of the process is known as comparison. If GRC, in fact, has in its records that sale against SF&R, then SF&R has a valid trade. In all likelihood, Giant Reckor & Crane has its own order match system. Therefore, it has a client who sold 100 shares of Cavalier for $2,900 through Giant Reckor & Crane to somebody whom the client does not know but whom we know as Stephan Nee of Stone, Forrest & Rivers.

IV-F-2 Equity Comparison

In recent years, great effort has been put into the concept of capturing the trade at the point of execution. As a result, we have systems like Super SOES from NASDAQ and Super DOT from the New York Stock Exchange that capture the names of the buying firm and the selling firm as well as the security involved, the quantity, the price, and the time the execution occurred.

Order Audit Trail System (OATS) is a NASD requirement that all clocks be set to the same time as NASDAQ prescribes. This requirement was brought about because of the discrepancies in times stamped on orders during various steps in the order processing and reporting phase of the operation. These discrepancies occurred both intrafirm and interfirm. As NASDAQ members had trade-reporting time requirements, these discrepancies made enforcement of the rules difficult. In addition, as clocks were not synchronized, responding to client complaints about bad executions was difficult. There were cases where the time stamp on an order at the point of execution was before the stamp placed at the time the order was entered. In other cases, the time the order was received at the trading desk was before it was sent by the branch office, and so on. As all clocks are now synchronized, the times at which various processes occur can be monitored.

NASDAQ employs a system called Automated Confirmed Trade (ACT). ACT has a hierarchy, which determines who reports the trade within 90 seconds after the execution. The hierarchy works as follows:

If the buy side and the sell side are both market makers, the sell side reports the details of the trade to ACT. If the buy side and sell side are both brokers, the sell side reports. If one side is a dealer and the other side is a broker, the dealer reports. The contra side to the trade must accept the terms of the trade before the trade can be processed. Once the terms of the trade are agreed upon, ACT deposits the trade details at the National Security Clearing Corporation (NSCC), to complete the comparison cycle.

The New York Stock Exchange uses a system called Designated Order Turnaround (DOT). DOT trades are compared in a slightly different fashion. The specialist firms, which are responsible for the fair and orderly marketing of the securities they are assigned to, maintain omnibus accounts. Omnibus accounts are offset accounts used for trade comparison. If SF&R is entering into a DOT trade, the order will be sent electronically from SF&R to the NYSE/AMEX Common Message Switch (CMS) to the post on the NYSE trading floor where the stock is traded. There it will appear on the Specialists' Display Book. When the order is executed, it is executed against an omnibus account and reported back to SF&R. The actual other side of the transaction is notified of the trade, and their trade is executed against a second omnibus account. At the end of the day, the specialists compare the two omnibus accounts for any discrepancies. The rules of the stock exchange dictate at what point there's a large enough discrepancy to cause the specialist to break a trade and at what point the specialist just takes it as a cost of doing business. Therefore, while it is not a true comparison, it is a locked-in trade.

There are six omnibus accounts: DOT, the offset side is called TOD; there is LOC, the offset side is LMT; and there is MKT, the offset side is OPN (DOT = TOD, LOC = LMT and MKT = OPN). In our example above, Stone, Forrest & Rivers bought stock through DOT. On the other side of the trade is another broker/dealer—let's say Knight and Knune, which sold the stock. If SF&R's trade is executed against the omnibus account DOT, Knight and Knune's transaction would be against the omnibus account TOD.

All transactions go through a comparison system with one exception, of course. That's a transaction done between a client and the trading account of the firm that the client belongs to. In that case, there is internal comparison, which is monitored by trade processing specialists. Different securities have different timing for their comparison cycles. However, as the number of days between trade date and settlement date shrink, the difference is becoming ambiguous. Therefore, several clearing corporations, at the writing of this book, have merged. Government Security Clearing Corporation (GSCC) and Mortgage Backed Securities Clearing Corporation (MBSCC) merged to form Fixed Income Clearing Corporation (FICC).

IV-F-3 Workings of the Clearing Corporation

The main purpose of a clearing corporation is, and always has been, to expedite the street side settlement function. This is accomplished by various means. Once upon a time, and not that long ago, the clearing corporations would perform comparison. That is, brokerage firms would submit trade data to the clearing corporation, giving their details of the street side part of their transactions. They would give complete trade details as well as the name of the contra broker/dealer that they traded with. The trade details included trade date, quantity, security, price, first money, and the nomenclature of the contra broker. Both firms were required to submit details to the clearing corporation before it would do a match, or comparison, and then produce reports, which were sent back to the submitting broker/dealers. These reports revealed which of the broker/dealer's submitted trade data had compared with the contra broker's and which had not. This system worked well while we were in a T+5 (trade date plus 5) business day environment. As the time between trade date and settlement date shrank, better systems were needed to accommodate this function.

First of all, if one were to stand back and look at the way we used to do comparison, we would find it kind of comical. The trade would occur at an exchange or an over-the-counter trading desk. Later that afternoon, an individual who had absolutely nothing to do with the trade, working in a different department, would read either the floor report (that's what the paper report coming from the exchange was called) or the trader's handwriting, and from this scribble a comparison form was prepared. That comparison form was sent to the contra firm. Therefore, a person who had nothing to do directly with the trade was responsible for developing the comparison agreements.

Later, systems were introduced that would automate some of that. First was the electronic data input from the respective broker/dealers to the clearing corporation. No longer were individual trade comparison notices the mainstay of this process. The clearing corporations, like National Securities Clearing Corporation, would take this input and prepare contract sheets. The contract sheets would show which trades were compared, which trades were uncompared, and which trades were what were called advisories (*advisories* (trades that are submitted against the broker/dealer receiving the contract sheet by a contra broker/dealer). The problem that the individual preparing the data for the clearing corporation had absolutely nothing to do with the actual trade still persisted.

As technology advanced and more responsive systems such as order match were introduced throughout the industry, this problem dissipated. Under the order match system, as stated earlier in this book, the report is locked to the trade and therefore all details, both street side and customer side, become one unit. The street side of the trade could now be electronically submitted to the clearing corporation for comparison. The individual in another department who had nothing to do with the trade was eliminated.

However, there still existed a time lag between when the trade occurred and when comparison was attempted. Over time the industry has tried to push the process back to where the names of the contra parties to the trade and the terms of the trade were captured at the point of execution. This would make sense, since the parties making the transaction know exactly what to place. One of the first attempts at accomplishing this was the New York Stock Exchange's Designated Order Turnaround (DOT) system. Under this system, specialists monitor omnibus accounts, which offset the broker/dealers' trades. Therefore, Stone, Forrest & Rivers entering an order on the DOT system would receive an execution against one of these omnibus accounts. The actual firm that it traded with would also receive an execution, but against another omnibus account. At the end of the day, the specialists would balance the two omnibus accounts. This process was called a *locked-in trade* and (unless there was a price discrepancy in the omnibus account over a certain amount set in the exchange rules), the trade stood. These locked-in trades were then forwarded to NSCC for comparison.

NASDAQ came out with their version, under which, based on some hierarchy, trades would be submitted to a system called Automated Confirmed Transaction (ACT). Only those trades that were compared in ACT would be forwarded to the clearing corporation for later processing. The hierarchy for trade submission is:

> If both sides of the trade are dealers, the sell side submits trade details to ACT.
>
> If both sides of the trade are brokers, the sell side submits trade details to ACT.
>
> If one side of the trade is a dealer and the other side is a broker, the dealer submits trade details to ACT.

The reporting side has 45 seconds to submit the trade details. The nonreporting side must accept or *DK (don't know)* the trade promptly thereafter.

The NASDAQ Small Order Execution System (SOES) is a trading system that locks the trade in at the time of execution. Market makers or dealers submit their quotes to NASDAQ. Orders entering the system are routed to the best bid, or best offer, at the time and executed. The system captures the order, the firm entering the order, the execution, and the dealer who is trading. Then comparison occurs.

IV-F-3-a *National Securities Clearing Corporation*

National Securities Clearing Corporation (NSCC), a division of Depository Trust and Clearing Corporation (DTCC), is responsible for expediting settlement on all New York Stock Exchange, American Stock Exchange, and NASDAQ equity transactions. They also perform the same process for corporate bonds and notes and municipal debt. Today almost 100% of all equity trades being submitted to NSCC are already compared. This process has taken place either at the point of execution or shortly thereafter. The individuals responsible for the transaction are also responsible for the comparison process. NSCC accepts this data in electronic format and produces contract reports. These reports are in electronic form also. As of the writing of this book, it has been proposed that these comparison reports be produced on a multibatch basis. In other words, instead of the reports being produced overnight in a batch mode, they would be produced during the course of the day in a smaller batch mode and transmitted to the respective broker/dealers during the course of the day.

Stone, Forrest & Rivers receives the current version of the contracts, which is received at the workstation in the trade processing section. The information contained therein includes Stone, Forrest & Rivers' clearing number and its full name, the trade date, the settlement date, and the unique number that is assigned to that particular trade by NSCC. Also included are the security's unique CUSIP number as well as the terms of the trade and the name or symbol of the contra firm. These reports are received during the course of the day. Let's step back for a second and verify where we are. There are four types of trades that Stone, Forrest & Rivers processes: principal transactions, market maker trades, agency transactions, and principal transactions (modified).

IV-F-3-a-i Principal Transactions

In a principal transaction, the customer's order is executed against the firm's trading account. Since these transactions are contained internally within Stone, Forrest & Rivers, there isn't any need to send details to the clearing corporation for further processing. The entire process will be handled within SF&R.

IV-F-3-a-ii Market-Maker Trades

A variation of a principal trade takes place when the firm's traders are market makers or dealers, and they trade not only with the firm's customers but with other nonmarket-making firms in those particular securities. These are *market maker trades*. The firms are buying or selling securities against Stone, Forrest & Rivers' trading accounts, either for themselves or for their customers. As these transactions involve two broker/dealers, these transactions will be submitted to the clearing corporation for further processing.

NATIONAL SECURITIES CLEARING CORPORATION OTC S A L E CONTRACT - TRADE DATE T

MEMBER NO X035 MEMBER NAME STONE RIVERS AND FORREST CORORATION TRADE DATE 02/16/20XX SETTLEMENT DATE 02/22/20XX

NON NP/ CNS SP	QUANTITY	CONTRACT MONEY	SELL EXEC	MATCH IND	PRICE	BUYER	BUY EXEC	TRADE SRCE	TRADE ORG	REF NUM	BRANCH ID-SEQ	EXEC TIME	BA/ST IND	RV IND	CAP CDE
APD - AIR PROD&CHEM INC															
009158 10 6															
	100	6,345.00	SFR	M1	63.450000	CONTRA BROKER ID AND CLEARING NUMBER		ACT		065BE9	BFEH-4299	13:57			A
TOTAL	200	12,692.00													
APH - AMPHENOL CORP (NEW) CL-A															
032095 10 1															
	100	5,000.00	SFR	M1	50.000000			ACT		04DA50	BFAD-8299	12:29			A
APN - APPLICA INC															
03815A 10 6															
	1,000	1,340.00	SFR	M1	1.340000	XX590	GRC	ACT		046B6E	BEJA-8499	12:05			A
	100	132.00	SFR	M1	1.320000	XY325	KK	ACT		069BB7	BFFB-8599	14:09			A
TOTAL	1,100	1,472.00				ETC.									
ARG - AIRGAS INC															
009363 10 2															
	200	7,314.00	SFR	M1	36.570000			ACT		017F5A	BEAG-2599	10:02			A
	200	7,314.00		M1	36.570000			ACT		017F43	BEAG-2799	10:02			A
	100	3,642.00		M1	36.420000			ACT		0964A6	BGAF-5099	15:57			A
	700	25,480.00		M1	36.400000			ACT		03E4C0	BEHG-2699	11:39			A
	100	3,640.00		M1	36.400000			ACT		0864FE	BFJB-8599	15:31			A
	100	3,640.00		M1	36.400000			ACT		08B20B	BFJG-9099	15:40			A
	100	3,640.00		M1	36.400000			ACT		08B1F6	BFJG-9399	15:40			A
	100	3,640.00		M1	36.400000			ACT		08CD94	BFJI-5899	15:43			A
	100	3,640.00		M1	36.400000			ACT		08CD51	BFJI-6099	15:43			A
	100	3,640.00		M1	36.400000			ACT		05EDE2	BFDC-8699	13:34			A
	400	14,556.00		M1	36.390000			ACT		03E28F	BEHG-9799	11:40			A
	100	3,639.00		M1	36.390000			ACT		04343B	BEIF-5999	11:56			A
TOTAL	2,300	83,785.00													
ARJ - ARCH CHEMICALS INC.															
03937R 10 2															
	100	2,910.00	SFR	M1	29.100000			ACT		035F35	BEGD-4199	11:18			A
	100	2,903.00		M1	29.030000			ACT		05FA95	BFDE-4399	13:37			A
TOTAL	200	5,813.00													
ASF - ADMINISTAFF INC															
007094 10 5															
	200	9,546.00		M1	47.730000			ACT		027FA1	BEDG-9699	10:40			A
AT - ALLTEL CORP															
020039 10 3															
	500	31,875.00		M1	63.750000			ACT		069CD1	BFFB-8999	14:09			A

IV-F-3-a-iii Agency Transactions

In an agency transaction, Stone, Forrest & Rivers acts as a broker or agent. The firm itself buys or sells securities for its customers against another firm and charges the client a commission for the service. In this case, the firm must compare the transaction with the opposing or contra firm to ensure that all of the details of the transactions are known and agreed to.

IV-F-3-a-iv Principal Transactions (Modified)

The fourth type of transaction is one in which the firm buys securities from a market maker, passes them through its own trading account, marks it up as a principal transaction, and sells it to the client. Or in the case where the client is selling, the client will sell it to the trading account and then the trading account will turn around and sell it to a market maker. The firm is holding the stock for a matter of seconds before it is released from its trading account in either direction. As the firm is holding the position in its trading account, even though it's for a very short period of time, it will act as a principal and charge a markup. This type of trade is usually conducted where the firm is selling a debt instrument on a yield basis.

- When Stone, Forrest & Rivers quotes a bond yield to the client, that bond yield is based on the amount of money the client will pay for the purchase of the bonds or other debt instrument or the proceeds received for a sale of same. If the firm acted on a purely agency basis and charged commission, then the amount of money that the yield is based on would be the bond's first money and the commission would be added afterwards. Therefore, the client would not be receiving the actual yield that was discussed. By taking the transaction through the trading account, even though it's a very short period of time, the money that the customer is paying, first money and the net money, are the same and therefore that is the yield that the customer would receive.

- In addition, in some cases where Stone, Forrest & Rivers is an active market maker, it may have a policy that in that particular type of security or in a particular marketplace, all the transactions, whether or not it is a market maker in that particular security, will be done on a principal basis. This is done to avoid confusion with the client receiving trades that are done on a principal basis and then later receiving trades that are on an agency basis. This is strictly a sales/marketing/public relations tool. For example, traders make markets in securities when those securities are actively traded or there is a general interest in those securities. Each firm that's a market maker sets its own standards as to which securities would be acceptable for making markets. This has nothing to do with the value of the securities or the financial situation of the corporation. It has to do with the ability of the traders to stay within the framework of the broker/dealers' culture, and make a profit trading securities.

- Let's suppose Jerry Riggs, a client of Stone, Forrest & Rivers, buys 1,000 shares of Focus Tech Incorporated at $37 a share. During this period of time one of SF&R's traders is making a market in this security. Over time, the security becomes less actively traded, causing the trader to widen the spread between bid and offer (the more interest there is in a security, the tighter the spread; the less interest, the wider the spread). As the market changes and as the traders look for opportunities in which to make markets, the SF&R trader decides to stop making markets in Focus Tech and make markets in some other security. Later, SF&R's client Jerry decides to sell the stock. As Stone, Forrest & Rivers is no longer a market maker in Focus Tech, they will be buying from and selling stock to other market makers for SF&R clients and will act on an agency basis. Therefore, when Jerry bought the stock, since the firm was a principal, the markup was included in the first money (shares × price including markup) that Jerry paid. When Jerry sells the stock, since the firm is now acting as an agent, it will charge a commission.

- When Jerry gets the second confirm, the sell confirm, he notices that there is commission charged, whereas when the security was purchased, there was no commission charged. He queries his stockbroker. As the stockbroker explains what took place, Jerry wants to know this: when the market maker got out of Focus, why did the firm take him "out of Focus." The fact that the firm decided to stop market making in Focus Tech has nothing to do with the value of the security or anything that concerns Jerry and Jerry's account. It was a business decision. It could be as simple as the trader who was making a market in Focus has left Stone, Forrest & Rivers to go to another firm, and the trader that replaced him was not interested in trading Focus. This happens from time to time.

- Therefore, to avoid confusion with Jerry and to alleviate the possibility that he'll start to look at SF&R with a jaundiced eye, the firm has a policy of charging principal on these types of transactions. So, when Jerry bought the stock, he was charged a markup; later, when he sold the stock, he was charged a markdown. On neither confirm does the word *commission* or *agency* exist. While Jerry has received the same proceeds moneywise as he would have with an agency trade, the question, "Why commission on the sell side?" is never asked.

Of the four types of trades we discussed, three will be sent to the clearing corporation for final resolution. They are (1) the agency transaction, where Stone, Forrest & Rivers acted as a conduit between the client and the contra firm; (2) where Stone, Forrest & Rivers is a market maker and another broker/dealer trades against it; and (3) where Stone, Forrest & Rivers buys the security or sells the security for a client against another firm but "runs" it through its trading account so that it can act as a principal on the transaction.

IV-F-3-b *Equity Transaction Comparison*

IV-F-3-b-i What Is Being Compared?

Example: Stone, Forrest & Rivers purchases 100 shares of RAM at $46 from Chuck, Spear & Dukk (CSD). Since this is an agency transaction, SF&R's client, Al Luminum, will pay $4,600 plus commission. Because commission rates are not set by the industry, each firm maintains its own commission schedule. Against this commission schedule, clients can negotiate a commission rate. SF&R charges Al $75 for this transaction. The total cost to the client is $4,675. The commission charged is SF&R's income, or revenue. The $4,600 (100 shares × $46) is what SF&R owes the contra firm, CSD. Here's what comparison between SF&R and CSD involves:

1. SF&R bought 100 RAM @ $46 for $4,600 from CSD.
2. CSD sold 100 RAM shares @ $46 for $4,600 to SF&R.

All details of the trade must agree. Whether Chuck, Spear & Dukk has sold the securities for their client or for their own proprietary account is their business and does not concern SF&R.

IV-F-3-b-ii Types of Comparison

Comparison can occur in many ways. The procedures are usually set by the nature of the product and the marketplace in which it trades. It can range from a manual exchange of comparison notices on a trade-for-trade basis to an online real time computerized comparison that locks in the details of the trade at the point of execution.

Trade for trade. Some products, because of their comparatively low trading volume or substantial size or customization of terms, may compare on a trade-for-trade basis. This means that each transaction is compared between buying and selling firms on a trade-for-trade or item-for-item basis. Each transaction is compared individually.

In this method, buyer and seller exchange trade detail notices. After reviewing the trade notices, the contra party determines whether it agrees with the terms as they are presented. If so, the contra broker acknowledges the confirmation and returns it to the originator.

If the contra broker does not agree with the terms of the trade, a DK, signifying *don't know,* is reported back to the submitting firm. The phrase *DK* is the official notice that the contra firm does not agree to the terms of the transaction. Upon receipt of the DK notice, the trade-processing specialist will take the terms of the trade that they possess back to the trader who entered into the agreement to get the dispute resolved.

The reason for the DK is manifold. The trader may have copied the wrong contra party's name. The contra party may have forgotten to process the transaction. There may have been confusion over the security traded and/or the price. Or the trader may have thought a trade occurred when it really hadn't. Whatever the reason, the discrepancy must be resolved for the transaction to complete the settlement cycle.

Systematized comparison. In *systematized comparison*, trade data that has been compared by the marketplace where the trade occurred is submitted to the clearing corporation. We will look at National Security Clearing Corporation (NSCC) first. Those trades that were consummated on the New York Stock Exchange or on the AMEX via the exchange's electronic order routing and reporting mechanisms are called locked-in trades. The New York Stock Exchange's DOT (AKA Super DOT) trades mentioned earlier in the book are locked in at the point of execution. Non-DOT trades are entered into NYSE's Online Comparison System (OCS) by the executing broker/dealers during the trading day and compared before being sent to NSCC. AMEX and other exchanges have their own systems for reporting compared trades to NSCC. Another source of trades sent to NSCC is the over-the-counter environment, including NASDAQ. These trades have been compared through NASDAQ's various comparison systems, the primary one being Automated Confirmed Transaction (ACT). Under this system, if both broker/dealers are dealers, the selling dealer reports the trade; if both are acting as brokers, the selling broker reports the trade; and if one side is acting as a dealer and the other side is a broker, the dealer reports the trade to ACT regardless which firm bought or sold. The reporting firm has 45 seconds to "print" the trade. The contra party has 20 minutes to affirm or DK the trade. NASDAQ's Small Order Execution Systems (SOES) automatically compares the trade at the point of execution so that it bypasses ACT. The third source is known as two-sided input. For whatever reason, these trades were not processed through the aforementioned methods, and the buying firm and selling firm must submit trade data. In this case, National Security Clearing Corporation does the actual comparison. Three results could occur from the latter method. One, the submitter and contra side agree. Two, the contra party does not agree with the submitter. Or, three, the contra party transmits details of a transaction that the submitter does not know. (Remember, we are considering one firm's contract sheets.)

IV-F-3-c *Regular Way Contract*

Stone, Forrest & Rivers is a participant at National Security Clearing Corporation. Therefore, it is known as a clearing firm. Each business day, their trade data is submitted to the clearing corporation using the aforementioned processes. NSCC accepts this data and runs a series of programs, which result in the publishing of a computer-generated report, which is distributed to the member firms. Stone, Forrest & Rivers, as one of these clearing member firms, receives its results on a report called a *Contract Sheet*. The contract sheet contains the following trade information:

1. *Compared*. SF&R's trade detail equals a contra broker's: SF&R = contra side.
2. *Uncompared*. SF&R's submission of details does not match what the contra firm thinks occurred: SF&R≠contra side.
3. *Advisory* (AKA *adjustment*). Opposing firm has submitted trade data that SF&R does not know or does not agree with: contra≠SF&R.

Examples: Trades that SF&R and the contra firm agree with are called *compared*.

SF&R bought 1,000 shares of POW @ $86 per share from GRC.

GRC sold 1,000 shares of POW @ $86 per share to SF&R.

A trade that SF&R believes to be a valid trade, but that the contra party does not agree with, is referred to as *uncompared*.

SF&R bought 1,000 shares of POW @ $86 per share from GRC.

GRC sold 0.

A trade submitted against SF&R by a contra broker that SF&R doesn't agree with is referred to as an *advisory* or *adjustment.*

SF&R bought 0.

GRC sold 1,000 POW @ $86 to SF&R.

Another variation of an *uncompared* or *advisory* situation would exist if:

SF&R bought 1,000 POW @ $86.10 from GRC.

GRC sold 1,000 POW @ $86.20 to SF&R.

In this case, SF&R's version of the trade would be *uncompared*; Giant Reckor & Crane's version of the trade would be an *advisory* on SF&R's contract sheet. It would be a mirror image (opposite) on GRC's contract sheet.

While the number of trades entering NSCC that are not previously compared or matched is diminishing every year, problems still exist. To maintain control and sanity, NSCC does not permit its submitting clearing firms to alter or change their submissions once those submissions have been made. However, the contra party named in this submission has the ability to accept the proposed trade. By this method, SF&R and the contra party can research trade differences. SF&R will verify its uncompared trades against its advisory transactions and, where the contra broker/dealer's version may be correct, accept that version. If this situation exists, SF&R will submit an acceptance notice to the clearing corporation. A copy of that notice is also sent to the contra firm. Other trades appearing in the adjustment column will be checked against unexecuted orders at Stone, Forrest & Rivers to make sure that a transaction has not been overlooked.

The contra firms perform the same function. Trades that SF&R has submitted and that the contra firms originally did not agree with but now do, will be accepted by the contra party. They will submit to the clearing corporation acceptance notices with copies going to SF&R.

Trades that SF&R believes are valid trades, but for some reason cannot get the contra to agree to, are returned to the point of execution for reconcilement between the executing parties. The broker who executed the trade on the floor of an exchange or the trader who was involved with the transaction from an upstairs trading desk and reported the execution must contact the contra party to resolve the discrepancy. Again, we are not talking about transactions that have been compared through electronic processes such as DOT and ACT. Those transactions, should there have been a problem at that point in the process, would have been resolved immediately. The traders trading equity securities on the NASDAQ system would have had a set period of time to acknowledge the transaction as a good transaction under the ACT rules. If the trade was not submitted by the party whose responsibility it was to submit the trade, then the contra side would have queried almost immediately. If the contra side did not acknowledge the trade from the submitter, than the submitter would have queried the contra side. So when those transactions done through ACT, DOT, and other electronic comparison systems that are maintained at the point of execution leave those facilities, they are for all intents and purposes compared.

The process of having the contracting parties resolve discrepancies has different names in different marketplaces. As we are focusing on National Security Clearing Corporation, those trades executed on the New York Stock Exchange that do not compare are returned to the floor broker or its designee, and are known as *question trades (QTs)*. The same process on the AMEX exchange is called a DK as it is for NASDAQ securities. On the CBOE, these are called *rejected option trade notices (ROTNs)*. And in the future, market by rejected trade notice. Regardless of the outcome, the client's order that was entitled to an execution must be executed regardless of the cause of the discrepancy. Should a trade not have actually occurred but the client was entitled to an execution, the broker/dealer must "cover the mistake" and execute the transaction on behalf of the client. The client is entitled to receive the original execution price or the cover price, whichever is better.

The reports from NSCC to SF&R are transmitted electronically. They appear on the trade processing staff's workstation. All communication between SF& R's trade processing personnel and NSCC's clearing personnel is conducted electronically.

IV-F-3-d *Trade Reporting and Compliance Engine (TRACE) Comparison*

Exchange- and NASD-eligible investment-grade corporate bonds are reported to NASDAQ's TRACE system. Participants have 45 minutes to report the bond trades to TRACE. Trades that have been compared in TRACE are reported to the NSCC's comparison system.

IV-F-4 Netting

At the end of the comparison process, the function of netting begins. The purpose of netting is to minimize the number of interfirm receives and deliveries that must take place. As all the trades at this point are compared, the only difference between the various trades are the prices at which they were executed. The function that neutralizes that difference is called the Clearing Cash Adjustment (CCA).

The following transactions occurred between these broker/dealers, operating for their clients, on Monday, May 25.

1. Stone, Forrest & Rivers (SF&R) bought 100 shares of RAM @ $27 per share from Overland & Underwater [OU].
2. Giant Reckor & Crane (GRC) sold 100 shares of RAM @ $28 per share to Moore Orless and bought 100 shares of RAM @ $29 per share from Chuck Spear & Dukk (CSD).
3. Knight and Knune (KK) sold 100 shares of RAM @ $29 per share to Overland & Underwater (OU) and bought 100 shares of RAM @ $27 per share from Moore Orless (MO).

There is a total of 5 trades.

Example

Broker/Dealer

Buy Side	Price	Sell Side

SF&R

100	27	

GRC

	28	100
100	29	

OU

100	29	
	27	100

CSD

	29	100

KK

	29	100
100	27	

MO

	27	100
100	28	

Let us assume the last price of the day was $28 p.s. and NSCC is using this as a settlement price to homogenize the differences. By removing the price differences, all the trades become the same. Note that NSCC is not changing the contract price at which the transactions took place.

Commission and taxes are omitted in the following:

1. SF&R's client is going to pay $2,700 for the stock. NSCC is telling SF&R to pay $2,800 (the settlement price) for the purchase. NSCC gives $100 to SF&R to make up the shortage.
2. The GRC client that bought RAM is going to pay $100 more than the client who sold the stock is expecting from the proceeds of sale. NSCC charges (takes it away) and tells the firm to use the seller's stock to satisfy their client that purchased RAM.
3. The OU client that bought RAM is paying $200 more than the selling client is expecting from their sale. NSCC takes the $200 away and tells the firm to use the seller's stock to take care of the buyer.
4. CSD has a client who sold $2,900 worth of stock. When CSD makes delivery, they only receive the settlement price of $28 p.s. ($2,800). NSCC gives the firm $100 to make up the shortage.
5. KK has a client who sold stock for $200 more than the client that purchased it paid. NSCC gives the $200 to KK and tell them to use the seller's stock to satisfy the purchase.
6. MO's purchasing client is paying $100 more than their seller is due to receive from their sale. NSCC has charged them and they can use the seller's stock to satisfy the purchase.

In this example, five buys and five sells are reduced to one receive and one deliver; SF&R is to receive 100 shares of RAM at the adjusted price of $28 from CSD.

Imagine the impact on several hundred clearing firms and several thousand trades of RAM a day.

SF&R		
100	27	
+$100		

GRC		
	28	100
100	29	
−$100		

OU		
100	29	
	27	100
−$200		

CSD		
	29	100
+$100		

KK		
	29	100
100	27	

+$200

MO		
	27	100
100	28	

−$100

Settlement price: $28 per share.

At the end of the netting process SFR is to receive 100 shares of RAM at the adjusted price of $28 from CSD, and the money adjustments become part of the total settlement money of each firm that day:

SF&R		
	30	100

MO		
100	30	

If CSD delivers the stock to SF&R on settlement date, SF&R will pay $2,800 and the trade is settled. If, however, CSD cannot deliver the stock, SF&R will have a *fail to receive* on their books from CSD, and CSD will have a *fail to deliver* against SF&R on their books. (Note: Anytime a trade doesn't settle at the contracted time (settlement date) it becomes a "fail" item.)

IV-F-5 Continuous Net Settlement (CNS)

Before the industry employed continuous net settlement, fails would remain open until they were cleaned up (the security was delivered to the buying broker/dealer, who in turn paid the settlement price). It would be possible for SF&R to have a fail to receive open against CSD one day and have a fail to deliver against CSD for the same stock on another day. The open fail items grew to an alarming amount and were one of the main contributors to the "paper crisis" of the late 1960s. Something had to be done. The certificate had to be immobilized and settlement had to be performed by electronic, not physical, movement of securities. And that was the beginning of the Depository Trust Company (DTC) division of DTCC.

Prior to Depository Trust Company, NSCC or its predecessors, such as Stock Clearing Corporation (SCC), would issue balance orders instructing the firms which firms they owed stock to or which firms owed stock to them. Once the balance orders were issued, only the firms involved in that particular set of balance orders knew which trades settled and which trades failed. Therefore, the fail problem grew. With DTC in place, NSCC could instruct DTC which firms owed stock and which firms were owed stock. Those firms that couldn't make delivery would create a set fails. Those fails would reside on NSCC's stock record as open items and, for the first time, the industry knew what was happening.

With this new entity and the control it gave to the industry, it was decided that fails prices should be updated (marked to the market) daily by the settlement price used by NSCC. Once this was done, it became apparent that a fail to receive had the same structure as a new buy trade, and a fail to deliver had the same qualities as a new sell trade. Why not roll the open fails into the next day's settling trades and the new positions through the netting process? This concept is called *continuous net settlement*. Under this concept a broker/dealer can only have one position per security. Either the firm will have a fail to receive, or a fail to deliver, or they are flat (have no fail position open).

In the above example, let's assume SF&R had a fail to receive against CSD. The next day's trading activity revealed the following:

SF&R		
	29	100
	−$100	

GRC		
		28
100	30	
	−$200	

OU		
	100	29
	27	100
	−$200	

CSD		
	100	27
	30	100
	+$300	

KK		
	29	100
100	29	
	+$0	

MO		
100	28	
	−$200	

Settlement price: $30 per share.

As a result the security settlement positions are:

SF&R

100	28	

CSD

	28	100

At the end of this day SF&R would have a fail to deliver at 30 against MO if delivery was not made.

SFR's fail record would reflect:

> Fail to receive of 100 shares at $28, settlement date May 28 against CSD
>
> Fail to deliver of 100 shares at $30, settlement date, May 29 against MO

If the fails from May 28 were rolled into the May 29 settlement date, the following would happen:

SF&R

	29	100
100	***28***	

+$100

GRC

	28	100
100	30	

–$200

OU

100	29	
	27	100

–$200

CSD

100	27	
	30	100
	28	***100***

+$100

KK

	29	100
100	29	

+$0

MO

100	28	

+$200

Settlement price: $30 per share.

* Previous day's fails are ***italicized in bold.***

SF&R would net out securitywise and CED would have an updated fail against MO. This rolling of the previous day's fails into today's settlement accomplishes two desired goals. One, it reduces the number of open items that could be outstanding at one time. And two, it updates market value of open items to reflect the current market value while charging or crediting the open fail position firms' mark to market.

Note: As the fail positions are updated pricewise every day, they are refferred to as open trades for regulatory reasons.

IV-G *BALANCING OF THE CUSTOMER SIDE*

As most of the transactions executed on the exchanges and/or the over-the-counter market are compared at the point of execution, and as firms like SF&R have automatic systems that lock the execution report to the customer's side of the trade, the need to verify what SF&R's record shows as to the customer side versus the street side has been eliminated as has the need to verify what SF&R's internal records show as street side versus what NSCC shows as street side. This may be confusing, but remember we are looking at different processing streams. The following may clarify any confusion:

One, the customer has entered an order. That order has specific information on it: what the customer wanted to do (buy or sell securities, the name of the security, customer's account number, customer's name, etc.). That trade was executed in a marketplace. That execution formed the second set of data. SF&R's personnel used to verify the client's side of the trade (the first data stream) against the trade execution information that SF&R sent to NSCC (the second data stream). This checkout was to ensure that both data streams had the same information. The firm that SF&R traded with had their version of the transaction that they submitted to NSCC. This is the third data stream. An SF&R employee would have to verify that the data SF&R submitted to NSCC agreed with the data the contra side was submitting. The broker/dealers used to have a staff that would verify what one firm's records revealed as the customer side versus what the other firm's records revealed as the street side. That was the first checkout (pairing off). The second pairing off would be what SF&R's

street side reveals versus what the clearing corporation representing the contra firm shows took place. SF&R's order match system has negated the first match, and the comparison mechanisms of the marketplace in which the trade took place eliminated the second match. SF&R now has one unified record, it has a customer, it has a street side, and it has the street side's version of the same transaction, all in agreement. The trade processing staff works on exception basis. Other than those exceptions, the SF&R trade specialist in the trade processing section does not do any "manual" checkouts. They do verify, by the way, that the totals agree. It is estimated that over 99% of the trades will go through the processing streams, both at the clearing corporation and at the broker/dealers, without human intervention.

IV-H *FIXED-INCOME CLEARING CORPORATION*

The Fixed Income Clearing Corporation was formed when Mortgage Backed Securities Clearing Corporation (MBSCC) and Government Securities Clearing Corporation (GSCC) merged. MBSCC primarily compares TBA transactions whereas GSCC compares transactions in U.S. Treasury, Government National Mortgage Association (GNMA), Federal Home Loan Mortgage Corporation (FHLMC), Federal National Mortgage Association (FNMA) securities, and other agencies.

IV-H-1 Forwards and TBAs

As stated earlier, the aforementioned securities are brought to market before the actual instruments are fully in force. In the case of GNMA, mortgages have been approved for the homebuyers but are not in force as the home building has not been completed. As the mortgage lender does not want to experience interest risk, they sell an interim instrument to mortgage-backed securities traders. This product is known as a TBA (to be announced). At the appropriate time, the mortgage banker takes the approved and now in force mortgages to the government agencies, which assign a unique number to that pool of mortgages. The issue then trades as a debt instrument paying interest and principal on a regular basis. The time difference between when the TBA is first brought to market and when the actual security is issued can be between three and six months, during which time the product trades in the TBA state.

Due to the rapid growth of securitized mortgages issued by GNMA (Ginnie Mae), FHLMC (Freddie Mac), and FNMA (Fannie Mae), and because these instruments settle once a month, controls had to be put in place to even out the delivery cycles. The delivery cycle process is determined by the Bond Market Association (BMA). A schedule is produced showing which instruments settle on what day of the month. (Note: See Notification and Settlement Dates example, below). The instruments we are referring to are TBA or when-issued trades. MBSCC performs a comparison of these instruments, which is accomplished on a trade-for-trade basis.

Notification and Settlement Dates

Class A 30 Year	**Class B 15 Year**	**Class C 30 Year**	**Class D Balloons**
Freddie Mac Fannie Mae	Freddie Mac Fannie Mae Ginnie Mae	Ginnie Mae	Freddie Mac Fannie Mae All ARMs/VRMs/ Multifamily/GPMs/ Mobile Homes Ginnie Mae
December 20XX			
Notification Date			
Friday 9	Tuesday 13	Thursday 15	Tuesday 20
Settlement Date			
Tuesday 13	Thursday 15	Monday 19	Thursday 22
January 20XX			
Notification Date			
Tuesday 10	Friday 13	Thursday 19	Friday 20
Settlement Date			
Thursday 12	Wednesday 18	Monday 23	Tuesday 24

February 20XX

Notification Date

Thursday 9	Tuesday 14	Thursday 16	Friday 17

Settlement Date

Monday 13	Thursday 16	Tuesday 21	Wednesday 22

March 20XX

Notification Date

Thursday 9	Tuesday 14	Friday 17	Monday 20

Settlement Date

Monday 13	Thursday 16	Tuesday 21	Wednesday 22

April 20XX

Notification Date

Monday 10	Thursday 13	Tuesday 18	Thursday 20

Settlement Date

Wednesday 12	Tuesday 18	Thursday 20	Monday 24

May 20XX

Notification Date

Tuesday 9	Friday 12	Tuesday 16	Friday 19

Settlement Date

Thursday 11	Tuesday 16	Thursday 18	Tuesday 23

When a customer buys a TBA of GNMA or other mortgaged-backed issuers, he receives a confirmation without money. A TBA transaction will settle at a later date, when the mortgages involved in that TBA are alive and the homeowners are paying their monthly mortgage bills. If the customer closes out or sells the position while the instrument is still in TBA form, the trade processing system will produce another confirmation without money and the profit or loss is settled when the TBA becomes *regular way*. Any customer still maintaining a position when the TBA goes regular way receives a cancel (CXL) confirmation for the TBA and a regular-way confirmation containing pools of mortgages to be delivered or received as well as the complete figuration necessary to settle the transaction on the actual settlement date.

Mortgage-backed securities are traded as regular pools or forwards. Regular pool transactions involve the exchange of established pools, forwards, which also include TBAs, and are traded in "out months" at the time of the transaction. The term *out months* refers to when the mortgages contained in the pool are to be alive. For example, SF&R's client Woodrow Holmes enters into an interest rate position when he buys $5,000,000 worth of GNMA 6% TBA. The TBAs are due to settle in six months. Woody has no intention of taking delivery of the actual pool of mortgages, so after five months he sells the position. The changes in interest rates from the time Woody took on the position to the time he closed it out will determine whether there is a profit or loss on the transaction. If there is a loss, most firms, like SF&R, would ask Woody to deposit the loss immediately. If there is a profit, Woody would have to wait until the actual TBA settles. This might seem unfair, but since Woody is an individual and not an institution, the firm is at risk that Woody could easily disappear in the case of a loss, though they know that Woody will still be around in the case of a profit. Therefore, they employ this process. This process of collecting losses when the position is closed out is often hidden in the margin requirement that Woody, being an individual, must deposit. SF&R reviews every account that does this type of business to determine whether margin is applicable. These products are not covered by Regulation T of the Federal Reserve.

IV-H-2 Mortgage-Backed Security Division of Fixed Income Clearing Corporation

Forward or TBA interfirm transactions are processed through Fixed Income Clearing Corporation's MBSCC (Mortgage-Backed Security Clearing Corporation Division). MBSCC, or as it's known now, MBSD, carries each firm's positions by the issuer or guarantors, type of instrument, coupon rate, the delivery month of the forward or the TBA transaction. We will assume the following example: a GNMA passthrough with a 6% coupon settling in six months is a current forward trade.

Stone, Forrest & Rivers is a member of MBSD. Each day it submits its interfirm forward transactions to MBSD. Among the transactions are its GNMA 6% forward transactions due to settle in six months.

The transactions go through comparison with the other MBSD member firms. MBSD has two categories of members: those that use the facility for comparison only and those that use the facility for comparison and for settlement. The process used for comparison is called *Real Time Trade Match (RTTM)*. Both parties to the trade submit trade data to MBSCC, which in turn does a match and reports the results back to the submitting firms. Under this process, submitting firms know the results of the comparison immediately, thereby reducing risk and exposure. Once the trade is agreed to, the trades become part of each member firm's per issue *rolling balance.* SF&R, being a GNMA dealer, has many different positions running concurrently. In addition to its proprietary positions, it also maintains the position of its clients at MBSD. Each day its trades are added to or subtracted from the individual securities' balances and the money side is adjusted for the amount of each transaction. These rolling balances reflect the exposure each firm has to the industry. As these are forward transactions, the amount of money involved in the trade is not exchanged until final settlement.

Example: On day 1, SF&R bought $50,000,000 worth of GNMA 6% passthrough TBAs due to settle in six months. It also sold $30,000,000 worth of the same issue on that day. All transactions are compared and, therefore, SF&R's closing position is long $20,000,000 worth of GNMA 6% TBAs due for delivery in six months. On day 2, its transactions reflect a net purchase balance of $10,000,000 worth of GNMA 6% TBAs for the six-month settlement. Therefore, SF&R's balance is now long $30,000,000 worth of GNMA 6% TBA six months out. On day 3, SF&R bought $40,000,000 worth and sold $80,000,000 worth of GNMA 6% TBA due in six months for the net trading balance of short $40,000,000 GNMA 6%. When this trade balance is added to SF&R's rolling balance, what will be the new position?

Net Balance

Day 1: $20,000,000 long (bought $20,000,000 more than it sold that day)

Day 2: $30,000,000 long (bought $10,000,000 more than it sold that day)

Day 3: $10,000,000 short (sold $40,000,000 more than it bought that day)

Its new position is short $10,000,000 worth of GNMA 6% TBAs due for settlement in six months. The money balances are marked to the market every day, even if SF&R didn't trade that particular issue that day.

The process continues until the actual settlement date when MBSCC notifies the participants who have positions of their receive/delivery and monetary obligations.

As the trades have been netted interfirm and the results added or subtracted from the firm's position at MBSD, final settlement will most likely not occur with the same firms that were originally involved with the trade. Therefore, MBSD, which has maintained these rolling balances, will issue *settlement balance order (SBO)* instructions to its participants. As these are compared trades, each buy has a sell, and therefore, the resulting netting should leave a balanced position between firms that end up net buyers and those that end up net sellers. Settlement is at the Fed.

Settlement of passthrough securities is different than that of other issues. Passthrough issues pay interest and principal periodically. Also included in the principal paydown is prepayment of debts. When someone recalculates or refinances a home, the "old" mortgage is paid off by the "new" mortgage. This paying down of the old mortgage is known as a *prepayment.*

As the amount of principal in a pool is not constant, it is almost impossible to deliver the exact amount required by the transaction. Therefore, as of the writing of this chapter, the seller can deliver up to three pools per million dollars as long as they are over or under $1,000,000 by .01% and none of the three or fewer pools total the lower threshold of $999,900 (.01% of $1,000,000 = $100; $100,000,000 − $100 = $999,900). Because of the ability to mix and match pools, firms can maximize profits or minimize losses. For example, using a made-up standard product, the following trades occurred:

Bought	Sold	Profit
1,000,000 @ 96	1,000,000 @ 96⅛	$1,250,000
1,000,000 @ 96½	1,000,000 @ 96⅝	$1,250,000
1,000,000 @ 96¾	1,000,000 @ 96⅞	$1,250,000
	Total profit	$3,750,000

The passthrough securities received against each of the above purchases were:

@ 96	$1,000,095 principal
@ 96½	$ 999,995 principal
@ 96¾	$ 999,900 principal

IV-H-2-a *The Allocation*

By allocating the deliveries of highest principal in, to highest price out, we can maximize the profit:

Purchase side	*– Sale side*	*= Profit (loss)*
$1,000,095 principal × 96	vs. Sale 96⅞	
= $960,091.20	= $968,842.03	= $8,750.83
$999,995 principal @ 96½	vs. Sale 96⅝	
= $964,995.18	= $966,245.17	= $1,249.99
$999,000 principal @ 96¾	vs. Sale 96⅛	
= $966,532.50	= $960,288.75	= ($6,243.75)
	Total:	$3,757.07

By matching the highest principal amount received in against the highest price out, we were able to increase our profits from $3,750 to $3,757.07. The $7.07 extra profit may not appear to be worth the effort, but remember, it was only on three trades. What if the firm had 30,000 trades involved in the settlement process? Just multiply $7.07 by 10,000 and you get a very handsome return. This method of settlement is known as *allocation*.

IV-H-3 Government Security Division of Fixed Income Clearing Corporation (GSCC)

Like other clearing corporations, GSCC offers comparison and netting along with other services. The products that it handles are U.S. Treasury bonds, notes, bills, and strips, as well as book entry nonmortgage-backed agency securities (the regular debt of Freddie Mac and Fannie Mae discussed earlier in this chapter). It also handles repos and reverse repo transactions. The comparison system runs on a real time basis so that input into GSD is compared and the results are known almost immediately. SF&R has an opportunity to receive these results momentarily or at the end of the day. SF&R, because of its sophisticated systems, receives the information immediately, thereby minimizing risk of loss due to an erroneous transaction. In addition, as Stone, Forrest & Rivers is a government dealer, it participates in the auction of U.S. Treasury instruments. It uses GSD as a method of distribution and settling these transactions.

Like NSCC and OCC, GSD guarantees settlement of all transactions entered into its netting system. Like other clearing corporations, GSD places itself between buying firm and selling firm once the trades are agreed to. The only clearing corporation that we have discussed so far that does not offer this feature is Mortgage Backed Security Division (MBSD). Compared trades are netted down by type of instrument, coupon rate, maturity date, and settlement date. At the end of the process, GSD substitutes delivery and receive instructions in place of the netted balances. All securities, whether to or from GSD's clearing banks, are made against full payment over the Fedwire, or intrabank if the participants have accounts at GSD's clearing banks. All securities delivered into GSD's clearing banks are instantaneously redelivered to the participants that are due to receive the securities.

IV-I *OPTIONS*

IV-I-1 OTC Options Comparison

Over-the-counter options are custom made in a negotiation between the holder and the writer. As each one is different, they are highly illiquid and do not trade as listed options do. The contract generally remains between the buyer (holder) and the seller (writer). Comparison is accomplished by both parties exchanging comparison notices, detailing the terms of the option contract. There isn't any clearing corporation or other central party involved with the trade.

IV-I-2 Listed Option Comparison

SF&R trades options on behalf of their clients. The vast majority of these transactions are in listed options. Let's follow the listed option comparison process. (The comparison procedure for options is an intelligent and simple one.) Because listed options settle next day—that is, on the next business day—comparison takes place on trade date. All option transactions are sent to the comparison facility of the exchange of execution. Comparison takes place at these locations and not at a national clearing corporation.

As SF&R is a member of the Chicago Board Option Exchange, the firm executes its options transactions on the CBOE and sends the trades to the exchange's facility for comparison late in the afternoon of trade date. Each client side transaction must have a street side (an opposing broker), and those sides must agree to the terms of the trade. It's important that SF&R records reveal whom it traded with. More important is that the opposing firm agrees with the details of the trade.

The trade data submitted for comparison on behalf of SF&R consists of the following information:

1. Its unique clearing number.
2. The opposing firm's clearing number.
3. Whether SF&R bought or sold.
4. The terms of the trade:
   a. Option description, including the class of option and series.
   b. The quantity or number of contracts that were traded.
   c. The price of the option and/or first money.
5. Trade date and settlement date.
6. The identity of the principal behind the trade. Is it a client, is the firm trading for its own account, or is SF&R comparing this trade for a market maker or a specialist?
7. The effect this trade will have on SF&R's positions at OCC. Is it opening a position (in other words, creating a position), or is it closing out a previous open position?

For comparison, only the first five items are necessary. The opposing firm should be submitting the same details, except, of course, if SF&R bought, they should be saying they sold, but the rest of the data that they are providing should be the same as SF&R's. Items 6 and 7 are important in later processing.

Either the comparison system of the exchange on which the trade took place receives the data from the clearing firms or it is captured at the point of execution. Once the data is collected, the comparison is performed. Each clearing firm then receives a report showing which trades compare and which do not.

SF&R receives these reports in the early evening of trade date. The results are verified against their internal records. As SF&R uses an automated system, their client side and their street side are one stream of data. What they are verifying is that the data about to be sent from the clearing facility of the option exchange in which the trades were executed to Option Clearing Corporation (OCC, which is responsible for the clearance and settlement of all exchange-traded options) agrees with their internal records. Any discrepancies that should appear in this checkout are reviewed immediately. SF&R and other option clearing firms are all doing the same checkout at the same time. They are trying to make as many corrections as possible so that the data going to OCC is as accurate as possible.

IV-I-2-a *ROTNs*

Any trade that SF&R still shows as a good trade, but whose terms the contra party has not agreed to, is sent back to the floor of execution. In the case of trades occurring on the Chicago Board Option Exchange, these are known as *rejected option trade notices (ROTNs)*. On the AMEX they are known as DKs (Don't Knows).

On the morning after trade date before the exchanges open, the various option exchanges go through a procedure by which discrepancies are identified and corrective action is set up to be taken once the market is open. For example, Stone, Forrest & Rivers knows of a trade that it did with Chuck, Spear & Dukk. Unfortunately, there has been a mix-up on the side of CSD and they have not agreed to the trade on trade date. Representatives of SF&R meet with representatives of CSD and reconcile the difference. In this particular case, Chuck, Spear & Dukk knows of the trade but just did not process it properly. Therefore, with the ROTN process the trade is rectified. However, SF&R has another trade that it believes it did with Knight & Knune. When their representatives meet, Knight & Knune checks its records and determines that they did not trade that day with SF&R. Apparently there was a mistake by the SF&R broker, who believed the trade had been consummated when it actually wasn't. SF&R now must make sure that the client is entitled to the trade and, if so, must go into the market on the next day and perform the transaction while holding the client harmless. In other words, if the price that the client should have received that trade date is better than the price SF&R receives when it makes the corrective trade on the day after trade date, an adjustment will be made to that trade so that it reflects the proper price the client should have received on trade date. On the other hand, if the corrective trade has the better price of the two, then that is the price the client will receive.

Once the trade processing system receives the corrected data from the floor personnel, it processes the trade. Some corrections affect the client transactions, while others affect the street side entries. Still others do not affect SF&R's books and records at all, because the opposing firm has to make the corrections.

Corrections being made against the client's positions are very expensive to process. The firm earns its income when the original trade is processed. Changes to the original trade necessitate the processing of a cancel and a rebill (two separate entries) for which no additional revenue is obtained. The two entries follow the same operating cycle as the original transaction, but the client only pays commission one time.

Option trades (and futures and forwards for that matter) have two cycles (lives). The first is the trade, which must be compared against the opposing firm. The second is the effect the trade has on an existing or assignable position. Remember that a holder, or owner, of an option has the privilege of exercising, whereas a writer, or seller, has the obligation to perform the terms of the contract, should the position be assigned.

This is different than the standard stock, or buy, transaction. A client buying a stock pays for it at the end of the transaction. A client selling a stock delivers it, unless it's in his account already, and that is the end of the transaction; there is no follow-through. However, with options and futures, the initial transaction is part of a process. In other words, a client buying a call option and settling that trade now has a period of time until expiration in which to exercise that option. So, as stated earlier in this chapter, the option and the future have two lives.

IV-I-3 Position Reconcilement

When a client or the firm's proprietary account buys an option, the purchase may be to establish a holder's position or to close out (trade out) of a previous written position. In a similar fashion, the seller of an option may be establishing a written position or closing out (that is, trading out of) a previous owner's, or holder's, position.

A buyer of an option who wants to establish a position (that is, be an owner) is said to be *buying open*. To unwind (that is, close out or trade out of the holder's position), the holder can exercise, or *sell closed* (sell to close). On the other side, where a position is established, a writer is said to be *selling open* (selling to open the position). To unwind, or close out, or get out of this written position, the writer can *buy close* (buying to close). A writer's position may also be terminated by OCC by assigning an exercise. Therefore, positions can be maintained by the following instructions being carried on the orders being entered.

Buy open	= Sell close, or exercise
Buy close, or assignment	= Sell open

or

Bo	= Sc, E
Bc, A	= So

Because all options expire, expiration is not included in the equation. All unexercised positions in an expired option series will be negated and the position will go "flat." Any option remaining in position after its expiration date has passed is virtually worthless, as the contract has expired.

The importance of the buy open–sell close regimen is how Stone, Forrest & Rivers, all of the other option clearing firms, and Option Clearing Corporation reconcile positions.

After trade comparison and position adjustments have occurred, all long (holders', buyers') positions are against Option Clearing Corporation, as are all sellers' (writers' or short) positions. In other words, after comparison Option Clearing Corporation stands between all holders and all writers. Exercises by holders of options are made against OCC, and OCC turns them around and makes assignment on a random basis to writers. This feature permits option users to go into and out of positions with ease, with the contra parties to the trade not caring. In the over-the-counter option market, the buyers and sellers stay locked; to trade out of a position usually means that both sides of the original trade must agree to the closeout. Or, if one side trades out of the position, that side is said to *go long and short*, since the original contra party is not obligated to accept the new contra party and therefore another option position is created.

Examples:

Listed option

1. Frei & Cook buys a call from Wellington & Co.
2. The trade compares.
3. Frei & Cook is a holder against OCC.
4. Wellington & Co. is a writer against OCC.

Frei & Cook sells the call to Bahl & Puck, which has no previous position.

1. The trade compares.
2. Bahl & Puck is a holder against OCC.
3. Wellington & Co. remains as a writer against OCC.
4. Frei & Cook is flat (i.e., has no position).

In the case of an over-the-counter option, which does not use the facility of a clearing corporation, the result would be different.

1. Frei & Cook buys a call from Wellington & Co.
2. The trade compares.
3. Frei & Cook owns a call written by Wellington & Co.
4. Frei & Cook wants to close out position and contacts Wellington & Co. If Wellington & Co. is interested, it will buy the call back from Frei & Cook. Both go flat. If Wellington is not interested:
   a. Frei & Cook sells the call to Bahl & Puck.
   b. Frei & Cook remains long against Wellington & Co.
   c. Frei & Cook is now a writer against Bahl & Puck.

Option trades originate either with clients, a firm's proprietary account, a specialist, or a market maker. As these four types of accounts represent distinctly different interests, their positions must be maintained separately and not commingled. This is true of a firm's own records as well as the positions at OCC. To maintain control of the firm's internal records as well as the external records maintained by OCC, trades being processed through the system carry specific designations so that they will be segregated into the correct categories and accounted for properly.

Firms that enter orders for their clients and have these orders executed will make certain that the effect of the order will be represented in the code and that code will be carried on the order into OCC. In other words, if a client of Stone, Forrest & Rivers is purchasing option contracts to own them, that client's order will carry a designation "buy open," or BO. This will be reflected in SF&R's own records as well as be channeled properly at Option Clearing Corporation. If a client, on the other hand, is buying options to close out a previous written position, that client's order will say, "buy closed" or "Bc." Again, this will be carried on Stone, Forrest & Rivers' records as well as be used as an instruction at OCC to reduce the number of writers OCC has in their client positions. For this reason, every client order being entered by SF&R carries the designation code as to what effect it will have on the client's position or what standing it will have in the client's account.

This does not hold true in the proprietary world. Some firms do not code their trades when they are trading for their own accounts. The reason is that their net position is the position they want to carry. For example, Stone, Forrest & Rivers' option trading desk is trading calls on RAM Apr 80s. If, in that particular option, they buy more than they sell, then they are holders; if they sell more options than they own, then they are writers. The traders use this method to expedite their positions. In some of the other trading areas of SF&R, for control purposes, they maintain separate accounts at OCC and follow the client's methodology of putting in "buy open," "sell close," and so on. This, again, is a choice of the firm.

The firms that trade for themselves are given a lot of latitude on how their OCC reports are presented. A firm may want a *net* report, that is, all proprietary trading netted into one total position, or a *broad* report, with total long and total short per account per position. The firm may also request separate reports for each trading account.

The daily position reports submitted by OCC to their members reflect the data that the corporation has received from the various comparison facilities. This data, in turn, represents the information received from and/or agreed to by the specific clearing firms.

Here's an example: Stone, Forrest & Rivers is one of the clearing firms. It enters orders for and reports option executions to its clients, as well as trade options for its own proprietary accounts. Therefore, it receives two sets of reports each day: one for its client positions and one for its proprietary positions. We will review the proprietary position first:

	Holders	*Writers*
Previous position		30
	3	
		5
	10	
		25
	50	
		5
	20	
Closing position	18	

All of the transactions under the heading *Holders* are buys, whereas all the transactions under the heading *Writers* are sales. As SF&R nets its proprietary trading, it doesn't matter if the trade is to buy open, buy closed, sell open, or sell closed. Buy transactions simply increase a holder's position or reduce a written position, whereas sell transactions increase a written position or reduce a holder's. The result is always a net of either a holder's or writer's position.

Client positions are different. As each client's transaction affects that client's position, the effect of the transaction must be noted on the original ticket. This notation of effect on a position carries through to the OCC daily position report. Here's an example:

OPTION CALLS ZUP OCT 40—CLIENT, APRIL 25, 20XX

	Holders	*Writers*
Previous position	30	15
O		5
O	3	
O	4	
C		6
C	10	
E		2
A	5	
Closing position	29	5

SF&R client's position at the beginning of the day was holders 30 and writers 15 contracts. The activity for the day affecting holders consisted of the buy open of (3+4) contracts, the sell close of 6 contracts, and an exercise of 2 contracts. Transactions affecting writers consisted of a sell open of 5 contracts, a buy close of 10 contracts, and an assignment of 5 contracts.

Applying the activity to the opening position, we have 29 holders (30+3+4−6−2) and writers 5 (15+5−10−5). The SF&R closing client's position for the day is holders 29, writers 5.

The premiums involved with all of the option transactions for SF&R's clients and their proprietary positions are also netted into one balance figure per category. This net is added to or subtracted from the previous day's balances. For example, suppose that SF&R's clients' netted balance (a result of all activity in all option positions) was a debit and this day's balance was also a debit. The two would be added together and SF&R would owe the difference. If, on the other hand, the daily balance was a credit, it would be applied to SF&R's debit, and OCC would owe SF&R the difference. Should SF&R be running a credit balance, then the reverse would be true.

In addition to balancing the daily position, SF&R must also *post margin* at OCC. This margin is different from client margin. In computing the margin, OCC takes into account what its exposure is compared to SF&R clients' position and what its exposure is compared to SF&R proprietary trading. The two balances may not be netted. An example of this margin computation is that all client-owned positions are excluded since they do not pose any risk to OCC. Options that are written against security (by "covered" writers) are also excluded from the client account margin at OCC because they don't pose any risk either. Then OCC minimizes its risk by offsetting option positions in each option type and class, for example all call options in ZAP that are in client accounts and not either fully paid for or fully covered are offset against each other.

IV-I-4 Option Exercise

When an option is exercised, it is exercised against OCC. OCC then turns the exercises around and assigns a writer, or writers, in that option series. The settlement of the exercise follows the usual path of the underlying issue.

Exercises of equity options result in the delivery of the underlying, usually 100 shares against payment in U.S. dollars. This is accomplished by delivering the issue through DTCC's division, NSCC, as part of the firm's settling trades. The exercises eventually become part of that firm's CNS balances and flow through to DTCC's division DTC. Exercises follow the normal settlement cycle of the equities. Therefore, if we are in a T + 3 environment, the exercise will settle in three business days. If we are in a T + 1 environment, the exercise will settle next business day. Because the firm that receives the assignment is notified the next morning of the exercise, they have the normal settlement cycle to satisfy their requirements. Due to the fact that the settlement cycle of the equity trade is longer than the period given in an assignment, the party being assigned is given a one-day grace period to honor the assignment.

Example: Monday, July 14, an account of SF&R exercises a call on PIP with an exercise price of $50. The exercise is against OCC, which processes it that evening. On Tuesday morning, the firm of Overland & Underwater is notified that the assignment has been made against their written proprietary position. (An exercise can be assigned to any writer per option series.) OU goes into the market on Tuesday to acquire the 100 shares of PIP. In a T + 1 environment, that trade will settle on Wednesday; in a T + 3 environment, that trade will settle on Friday. In any event, the trade that OU entered into to satisfy an option obligation would settle one day after the security is due at SF&R. OU is not penalized for this delay, as they did what they had to do as prescribed by the OCC and regular stock rules and regulations.

Exercises of index options or other cash-settling options settle next business day. Exercises on Monday, July 14, will be assigned Tuesday, July 15. At the same time this assignment "hits" the writer, the account is charged the amount owed. In a cash-settling option, the writer always pays.

Example 1: A call on the IND Index, with an exercise price of $350, is exercised when the IND index closes at $357. As each IND Index has a multiple of $100, the 7-point difference between exercise and index value is equal to $700. Therefore, the writer pays the holder $700 on the next business day.

Example 2: A put on the IND Index, with an exercise price of $360, is exercised when the IND Index is at $357. The writer will pay the holder the $300 difference ($360 − 357 = 3 points × $100 = $300) on the next business day.

Currency options trade in the currency of denomination, but are exercisable in the underlying currency. The British pound contract, traded on the PHLX, is denominated in dollars, but when exercised, the British pound sterling is the deliverable. Since the dollar-denominated contract is based on 31,250 GBP, exercise of the option requires payment of dollars for pounds. These exercises must be accomplished two days after exercise within the country whose currency is being traded. Any firm offering currency options as a product to its clients, or for its own proprietary interest, must have arrangements with an OCC-acceptable bank to transact the exchange of currency in that country.

Unlike other listed options, currency options have one of two expirations per month. They expire the Saturday before the third Wednesday or on the last Saturday of the month. Other listed options expire the Saturday after the third Friday of the expiration month.

IV-I-5 Ex by Ex

Finally, as equity options expire on the Saturday after the third Friday of the expiration month, a discipline known as *exercise by exception (ex by ex)* exists. Under this rule, options that are in the money by $.15 or more for proprietary options, or $.25 or more for clients, will automatically be exercised at expiration if no counterinstructions are received. The ex by ex rules avoid confusion about what is to be done when an "in the money option" is about to expire and no instructions have been received in the trade processing area from stockbrokers representing their clients, or traders, at the firm.

IV-J *FUTURES COMPARISON*

Like options, futures are compared on trade date. But because the comparing facility also acts as the clearing corporation, no central clearing corporation exists. Future comparisons occur during the trading day. The various future exchanges have established time zones, by which the seller of the contract must input the terms of the trade and the buyer must accept or reject those terms. The seller usually has two time zones in which to submit the details of the trade. The buyer likewise has the period to accept or reject the terms of the trade. Should a seller not input the details of the trade in time, the buyer will either come looking for the details themselves or call a floor official to find out what the problem is. This methodology of comparing trades within time zones is very efficient. When the scalpers, also known as locals, or brokers, hedgers, spreaders, and traders of any sort go home from the exchange that night, they know exactly what their positions are and what problems they may have.

IV-K *TRADE CONFIRMATION*

After the trade occurs the client must receive a confirmation of the trade. Retail clients receive paper confirms, whereas institutional clients receive notification electronically.

The confirmation notice must contain the following information.

Transaction code

CUSIP number

Trade date

Settlement date

Activity date if not processed on trade date (known as an "of trade")

Buy, sell long or sell short

Quantity

Security description

Price

All money calculations

Client's account number, registered representative number

Client's name and address

Standing instructions

SF&R systems compute the trade monies almost instantaneously and put it on the Web for the client to view. However, the paper confirm in the case of retail clients must still be sent.

Institutional account trades are confirmed through one of three processes. Trade Suite, OASYS or Omgeo. These processes are explained in Chapter VII. Under the processes, the broker/dealer notifies the institution of the trades as they occur during the trading day. Since institutions usually enter orders of substantial size it is likely that an order's entire quantity may not be executed. The institution waits until the start of the day to allocate the executions among their clients' accounts. When the broker/dealer receives the allocation, usually on trade date + 1, the trades are entered into the trade processing system.

Exhibit 4 Client Confirmation

STONE, FORREST & RIVERS INCORPORATED

CLIENT CONFIRMATION   TRADE DATE: 05-11-XX   SETTLEMENT DATE 05-14-XX

YOU BOUGHT   1000 DYNAFLOW   TECHNOLOGY INC.   35.45

CUSIP   342671103 SYM DYN
TID 1N05110006234

FIRST MONEY	ACCRUED INTEREST	COMMISSION	HANDLING FEE	NET MONEY
$35,450.00		$709.00	$5.00	$36,164.00

MR. ERNEST PERSONS 315 SEVILLE LANE WOODS IL 60632	STONE, FORREST & RIVERS INC 115 MONTGOMERY BLVD CHICAGO IL. 60604-0115 1-312-555-6000
A/C# 4CG000524 RR# CG15	SI H

CHAPTER V

Margin

Member firms are subject to—and base many of their procedures on—the rules and regulations of the Securities and Exchange Commission, the exchanges, and other self-regulatory authorities. While some of these many directives govern firm-to-firm dealings, others affect customer-to-firm relationships. Yet rarely are customers aware of all the rules and regulations that affect them. The brokerage firms must therefore act as watchdogs for their clients, maintaining their clients' accounts in accordance with all applicable rules, if they are to conduct a violation-free business.

The majority of customer-firm rules are enforced by a department known as the *Margin* (or *Credit*) *Department*, which monitors the current status of each customer's account. The employees in this area review the firm's customer accounts to make certain that each one is operating within the framework of the rules and regulations applicable to a customer purchasing and selling securities. The rules determine when the customer must pay for the securities purchased and how much must be paid. In the case of a sale, the rules determine when the securities must be delivered and how much of the proceeds from that sale the customer may withdraw.

V-A *CASH VERSUS MARGIN PURCHASES*

Customers may acquire securities in two ways:

1. In a *cash account purchase*, they must pay for the acquired securities in full.

2. In a *margin purchase*, they pay for some of the acquired securities and use the remaining newly purchased securities to finance the part of the money that is still owed. These securities may be placed at a bank and the firm borrows the money from the bank and in turn lends it to the customer. Or, the money may be obtained by lending the stock to another user, or using the stock to clean up (settle) someone else's transaction. In any event, in a margin purchase, the client making the purchase has to have on deposit a portion of the purchase price; the firm will finance the rest.

Not all securities may be purchased on margin. The security must meet certain federal criteria before it can be marginable. Generally, all securities listed on national exchanges, such as the New York Stock Exchange, are marginable, as are NASDAQ securities that have been approved for margin by the Federal Reserve Board. The brokerage firm, however, has the final say in determining which securities it permits its customers to purchase on margin. A member firm can never permit a customer to margin an unapproved margin security, but it could prohibit a customer from margining an approved one.

Not all clients and/or their accounts may qualify for a margin account. Custodians are not permitted by law to have margin accounts for minors, for example. A firm may choose not to permit margin on a large single-security-position account where the security in question fails to meet certain firm requirements. The firm may also place restrictions on highly volatile securities.

V-B *TERMINOLOGY*

Before we delve into margin, let us understand some of the terms that we will be using:

Credit balance: Money balance in an account representing funds owed by the firm to the client.

Current market value: The present market value of the securities that are in position in an account.

Debit balance: Money balance in an account representing funds owed by the client to the firm.

Equity: That portion of the account that represents what proceeds the client would receive if all security positions were converted and added to cash.

Loan value: The maximum amount of money a firm can lend on the securities in a margin account.

Maintenance requirement: The monetary level to which equity in an account can fall after which the client would need to deposit additional collateral in the form of cash or securities.

Margin requirement: The minimum amount of available cash that the client must have in an account to satisfy a transaction.

Minimum equity requirement: The amount of equity that must be present in the account before a firm can lend the client any funds. Regulation T states that a client must have a minimum of $2,000 equity after which the firm can lend money. Most broker/dealers have higher requirements.

Special memorandum account (SMA): A memorandum field accompanying a margin account that records funds available for the client's use under certain circumstances.

V-C CASH ACCOUNT

When making a purchase in a cash account, the customer pays for securities in full. When making a sale, the client receives payment in full.

Example: Della Kattessin, a client of SF&R, buys 100 shares of ZAP @ $42. The market value of the securities is therefore $4,200 (100 shares of ZAP × $42 per share). (Ignore commission and other expenses.) The client pays for the purchase in full, and the equity in the account is therefore $4,200. If ZAP rises to $60 per share, the market value becomes $6,000 (100 ZAP × $60 per share), and the client's equity becomes $6,000.

Della purchases the stock:

Buys 100 shares @ $42 per share =	$4,200 CMV	(current market value)
–	0 EQ	(equity)
Client owes =	$4,200 Dr	(debit balance)

Della pays for the stock:

Long (owns) 100 shrs. @ $42 =	$4,200 CMV
=	4,200 EQ
	0 Dr/cr balance

The stock rises to $60 per share:

Long (owns) 100 shrs. @ $60 =	$6,000 CMV
=	6,000 EQ
	0 Dr/cr balance

While Della has an $1,800 profit, it is a paper profit as the increased value is locked in the security that she owns. If Della sold the stock, she would receive proceeds of $6,000.

Trades purchased in a cash account must be paid for in full by settlement date and no later than the second business day thereafter.

V-D MARGIN ACCOUNT

In a margin account, however, the customer can pay only part of the cost of purchase, and the brokerage firm lends the rest to the customer. Many securities are *marginable*, that is, the firm can lend the client money on them.

Note: Regulation T of the Federal Reserve covers the lending of money by brokerage firms. The amount that a firm can lend is established by the Federal Reserve Board.

Example: Jay Walker, a margin client of SF&R, is interested in purchasing 100 shares of RAM, which is presently trading at $50. The client wants to invest the minimum amount permitted by Regulation T. At the time of purchase, the margin rate is 50%. The loan value is, therefore, also 50%.

Margin rate % + Loan value rate % = 100%
50% + Loan value rate % = 100%
Loan value rate % = 100% – 50%
Loan value rate % = 50%

On a $5,000 purchase (100 shares of RAM at $50), the minimum Jay has to pay is $2,500 (50% of $5,000). Jay purchases the shares of RAM and pays $2,500, while the firm is lending the remaining $2,500, which becomes the debit balance. As with all loans, the client pays interest on the outstanding principal.

Jay purchases the stock:

Buys 100 shrs. @ $50 per share = $5,000 CMV
– 0 EQ
Client owes = $5,000 Dr

Jay pays for 50% of the purchase:

Long (owns) 100 shrs. @ $50 = $5,000 CMV
–2,500 EQ
$2,500 Dr

Equity + Debit balance = Market value
$2,500 + $2,500 = $5,000

The customer's $2,500 and the firm's loan of $2,500 are sent to the broker/dealer that SF&R purchased the stock from. There isn't any cash in the client's account, just a security position worth $5,000. Of the $5,000 in market value, $2,500 is the client's equity and $2,500 is the client's debit balance (loan). Assume the stock that Jay purchased rose in value to $75 per share. Jay's account would have these balances:

Long (owns) 100 shrs. @ $75 = $7,500 CMV
= 5,000 EQ
$2,500 Dr

The debit balance (loan) remains the same because no money entered the account. The increased value of the security is reflected in Jay's equity.

V-E *A BRIEF LESSON IN MARGIN*

V-E-1 Regulation T (Reg T)

The backbone of all margin rules is a Federal Reserve Board regulation known as *Regulation T*. The Federal Reserve Board writes and changes Regulation T. The SEC, NYSE, and NASD enforce it.

One of Reg T's provisions stipulates the percentage of margin (that is, the amount that the customer must put into the account), which is known as the *margin rate*. The rate is determined by the Federal Reserve Board (FRB).

Example: Given a margin rate of 50% for common stock, customer William Board must pay at least 50% of any purchase that he makes. If Bill purchases $30,000 worth of common stock, he must put up 50% ($15,000) of his own money into his account by settlement day. The brokerage firm will lend the remaining $15,000, on which the customer will pay a monthly interest charge.

The margin rate is therefore part of the system of controls that the Fed uses to regulate money and, in turn, the economy.

Another Regulation T requirement is known as the *minimum equity requirement*. It states that a broker/dealer may not lend a client money if the equity in the account is below $2,000. Many broker/dealers have set their minimum equity requirements at a higher amount. A client, Lauren Auder, wants to purchase $1,500 worth of stock in her new margin account. Because the purchase price is below $2,000 she must pay for the entire purchase. Suppose Lauren's initial stock purchase was for $2,100 in her new margin account. Lauren must deposit $2,000 and the firm can lend $100. Therefore, not until the client has purchased $4,000 or more worth of equity and/or convertible debt securities does the margin rate of 50% supplant the minimum equity requirement.

V-E-2 Maintenance Rules

While Regulation T dictates the obligation of the customer at the time of trade, the exchanges and self-regulatory associations have instituted rules that not only augment Reg T, but also establish procedures to be followed after the initial transaction. Rules 431–432 of the New York Stock Exchange and 2520–2522 of the NASD are two such sets of rules. Among the areas covered by these rules are the minimum maintenance requirements.

To understand minimum maintenance requirements, we must focus on the three primary elements of an account:

1. *Current market value*, which is the total of the current market values of all securities maintained in the account.
2. *Equity*, which is the amount, in either a dollar value or a percentage, of the total current market value in the account that the customer would receive, should the account be liquidated.
3. *Debit balance*, which is the amount of money loaned by the firm or owed by the customer. A *credit balance* is the amount of money in the account belonging to the customer. In some types of accounts, such as margin accounts, there cannot be a debit and credit balance at the same time; either the client owes the firm money in that type of account, or the firm owes the client money, or there isn't any money balance.

These three components are related by a mathematical formula:

$$\text{Current market value} - \text{Debit balance} = \text{Equity}$$

$$\text{Current market value} + \text{Credit balance} = \text{Equity}$$

As the current market value fluctuates, so does the customer's equity. Not subject to market fluctuations is the debit balance, which is the amount loaned by the firm to the customer. Because the customer must repay this debt at a later time, it is therefore an obligation of the customer. Should the client have a credit balance (money owed by the firm to the client), it too would not be affected by market fluctuations. It is simply added to the client's equity.

In a cash account purchase (when the customer pays for the purchase in full), no debit balance is incurred, and the customer's equity always equals the current market value.

Example: Customer Shelly Fish purchases 100 shares of BOW at $15 for $1,500, paying for the purchase in full. (For all examples, disregard commission and fees.) The current market value is $1,500, and the customer's equity is $1,500.

$$\text{Equity} = \text{Current market value} - \text{Debit balance}$$
$$\$1{,}500 = \$1{,}500 - \$0$$

If the stock appreciates in value to $2,000, the equity increases to $2,000. Should the stock decline in value to $1,000, the equity will decline to $1,000.

V-E-3 Loan Value

The complement of the margin requirement is known as the *loan value*, which is the amount that the customer may borrow on the security. Together, the margin rate and loan value, both expressed as percentages, must total 100%. If the Federal Reserve Board establishes a margin rate of 60%, then the loan value of the security is 40%. If the customer is required to pay 70%, then the loan value is 30%.

Example: A customer, Scott Chensoda, wishes to purchase 100 shares of JAM at $60 per share. The purchase would cost a total of $6,000. Chensoda can pay any amount of cash that represents a percentage between the current margin rate and 100%. If the margin rate is 60%, the minimum he has to pay is $3,600 (.60 × $6,000). The loan value here is 40% or $2,400 (.40 × $6,000). Chensoda deposits a check for $3,600 by settlement day, and the firm lends the remainder.

Chensoda's $3,600 and SF&R's $2,400 go to the selling broker/dealer. The customer who sold the stock then receives $6,000 and doesn't care how Chensoda pays for it.

Chensoda's account has the following balances:

Long 100 shares JAM @ $60	$6,000
Less debit balance	2,400
Customer equity	$3,600

If JAM appreciated in value to $100 per share, the account would have these balances:

Long 100 JAM @ $100	$10,000
Less debit balance	2,400
Customer equity	$ 7,600

Chensoda borrowed only $2,400 and therefore only owes that sum to the brokerage firm.

With the value of account now at $10,000, the loan value has increased $4,000 (.40% × $10,000). Chensoda can borrow an additional $1,600 if he wishes. ($4,000 loan value minus the $2,400 already borrowed = $1,600.) If he *borrows* this sum, then:

Long 100 JAM @ $100	$10,000	
Less debit balance	4,000	(40%)
Customer equity	$ 6,000	(60%)

The account has returned to maximum loan value.

V-E-4 Margin Excess and Buying Power

Any time the loan value is greater than the debit balance or the equity is above the margin rate in the account, the difference is known as *Reg T excess*, which can be used to calculate *buying power.*

Example: With JAM still at $100 per share, the debit balance is still $2,400 as Chensoda has not borrowed the $1,600. He wants to purchase TIP common stock that is selling at $26.60 per share, or $2,660 per 100 shares. How much additional money must he deposit to meet the margin requirement of the new purchase?

$2,660
× .60 (Margin requirement)
$1,596 (60% of TIP's market value)

The client would need $1,596 to satisfy the margin required on the purchase. Does Chensoda have enough "excess" to make the purchase on the margin? Yes, he does:

Current market value	$10,000
Loan value rate	× .40
Maximum loan value	$ 4,000
Debit balance	− 2,400
Excess	$ 1,600

The $1,600 can be used to purchase the additional securities. The $1,600 excess represents the customer's investment in that new purchase, or 60% of the new purchase. As Scott Chensoda is purchasing $2,660 worth of stock, he can use $1,596 of his excess to satisfy 60% of the purchase. The firm will lend the remaining 40% ($1,064) on the value of the new purchase.

Example: After Chensoda purchases TIP common stock at $26.60, the account has the following balances:

Original debit balance	$2,400.00
Excess supplied to TIP purchase	1,596.00
Additional loan the firm will make on the purchase	1,064.00
New debit balance	$5,060.00

100 JAM @ $100	$10,000.00
100 PIP @ $26.60	2,660.00
Current market value	$12,660.00
Less debit balance	5,060.00 (approx. 40%)
New equity	$7,600.00 (approx. 60%)

Let's look at another example with a different angle.

Example: The margin rate is 50%; therefore the loan value has to be 50% also. Scott buys 100 JAM at $50 and deposits the entire amount. Then:

100 JAM @ $50	$5,000
Less debit balance	0
Customer's equity	$5,000

Scott then decides to purchase another 100 shares at $50 for an additional $5,000, and he asks, "What is my buying power?"

Current market value	$5,000
Loan value rate	× .50
Loan value	$2,500
Less debit balance	0
Total	$2,500

Scott has $2,500 excess that represents 50% of a new equity transaction. Therefore, Scott can purchase $5,000 worth of equity securities. ($2,500/.50 = $5,000.)

Chensoda purchases the additional stock, and the account reveals:

Current market value (200 JAM @ $50)	$10,000
Less debit balance (50%)	5,000
Equity (50%)	$ 5,000

Had he purchased 200 shares originally with a 50% margin requirement (and 50% loan value), the account would have been:

Current market value (200 JAM @ $50)	$10,000
Less debit balance (50%)	5,000
Equity (50%)	$ 5,000

This is exactly how the account's positions appear after the two purchases.

V-E-5 Minimum Maintenance Requirement

Unfortunately, securities don't always increase in value. Sometimes they decrease, creating an altogether different set of problems. In a cash account, as the client has paid for the purchase in full, Stone, Forrest & Rivers does not have any market or credit risk. However, in a margin account, where the client has borrowed funds from the firm, SF&R has concern as its loan is at risk. Therefore, to what level can the securities' market value in an account fall before the brokerage firm must "call" for additional money or collateral? The exchanges and NASDR (National Association of Security Dealers–Regulatory) rules state that the call must go to the client when the equity in the account is less than 25% of the market value. Most firms maintain even more stringent requirements.

Example: Customer Phil O'Dendrin purchases 200 shares of ROCO at $60 for a total cost of $12,000. With the margin rate at 50%, the brokerage firm receives Phil's check for $6,000 and lends him the rest. Then:

Current market value (200 ROCO @ $60)	$12,000
Less debit balance	6,000
Equity	$ 6,000

If ROCO falls in value to $20, the account balances are:

Current market value (200 ROCO @ $20)	$4,000
Less debit balance	–6,000
Equity	($2,000)

As shown, there is a *deficit* in the account of $2,000. This is known as an *unsecured debt balance.*

In this case, the firm risks losing $2,000 of its own funds should the customer be unable to pay back the $6,000 loan or even the $2,000 shortfall. Even if the firm liquidated Phil's securities ($4,000) the firm would still be short $2,000. To prevent this from happening, the minimum maintenance requirement rules are enforced. When the equity value falls below 25% of the market value, which is the same as when the equity falls below one-third of the debit balance, firms send "calls" to customers for additional collateral. In our example, because the debit balance in the account is $6,000, the equity can decrease to only $2,000 (a third of the $6,000 debit balance). If it drops below this figure, the firm issues a *maintenance call* for additional money, or collateral, to be deposited by the customer. If the customer does not meet the needs of the call, the firm must liquidate enough securities to satisfy the requirement. With the equity at $2,000 and the debit balance at $6,000, the market value would be $8,000. ($2,000 is 25% of $8,000.) The maintenance rules from the SROs state that the equity cannot be less than 25% of the market value.

Let's run through another example using all the tools discussed above. Client Ellie Fant opens a new margin account and purchases $2,000 worth of KIP securities. Ellie must pay the full amount (minimum margin requirement) and does. The minimum equity rule states that a firm cannot lend any funds until the client satisfies the $2,000 equity requirement. As this first purchase is for only $2,000, Ellie must pay for it in full.

CMV of KIP = $2,000
less EQ = 2,000
Dr balance = $ 0

She then purchases $6,000 worth of RAM common stock:

$2,000 (KIP)
+6,000 (RAM)
CMV = $8,000
less EQ = 2,000
Dr bal. = $6,000

The loan value on securities worth $8,000 is $4,000 ($8,000 × .50 = $4,000). Ellie has a debit balance of $6,000 and therefore must deposit $2,000. Upon receipt of the $2,000, the debit balance would be reduced to $4,000 and the equity would increase to $4,000. The account would be:

CMV = $8,000
Less equity = 4,000 (50%)
Debit balance = $4,000 (50%)

Ellie's purchase of $6,000 worth of RAM was satisfied by the release of $1,000 from the first purchase as the minimum margin requirement was satisfied by the second purchase and the T call for $2,000 that Stone, Forrest & Rivers sent to Ellie to satisfy the second purchase's requirement, which she paid.

The market value of Ellie's portfolio increases to $14,000. Her debit balance remains $4,000, as no additional money came into the account. The increase in market value has caused an increase in Ellie's equity. Her equity has increased to $10,000.

CMV = $14,000
Less equity = 10,000
Dr = $ 4,000

The loan value on $14,000 market value is $7,000. Ellie borrowed $4,000, so she can borrow $3,000 more. She does and uses it to purchase $6,000 shares of BUPP on margin. Her account has the following balances:

CMV	$14,000	(New purchase)	→ +$6,000 = $20,000
Equity	10,000 – $3,000	(Borrow of excess)	→ + 3,000 = 10,000
Debit bal	$ 4,000 + 3,000 ↲	(New loans)	→ +$3,000 = $10,000

With the account as it now stands, to what market value can it fall after which Stone, Forrest & Rivers would have to call for additional collateral?

As equity and market value change dollar for dollar, we must use the part of the account that doesn't change when the market value changes.

The debit balance remains constant so we calculate from that figure. If equity cannot fall below 25% of market value, then the debit balance cannot rise above 75%. A ratio can be developed between equity and debit balance of 1 to 3 (25:75) or equity cannot be less than ⅓ of the debit balance ($25/25 = 1, 75/25 = 3$).

Ellie's account has a $10,000 debit; ⅓ of $10,000 is $3,333.33. The equity in Ellie's account cannot fall below $3,333.33. Therefore, the market value in the account cannot fall below $13,333.33 ($10,000 debit balance plus $3,333.33 equity equals $13,333.33 market value).

Please note that 25% of $13,333.33 is $3,333.33. The maintenance equity requirement is that the equity cannot be less than 25% of market value.

V-E-6 Restricted Accounts

An account may not have excess and yet still not be on call. Such an account has a debit balance that is higher than the current loan value.

Example:

Current market value	$10,000
Less debit balance	6,000
Equity	$ 4,000

With a 50% loan value, the account is currently undermargined, but not enough to justify a maintenance call.

The self-regulatory agencies refer to this type of account as *restricted*.

Should the customer decide to purchase additional stock, the brokerage firm requires margin only for the new purchase. It does not compel the customer to deposit sufficient funds to bring the entire account up to the margin requirement.

When a client sells a security from a restricted account, the client is entitled to withdraw 50% of the proceeds of sale whether or not the account remains in the restrictive stage. The sale could also cause the account to change to having excess when the proceeds of the sale are applied to the money balances. The customer may withdraw 50% of the proceeds of sale, or all of the recomputed excess, whichever is a greater amount. However, we are discussing a margin account that has a debit money balance. On that balance the firm is charging interest. Therefore, when the proceeds of the sale are posted, the debit balance is reduced. Any withdrawal of funds will increase the debit balance.

Example: Sandra Beech's account reflects the following positions and balances:

Long 100 BOO @ $90	$ 9,000.00
Long 100 MAW @ $30	3,000.00
Long 100 ZOW @ $60	+ 6,000.00
Current market value:	$18,000.00
Less debit balance:	−11,000.00
Equity:	$ 7,000.00

The account is restricted as the equity is less than 50% ($9,000) but greater then 25% ($4,500).

Sandy sells MAW at $30 per share. Her account balances change to:

Long 100 BOO @ $90	$ 9,000.00
Long 100 ZOW @ $60	+ 6,000.00
Current market value:	$15,000.00
Less debit balance:	− 8,000.00
Equity:	$ 7,000.00

Sandy can withdraw 50% of the proceeds ($1,500) even though the account is restricted. The removal of the $1,500 would raise the debit balance to $9,500 and reduce the equity to $5,500. Sandy can also use the $1,500 proceeds to purchase up to $3,000 worth of common stock on margin.

Let's say that instead of selling the MAW, Sandy sold BOO shares @ $90 per share. Her account would reflect the following balances:

Long 100 MAW @ $30	$3,000.00
Long 100 ZOW @ $60	+6,000.00
Current market value:	$9,000.00
Less debit balance:	−2,000.00
Equity:	$7,000.00

The proceeds from the BOO sale would bring $9,000 into the account. Sandy could withdraw 50% of the proceeds or the excess, whichever is greater. In this case, the $4,500 representing 50% of the proceeds could be withdrawn.

The excess in the account is $2,500. Caution: depending on the structure of the account, the removal of the full 50% of the proceeds could cause the equity to fall below maintenance and trigger a maintenance call. In this situation, the client may withdraw up to the amount that would cause the call.

V-E-7 Special Memorandum Account (SMA)

As the margin and/or short account is operating, different entries are being posted to them. This includes buys, sells, and dividend and interest payments, to name but a few. In addition, the value of the securities in the clients' accounts changes over time. To track entries that enable the client to borrow or use funds, margin accounts utilize a memorandum field known as the *special memorandum account (SMA)*. First, the margin rules state that a client may withdraw 50% of the proceeds of any sale as long as the account was not on call for additional collateral at the time of the sale. Second, the client may withdraw 100% of any dividend or interest payment credited to the account, provided the account was not on maintenance call when the entry was made. Third, as we have seen, when the market price of a security owned by the client increases in value, Reg T excess is developed. This excess is "booked to the SMA." The only time the balance in the SMA can be reduced is when the client uses it. Remember, it is a bookkeeping entry. Should the client decide to utilize it, the debit balance in the margin account would increase (or the credit balance, should one exist, would decrease).

When a sale is made in a margin account, the security position is dropped from the account, and the money received is applied against the debit balance or credit balance. After the sale has cleared the books, the account does not reflect the sale. It would take a margin employee a good amount of time to determine if, first, a sale had taken place and, second, whether the releasable funds had been previously withdrawn. The SMA saves the margin department this waste of time by recording such events, which could have taken place but didn't.

Example: A restricted account sells $5,000 worth of stock. On settlement date, the client can withdraw 50% of the sale's proceeds, or $2,500. If the client doesn't withdraw the $2,500, it is posted to the SMA.

If at a later date the client decides to withdraw the money, the margin department checks the SMA, sees the $2,500 entry, and approves the payment.

In addition to watching minimum maintenance and sending "house calls," margin employees use the SMA to determine what is permitted in the accounts. The SMA is essential to the working of the margin area.

V-F *MARGIN—LONG POSITION*

Let's review margin applications again from a slightly different perspective.

V-F-1 Reg T Excess

The market value of stocks, purchased on margin, may rise. When it does, the increased value is known as *excess equity*. It is "excess" because it is more than the equity required by Reg T. It is *Reg T excess*.

Example: Assuming a margin rate of 50%, customer Sara Toga buys 100 shares of DUD at $50. Sara deposits $2,500 (50%) and borrows $2,500 (50%).

Margin rate + Loan value = Market value
$2,500 + $2,500 = $5,000

After the trade:

Equity + Debit balance = Market value
$2,500 + $2,500 = $5,000

The market value of DUD increases to $100 per share, so the current market value of the 100 shares in the account is $10,000 ($100 × 100 shares). Since the customer borrowed only $2,500 for the original purchase, the equity is $7,500.

Equity + Debit balance	= Market value
Equity + $2,500	= $10,000
Equity	= $10,000 – $2,500
Equity	= $7,500

Market value	= $10,000
Loan value %	= × 50%
Loan value $	= $ 5,000
Debit balance	= –2,500
Available for loan	$ 2,500 (Reg T excess)

Ms. Toga does not have access to her account online so she calls Stone, Forrest & Rivers' stockbroker to determine if any money can be borrowed. The stockbroker looks up the customer's account on his workstation and sees that she does have $2,500 Reg T excess available in her SMA. The stockbroker informs Ms. Toga that she can withdraw $2,500. Please note that the customer is *borrowing* the $2,500 as the value of stock in the account has increased—cash has come into the account. If Ms. Toga borrows the $2,500, the equity in the account will decrease and the debit balance will increase.

			Loan ↓		
Market value	$10,000			=	$10,000 Market value
Equity	– 7,500	–	$2,500	=	–5,000 Equity
Debit balance	$ 2,500	+	$2,500	=	$ 5,000 Debit balance

V-F-2 Buying Power

Sara may also apply the Reg T excess in the account to a margin purchase. The excess equity is then said to have *buying power*. It represents the part of the purchase price that the client can use instead of cash.

What, then, is the maximum dollar purchase of common stock that the client can make on margin? To arrive at that amount, simply divide the margin rate into the excess dollar amount.

Example: The client can apply the $2,500 excess to a new common stock trade. The excess equals 50% of what can be bought.

$$\text{Buying power} = \frac{\text{Reg T excess}}{\text{Margin rate}} = \frac{\$2{,}500}{.50} = \$5{,}000$$

In other words, the current market value of any new purchase can be up to $5,000 without the client having to deposit more equity. Of that total value, $2,500 (50%) is equity applied from the client's excess equity, and $2,500 (50%) is a new loan from the brokerage firm. The client decides to buy $5,000 worth of ROS. The client can purchase $5,000 worth of marginable securities.

Current market value	
DUD	$10,000.00
ROS	+ 5,000.00
Total	$15,000.00
Less equity	
DUD	$5,000.00
ROS	2,500.00
Total	7,500.00
Debit balance	$7,500.00

The client has substituted securities for the excess loan value ($2,500). The debit balance of $7,500 is the equivalent of the loan value of 50% ($15,000 × .50). The equity of $7,500 is the equivalent of the margin rate of 50% ($15,000 × .50).

V-F-3 Minimum Maintenance Requirement

If a rise in market value creates Reg T excess (equity), what effect does a decrease in value have? To answer that question, we must explain minimum maintenance.

Minimum maintenance margin is the minimum amount of equity that a customer must have in a margin account based on the market value and the size of the debit balance (loan). The New York Stock Exchange in rule 431, NASDR in rule 2520, and other exchanges prescribe the minimum amount. As the market prices of securities fluctuate, they create changes in a margin account's equity. (Don't forget the formula: Equity plus Debit balance equals Market value.) If the market value goes up or down, the debit balance will remain the same; therefore, the equity has to change. If the equity in an account falls below 25% of the market value or becomes ⅓ of the debit balance, the customer will be asked to provide additional collateral and bring the account up to the *minimum* level. The customer must somehow restore the level of equity to satisfy these minimums. It may appear confusing, but if the equity cannot be less than 25% of the market value, then the debit balance cannot be greater than 75% of the market value. The relationship between the 25% and the 75% is one to three, or ⅓. The previous sentence, therefore, is saying the same thing, but from two different points of view. It says the equity in the account cannot fall below 25% of the market value or become less than 1/3 of the debit balance.

V-F-3-a *A Working Illustration*

Let's follow an account through several transactions to see how a margin account works.

With the margin rate at 50%, customer Stephan Nee (account 4CG001243) wants to open a margin account with the purchase of 100 shares of PIP common stock at $50 per share. After the new account paperwork is completed, an order is entered and executed, and the trade is settled, the account reflects the following figures:

Long 100 PIP @ $50	
Current market value	$5,000
Less equity (customer's cash)	−2,500
Debit balance (loan from firm)	$2,500

Within a few days, the stock increases in value to $80 per share:

Current market value	$8,000
Less equity	–5,500
Debit balance	$2,500

On $8,000 worth of market value, Reg T permits SF&R to lend 50%, or $4,000, but SF&R has already loaned the customer $2,500. Now that the market value has gone up, so has the equity. The customer may borrow $1,500 more. When the stockbroker or the client accesses the client's account on the workstation or CRT, the account will pop up and the Reg T excess field will show $1,500. The computation is as follows:

Current market value (CMV)	$8,000
Loan value rate (LVR)	× 50%
Loan value (LV)	$4,000
Less debit balance (Dr)	–2,500
Reg T excess	$1,500

Stephan can remove the $1,500 excess from the account—that is, borrow it—or apply it to the new purchase. If he removes it, the account is:

Long 100 PIP @ $80	
Current market value	$8,000
Less equity	–4,000
Debit balance	$4,000

But Stephan is interested in purchasing shares of WOW, which is trading at $30 per share, and he does not want to put in any more money. Stephan's $1,500 from the loan value of PIP is used to buy WOW, and the firm lends the other 50% of the value of WOW. The customer can therefore purchase $3,000 worth of WOW.

Long 100 PIP at $80	
Current market value of PIP	$ 8,000
Long 100 WOW at $30	
Plus: Current market value of WOW	+ 3,000
Total current market value	$11,000
Less equity	– 5,500
Debit balance	$ 5,500

Now our customer wants to purchase 100 ZAP at $70. SF&R's stockbroker informs Stephan that there isn't any excess:

CMV	$11,000
Times margin rate	× .50%
Loan value	$ 5,500
Less debit balance	– 5,500
Excess equity	$ 0

The client orders the purchase and, as there isn't any equity excess, must deposit 50% of the total value by settlement day, but no later than two business day after settlement. Instead of sending SF&R a check for $3,500 (50% of $7,000), Stephan deposits fully paid for, marginable shares of MAM common stock. With MAM currently trading at $17.50 per share, the customer sends 400 shares, for a market value of $7,000 ($17.50 × 400 = $7,000). The loan value on $7,000 worth of marginable stock is $3,500 (50%). SF&R may now lend Stephan $3,500 based on the MAM securities that were deposited to cover his obligation on ZAP. The account now is as follows:

Long	
400 MAM at $17.50	$ 7,000
100 PIP at $80	8,000
100 WOW at $30	3,000
100 ZAP at $70	+ 7,000
Total current market value	$25,000
Less equity	–12,500
Debit balance	$12,500

The lending, step by step, took place as follows:

1. Client bought 100 shares of PIP @ $50	CMV	$5,000
Deposits	EQ	–2,500
Borrows	Dr	$2,500
2. PIP increases in value to $80 per share	CMV	$8,000
	EQ	–5,500
	Dr	$2,500

3. Account has Reg T excess.

CMV	$8,000
LV rate	× .50
LV	$4,000
Dr	−2,500
Excess	$1,500

4. Client uses excess to buy WOW stock on margin.

	Account	Borrow		WOW		Account
CMV	$8,000		+	$3,000	=	$11,000
EQ	−5,500	−$1,500	+	−1,500	=	− 5,500
Dr	$2,500	+$1,500	+	$1,500	=	$ 5,500

5. Client buys ZAP @ $70.

	Account	Borrow		ZAP		Account
CMV	$11,000		+	$7,000	=	$18,000
EQ	− 5,500	$0	+	0	=	− 5,500
Dr	$ 5,550	$0	+	$7,000	=	$12,500

6. Client pays fully for MAM stock.

	Account		MAM		Account
CMV	$18,000	+	$ 7,000	=	$ 25,000
EQ	− 5,500	+	−7,000	=	−12,500
Dr	$12,500	+	$ 0	=	$ 12,500

1. Borrowed to buy PIP	$2,500
2. Excess from PIP to acquire WOW	1,500
3. Borrowed on value of WOW	1,500
4. Borrowed against MAM to buy ZAP	3,500
5. Borrowed on the value of ZAP	+3,500
6. Debit balance	$12,500

The market value in the account falls from $25,000 to $23,000. The account is as follows:

Current market value	$23,000
Less equity	−10,500
Debit balance	$12,500

Note how the $2,000 drop in market value is offset by the $2,000 drop in equity.

The customer wants to purchase 100 shares of POP at $20 per share. Despite the drop in market value, Stephan can purchase POP just by depositing 50% of the *purchase price.* He does *not* have to bring the account up to 50%. With the purchase of 100 shares of POP at $20, the account has a market value of $25,000, an equity of $11,500, and a debit balance of $13,500.

	Account		POP		Account
CMV	$23,000	+	$2,000	=	$25,000
EQ	−10,500	+	−1,000	=	−11,500
Dr	$12,500	+	$1,000	=	$13,500

With the debit balance of $13,500, to what level can the equity fall before client Stephan is called for more money? Under the maintenance rules, the equity in the account cannot be less than one-third of the debit balance.

$$\frac{1}{3}\times\frac{\$13{,}500}{1}=\$4{,}500$$

Debit balance plus equity equals market value. Here, $13,500 plus $4,500 = $18,000.

With the debit balance at $13,500, the equity cannot fall below $4,500; said another way, the market value cannot fall below $18,000. Please note that 25% of $18,000 is $4,500.

Should the account fall in value below $18,000, the client would get called for additional funds. Let us assume that the market value drops in value to $16,000. The account would have the following balances:

CMV = $16,000
Less equity = − 2,500
Debit balance = $13,500

At this point the equity in the account is approximately 15%. The client would have to add additional value. A market value of $16,000 requires equity of 25%, which is $4,000. As the client's equity is only $2,500, the client would receive a maintenance call for $1,500.

An easy way to remember which of the two formulas to use is to key off the item that won't be changed by the event. If the concern is the level to which the value in an account can fall, the debit balance isn't changing in this event and therefore the debit balance cannot be more than three times the equity. If, on the other hand, money is being called for, the market value won't change by this event and therefore the equity must be 25% of market value.

V-G *MARGIN—SHORT SALES*

V-G-1 Required Margin

Customer Lawrence Ott (account 3MI013412) from SF&R's Miami office believes that BUM, currently at $80 per share, is about to fall in value—that is, he thinks it is overpriced. After making certain that Larry has a margin account and that the stock is available for loan, SF&R's Miami stockbroker, Carl Lee, enters an order to sell short 100 BUM at the market. The trade is made. Larry must deposit 50% of the short sale value, or $4,000, which is placed in the margin-type account. When properly margined, the account is:

Margin account (type 2)	Short account (type 3)
Equity (credit balance) = $4,000	Short 100 BUM @ $80 = $8,000 Cr

Because the customer has borrowed the stock through SF&R, 100% of the value must be frozen to protect the firm against the customer's inability to "buy back" the borrowed or sold stock. As the price of BUM fluctuates, SF&R is moving money between the customer's equity in the margin-type account and the current market value of the stock in the short-type account. BUM rises to $85 per share. $500 is removed from Larry's equity and placed in the short position. The account is as follows:

Margin account (type 2)	Short account (type 3)
Equity $3,500 cr.	Short 100 BUM @ $85 = $8,500 Cr

If BUM continues to rise in price, the customer's equity will be depleted. (Note how a rise in market value "hurts" a short position, whereas it enhances a long position.)

Once a short sale is made, two factors may come into play as the market value of the stock fluctuates: mark to the market and the maintenance requirement.

V-G-2 Mark to the Market

Mark to the market is a process by which the value of a security position is adjusted to reflect the current market price. As the market value of the borrowed stock increases, the brokerage firm will take money from the customer's equity and freeze it in the short position. Should the market value decline, the brokerage firm will unfreeze funds and credit, or give money, to the customer's equity. Either way, the account is marked to the market price on a daily basis.

V-G-3 Maintenance Requirement

To protect SF&R against unfavorable movements in price, self-regulatory agencies have established a minimum equity *maintenance requirement* for a short position. If the equity falls below the maintenance requirement, the customer must be called for more collateral. In a short sale, the maintenance requirement is that equity be at least 30% of market value. Brokerage firms may require a higher minimum than the SRO's requirement, but never less.

With BUM at $80 ($8,000), Larry had to deposit 50% of the sale, or $4,000. The maintenance requirement is $2,400 ($8,000 × .30 = $2,400); therefore, the account has "surplus" over maintenance of $1,600 ($4,000 − $2,400).

If BUM rises to $81 per share, SF&R deducts $100 from the customer's equity and places it into frozen funds:

Margin account (type 2)	Short account (type 3)
Equity $3,900 cr.	Short 100 BUM @ $81 = $8,100

At the same time, the maintenance increases from $2,400 to $2,430 ($8,100 × .30). The one-point move reduces the surplus of equity over maintenance by 130%, or in this case $130 (from $1,600 to $1,470).

	Was	*Is*
Equity	\$4,000	\$3,900
Maintenance	−2,400	−2,430
Excess equity	\$1,600	\$1,470

SF&R's margin system monitors the customer's accounts and will alert the margin/credit specialist should the equity fall below the 30% minimum maintenance requirement. To determine when a minimum maintenance call is necessary, the margin specialist can perform a simple computation. The specialist will divide the surplus equity (the amount that the current equity is over maintenance) by the maintenance rate of 30%, plus 100%, which is the dollar-for-dollar movement of the security price between the frozen funds and the customer's equity. With that done, the resulting answer reveals the number of points the stock can move against the customer's position. In our example here, if you divide the \$1,600 by 130, you arrive at an answer of 12.31 points.

$$\text{Price rise to a maintenance call} = \frac{\text{Excess equity}}{\text{Maintenance rate} + 100\%}$$

$$= \frac{\$1{,}600}{30\% + 100\%} \text{ or } \frac{\$1{,}600}{.30 + 1.00}$$

$$= \frac{\$1{,}600}{1.30}$$

$$= \$1{,}230.77$$

This amount represents the dollar amount of a rise in market value for 100 shares of BUM. To arrive at the rise per share, the margin employee simply divides \$1,230.77 by 100 shares.

$$\text{Price per share} = \frac{\$1{,}230.77}{100 \text{ shares}}$$

$$= \$12.31 \text{ per share}$$

In other words, if BUM were to trade at \$92.31 (\$80 + \$12.31), the equity in the account would be close to the required minimum, and a maintenance call might have to be issued to the customer.

Let's see why this is so. With BUM at \$80, the maintenance requirement is \$2,400 (\$8,000 × .30). The customer has \$4,000 in the account—plenty of equity. Should the value of 100 shares of BUM rise to $9,237.50, the maintenance requirement would be $2,771.25 ($9,237.50×.30). The customer still has $4,000 in the account, so he still has plenty of equity, right?

Wrong. Since this is a *short* position, the rise in a price *decreased* the equity in the account. The price rise in a short position is like a price decrease in a long position. As a result, the firm will have to deduct the dollar value of the price change from the equity:

Equity	$4,000.00
Less adjustment for price rise	−1,237.50
Reduced equity	$2,763.50

Larry Ott does not have enough equity to cover the minimum requirement—but just barely. The minimum required is $2,771.25, and his reduced equity is $2,763.50. A maintenance call would be sent to the client. However, in reality, the firm would not send out a maintenance call for $7.75 as the amount is so small but would issue one if it grew to $500.

Let's run through another example:

Another client of SF&R, Lester Ismoore (account 6PT000657), believes JAB common stock is overpriced and will have poor earnings over the next year. To take advantage of this, Les wants to sell short 1,000 JAB, which is currently trading around $40 per share. He calls his broker, Carole Ling, at SF&R, who in turn verifies the availability of JAB shares for loan purposes on her workstation. The list of available securities is maintained online by the Stock Loan/Stock Borrow section of the Settlement Department. Carole locks in the 1,000 shares and, on direction from Les, enters an order to sell short 1,000 shares of JAB at the market. As short sales require "uptick," the trade cannot take place at a price lower than the last sale or the last different sale price. (See "Short Sales" on page 149.)

With the last sale at $39.90, SF&R enters the order into the Super DOT system at the NYSE and is able to effect a trade at $40.

Les would have to deposit $20,000 into his account, which represents the margin requirement of 50% of the short sale. The account would have the following balances:

Margin type	Short type
6PT000657-2	6PT000657-3
$20,000 Cr	SS 1,000 JAB @ $40 = $40,000 Cr

Should Les be wrong and JAB rises in price, at what price level will Les's account be on call? The maintenance requirement is 30% of market value.

$40,000
× .30
$12,000

As stated above, each rise in the stock price requires an adjustment from the balance in the margin account to the balance in the short account. Therefore, a one-point rise to $41 per share would cause $1,000 (1,000 shares × $1.00) to be moved from the margin account to the short account, leaving a balance of $19,000 in the margin account and a balance of $41,000 in the short account. (Should JAB fall in value, the reverse would occur.)

At $40 per share, Les's margin account was over maintenance by $8,000:

$20,000 margin account
−12,000 maintenance
$ 8,000

At $41 per share, the balance in the margin account went down to $19,000 and the maintenance rose to $12,300 ($41,000 × .30). The difference between the balance in the margin account and the maintenance requirement is now only $6,700, a decrease of $1,300, or $1.30 per share. Therefore, if we divide $8,000 (or even $6,700) by $1,300 ($1.30 per share × 1,000 shares), we see how much the stock can increase in value before Les's account is on maintenance call.

$8,000 divided by $1,300 = $6.15+. If the price of JAB rose from $40.00 per share to $46.16, the account would be on call.

Margin type	Short type
6PT000657-2	6PT000657-3
$13,840 Cr	SS 1,000 JAB @ $46.16 = $46,160 Cr

Maintenance requirement at $46.16:

$46,160
× .30
$13,848

As the maintenance requirement is $8 higher than the balance in the margin account, the account is now on call. SF&R wouldn't issue a call for $8, which is too small an amount, but would consider several factors such as other securities in the account and their own research department's opinion of JAB in deciding the amount that would be called for. Remember, the 30% maintenance requirement is set by the SROs and is used in this book. SF&R, as do other broker/dealers, sets higher requirements.

V-H *MAINTENANCE EXCESS*

As the margin account is being operated, over time there could be generated an excess greater than the maintenance requirement. Previously, when the maintenance requirement was discussed, we said that the equity in the account cannot be less than 25% of the market value. Therefore, any Reg T excess that would not trigger a maintenance call is known as *maintenance excess*. This figure is maintained in the SMA. A client may use this maintenance excess. Let's take an example:

Current market value	= $50,000
Less equity	= −25,000
Debit balance	= $25,000

The account increases in value to $75,000. At that level the account has Reg T excess of $12,500.

1. | | |
   |---|---|
   | Current market value | = $75,000 |
   | Less equity | = −50,000 |
   | Debit balance | = $25,000 |

2. | | |
   |---|---|
   | Loan value on $75,000 | = $37,500 |
   | Less debit balance | = −25,000 |
   | Reg T excess | = $12,500 |

If the client doesn't apply the excess, a bookkeeping entry will be made to the SMA recording the $12,500. The client can employ all of it or part of it, as long as the amount being used will not trigger a maintenance call. Remember, the excess is the amount the client can borrow. Its usage will increase a debit balance or decrease a credit balance.

Let's assume the market value falls to $40,000. At that level the account would have the following balances:

Current market value	= $40,000
Less equity	= −15,000
Debit balance	= $25,000

If the client decided to withdraw the $12,500 at this point, the debit balance would increase to $37,500, and the account would be on call for $7,500.

Current market value	= $40,000
Less equity	= − 2,500
Debit balance	= $37,500

A $40,000 market value requires an equity balance of $10,000 (25%). To prevent the release of funds from the margin account and the resulting immediate maintenance call for money back to the account, we must calculate the amount of the SMA that can be used. To what level can the debit balance be increased after which a maintenance call would be issued? The maximum debit balance that a $40,000 market value can support is $30,000 (75% of $40,000). The debit balance is currently $25,000, so the client can use $5,000 of the $12,500 that is in the SMA. That $5,000 is known as maintenance excess.

Example: Cliff Hainga has the following account balance:

Current market value	= $50,000
Less equity	= −25,000
Debit balance	= $25,000

From previous account activity, let us assume the SMA has accumulated $12,500.

The maintenance requirement on an account with $50,000 market value is $12,500 ($50,000 × .25 = $12,500).

As the client currently has $25,000 equity and a maintenance requirement of $12,500, the customer has usable SMA $12,500. This is also maintenance excess:

Equity	$25,000
Less maintenance requirement	−12,500
Maintenance excess	$12,500

V-I *DAY TRADING*

In recent years, a new type of client has appeared in the financial industry. These individuals are known as *day traders.* They sit at their homes or at certain brokerage firms and trade in and out of securities during the course of the day. In pure day trading, they do not maintain security positions overnight. In other words, whatever they buy during the day, they sell; and whatever they sell during the day, they bought that day. So at the end of the trading day, they do not have any positions. In securities industry parlance, they are "flat."

There is a set of special rules governing day trading. First of all, day trading is divided into two distinct groups. First is the customer who executes an occasional day trade. Second is what is known as the *pattern day trader*—someone who day trades on a regular basis. We will focus first on the customer who does an occasional day trade in his margin account.

Day trading is not permitted in a cash account because of the rule governing *free riding.* When a customer purchases and then sells stock before it is paid for, it is known as *free riding.* This process is illegal under SEC rules. In other words, a client cannot buy stock, immediately sell it, and either take the profit or pay the loss and walk away from the trade. Regulation T mandates that the purchase be paid for. Therefore, day trading is not permitted in a cash account.

A client can use maintenance excess that has accumulated in the SMA of a margin account to day trade. As the client is not a pattern day trader, he may during the course of the day utilize up to four times this amount of money to transact securities.

Here's an example: Clifford Hainga is a retail customer who does occasional transactions through SF&R. Cliff decides to do a day trade. His account has $50,000 market value and over time he has accumulated $25,000 in his SMA account. The account has a $25,000 debit balance. As stated above, his maintenance requirement would be $12,500, or 25% of $50,000. With the account in this position, Cliff has available to use in day trading $12,500 of maintenance excess. He may use, under the regulations, four times that amount ($50,000), so Cliff can buy up to $50,000 worth of stock during the day. Let's suppose Cliff enters into a transaction to buy $50,000 worth of stock in the morning and sells it later in the afternoon for $55,000. As he has utilized his limit, he is not penalized in any way and has made a $5,000 profit, which he may keep in the account or withdraw. However, let's suppose that Cliff purchased $50,000 worth of stock and at the end of the day sold it for $45,000. He would be obligated to put up 100% of the loss.

Instead of buying $50,000, Cliff purchases $60,000 worth of stock during the day. Cliff would have to put up 25% of the $10,000 by which he exceeded his maintenance excess. In other words, he would have to deposit $2,500. That could come from cash or marginable securities.

SF&R also has several *pattern day traders*. One of these individuals, Justin Tyme, has these current balances in his account:

Current market value	= $ 40,000
Less equity	= −15,000
Debit balance	= $ 25,000

As Justin is a pattern day trader with a market value of $40,000, his maintenance requirement is $10,000 (25% of $40,000 = $10,000). Over time Justin has accumulated $15,000 in his SMA. Justin has a current equity of $15,000. Therefore, Justin has $5,000 maintenance excess over the maintenance requirement. As he is a pattern day trader, he may transact two times that amount of money during the course of the day. Therefore, Justin can buy $10,000 worth of stock and sell it during the course of the day. Let's suppose that instead of buying only $10,000 worth of stock, Justin actually purchased $12,000 worth of stock. As his buying power, as applied to this particular situation, is two times the maintenance excess, he would have to bring in $1,000 (50% of the overage). At the end of the day, if Justin Tyme has a profit, he may withdraw the profit; if he has a loss, he must deposit 100% of the loss.

The rules are very strict regarding day traders. The firm must be able to prove what time the purchases and sales, or sales and purchases, took place during the course of the day. By being able to pair off transactions timewise, the firm can state the largest amount of money in use at one time. This affects the day traders' requirements. Should the firm not be able to state the largest amount of capital in use at one time, then Mr. Tyme would be responsible for the total amount either purchased or sold, whichever is greater during the course of the day.

This may be confusing, but let's suppose the following trades took place in Justin's account. (Remember, Justin can use up to $10,000 during the course of the day without having to deposit any additional funds.) Justin:

Buys 300 shares of RAM at $30 a share for $9,000 at 10:15 A.M.

Sells the 300 shares of RAM at $31 for $9,300 at 11:00 A.M.

Buys 400 shares of ZAP at $20 a share for $8,000 at 11:30 A.M.

Sells the 400 shares of ZAP at $19 for $7,600 at 1:15 P.M.

Buys 500 shares of PIP at $15 a share for $7,500 at 2:50 P.M.

Sells the 500 shares of PIP at $18 a share for $9,000 at 3:30 P.M.

To summarize the transactions:

Buys 300 shares of RAM @ $30 = $9,000	10:15 A.M.
Sells 300 shares of RAM @ $31 = $9,300	11:00 A.M.
Profit: $ 300	
Buys 400 shares of ZAP @ $20 = $8,000	11:30 A.M.
Sells 400 shares of ZAP @ $19 = $7,600	1:15 P.M.
Loss: $ 400	
Buys 500 shares of PIP @ $15 = $7,500	2:50 P.M.
Sells 500 shares of PIP @ $18 = $9,000	3:30 P.M.
Profit: $1,500	
Profit for the day: $1,400	

Since Cliff never exceeded the $10,000 excess he had over maintenance, then at the end of the day he can withdraw the $1,400 profit. Had the trades gone the other way and resulted in a $1,400 loss, Cliff would have had to deposit that money immediately. In addition, had Cliff exceeded the $10,000 on any one of these trades, he would have had to put up 50% of that overage to compensate for the excess that he used.

Suppose SF&R did not have the ability to monitor the time of the trades—which is very rare but could happen. In that case, Cliff would be responsible for the largest amount, buy or sell, that was outstanding at any one time during the course of the day. Remember, the firm cannot tell the time of the trades, they cannot tell whether the buys took place before the sells; therefore, if the sell side has a greater amount or the buy side has a greater amount and it exceeds $10,000, Cliff is responsible for 50% of that overage.

V-J *THE MARGIN/CREDIT DEPARTMENT AS PART OF CLIENT RELATIONSHIP MANAGEMENT*

V-J-1 Account Maintenance

The margin/credit function ensures that all of the customer accounts are operating in accordance with the regulations and firm policy. Through SF&R's real time systems, accounts are reviewed continuously, computing excess and/or buying power and updating money line balances. In addition, the systems monitor the resolution of account deficiencies. Some broker/dealers use less current systems and may adjust only the clients' security positions on a real-time basis but the money balances are adjusted in a batch process or vice versa. The degree of system support varies from firm to firm.

V-J-2 Sales Support

Any one of a thousand questions may be directed to the margin/credit personnel in the course of a day. Reliable, accurate responses to these questions are vital to the overall operation of the firm. The stockbroker or Web-based client relies on these automated systems and on margin/credit personnel for information when verifying the balances in a particular account. For example, a stockbroker may be discussing a possible transaction with a client, such as buying 100 shares of ZAP or selling (writing) a call option on a particular stock. The stockbroker has to know what effect the transaction will have on the overall account.

V-J-3 Clearance for Issuance of Checks

In most retail firms, margin systems keep track of the money available to be paid to clients. In an era when a client can access her account and request that checks be drawn without approval of the firm, these systems must be maintained in a controlled fashion. Generally, the firm will allow the client to withdraw checks from their accounts up to a certain amount, without the registered rep's and or client relationship manager's verification, but once a certain limit has been reached, approval must be sought from the margin/credit professional. The amount of money that can be taken on a customer's request without such approval varies from firm to firm. Those firms that do not have complex interactive real time margin systems still rely on either a registered rep and/or the margin personnel or the margin supervisor to approve payments of checks out of a customer's accounts.

Many firms have rules as to how these checks can be drawn. Most firms maintain that checks being paid from a customer's accounts can only be drawn in the name of the account. The ability to draw checks from the customer's account should not be used to pay bills and so on.

In recent times SF&R, as have many other firms, has allowed their customers to maintain checking accounts and money market funds as well as their investment portfolios under one roof. In such cases, there is generally a minimum amount of equity the customer must have to open and maintain such an account. These accounts, which combine the avenues of banking and brokerage, allow customers to draw checks as if they were regular, ordinary checking accounts.

Broker/dealers that offer the clients unrestricted checking accounts have generally made arrangements with a commercial bank to actually service the checking account. SF&R has such arrangements with First Continental Bank. While SF&R offers their clients full service, the check-writing portion of the account is maintained by the bank. Both entities have real-time systems that communicate with each other, moving funds back and forth in the clients' accounts as needed.

To summarize, depending on the level of service, clients can have checks drawn out of their accounts made payable to the name appearing on the accounts. Any other payee is an exception. They may also draw checks from their money market fund payable to anyone of their choice, but there are usually minimum and denomination restrictions (e.g., $500 minimum and multiples of $100 thereafter). Or the client may have a regular checking account offered by the broker/dealer but serviced by a commercial bank.

V-K *MARGIN DEPARTMENT'S DAILY ROUTINE*

The margin function, like all operations procedures, is an ongoing process. Every business day, some customers enter into new commitments and others settle transactions. Securities and funds are paid, received, or delivered. Stock dividends and bond interest are credited or charged to customers' accounts. Legal papers are received. Sell-outs and buy-ins are issued. T calls and maintenance calls are sent. All the while, the markets are open for trading and securities' prices are fluctuating. With all this happening at once, accuracy is a must. The margin/credit employee must be able to deal quickly with figures and understand the applicable rules.

Few firms, and they are very rare, operate without a computer-generated exception listing. In those firms, a margin clerk has to review each and every account to determine which ones are operating within the framework and guidelines provided by the regulators and the firm's own procedures, and which ones need attention. The vast majority of margin computations are performed by the margin system's programs. Therefore, the margin/credit function now operates on an exception basis. There is no longer a need to look at every account and compute the values to determine if the account has excess, if it's restricted, or if it's on call for money. The system takes care of that. The system also alerts margin/credit personnel of deficiencies that could be present in customers' accounts. Through the use of these systems, messages are sent between the margin/credit personnel and sales branch offices staff (or, in the case of a Web client, the customer relationship management centers) as to the disposition of the various items. Messages sent to the branch are forwarded by the branch operations personnel to each stockbroker concerning accounts that they are responsible for and what their current problems are.

V-K-1 Reports to Produce

Each morning when SF&R's margin/credit personnel report to work, they find *exception reports* and the *items due lists* on their workstation. Most firms have this as a computerized interactive function. Some firms, however, still produce the reports in paper format.

V-K-1-a *Exception Report*

The exception report covers:

1. Any account that has less equity than is required. (A new maintenance call is to be issued.)
2. Clients that sold a different class of security than the one that was in position in the client's account (e.g., the $8.56 preferred vs. the $8.35 preferred). It may be a valid trade, but it has to be verified with the rep or the client.
3. A client's check that was returned marked "NSF" (nonsufficient funds).
4. A client that sold an option marked "opening" transaction and is long (owns) the same option series in position. (The sale should have been marked "close.")
5. Deficiencies in name and address documentation.
6. Any account involved with a legal proceeding with or against Stone, Forrest & Rivers.
7. Any arbitration underway between principals of an account.
8. A client's violation of a restriction imposed by the firm on its account.
9. Other problems.

V-K-1-b *Items Due*

Due to the nature of the industry, the credit department staff spends a good part of its time working with branch office and customer service center personnel on *items due*. This includes items that are pending and items that are actual deficiencies in customer accounts. Included in the items due report are:

1. Money due on T calls—the sum owed by a customer on a new transaction.
2. Money due on house calls—the sum that a customer owes to satisfy an equity deficiency (that is, the equity is below the firm's minimum maintenance).
3. Stocks or bonds due to be delivered by the client against a sale in the account.
4. A client's extension of time for payment that is about to expire.
5. A client that was supposed to liquidate securities to satisfy a T call or maintenance call but didn't.
6. Legal papers needed to effect transfer.
7. Any other pending problem.

Someone at a sales branch—usually a stockbroker or an individual in the client relationship management center—has to contact the clients and advise them of the discrepancies. The client's obligation is to then satisfy the discrepancy promptly or the firm may take market action against the account.

V-K-2 Extensions

Occasionally, clients enter into a security transaction and, due to circumstances beyond their control, cannot satisfy the obligation by settlement day. Usually, clients have a grace period after settlement day to satisfy the problem before the firm must take action. In such a case, the firm, on instruction from the stockbroker or from the client relationship manager, may request an extension of time with the NASD Regulation Division. If the request is granted, the client has additional time to satisfy the commitment. A customer is permitted to have five extensions per year, on an industrywide basis.

V-K-3 Close-Outs

If a request for extension of time is turned down, the firm has to take the appropriate action and *close out* the transaction. If the client has failed to pay for a purchased security, the security is liquidated. In closing an unsatisfied purchase, the brokerage firm is said to *sell out* the purchased security. If the client has failed to deliver a sold security, the firm closes out the commitment. In closing out an unsatisfied sale, the firm is said to *buy in*; that is, the firm buys the security elsewhere and delivers the securities to the original buying firm.

Because the problem arises with the customer, the closing transaction must be effected in the customer's account. However, a customer cannot profit from a trade he did not pay for. Therefore, if the liquidating transaction results in a profitable trade, the original trade will be moved from the customer's account to a firm's error account and liquidated through that facility. If, on the other hand, the liquidating transaction results in a loss, both the original trade and the liquidating trade will take place in the customer's account. (It is very seldom that a customer will not pay for a trade that is in a profitable position. Therefore, the vast majority of these transactions that are not satisfied by customers are because of a resulting loss that has occurred.)

V-K-4 Delivery of Securities

The customer's account reflects the firm's obligation to the customer and the customer's obligation to the firm. Once the obligation ceases to exist, it is no longer reflected in the account. The obligation can be for either money or securities.

For fully paid-for securities that remain in the firm's possession, the firm owes the securities to the customer so the firm assumes a custodian obligation. The margin/credit personnel have the responsibility of releasing securities for delivery to clients. (A few customers still request physical delivery of the securities.) These securities can be delivered only if the client has paid for them in full.

On sales, the client can owe the firm delivery of the securities sold. Once the delivery of the securities is made in good form (in other words, once the securities are made negotiable), the firm owes the customer the proceeds of the sale.

Most securities are in registered form. This means that the face of the certificate contains the name of the legal owner or its nominee. Certificates must be endorsed (signed) by the registered owner (whose name appears on the face of certificate) to make them negotiable. There may still be, in certain products, *bearer certificates.* These certificates do not bear any name and are assumed to be the property of the person presenting them. They are very rare and are dying out as each year passes. Clients requesting delivery of their securities require *registered securities* to be sent by the brokerage firm, or by the depository, to a transfer agent that represents the issuer to effect the change in registrations. The transfer agent reregisters the security in the customer's name and mails it to the depository or the brokerage firm for delivery to the customer. Once these securities are delivered to the customer, the security position is no longer reflected in the customer's account.

The margin/credit personnel keep track of all these entries, making sure that accounts reflect the correct balances. Margin/credit personnel have the dual responsibility of protecting the firm's funds *and* the customer's funds. They must be aware at all times of *all* the rules affecting brokerage-customer relationships.

V-K-5 The Margin/Credit Workstation

The typical account that appears on a workstation will contain the following information:

1. Client's account number, registered rep number, and a condensed version of the client's name, known as the *short name.*
2. The trade date and settlement date money balances by type of account. Some systems also show the money balances for T+1 and T+2.
3. The trade date and settlement date security positions.
4. The client's SMA.
5. The amount that equity exceeds the house requirement.
6. The amount of excess and buying power in the account.
7. Any restrictions currently imposed.
8. In the case of a margin account with a debit balance, the amount of accrued interest being charged up to that point of the month.
9. Total of any dividend and interest received during the month.

Margin/credit personnel (as well as the branch office's staff) can also bring up a recent history file of all activity in the client's account. This is generally for the past 90 days. They can also access previous months' statements.

These statements are designed to conform to computer specifications and cannot be used in place of the regularly produced monthly statement sent to the client. The latter is a legal document conforming to regulatory requirements.

There is much more to margin. This basic presentation should, however, provide some insight into the workings of a margin account. The margin department employee has a much more detailed understanding of these regulations, and the department manager must be cognizant of all the rules and regulations as well as their interpretations and applicability. If these regulations are not enforced, the firm can face possible loss through unnecessary exposure to risk or fine in addition to suspension from the regulatory agencies.

V-L *OPTION MARGIN*

Stone, Forrest & Rivers has many clients who transact business in the various option products. These clients have filled out the proper documentation required for such transactions and have been approved for trading by the senior registered option principal (SROP) of SF&R. Stone, Forrest & Rivers has a policy that any client wishing to conduct business in options, regardless of the nature of that trade, not only must promptly sign the option agreement, but also must have completed a margin agreement. The reason for this policy is that customers who trade with options will eventually enter into option strategies that require their being held or maintained in a margin account. Option positions are different from equity and debt positions in that the former represent *intent* while the latter represent *actual ownership* of an issue. The exception is IRA accounts, where clients who want to enter into option spread positions are permitted to do so in a cash account. Option spreads must be maintained in a margin account for non-IRA accounts.

V-L-1 Option Margin Theory

Option margin is firm protection. If there isn't any risk to the firm, either real or perceived, there isn't any margin. Recently option margin rules were altered to permit options having a life span of more that nine months to be acquired on margin. However, the vast majority of option trades are short term and purchases of these must be paid for in full. If there is risk to the firm, a margin formula is then applied.

Example 1: Account 1BS044291 owns 100 shares of KID at $50 per share. The client sells a call on KID and receives the premium. If the option is exercised against this account, the firm will deliver the client's security. (The owner of a call has the privilege of "calling in," or buying, the underlying security. The seller, or writer, of a call option must deliver the underlying security, which in this example is KID, on exercise.) Since the firm is not exposed to any risk with this position, there isn't any margin applied to the option. This is known as a *covered option position.*

Example 2: Account 1BS049682 is anticipating a drop in the price of ZAP. Since puts increase in value as the underlying issue value falls, the client expects the profit from the decrease in ZAP's market value by buying puts on ZAP. If ZAP actually increases in value, the market value of the put will fall and the option could expire worthless. In any event, the firm is not at risk because the client must pay for the purchase of the put options. Let's assume our client Victor Torri, account 1BS049682, purchases 10 puts at a premium of 3. Those 10 puts would cost Vic $3,000 plus commission (10 puts × 100 shares × 3 = $3,000). If the option had a duration of nine months or less, Vic would have to pay for the put purchase in full.

As stated previously, recently the rules were altered so that any option issued for longer than nine months could be acquired on margin. In other words, a firm may advance a customer the margin requirement of 75% of the purchase price. So if Vic had purchased long-term options called LEAPS (Long-term Equity AnticiPation Securities), he would have to deposit 75% of the $3,000 required, or a total of $2,250. The firm would lend him the other $750.

Example 3: Another account, 4CG002731, sells (writes) 10 calls POW Apr 60 at 2. POW is currently at $59 per share. The client believes that POW will fall in value; therefore, the call premium will fall also (the call's market value rises and falls with the underlying's value). Since the client does not own 1,000 shares of POW, this option position is considered uncovered (naked), and margin must be charged. Margin is needed in case the market value of POW rises and the firm has to respond to an exercise and cover the loss.

Let's assume POW rises to $70 by the option's expiration. A call with a strike price of $60 would be worth 10 points, because the owner of the call option could call in a stock worth $70 per share and pay the option's strike price of $60 per share. Since the client, in this example, received only $2 per share ($200 per option), the firm would be at risk because the underlying stock rose against the client's position. The firm will collect margin from the client to cover the risk and, as the market value continues to rise, more margin will be required.

V-L-2 Margin Calculation for an Uncovered Equity Option

The margin calculation for an uncovered equity option position is 20% of the underlying value, plus the premium, less the out-of-the-money sum, if any, with a minimum requirement of 10% of the underlying plus the premium. Both calculations are performed and the higher amount is applied. In this example, the option(s) are out of the money, since no one will call in (buy) stock at $60 (the strike price) when the security is trading at $59.

In the margin calculation:

1. Each option has 100 shares of stock underlying it.
2. The position is for 10 options.

	Margin Req.	Maintenance Req.
Current market value	$ 5,900	$ 5,900
× number of options	× 10	× 10
	$59,000	$59,000
× appropriate percentage	× .20	× .10
	$11,800	$ 5,900
Plus premium 2 × 100 × 10 =	+ 2,000	+ 2,000
	$13,800	$ 7,900
Less out-of-money amount	− 1,000	—
	$12,800	—

Since the $12,800 figure is higher, it becomes the margin requirement.

Example 4: Account 2BW106341 sells 5 puts WAM Jun 40 at 3. WAM is at 39. Is the WAM put option in, at, or out of the money? The margin calculation is:

	Margin Req.
$39 × 100 shares per option × 5 options =	$19,500
× 20% (the margin percentage)	× 20%
	$ 3,900
Plus the premium: 3 × 100 × 5 =	+ 1,500
Less the out-of-the-money sum, if any (these options are in the money since anyone who owned one "free" could buy the stock at $39 per share and put it out at $40, strike price)	0
Total	$ 5,400

In puts, the minimum computation is 10% of the *exercise price* and not the market value of the underlying, plus premium:

5 put options × $40 strike price	=	$20,000
$20,000 × 10% margin requirement	=	$ 2,000
Premium	=	+ 1,500
		$ 3,500

Since $5,400 is the higher requirement, it is the one that is utilized to carry this position.

Here's one more example:

Let assume SF&R's client, account 2BW106341, sold 5 puts WAM Jun 40 at 3 when WAM was at $39 per share. The stock has risen in price to $55 as of last night and the option was trading at $.20. The margin calculation would be:

$55 × 100 shares per option × 5 options	=	$27,500	
× 20% (the margin percentage)		× 20%	
		$ 5,500	
Plus the premium: $.20 × 100 × 5	=	+ 100	
Less the out-of-the-money sum, if any (the options are out of the money by 15 points × 100 × 5)	=	− 7,500	
Total		($1,900)	negative figure

Maintenance calculation:

5 put options × \$40 strike price	= \$20,000
\$20,000 × 10% margin requirement	= \$ 2,000
Premium	= + 100
	\$ 2,100

The requirement is the maintenance requirement of \$2,100.

V-L-3 Margin for Spread Positions

For margin purposes, spreads exist whenever a client is long *and* short (has bought and sold) equal numbers of puts *or* calls on the same underlying, but with different expiration months and/or strike prices. The positions do not have to be developed at the same time, but they must be in position at the same time.

Examples: The following are spreads:

1. Long 1 Call EEK Jun 40
   Short 1 Call EEK Jun 45

2. Long 1 Call EEK Jan 40
   Short 1 Call EEK Feb 40

3. Long 1 Put MIP Sep 30
   Short 1 Put MIP Sep 25

4. Short 1 Put TOP Apr 35
   Long 1 Put TOP Mar 35

The following are not spreads:

1. L 1 Put ZAP Apr 40
   S 1 Call ZAP Apr 40

2. L 1 Put PIP Oct 40
   S 1 Put POW Oct 40

3. L	1	Call	RAP	Sep 35
L	1	Call	RAP	Oct 30

In a spread, one option (the more expensive one) is the *main option*. If the main option is long (bought), the other option acts to reduce the premium or cost.

Example:

L	1	Call	PAM	Nov 40
S	1	Call	PAM	Nov 45

The lower strike price call, with the longest time remaining, always has the most value, because it will "go" into the money first. If the stock PAM is above 40 but less than 45, the 40 strike price call option is in the money; the 45 strike price call is out of the money.

Let's assume that PAM is currently trading at $40 per share. The Nov 40 call is trading at 4 ($400 per option), and the Nov 45 call is trading at 1.50 ($150 per option). The client believes that PAM will rise in value but would not rise above $45 per share so he could buy the 40 and sell the 45 for a "net" cost of 2.50, or $250 per option ($400 premium for the 40 strike price option less $150 premium for the 45=$250). The breakeven, should the stock rise in value, is $42.50.

If, on the other hand, the more expensive option was the one that was sold, the other option in the spread acts as an insurance policy. For example:

S	1	Put	PAT	Nov 30
B	1	Put	PAT	Nov 25

In puts, the higher strike price option, with the longest time to go, has the most value, because it will go into the money first.

Example: Refer to the previous example. If the stock was between $25 and $30 per share, the Nov 30 put would be in the money, and the Nov 25 would be out of the money. In this position, the client would want the price of PAT to rise so that both options would expire out of the money.

Let's assume PAT was at $30 per share. The PAT Nov 30 option was trading at $4; the PAT Nov 25 option was trading at $1. If the client is correct, the market value of PAT stays at $30 or rises, both options expire worthless, and the client keeps $300 per spread ($400 for the 30 strike price put option, less $100 for the 25 strike price option). If, however, the client is wrong, the price of PAT falls below 25; whatever the client lost on the Sold or Short 1 put PAT Nov 30 when the stock went below 25 is made up by gains in the Bought or Long 1 put PAT Nov 25. For instance, if at expiration PAT is trading at 20, the Nov 30 is worth 10 points, and the Nov 25 is worth 5 points. The client would be facing a 5-point loss, less the 3 points of premium received for a real loss of 2 points. If the stock was at $15 per share at expiration, the 30 strike price put would be worth 15 points, and the 25 strike price put would be worth 10 points. The client would be losing $1,500 on the sale of the 30 put, but earning $1,000 on the buy of the 25 put, for a spread difference of $500. When the $300 premium, which was received on the original trade, is subtracted, the client is left with a $200 loss.

Margin charged on option positions, as already stated, is required when there is real or perceived risk to the firm. Due to the "perceived" part, any spread in which the sold option expires after the bought option is automatically charged margin, based on an uncovered position from day 1. The reason is that, at some later date, the long (bought) option will expire and the client will be left with a short (sold) uncovered option.

In spread positions where the long (bought) option expires on or after the short (sold) option and has the greater value, the client pays the difference (spread), because the firm doesn't have any risk; there isn't need for margin.

If, however, the long option expires on or after the short option with the short option as the main option, the margin requirement is the difference between strike prices, or the calculation for an uncovered option, whichever is less.

Example:

S	1	call	JAY	Oct 40 = 6
L	1	call	JAY	Oct 45 = 3

JAY common stock is trading at $40 per share.

Step 1: Calculate the difference between strike prices:

Long	45	strike price
Short	40	strike price
	5	points × 100 shares = $500

Step 2:

		Margin	Maintenance
Market value of 100 shares JAY	=	$4,000	$4,000
times the margin rate	=	× .20	× .10
		$ 800	$ 400
Plus the premium	=	+ 600	+ 600
		$1,400	$1,000
Less the out-of-the money amount		− 0	− 0
		$1,400	$1,000

The margin requirement for an uncovered option is the greater of the margin or maintenance requirement ($1,400). This is applied against the difference between strike prices ($500), and the lesser amount is applied. The margin required is $500 (computation does not take into consideration the $300 premium received and other expenses).

V-L-4 Margin for Straddle or Combo Positions

The final option position is a *straddle* or *combo*, either of which is defined as buys or sells of equal numbers of puts and calls, all having the same underlying. If both have the same series description, the position is a *straddle*; if the series descriptions are different, it is known as a *combo*.

Example: The following are straddles:

1. B 1 Put BOB Jan 60
   B 1 Call BOB Jan 60

2. S 1 Put SAN Jun 30
   S 1 Call SAN Jun 30

The following are combos:

1. B 1 Put SRA Oct 35
   B 1 Call SRA Oct 40

2. S 1 Put MEL Jul 50
   S 1 Call MEL Oct 55

The following are not straddles or combos:

1. S 1 Put LEE Mar 15
   S 1 Put LEE Mar 17½

2. B 1 Put LAR Nov 25
   B 1 Call MAR Nov 25

3. B 1 Put LAR Oct 35
   S 1 Call LAR Oct 55

In the case of a straddle or combo, if the position is bought, the client pays the premiums in full, and no margin is charged as long as there is no risk to the firm. The client owns both positions.

If, however, the straddle or combo is sold, both positions are computed as uncovered options. The margin requirement is the requirement of the greater side, plus the premium of the other side.

Example:

S 1 Call LAR Oct 35=5
S 1 Put LAR Oct 40=3
LAR is selling at 38.

Call		Put	
100 LAR 38		100 LAR 38	
$3,800		$3,800	
× .20		× .20	
760		760	
500	Premium	300	Premium
$1,260		$1,060	
0	Less out-of-the-money amount	0	Less out-of-the-money amount
$1,260		$1,060	

The margin requirement is the "greater" side (the call), plus the premium amount from the other side (put, 3 points premium).

$1,260	Margin requirement, call
+ 300	The premium of the put
$1,560	Margin required for the position

Note: Reviewed here is the margin required for equity options. The margin required for other products requires the application of different amounts and/or percentages. In any event, the firm's requirement may be higher or more restrictive.

V-M *FUTURE MARGIN*

Future margin is based on a product (commodity, debt instrument, index, currency, metal) that is to be delivered at a later time. The buyer and seller of the future are really involved with a promise. The buyer is relying on the seller's "promise" to deliver; the seller is relying on the buyer's "promise" to pay upon receipt. Between the two parties are the clearing firms and clearing corporations that must make good the terms of the contract.

Futures, like many other products, give the participant the ability not only to receive or deliver, but also to trade out of, or liquidate, positions. Between the time the position is opened and the time it is finally settled, the price on which the future product itself is based can change drastically.

Because the future is a "promise," the amount of margin must be enough to protect all interested parties. Yet it must not be so high as to prevent participants from being able to benefit from the product.

Future margin is usually maintained between 3% and 5% of the value of the underlying contract. This sum may be reflected as a fixed dollar sum or as a percentage. Index futures have the highest requirement, 10%. Again, as with all margins, regardless of product, the brokerage firm, commodity house, or other entity may charge higher rates.

V-M-1 Standard and Maintenance Margin

The gold contract is 100 troy ounces. If a particular gold future is trading at $350 per ounce, then a contract on gold at that price would have a value of $35,000. Assuming 5% margin, the margin per contract would be approximately $1,750. Therefore, the buyer and seller of a gold futures contract would be expected to deposit $1,750 for the contract. This is known as *standard margin.*

When the exchange on which the future trades establishes the standard margin, it also establishes *maintenance margin.*

Example: Assume that the maintenance margin for gold is 2% and that it sells for $350 per ounce. This means that the amount of margin in a client's account may not be less than $700 ($35,000 × .02 = $700). We will keep margin at these rates throughout the following examples.

The 6-month gold future is trading on the New York Commodity Exchange (COMEX) at $350 per ounce when a client of SF&R decides to buy one contract. The client, Nathan Lee, must deposit standard margin by the next business day. Nat would deposit $1,750.

V-M-2 Mark to the Market

Another firm, Giant, Reckor & Crane, has a client, Emily D'Elder, wanting to sell one contract. Emily will also have to deposit $1,750 when the trade is made.

Nat	Emily
Long 1 gold 6-month @ $350	Short 1 gold 6-month @ $350
Standard margin $1,750	Standard margin $1,750

Assume that, at the end of the trading day, the gold 6-month future contract closes at $350.50. Both firms would have to "mark" their client's account to the market. This means the money balances in the accounts must be altered to show the proper adjustment for profit or loss that resulted from that day's trading.

V-M-3 Variation Margin

Since Nat took the contract on at $350.00, and the price is now $350.50, Nat's account is credited (given) the 50 cents × 100 = $50.00. Emily's account would reflect a decrease of 50 cents × 100 = $50.00. At the end of the day's trading, Nat has an $1,800 balance; Emily has $1,700.

This daily *mark to the market* (or P&S-ing) is important, because it brings all of the positions in a given contract to the same price. The adjusted money position is called *variation margin.*

Just as these two illustrative accounts were adjusted to show the price difference, so would every other account that held positions in this contract, regardless of the price or time of commitment. All prices in this particular contract would be adjusted against the $350.50 settlement price.

Example: Nat has a $50 profit at this point. If the position is "liquidated" or closed out, Nat receives the $1,800 from the account. Since he only put up $1,750, the $50 profit is reflected in the difference. If Emily, on the other hand, liquidates the position, she receives a check for $1,700, reflecting the $50 loss. (Commission is ignored in these examples.)

Should the participants decide to maintain the positions until delivery, Nat is *contracted* to buy 100 troy ounces of gold for $35,000 (100 × $350), and Emily is contracted to deliver 100 troy ounces of gold and receive $35,000. As Nat already paid $1,750 (standard margin), Nat would owe the difference: $35,000 – 1,750 = $33,250. Upon payment of the $33,250, Nat has fulfilled the terms of the contract.

Emily has to deliver 100 troy ounces according to the terms of the contract. When this is accomplished, Emily will receive $35,000 plus the standard margin of $1,750, for a total of $36,750 (the $1,750 is Emily's money).

V-M-4 Delivery and Payment

Example: Gold is at $350.50 an ounce at the time of delivery. When the account is marked to the market, Nat would have had a profitable position and his account would have been credited $50 (50 cents × 100 troy ounces). The account would have contained $1,750 standard margin and $50 variation margin, for a total of $1,800. If gold is settling at $350.50 an ounce, SF&R (Nat's firm) would take Nat's standard margin, $1,750, plus the additional money Nat owes, $33,250 ($35,000 – $1,750 = $33,250) and the variation margin, $50, and purchase the gold for their client, Nat, for $35,050 ($350.50 per ounce). Nat's profit is now hidden in the fact that Nat paid $35,000 ($1,750 standard margin plus $33,250 additional deposit) for $35,050 worth of gold; the variation margin made up the difference.

Emily, on the other hand, received $36,750 when the gold was delivered. This sum, from Emily's point of view, is made up of the $1,750 standard margin that she deposited and the $35,000 received from the gold delivery. In reality, Emily's account was charged $50 variation margin when the gold rose from $350 to $350.50. Emily's firm, Giant, Reckor & Crane (GRC), has taken Emily's gold and delivered it as required by contract. (Actually, GRC has instructed Emily how and where to deliver it, but that's a different subject not to be discussed here.)

Upon delivery of the gold, $35,050 is received. This sum, plus Emily's remaining standard margin of $1,700, would total the money owed to Emily ($35,050 + $1,700 = $36,750).

Nat's Account		Emily's Account	
B 1 gold 6 months @	$ 350	S 1 gold 6 months @	$ 350
Both deposit standard margin.			
L 1 gold 6 months @	$ 350	S 1 gold 6 months @	$ 350
Standard margin	$1,750	Standard margin	$1,750
	$1,750		$1,750

Gold rises to $350.50.

Long 1 gold 6 months @	$ 350	Short 1 gold 6 months @	$ 350
Standard margin	$1,750	Standard margin	$1,750
Variation margin	+ 50	Variation margin	− 50
	$1,800		$1,700

Standard margin accounts are adjusted to reflect current contract value.

If either party closes out the position at this market level, he or she would be trading at $350.50. Nat would have a $50 profit ($1,800 − $1,750 = $50). Emily would have a $50 loss ($1,750 − $1,700 = $50).

If Nat is still long the position at the time of delivery, he would have to pay $35,000 in total. Having deposited $1,750, Nat would owe the difference ($33,250). The firm would take Nat's $35,000 and the variation margin of $50, and acquire the gold at $350.50 per ounce.

$ 1,750	Standard margin
33,250	Additional deposit
$35,000	Total cost to Nat
+50	Variation margin
$35,050	Total cost for receipt of gold

Nat's contract stated that the cost to Nat for 100 troy ounces of gold would be $350.00 per ounce, and that is what it cost Nat.

If Emily is still short the position at the time of delivery, she would have to deliver the gold and receive $35,000 plus the standard margin that Emily had placed in the account, for a total of $36,750.

When Emily's gold is delivered, the firm will receive $35,050, the current value for gold. The firm takes the $35,050 plus whatever funds remain in the account, and delivers it to Emily.

Emily is contracted to deliver gold and receive	$35,000
Emily is to receive the standard margin deposit	+1,750
	$36,750

Emily will actually receive for the delivered gold	$35,050
Emily's deposit to standard margin	$ 1,750
Less variation margin	−50
Remaining standard margin	+1,700
	$36,750

Emily's contract term has been satisfied.

Had the price of gold fallen instead, the adjustments for variation margin would be reversed. Both parties would still be contracting for $35,000 worth of gold, but Nat would be paying $35,000 for $34,950 worth of gold:

Standard margin	$ 1,750	
Variation margin	−50	
	$ 1,700	
	+33,250	additional funds owed by Nat
	$ 34,950	

Paid by Nat = $35,000 ($1,750 + 33,250 = $35,000)

Value of gold = $34,950 ($1,700 + 33,250 = $34,950)

Emily would receive $35,000 plus the standard margin of $1,750 deposited, for a total of $36,750. In reality:

Standard margin	$ 1,750
Variation margin	+50
	1,800
Actually received for gold	+34,950
	$ 36,750

V-M-5 *STANDARD PORTFOLIO ANALYSIS OF RISK (SPAN) MARGIN*

Professional traders and hedgers offset their future positions with futures and put and call options on the same deliverable products. These combinations result in different market risks depending on how they are applied against one another. In addition, as the value of the underlying product changes, so does the relationship between the different options and futures that are overlying the product. SPAN margin was developed for the industry participants to use in computing their exposure through the use of a preset algorithm. Each trading day the future exchanges distribute the SPAN calculations to their clearing members who input the data into their systems so that the firms can compute the risk analysis on each client and proprietary account's position.

Let's look at a simplified example. Ron Divoo has sold 10 silver contracts. He has bought 10 at-the-money call contracts and wrote 10 out-of-the-money call contracts. He also bought 10 out-of-the-money put contracts and sold 10 at-the-money put contracts. At this moment SF&R would marry the puts to the short position and let the calls stand on their own. What is Ron's minimum margin requirement?

Assume that all options expire the same day.

Example 1. Marry the sold puts to the short silver contracts.
Treat the call options as a covered spread.
Treat the bought puts as uncovered.

Example 2. Treat the calls and the puts as separate spreads.
Leave the short silver contract uncovered.

Example 3. Treat the bought calls and puts as straddles.
Treat the sold calls and puts as straddles.
Leave the short silver contract uncovered.

Each of the above would result in a different requirement as well as represent different exposure to the firm. SPAN margin would calculate the margin required for the various examples above and that would giver SF&R the answer it needs. Missing from the above are the changes in market prices and the changes in positions that occur every day.

This concludes the chapter concerning the different types and applications of margin. We have only scratched the surface of this topic. Remember, broker/dealers, commodity and future firms, and other service providers can be more restrictive with their rules and policies than is required by regulators, and they usually are. However, their rules can never be more lenient than what the regulators have set.

CHAPTER VI

Settlement

After trade processing, the settlement function begins. The settlement function manages the firm's most critical assets: securities and cash. Specifically, this department must move securities as efficiently as possible so as to minimize the firm's need to borrow securities or cash, and it must maximize the firm's profit potential.

SF&R's settlement area consists of:

- Receive and deliver
- Fail to receive/fail to deliver
- Warehousing (vault, custodian bank, or depository)
- Financing
    - Stock loan/stock borrow
    - Bank loan
    - Repo
    - Letter of credit control
    - Unsecured loan

Adjuncts to these areas are custodian responsibilities:

- Security transfer
- Corporate action
- Dividend and bond interest

The sections of the settlement area work jointly to use the firm's securities and other resources as effectively and efficiently as possible. Note that while accuracy in security processing is very important, the money represented by these securities is equally important. As securities move in one direction, cash is usually moving in the opposite direction. Very seldom in operations do securities move without cash moving in the other direction and vice versa. In other words, when SF&R delivers stock to another broker/dealer, SF&R is going to be paid. Likewise, when another broker/dealer delivers stock to SF&R, SF&R must pay. The control and use of securities and the resulting cash movement is very important to the stability, control, and profitability of Stone, Forrest & Rivers.

The settlement department becomes involved in operations the day before settlement, on settlement day itself, and in the postsettlement period.

VI-A *SEGREGATION (SEG)*

Under the Federal Reserve Board's Regulation T, broker/dealers have certain requirements in the maintenance of client security. The rule states that the broker/dealer must have possession or control of clients' fully paid-for securities and may only use securities with market value of up to 140% of the client's debit (loan) balance in a margin account to finance the loan. The stock that is available for loan is known as margin stock, whereas the remainder is referred to in the rules as excess margin stock. A violation to the seg rules is a federal offense punishable by imprisonment.

The fact that a broker/dealer has to account for clients' securities doesn't mean that a particular certificate has to be assigned to a particular client, in the same manner that a bank doesn't have to assign a particular dollar that is on deposit to a particular depositor. Therefore, all of the shares of a particular company that are owned by SF&R's clients are pooled and the seg requirements are applied, per account, against the total position. Those securities not needed for seg are available to make deliveries to clients or other broker/dealers, to clean up fails to deliver, to lend to other broker/dealers, to cover other clients' short sales, and to pledge at a bank.

A broker/dealer can use clients' securities because the securities are registered in street name and are therefore *fungible*. A client's security that is registered in street name is said to be in *nominee name*. Stock maintained by SF&R in the client's name is said to be in the name of the beneficial owner and is not fungible because the client's name is unknown to the receiver and therefore may not be a valid delivery. (Think of someone who is buying something from you and paying for it with a check from someone that you do not know.)

To make sure that SF&R doesn't violate seg, at the beginning of the settlement cycle, all client accounts are updated to reflect the result of all activity. Clients' trades are assumed to have settled and fail items are added to maximize the possible seg requirement. The seg calculation is then performed. The previous seg requirement is compared to the newly calculated requirement. The result will be either a deficit or excess.

Stocks are then locked up in the following order:

1. Stocks registered in the client's name
2. Restricted securities
3. Nonmarginable securities
4. Stocks selling for under $5
5. Stocks locked up based on a preselected algorithm, which selects and locks up a security by highest market price first, or some other criterion selected by the broker/dealer

After the application of seg requirements, security positions are compared to delivery obligations. Where the value of stock exceeds that seg requirement, those shares are available to settle trades. During the settlement cycle, SF&R is receiving and delivering securities. Stocks being received are compared to the seg requirements and, if there is a deficit, the stock is locked up. As for those positions that have excess securities, the excess is used to clean up delivery obligations.

At the end of the cycle, SF&R's seg requirement is recalculated. If there is a deficit, SF&R will call back securities in bank loan first as these represent former *free stock,* where clients have either sold the stock or paid down their debit balances in their margin accounts. If the deficit still exists, SF&R will call back securities from stock loan. If the deficit still exists, SF&R will borrow the stock from another source. If, however, there is excess after all delivery obligations have been met, SF&R will try to lend the stock. Then, if an excess still exists, it will place the remaining excess in bank loan.

VI-B *RECEIVE AND DELIVER*

The length of the settlement cycle (that is, the number of days between trade date and settlement date) varies according to the instrument being traded. Obviously, the shorter the cycle, the less time SF&R has to prepare for the settlement function. For example, in commercial paper transactions, the settlement is the same day as the trade; therefore, processing time is minimal. Yet the trade must be entered into the system, money amounts figured and verified, the bank notified of the money sum to be paid or received, and the settlement area set up to receive or deliver. Once the receive or deliver instructions have been prepared and the actual issues have been received into or delivered from SF&R's account at DTC, money moves in the opposite direction and the trades are settled, all in one day.

Generally, for other products, SF&R's settlement staff begins preparing for the settlement prior to the actual settlement date. Reports are received from various clearing corporations and verified against SF&R's internally produced records. These external records are transmitted to SF&R electronically. SF&R maintains system programs that verify the external records against SF&R internal data as to the name of the securities, quantity, and monies involved in the settlement cycle. This "heads-up" beginning allows SF&R's staff to begin to line up securities that would be needed for delivery as well as to make sure that the funds that will be needed for settlement are going to be at the proper bank in the proper quantity and the proper currency.

SF&R keeps the majority of their securities at either Depository Trust Company, a division of DTCC, for corporates, munis, and other securities. U.S. Treasuries and government agencies are maintained at First Continental Trust, which acts as a clearing bank as well as assisting SF&R in financing its high-grade bonds, including governments and agencies. The bank has a process by which it accelerates repo processing. (*Repo* is a generic term for *repurchase agreement*, which is a method by which SF&R can finance high-grade bonds, including governments and agencies, at a lower interest cost than it would by financing through a bank.)

Transactions in corporate and municipal securities currently follow a three-business-day cycle. Using the T+3 scenario, notification of trades pending settlement enters the settlement area on the day before the actual settlement date. By this time, the transactions have been compared and netted by the various clearing corporations—and are being readied for settlement.

VI-B-1 Preparation for Settlement

National Securities Clearing Corporation (a division of DTCC) provides its participants with a report known as the *projection report*. It informs the settlement area of the remaining positions due for that day's settlement. Earlier in this book, when we discussed the continuous net settlement process, we covered NSCC's ability to net trades so that the number of receives and delivers that must be made interfirm are minimized. We also discussed "open receives" and "open delivers" from one settlement day being rolled into the next day's settling trades and netted with the next day's transactions. This process not only minimizes the number of receives and delivers but also minimizes the number of open trades (fails) that are awaiting settlement. The first part, the pairing off of transactions intrafirm to minimize receives and delivers, is known as netting. The second part, the rolling of open transactions into the next day's settling trades, is known as *continuous net settlement.*

After the netting process has been completed, clearing firms are either "net buyers" or "net sellers" or they are "flat" per security. As the industry is in a compared environment at this part of the trade processing cycle, the quantity owed to net buyers must equal the quantity owed by net sellers. Therefore the street-side settlement process can begin.

On the night before settlement (in the current world, the night of T+2), the actual settlement cycle begins. DTC and NSCC exchange information during this night cycle known as PDQ (pretty darn quick). It is in this cycle that the majority of settlement occurs.

VI-B-2 Settlement Cycle Begins

Early in the evening of T+2, SF&R instructs DTC which securities they have in position that can be used for settlement, and so on, and which are not to be touched. This is accomplished through "exemptions." At this point in the process, net buyers have been identified as have net sellers, and DTC knows what quantity of securities are available for settlement per security, per firm. NSCC sends instructions to DTC as to which firms are net sellers and the quantity they owe. DTC verifies this obligation against the net sellers (delivering firm) and takes from the firm's position the quantity it can access. The quantity taken is electronically transferred from the delivering firm's account to NSCC's omnibus account. NSCC then allocates the shares to the net-buying firms in chronological order of their positions. The oldest receive position gets filled first.

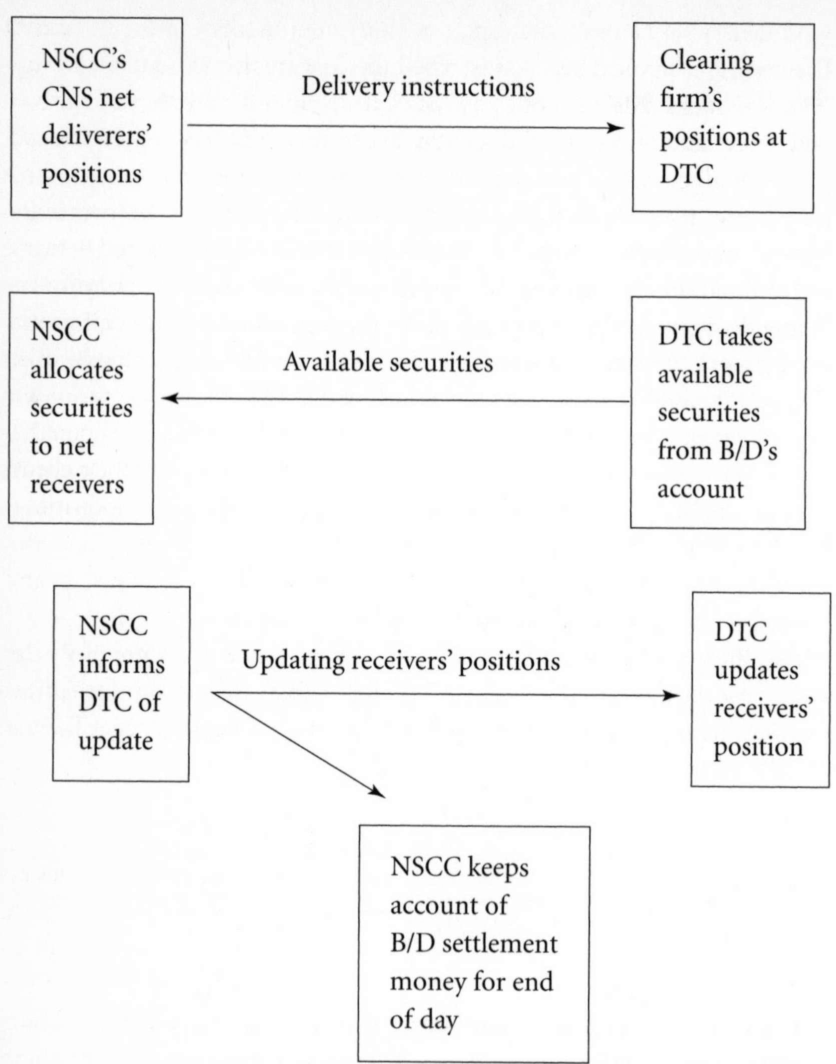

VI-B-2-a *The Projection Report*

The next morning after the conclusion of the PDQ night cycle, the day cycle known as *mainline* begins. Trades that are still open for settlement, as well as the trades due to settle the following business day are presented on the projection report from NSCC and given to the receive and deliver section. (In a T+1 environment the process will begin the night of trade date.) The receive and deliver staff use this report as a tool to guide them in the settlement functions for the next day. For example, let's assume that today, SF&R is supposed to make a delivery of Pan Kaick Tech common stock to another broker/dealer as a result of being a net seller. In looking at the report, the staff sees that in tomorrow's settling trades, they are supposed to receive the same quantity of the same security. They also see that they need the shares tomorrow to make a delivery to a client. If they make the delivery today to the other broker/dealer, as required, they may not get the security tomorrow because the firm that is assigned to deliver the security may fail to deliver it. If that occurs, they may be unable to satisfy the client's needs. On the other hand, if they fail to deliver the stock today, it will roll into tomorrow's receiving trades and net out at NSCC, leaving them with the security position they originally had. This will allow them to use that stock to satisfy their client's needs. This is just one example of security control and the use of securities to best benefit the firm and expedite settlement.

The projection report, as stated above, informs the firm of which transactions still require settlement today and which transactions are due to settle tomorrow. This valuable tool is used in conjunction with two other reports—the seg and the Needs Analysis Report—to maximize the firm's ability to move securities in such a way as to benefit the firm's cash flow.

VI-B-2-b *The Seg Report*

The *seg report* informs the receive and deliver staff as to what securities are available to be used to clean up trades and which are locked up in seg. As stated earlier in the book, the firm must maintain a certain percentage of securities belonging to customers who have margin accounts as well as all of the securities belonging to customers who have cash accounts. The term *locked up in seg* means that the firm has possession or control of the security and is not using it for other purposes besides the custodial function. Therefore, the seg report is a very valuable tool for the receive and deliver staff because it informs them what stock is available (or not locked up in seg).

VI-B-2-c *Seg Control*

SF&R maintains computer programs that automatically lock up certain stock and free other stock for loan or for other useful purposes. This is controlled by an algorithm that looks for securities that have little call for

DATE: 02/18/20XX
TIME: 01:31:48

NATIONAL SECURITIES CLEARING CORPORATION
CNS - PROJECTION REPORT
PROCESS DATE: 02/21/20XX
FOR SETTLEMENT ON: 02/22/20XX

PARTICIPANT: STONE FORREST AND RIVERS CORORATION
SUB-ACCOUNT: A REGULAR ACCCOUNT

	<------ T O M O R R O W ' S		------>				
TODAY'S CURRENT POSITION	SETTLING TRADES PURCHASED/ SOLD(-)	STOCK DIVIDENDS/ OTHER REC/DEL(-)	PROJECTED NET POSITION LONG/ SHORT(-)	PROJECTED MARKET VALUE LMV/SMV(-)	CURRENCY CODE	ISIN	SECURITY DESCRIPTION
	25-		25-	1,363.00-	USD	US-G0070K103-7	ACE LIMITED
3,000-			3,000-	175,590.00-	USD	US-G20045202-1	CENTRAL EUROPEAN MEDIA ENTRP-A
	1,123		1,123	58,171.40	USD	US-00163T109-7	AMB PROPERTY CORP
7,400-			7,400-	410,700.00-	USD	US-00508X203-6	ACTUANT CORP (NEW)
	23,000		23,000	1,101,930.00	USD	US-007094105-1	ADMINISTAFF INC
95-	15-		110-	11,137.50-	USD	US-00817Y108-2	AETNA INC.(NEW)
50-			50-	3,825.00-	USD	US-018804104-2	ALLIANT TECHSYSTEMS INC
	190		190	4,903.90	USD	US-02553E106-4	AMER EAGLE OUTFITTER INC NEW
	300-		300-	6,012.00-	USD	US-029066107-5	AMERICAN POWER CONVERSION CORP
	270-		270-	7,722.00-	USD	US-03060R101-4	AMERICREDIT CORP
	590		590	27,594.30	USD	US-039583109-4	ARCHSTONE-SMITH TRUST
	182		182	18,713.24	USD	US-053484101-2	AVALONBAY COMMUNITIES INC
	50-		50-	699.00-	USD	US-055472104-5	BISYS GROUP INC
	25-		25-	864.75-	USD	US-064057102-4	BANK OF NEW YORK INC
	109		109	9,151.64	USD	US-101121101-8	BOSTON PROPERTIES INC.
	50,000-		50,000-	1,222,500.00-	USD	US-101137107-7	BOSTON SCIENTIFIC CORP
	153,745-		153,745-	807,161.25-	USD	US-111621108-7	BROCADE COMMUNICATIONS SYS INC
	1-		1-	53.72-	USD	US-112585104-8	BROOKFIELD ASSET MANAGEMENT IN
135-			135-	10,847.25-	USD	US-12189T104-3	BURLINGTON NRTHRN SANTA FE(COM
300-	50-		350-	5,096.00-	USD	US-125896100-2	CMS ENERGY CORP
	125-		125-	3,575.00-	USD	US-126650100-6	CVS CORPORATION (HOLDING CO)
	830-		830-	20,750.00-	USD	US-12686C109-9	CABLEVISION SYS CP NY GRP CL-A
	720-		720-	8,064.00-	USD	US-140288101-5	CAPITAL LEASE FUNDING INC
	14,300-		14,300-	765,765.00-	USD	US-143658300-9	CARNIVAL CORPORATION (PAIRED S
	472		472	18,738.40	USD	US-144418100-2	CARRAMERICA REALTY CORP
	25-		25-	743.25-	USD	US-165167107-5	CHESAPEAKE ENERGY CORP
	800-		800-	33,880.00-	USD	US-169905106-6	CHOICE HOTELS INT'L INC(NEW)
	200-		200-	8,126.00-	USD	US-172908105-9	CINTAS CORP
	11,255-		11,255-	373,553.45-	USD	US-204149108-3	COMMUNITY TRUST BANCORP INC
869			869	37,775.43	USD	US-20441W203-5	COMPANHIA BEBIDA ADS (100 PF)
	1,740		1,740	82,197.60	USD	US-204412209-9	COMPANHIA VALE DO RIO DOCE ADS
285-	50-		335-	6,904.35-	USD	US-205887102-9	CONAGRA FOODS INC.
	350-		350-	22,095.50-	USD	US-20854P109-3	CONSOL ENERGY INC
	25-		25-	633.50-	USD	US-21036P108-4	CONSTELLATION BRANDS CL-A
	25-		25-	945.75-	USD	US-242370104-2	DEAN FOODS CO
	5,500-		5,500-	167,035.00-	USD	US-24702R101-4	DELL INC
200-	100-		300-	10,068.00-	USD	US-25385P106-6	DIGITAL INSIGHT CORPORATION
	25-		25-	672.75-	USD	US-254687106-0	WALT DISNEY CO-DISNEY COMMON
	761		761	26,551.29	USD	US-264411505-5	DUKE REALTY CORP

loans, or short sales and that keeps "free" securities that have a higher demand. Sometimes, however, there is a need for stock that the firm has automatically locked up in seg. As SF&R's seg system is an interactive system, it allows the receive and deliver staff to lock up stock that was available for loan and instead free up a stock that was automatically locked up and use the formerly locked-up stock in stock loan. As long as the dollar amounts of the securities involved in this switch are the same and the switch satisfies the seg requirement, there isn't any problem. This is known as *active seg*.

For example, one of SF&R's clients, Stanley Tahl, currently has shares of ZAP locked up in seg and shares of RAM available for loan. In Stan's margin account the RAM stock is being used to finance Stan's debit balance. The RAM stock is currently pledged at a bank as collateral against Stan's loan. In this particular case, RAM and ZAP are trading at the same price. SF&R receives a request to borrow ZAP stock from another broker/dealer. SF&R's receive and deliver staff checks the seg report and sees that Stan's account has 100 shares of ZAP locked up in seg and 100 shares of RAM free for delivery. The 100 shares of RAM are currently on bank loan. In other words, the RAM has been pledged at a bank with the money from that pledge used to support Stan's debit balance. SF&R's receive and deliver area gives instructions to Depository Trust Company (DTC) to release the ZAP stock from seg and use it for delivery and to pull the RAM stock back from the pledge account (where it had been used as collateral against the loan at the bank) and lock it up in seg. This whole process takes a few moments. However, as a result of this the ZAP stock is now free for loan. The firm receiving the ZAP stock will collateralize the borrow with cash. The money received for that borrow would be used to pay the bank for the loan that it had made on the RAM stock and is now supporting Stan's debit balance.

Here is an example of how the receive and deliver section moves securities to the best advantage of SF&R:

1. Stan Tahl owns shares of ZAP and RAM common stock.
2. The stocks were purchased on margin with Stan borrowing funds through SF&R.
3. SF&R locked up the ZAP shares in seg.
4. SF&R placed the RAM shares into their pledge account at DTC to borrow money from a bank with which it conducts business.
5. The bank lent SF&R money on the RAM shares to finance Tahl's margin loan for which it charged the broker's call interest rate.

6. Tahl's account is being charged the interest cost to borrow (broker's call rate) to SF&R plus an additional charge, by SF&R, to cover the expense of the loan.
7. The money that Stan deposited in his account plus the money that SF&R borrowed from the bank paid the sellers of the two stocks.
8. Later, SF&R pulls the RAM stock from the pledge account and locks it up in seg, replacing the ZAP stock that it needs to make a loan.
9. The ZAP stock is used to make the loan against another broker/dealer's client's sale, which the borrowing firm will pay SF&R upon receipt of the ZAP stock.
10. SF&R takes the proceeds from the ZAP delivery and pays down the bank loan.
11. Stan Tahl is still the owner of RAM and ZAP stock that has been purchased on margin.
12. Tahl can sell either stock whenever he wants to. If he wants to sell the ZAP stock, SF&R will borrow the stock from somewhere else or call in the loan.
13. The margin loan is now being financed by the loan of ZAP shares, whose proceeds are substituted for the bank loan.
14. SF&R will pay interest on the cash it received as collateral, but the rate will be much less than it was paying at the bank.
15. Tahl is paying the same interest rate as before on the margin loan.

The seg requirement is a federal regulation. It is covered by Regulation T of the Federal Reserve and enforced by the Securities and Exchange Commission. The term *locked up in seg* is a little misleading. What it means is that the broker/dealer has possession or control of the securities required to satisfy the segregation requirement.

The seg requirement affects only clients. Section 15c3–3 of the Securities and Exchange Act of 1934 defines the term *client* as a nonbroker/dealer or a nonprincipal of a broker/dealer. It affects retail and institutional accounts and, in the case where SF&R is a clearing firm for correspondent broker/dealers, it includes the clients of the correspondent nonclearing firms.

SF&R must have possession or control of the securities that clients have fully paid for. The securities that belong to these clients are maintained at DTC. DTC is known as a good control location. When a client deposits physical stock at any branch of SF&R for their account, the branch is said to have possession. SF&R and other broker/dealers maintain client securities in street name known as nominee name. Stock registered in the nominee name of SF&R or the nominee name of DTC is said to be in street name. There are four significant advantages to having stock registered in street name. First, it is accepted as "good delivery" at any broker/dealer or bank. Second, it can be maintained in electronic fashion. Third, it can be used by the broker/dealer in conducting its daily business. Fourth, clients don't have to wait until the stock clears transfer to get paid the proceeds of sales.

In speaking of use of the stock in the broker/dealer's daily business, I am referring to the stock's fungibility. Let's suppose a client owns 100 shares of Moovinslo and it is fully paid for. SF&R is maintaining the security at DTC. Another client has sold the same issue and the stock was in its name so it had to be transferred out of its name and into street name to make it good delivery. Security in transfer is considered to be in good location. Instead of having a fail to deliver to the buying broker/dealer, SF&R can take the fully paid-for stock from the first client and deliver it against the second client's sale. The first client's seg requirement is now satisfied by the stock that is in transfer.

Some clients of SF&R want to maintain their securities at SF&R but want them registered in their own name (beneficial owner's name). To do this, the stock must be fully paid for and maintained in a separate cash account. Margin account stock must be maintained in street name, regardless of whether the client has borrowed funds. In addition, as the stock is not fungible, SF&R cannot use it in expediting its daily work. Therefore, these clients are charged a service fee by SF&R for maintaining position. While stock registered in street name is fungible and placed in a pool with all the other street name stock of the same issue, SF&R must be careful not to violate seg requirements and use stock that they shouldn't.

Having *possession* is defined as having a security on the broker/dealer's premises, whether it is the main office or any branch. The term *control* includes the depository, the Fed, stock transfer, fails to receive or deliver, stock in transit between broker/dealer locations, security at a national clearing corporation, and securities maintained at custodial banks. Some of these accounts have position time constraints after which the positions are not considered good location.

VI-B-2-d *Needs Analysis Report*

The *needs analysis report* prioritizes the firm's delivery needs in terms of which give the greatest exposure to the firm. It is difficult for the specialist in the receive and deliver section to see the entire picture as to where stock is needed and where it can be best appropriated. Therefore, the firm produces a needs analysis report, which looks at all of the deliveries that have to be made and prioritizes them in terms of which give the greatest exposure to the firm, either from a cost basis or from a market exposure basis.

For example, one of SF&R's clients, the Reelibigg Trust Company, purchased 100,000 shares of PIP at $60 per share (100,000 shares × $60 = $6,000,000 worth of securities). Reelibigg will not accept a partial delivery of the security. At that moment in time, Reelibigg's delivery represents the greatest exposure to SF&R. Therefore, SF&R, while gathering the stock to complete the delivery, has to make sure that they accumulate all 100,000 shares or, if they do not, they will try find other uses for the stock that they have accumulated so as to make other deliveries. If they cannot accumulate all the shares they need, they will have to finance the accumulated position overnight. Remember, for whatever stock SF&R has accumulated from the 100,000-share trade they must pay the delivering broker/dealers; to obtain the funds to pay the delivering firms, SF&R has to finance the position at a bank that will charge SF&R interest. Assuming an interest rate of 6% and an accumulation of half the shares,

50,000 shares × $60 per share = $3,000,000
$3,000,000 × .06 × 1/365 = $493

is the daily interest payment. The $493 interest expense cannot be recouped by SF&R through other means. In other words, it is a total expense to SF&R.

Knowing that this delivery has to be made, the receive and deliver section has set up instructions at Depository Trust Company to accumulate the required amount of stock into SF&R's account before making deliveries for other commitments. In addition, they have alerted the stock loan/stock borrow section of the possible need of PIP shares. Due to past experience with its clients and other broker/dealers, the receive and deliver section can identify which will make deliveries and which have a habit of failing to deliver for one reason or another. In addition, if there are any sellers of a large quantity of PIP stock, SF&R's personnel will telephone them to verify that they are going to deliver the shares. Due to the fact that SF&R is facing the possibility of financing a rather large position overnight, the receive and deliver section is busy accumulating the stock to make the delivery. It will call stock back from bank loan and from stock loan if necessary; it will also borrow stock if need be. Through the use of these various tools it will have, in fact, accumulated 100,000 shares of stock by the end of the settlement cycle. SF&R will make the delivery and receive $6,000,000 as part of the customer's side settlement.

With the use of these three reports—the projection report, the seg report, and the needs analysis report—the receive and deliver section attempts to move securities in the most efficient manner, thereby minimizing the cost of carrying any position that's involved with a transaction to Stone, Forrest & Rivers.

VI-C *FAIL TO RECEIVE/FAIL TO DELIVER*

The fail control section plays a key role in protecting firm profits. Remember, as stock moves one way, cash is moving in the opposite direction. There are client fails and street side fails, and they are not connected. The fact that a client fails to deliver a security to SF&R does not mean that SF&R has an excuse for failing to deliver a security to the broker/dealer with whom the trade was consummated. In addition, fails pose potential risk to SF&R as prices change every day. Should a renege occur, SF&R has to make good on the other side of the trade.

Now let's look at the money side of fails. If SF&R is failing to receive securities, it means that SF&R has the money and the contra party has the security. If SF&R is failing to deliver the security, it means that SF&R has the security and the contra side has the cash. Obviously, it is better to have cash than securities. SF&R's fail control section has a two-prong mandate: On fail to delivers, clean them up as soon as possible. On fail to receives, mark them to the market to minimize exposure to the firm. The use of funds is important. Let's look at two scenarios.

Scenario 1. A client sold stock through SF&R on an agency basis; SF&R is failing to receive from the client, causing SF&R to fail to deliver to the contra broker/dealer.

1. Do not pay the client. Buy in client as directed by Regulation T and the rules of the SROs.
2. Borrow stock, make delivery to the contra firm, and get paid. There are three potential sources of stock:

a. Borrow stock from a proprietary account. The money received reduces the cost of financing the proprietary position.
b. Borrow stock from the client's margin account. The money received offsets the client's loan on that stock, thereby reducing the cost of financing the client's debit balance. The client continues to pay the same interest rate on the debit balance as before.
c. Borrow stock from another broker/dealer. Give the money received from delivery to contra broker as collateral for the borrowed stock. The broker/dealer pays SF&R interest on the money.

Scenario 2. A client bought stock through SF&R; the contra broker/dealer fails to deliver to SF&R.

1. A non-DVP (delivery vs. payment) client must pay within the allotted time under Regulation T and the rules of the SROs. As for the security position, clients with standing instructions to "hold securities in the account" do nothing. Clients with instructions to "transfer and ship" try to borrow the stock (using the same borrowing procedure as in scenario 1). DVP clients try to borrow using this procedure too.
2. Mark to market the street side fail and issue a buy-in notice should the position remain.

Note: Systems, such as NSCC's CNS, rebalance the clearing entity fail positions each day. Because of the clearing cash adjustment, all fails are marked to the same price every day. They constitute new fail positions. They are therefore not called fails but open position. Under this process, the oldest open position is allocated deliveries first. And these positions should not remain open for an extended period of time.

VI-D *FINANCING POSITIONS*

There are several ways for broker/dealers to finance the daily operation: stock loans, stock borrows, letters of credit, repos, and unsecured bank loans. Each day SF&R must finance both client and firm positions. It must also minimize the cost of processing transactions in order to be profitable.

It therefore seeks to arrange financing at the most advantageous terms and lend resources under the most beneficial terms it can arrange.

SF&R has proprietary positions. Their clients have margin accounts with debit balances as do nonclearing broker/dealers that use SF&R to clear and settle their street-side trades. The latter are known as *correspondent broker/dealers*. To finance these positions, SF&R uses bank loans, stock loans, and repos.

VI-D-1 Bank Loan

SF&R maintains accounts with several commercial banks. On a regular basis SF&R pledges *nonseg* securities at the bank and, after the appropriate *haircut*, the bank lends SF&R the funds. A bank will typically lend $.70 on every dollar of market value of equity collateral that is pledged. The remaining $.30, or 30%, is the haircut. For the loan the bank will charge SF&R interest. The published rate of interest is known as the *broker's call rate.*

The banks have their own rules as to credit limits to borrowers and as to the quality of the securities being pledged. While SF&R is a major broker/dealer, each bank that it conducts business with has a limit as to how much it can lend. The determination is a mixture of SF&R's creditworthiness and the pool of money the bank has available to lend to all of its clients. From SF&R's viewpoint, it makes good business sense to utilize the services of several banks, both for competitive reasons and for unencumbered sources of funds.

Quality of the securities could affect the haircut percentage. What if the stock's price is very volatile or if the issuing corporation has very weak financials? The bank may only be willing to lend $.50 on the dollar or less. In this case, SF&R will shop the loan to several banks and settle with the one that gives the best rate.

The flip side of the haircut is in the seg requirements, where a firm can use up to 140% of the client's securities to finance the client debit balance (loan). The 70% the bank will lend is the approximate complement of the 140% the broker/dealer can use.

$100,000	$70,000
× .70	× 1.40
$ 70,000	$98,000

The mix of the security being pledged could also affect the amount the bank is willing to lend. If one security makes up a major part of the loan, the bank may want to haircut the loan more severely.

The bank loan section of settlement must make sure that they are obtaining the best interest rates possible and that the proper value of collateral is pledged at all times.

VI-D-2 Stock Loan

While there are similarities, the stock loan has a different genesis than the bank loan. Under bank loans, SF&R takes loanable securities to the bank and pledges them. Under stock loans, there must be a need for a particular stock by the user. The personnel in stock loan are out marketing SF&R's ability to lend stock to current and potential users. The more stock they have available—both in number of different securities and in the amount of shares available—the more business they can do. This is a highly competitive part of the business for both lenders and borrowers. Timing is significant. Sometimes there is a large supply of stock and small demand; at other times there is heavy demand for stock and a small supply.

For example, rumors are circulating that AD Advertising Inc. is going to lose a major client's account. The price of their common stock is starting to fall. The questions are whether the rumor is true and, if so, how far the stock price will fall. There is a sudden surge of people wanting to sell short and, therefore, a sudden demand for stock from stock loan. SF&R has shares available, but some of the clients who own AD Advertising on margin and in their cash accounts are selling it. Suddenly there is an impasse. The supply of available stock has dried up. Everyone is scrounging around for shares. Shares that are available are being lent at a premium.

This raises the question, why stock loan? Shares of stock are needed for many reasons: to clean up fails, to complete client deliveries, for short sales, for arbitrage situations. Other financial institutions will come to SF&R to borrow stock for any of these or other reasons. Obviously, the institutions do not have what is needed so they come to SF&R and other security lenders to borrow the stock. SF&R is currently financing the shares, for both its proprietary and its clients' accounts, at a bank and paying broker's call rate. Under stock loan, the borrowing institution and SF&R negotiate the rate for the loan, which will be less than the broker's call rate. The shares go to the borrower, and the collateral for the loan (cash) comes to the lender. Because the lender got the cash, the lender pays the borrower interest. The rate of interest is less than SF&R was paying to the bank. So SF&R has reduced an expense. This is a win–win situation for the two parties.

VI-D-3 Stock Borrows

The flip side of stock loan is stock borrow. SF&R will borrow stock on an as-needed basis. There are times where SF&R will borrow stock on an anticipatory basis also. But these borrows must be justified to the firm's internal and external auditors as well as any to regulators who inquire. The need for the borrow is to avoid financing a partial delivery, or to clean up a fail to deliver, for short selling, for an arbitrage situation, for satisfying an underseg condition, or simply for satisfying a client's request for delivery of shares. In the case of a borrow, SF&R is borrowing the stock, sending cash as collateral to the lending firm, and receiving interest on the collateral money. Because this produces revenue in the form of interest payments, firms are monitored so they will only borrow stock on a needs basis. That is, to expedite some operational function.

VI-D-4 Repos

Repos (repurchase agreements) are a method of financing using high-quality securities. What differentiates a repo from bond loan (a form of stock loan) is that in a repo the entity with the security is seeking financing from a nonfinancial fund source, which will hold a security as collateral. Under a bond loan, the security is used for some operational purpose, such as cleaning up a fail to deliver. Another difference is that under a repo agreement, ownership of the security isn't changed. Interest and/or other payments made by the issuer go directly to the security owner. Under a bond loan, the borrower must pay the lender all interest and/or other payments as the security has been used for a business purpose, such as cleaning up a delivery, and is now in someone else's control. When the borrower receives the bonds that are owed, it will turn around and deliver them back to the lender.

As stated above, the purpose of the repo is to finance a position. Due to the requirement that these be highest-quality debt instruments, risk and exposure are at a minimum. Therefore, broker/dealers can tap other sources for funds besides the ones listed above. Corporations, for example, accumulate cash to meet specific deadlines, such as payroll. While the funds are in the accumulation stage, the corporation isn't permitted to put them at risk by investing them. In addition, there are very few, if any, money market instruments that either satisfy the quantity or the time restraints imposed on these segregated funds. However, they are available for repo "investing." There is actually more repo money available than any other source of financing. The repo money is among the lowest-cost funds available for loan.

There are three types of repos: physical, segregated, and third-party. Of the three, third-party has become prevalent. The third-party repo addresses one of the major problems in repo financing. The lender of the financing will not release the funds until it is sure that the collateral has been received from the borrower and that it is in good order. Should the securities not be properly received in the allotted time due to the fault of the borrower, the borrower must finance the securities elsewhere and still pay interest to the original lender. This means that interest must be paid twice: once to the original lender who tied up money for the loan and once for the actual, or final, lender. A lot can go wrong between the time instructions are given to deliver the security and the time the financing cash is received.

Third-party repo involves the entrance of a neutral party. SF&R enters into a repo agreement with The Loster Motor Corporation. Both entities maintain security and cash accounts at First Continental Bank. The bank is provided with the terms of the repo by both parties. At the appropriate time the bank removes the securities from SF&R's account and places them into its hold account. At the same time SF&R removes cash from The Loster Motor Corporation's account and places it in a hold account. If all is in proper order and correct as to identification of the securities and the money involved, the bank lets the repo settle. The same procedure is followed when the repo is closed out.

With seg repos (which broker/dealers rarely use anymore), the broker/dealer moves the security to a special location (segregates the issue) and the institution lends the funds. This is the most inexpensive way of processing a repo as it avoids the bank's movement and handling charges. However the broker/dealer is holding both the securities and the cash. Should something happen to the broker/dealer and it is suspended or put out of business, the institution has nothing. It must claim its money through legal procedures.

Physical (which includes electronic movement) between custodian banks for their client is the most expensive of the three ways to process repos. The custodial banks impose charges for the security and cash move-

Establishing the Repo

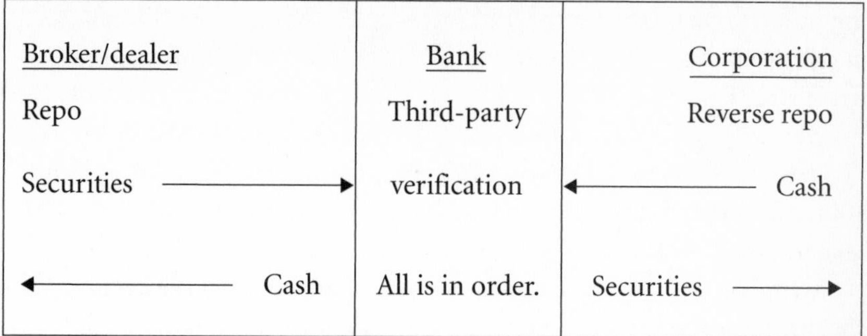

Closing out the Repo

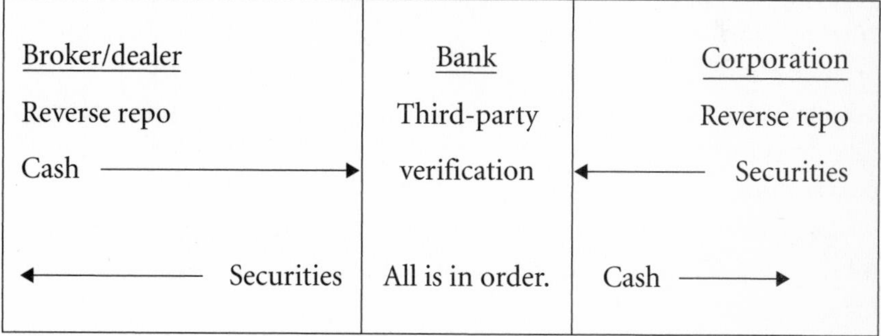

ments as well as handling and warehousing costs. Different banks have different charges. If the transaction involves a central depository, there are additional charges imposed by them.

If this were a real, physical repo, the exact same certificates that were sent out would be returned. In a pure repo, ownership of the instrument doesn't change.

Of the three methods, the third-party repo, while more expensive to process than the seg repo, offers safety and efficient processing. Of the three, it has the least risk as the third party will not release the collateral or the cash until all aspects of the transactions are correct.

There are three forms of repo employed by the industry: overnight, term, and open repo. The most common, the overnight repo, is used to finance traders' positions overnight. When SF&R enters into this type of transaction, there are two trades "booked" simultaneously. One trade setting up the repo is a cash trade (same-day settler); the other trade closing

Physical Repo

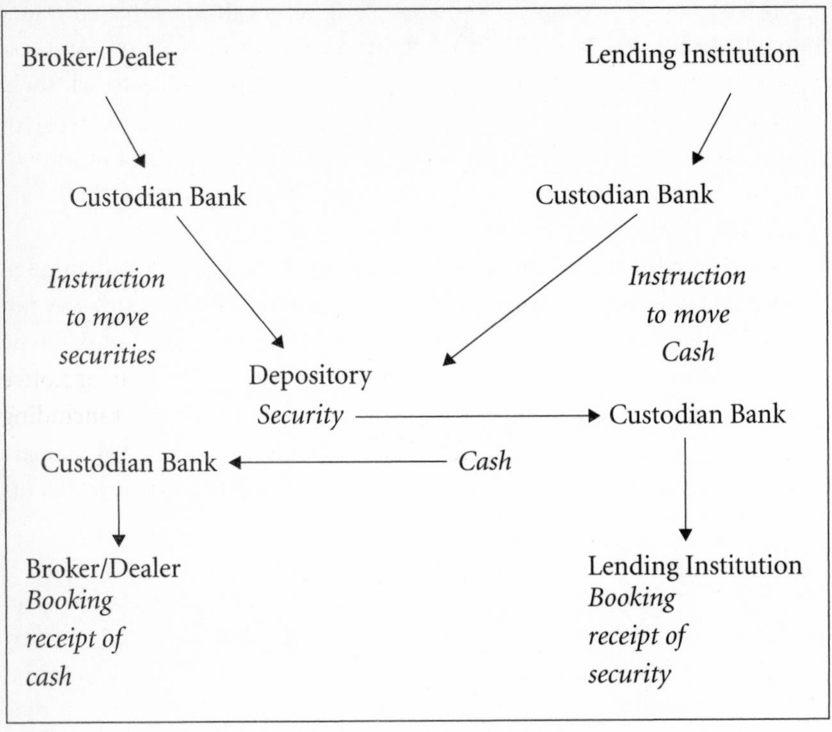

out the repo is a next-day trade. The money difference between the two trades is the interest SF&R is paying for the use of the money overnight.

Example: A repo at 2% interest

	Activity	Trade date	Settlement date	Issue	Amount
Trade #1	Deliver	05/11	05/11	100,000,000 GNMA @ $98	$98,000,000.00
Trade #2	Receive	05/11	05/12	100,000,000 GNMA @ $98	$98,005,444.45

$$\frac{\$98{,}000{,}000 \times .02 \times 1}{360} = \$5{,}444.45$$

With a term repo, both parties agree to the rate of interest and the longevity of the repo. SF&R is entering into a 30-day repo with the Indian

Apoliss Group. The repo is for $50,000,000 of U.S. Treasury bonds that are in SF&R's inventory account. SF&R may have to substitute other Treasury bonds for the ones initially on repo during the 30-day period. As these bonds are in SF&R inventory, they may have an opportunity to sell them during the 30-day period. To make the sale, SF&R will substitute the instruments. For this privilege, SF&R will pay a higher rate of interest to compensate the reverse repo side for the inconvenience. Again, two trades are booked to SF&R's records simultaneously.

An open repo is a bit more complicated to process. It is called an open repo because either the interest rate, the closeout date, or both are not known at the time of the agreement. The typical characteristic of this type of transaction is that it can be terminated by either party on 24-hour notice and the longer out it is likely to run, the greater the chances of it including rights of substitution. The main advantage to an open repo is that the parties to the transaction do not have to keep negotiating new agreements every few days.

SF&R is entering into an open repo with Payne Casualty Company. The terms of the repo include an open interest rate and open closeout date. The two parties agree that the interest rate should be reset weekly based on the Fed fund rate that is set every Wednesday. Again, two trades are booked simultaneously. One is a cash trade with the settlement date being the same as the trade date. The other has the same trade date as the first trade but has a settlement date way out in the future. Each week that the repo is in force, SF&R's and Payne Casualty Company's personnel verify the interest rates and the money balances. If during the period the value of the instruments pledged falls below the agreed-to amount, SF&R must either substitute the security with one that has more value or simply pay back some of the cash. The reduction in value can occur by a drop in the market value of the instruments or, in the case of mortgage-backed and asset-backed securities, paydown of principle. Should the value of the collateral increase, SF&R will take back collateral or borrow additional funds.

When the repo is eventually closed, personnel will cancel the fictitious trade and enter a good trade with the original trade date and the real settlement date. The booking of the fictitious trade initially serves several functions. First is control. With the delivery of the security against the cash trade, the security position is off the firm's books. If there are many repos, as is the usual case, it is difficult to make sure the proper account receives any payments made by the issuer. Second, as a reverse repo, it "pairs off " against the repo, thereby accounting for all repos. Remember, the reverse repo side of the agreement is "booked" the same day (trade date) as the repo itself.

VI-D-4-a GOVERNMENT SECURITY DIVISION (GSD) OF FICC GCF REPO SERVICE

The use of government and agency securities in the lending business serves the same purpose as any other security. A main difference is that the amount of money associated with each repo is large. To facilitate the processing of these repos, GSD offered the *General Collateral Financing Repo Service (GCF)*. Prior to this service the two participants to the repo had to settle each repo independently of other repo financing that they were involved in. In addition, the closeout of each repo, whether for overnight, term, or open contracts, required a repo-for-repo settlement.

SF&R is very active in the repo market. They use repos to finance their government and agency trading positions, to assist other broker/dealers in arranging finance through SF&R's match book business and assist institutional clients in financing their positions. As a clearing member of GSD, SF&R uses the GCF service to net positions and money balances each day, thereby saving time and expense, and reducing risks in the reconciling of internal and external accounts.

VI-D-4-b *Matched Book*

SF&R has many contacts from which it can raise repo money. Brock, Holly, Robb and Company, Inc. (BHR) is a smaller broker/dealer. BHR finds itself with the need to finance a $100,000,000 government bond position overnight. It can try to take the bonds to their lending bank and pay broker's call rate. However, if the amount is above their credit rating or if the bank cannot fund that big a loan because of other commitments, they may have to spread the loan over several banks. They are looking to minimize the interest expense while simplifying the loan process. The more pieces to the loan, the greater the chance that something could go awry. If that should happen, it could be very costly to BHR. SF&R has had dealings with BHR previously, so when SF&R receives the call, they have already performed due diligence on the firm. BHR wants to do a repo with SF&R. They are going to be part of SF&R's *match book.* A match book is where a broker/dealer acts as an intermediary by borrowing money from lenders for firms, clients, and so on, who need the financing. SF&R calls one if their money sources and negotiates a rate. They can borrow money at 3%, which is 2¼ % lower than the broker's call rate at this time. SF&R contacts BHR and tells them they will lend money at the rate of 3¼%. BHR takes the rate as they are saving 2% interest on the loan. That translates to a saving of $5,479.45 per day:

$$\frac{\$100{,}000{,}000 \times .02 \times 1}{360} = \$5{,}555.56$$

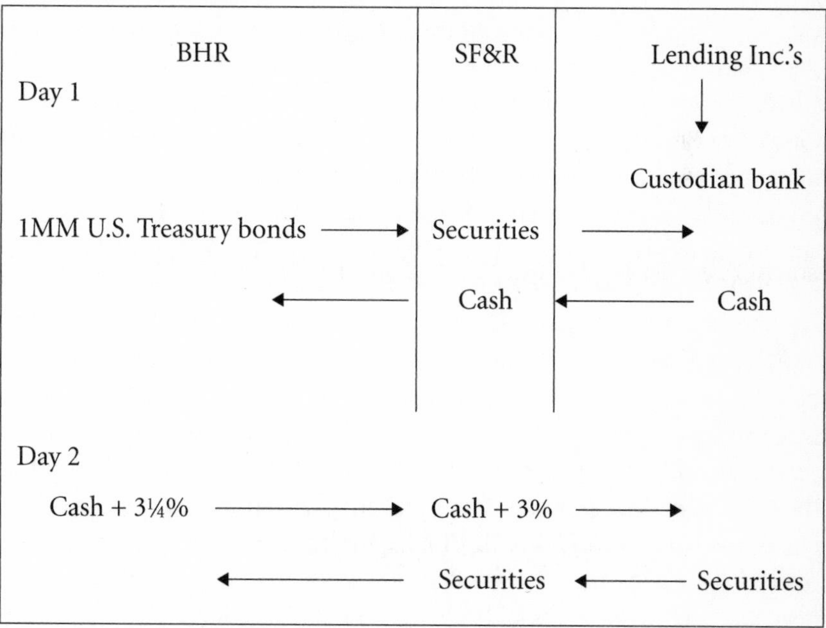

Meanwhile, SF&R has earned $684.93 for its efforts:

$$\$100{,}000{,}000 \times .0025 \times \frac{1}{360} = \$694.45$$

VI-D-5 Letters of Credit

SF&R must settle with a multitude of clearing facilities each day. Included with the settlement is the need to maintain a clearing fund to provide a cushion should SF&R stop conducting business. It is also used to satisfy its daily requirements in settling street-side trades and margin obligations at industry utilities. The amount necessary for the clearing fund is generally based on the daily activity of the broker/dealer. As the minimum amount of collateral necessary is generally stagnant, the broker/dealers meet this obligation by depositing U.S. Treasury bills instead of cash. The difference between the historical minimum and the amount needed that day is settled by the use of a letter of credit (LOC). Settlement money, on the other hand, fluctuates from day to day depending on the dollar amount that the broker/dealer bought and sold. The broker/dealers meet this requirement by depositing letters of credit. A letter of credit is issued and backed by a bank that states it is willing to lend an institution a set amount on demand. It is then given to another institution that has the power to "pull down" whatever funds are needed for settlement. This spares the borrowing institution the problem of refinancing loans every day. The borrower pays interest for the entire amount guaranteed by the letter of credit, whether or not any money is actually borrowed. The rate charged is minimal. If and when an actual borrow occurs, the borrower pays the negotiated rate for the loan.

SF&R has a letter of credit from First Continental Bank on deposit with Option Clearing Corporation. Each day SF&R must settle option trades with OCC as well as satisfy its margin requirement there. It uses U.S. Treasury bills for its base amount requirement (the minimum needed most of the time) and the letter of credit for the rest. Today SF&R clients purchased more than they sold. The difference is added to yesterday's balance. OCC "pulls" the extra cash collateral needed for settlement from the letter of credit. As SF&R is in balance with OCC, the figure borrowed is verified, and First Continental Bank and Stone, Forrest & Rivers adjust their internal records to reflect the current loan. Should SF&R's clients sell a dollar amount that is greater than what they purchased, the amount of the loan will be reduced.

VI-D-6 Unsecured Loans

Like any business, SF&R maintains a line of credit with several banks. These lines of credit are backed by nothing but the good name of SF&R and are therefore unsecured loans. The firm uses these lines of credit for many reasons, including general business that involves the administration of the company.

VI-E CUSTODIAL SERVICES

Stone, Forrest & Rivers maintains securities positions for its clients as well as its own proprietary positions. The client's security positions are primarily maintained in street name. That means that Stone, Forrest & Rivers is not the beneficial owner but is holding the securities for its clients who are the beneficial (or actual) owners. The vast majority, if not all, equities, corporate bonds and notes, municipal bonds and notes, as well as money market instruments, are maintained by the firm at Depository Trust Company (DTC). DTC actually carries the securities in its street (nominee) name, CEDE. So let's carry this through. Mr. Carl Lee Sing, a client of Stone, Forrest & Rivers, maintains his security positions with SF&R. SF&R maintains this customer's positions along with other customer positions at DTC. DTC maintains the positions in their nominee name. Let's go one step further. In all probability, DTC has sent the securities to the transfer agent that maintains that position on their computers. Therefore, the clients of all of the firms, which are participants of DTC, let's say, own PIP securities. The PIP shares are actually domiciled on a computer at the transfer agent that is operating on behalf of PIP Inc. (This makes me wonder why we need a stock certificate form in the first place, but that is another story.)

Some clients want the security registered in their name (beneficial owner) but maintained by Stone, Forrest & Rivers. Stone, Forrest & Rivers offers this service, which is called *safekeeping*. The firm charges clients a fee for this service. As the stock is in the client's name, it must be fully paid for and cannot be used by SF&R for any purpose. Stock that is maintained in seg or street name is fungible. Stock that is fungible can be substituted.

For example, SF&R is carrying a fully paid-for position of 1,000 shares of Car Leasing Corp. for client Jenna Raite. The stock is registered in street name and, since it is fully paid for, it is locked up in seg. Client Nicole Endyme sells 1,000 shares of Car Leasing Corp. and on settlement date brings the physical shares, properly endorsed, to her SF&R branch office and gets paid. The branch notifies SF&R's settlement area of the receipt of the securities via telecommunications. This process is known as *stock over the wire (SOW)*. It is too late in the day for SF&R to receive that stock and use it to settle the street-side part of the trade. However, as the firm has possession of fully negotiable stock (even though it is registered in Nicole's name), SF&R can instruct DTC to release the 1,000 shares that was "seged" to Jenna and deliver it against Nicole's trade. Jenna's fully paid-for seg stock is now at SF&R's branch office to be placed en route to the settlement area and then to DTC. SF&R needs 1,000 shares to satisfy its seg requirement for Jenna's position and it has possession of 1,000 shares. Nicole's trade has been settled on both the client and street sides. If Jenna's stock were registered in her name, it would not be fungible. As such, SF&R would have had to pay Nicole when she delivered the stock and risk not being paid that day as they were not able to turn the delivery around and satisfy their street-side obligation.

Stone, Forrest & Rivers also has a trading position. These are securities that Stone, Forrest & Rivers actually owns and the traders trade in and out of these positions. Those positions are segregated because firms are not allowed to commingle customer securities with the trading account or proprietary positions.

VI-E-1 Safekeeping

Customers who want securities registered in their name and maintained by Stone, Forrest & Rivers have to have fully paid-for securities; those securities are part of their cash account. For control purposes, SF&R separates those securities into a different type of account.

Let's examine this more closely. Each firm uses its own methods of doing this. SF&R's method is the account number and then the type. Type 1 refers to a cash account, type 2 to a margin account, and type 3 to a short account. Type 4 is used for dividends and bond interest collections, and type 5 is used for safekeeping. A client who wants their stocks and/or bonds registered in their name and held in safekeeping will see the positions carried on their monthly statements in type 5. SF&R systems are set up to prevent trades from occurring in type 5. Therefore, should the client sell the fully paid-for securities, the sale will take place in their cash account, type 1. As a result, the client will have a short position in type 1 and long position in type 5. This control prevents SF&R from accidentally paying the client the proceeds of the sale as the stock that is in type 5 is basically nonnegotiable. The client will have to send in a stock/bond power, which is affixed to the certificate to release the stock so that it can be transferred into street name. Once the stock is made negotiable, SF&R can use it to either clean up the transaction or use the stock as a substitute for some other client's security and use that client's security to clean up the trade.

VI-E-2 Customer Seg

It should be noted, at this time, that negotiable securities are as fungible in the industry as cash is universally. In other words, if SF&R has a requirement to maintain securities for customers with security positions in their cash account and/or the minimum allowable equity portion of their margin accounts in a "good location." Those securities are not physically locked against that account, item for item. It is a liquid position, similar to a bank holding cash for their clients. As long as SF&R has possession or control of the same securities in what is considered a good location and they are posted to the seg position on the stock record, the firm is in compliance with the law. In our example of clients who had stock registered in their name and maintained in their type 5 account, the security is automatically seged. Should the client sell the shares, they cannot be used for delivery against that sale. Therefore, the client will not receive the proceeds from the sale until the securities are made negotiable and can be reregistered into street name. SF&R can use another client's seg stock to settle the street side of the trade. Once the safekeeping stock belonging to the client who sold it is registered in the street name, the position will be changed from a Type 5 account to a Type I account. As this is the same account that the sale was made in, the position goes flat, the client can be paid, and the stock is again backing the owners, whose stock will be used to settle the trade. The securities can then be used for segregation purposes against the other client's position, whose fully paid-for stock was used for settlement purposes. Many people in the industry find this seg concept confusing.

Example: Account DTC100000 contains fungible securities. Account DTC100001 contains nonfungible securities.

1. Here are their starting positions:

Account	Position Type 1 long/short	Position Type 5 long	Seg	DTC's position short	Pay proceeds to client
1NY007832		1,000	1,000		
4CG008567	1,000		1,000		
DTC100000				1,000 (fungible)	
DTC100001				1,000 (nonfungible)	

2. Now the NY client sells stock and SF&R settles the street side of the trade by using fungible stock.

Account	Position Type 1 long/short	Position Type 5 long	Seg	DTC's position short	Pay proceeds to client
1NY007832	1,000	1,000			No
4CG008567	1,000		1,000		
DTC100000				0	SF&R gets paid on street-side delivers
DTC100001				1,000	

Note: the firm still has 100 shares locked up in seg.

3. The NY client's stock is now transferred into street name and the NY client's account is adjusted.

Account	Position Type 1 long/short	Position Type 5 long	Seg	DTC's position short	Pay proceeds to client
1NY007832	0	0	0		Yes
4CG008567	1,000		1,000		
DTC100000				1,000	
DTC100001				0	

VI-E-3 Exemptions

As mentioned earlier, SF&R notifies the DTC division of DTCC of which shares of stock may be used for settling trades and which shares must be seged. This process is accomplished through the transmission of exemptions. These exemptions are sent each day for each security via a process known as *memo seg*.

There are three levels of exemptions at DTC. The level 1 exemption, which we discussed above, has no exceptions at all. Whatever that figure is, DTC will not remove any stock from SF&R's positions until that quantity is reached or satisfied. The level 2 exemption is not as strict. There are exceptions to the exemption. For example, SF&R can make a direct deposit into DTC, called a CNS deposit, and that security can be used to settle trades. They will not be included in the exemption total. Also, stocks being returned from either stock loan or bank loan are also exempted from the exemption. In other words, if these stocks were "free to lend" previously, they are available now to settle trades or for other purposes. Finally, the level 3 exemption is no exemption at all. DTC can use all of the stock they needs to clean up trades that SF&R owes. An example of a level 3 exemption would be in securities for which SF&R is a market maker, as those are owned by SF&R and carried at DTC. This assumes that there aren't any positions for customer securities. Since SF&R owns all the securities in their trading account, there isn't any seg requirement and, therefore, unless there is a need to make a large delivery (as in the case of Reelibigg Trust Company) or some other internal need, SF&R will use level 3 exemptions on those securities. These securities are received against purchases and delivered against sales, and are free to be used as SF&R deems necessary.

As exemptions control the deliveries at DTC, SF&R uses *priorities* to control receives. Naturally, like most firms, SF&R wants to receive the majority of the stock in the evening PDQ cycle. The more stock they can receive early in the cycle, the more stock they can turn around and deliver or use for other purposes. Therefore, they set priority 1 (the evening cycle) and priority 2 or 3 (the remaining cycles). With the exemptions and priorities in place, DTC can now move securities in and out of SF&R's various positions as required by law and as required by SF&R's various needs. One final note: all of the movements that we discussed at DTC with exemptions and priorities are done electronically. Therefore, between broker/dealers and between the custodial banks representing institutional clients, all transaction settlements are done by bookkeeping entry, negating the need to move stock certificates and issue checks.

VI-F *SETTLEMENTS OF MORTGAGE-BACKED SECURITIES*

SF&R is a participant at Depository Trust Company as well as at the Federal Reserve Bank. Ginnie Maes are domiciled at the Federal Reserve (the Fed) along with Freddie Macs, Fannie Maes, and, of course, U.S. Treasury instruments. Settlement, therefore, will be at the Fed.

VI-F-1 GNMA Passthrough Securities

Settlement of passthrough securities is different from that of other issues. Passthrough issues pay interest and principal periodically. Included in the principal paydown is prepayment of debts. When homeowners relocate or refinance their home, the old mortgage is paid off by the new mortgage. This paying down of the old mortgage is known as a *prepayment.*

Most of the mortgage-backed securities settle once a month. Due to the number of instruments outstanding, it would be almost impossible to settle all the trades in one day. Therefore, the Bond Market Association publishes a monthly settlement schedule. Here's an example:

Class A 30-year	Class B 15-year	Class C 30-year	Class D balloons
Freddie Mac Fannie Mae	Freddie Mac Fannie Mae Ginnie Mae	Ginnie Mae	Freddie Mac Fannie Mae All ARMs/VRMs/ Multifamily/GPMs Mobile homes Freddie Mac Fannie Mae Ginnie Mae
Notification Date			
Thursday 12	Tuesday 17	Thursday 19	Monday 23
Settlement Date			
Monday 16	Thursday 19	Monday 23	Wednesday 25

VI-F-2 Electronic Pool Notification (EPN)

Clearing firms of MBSCC notify each other of pending deliveries through a process known as *electronic pool notification (EPN)*. This process is employed 48 hours before the actual settlement occurs. Settlement is processed through the Fedwire.

Broker/dealers and clients, which do not use EPN, notify each other via fax, e-mails, or telephone calls. Clients of SF&R are notified electronically over SF&R's Web site and through their CRM network.

Because an issue always retains its original face value, SF&R settlement personnel are especially vigilant in verifying the current outstanding principal being delivered against a trade. They all make sure, in the receipt of multiple pools against a trade, that the delivery conforms to the Bond Market Association's acceptable delivery standards. This includes not only the .01% over-or-under allowance, but also the number of pools being received per million dollars, and that the pools conform to the minimum standard. In the case of a GNMA delivery against a trade having a coupon rate of less than 11%, a maximum of three pools may be delivered as long as two of the pools do not exceed the minimum threshold. In the case of two pools being delivered, neither one may reach the minimum threshold.

VI-G *SETTLEMENT WITH GSCC AND THE FED*

Trades in U.S. Treasury securities, Government National Mortgage Association (GNMA), Federal National Mortgage Association (FNMA or Fannie Mae), and Federal Home Loan Mortgage Corp. (FHLMC or Freddie Mac) are compared and settled through the Government Security Clearing Corporation. These transactions settle at the firms' clearing banks via the Federal Reserve Wire Network. Securities carried by the Fed are in bookkeeping form only—certificates are never issued that represent these issuers. Settlement at the Fed follows pretty much the same process as used by DTC. GSCC will perform the netting process, resulting in certain firms owing government or agency debt while other firms are owed agency or government debt. Final money settlement for these transactions is accomplished over the Fedwire. The Fedwire is a communication network between the 12 member Federal Reserve Banks. Monies transferred over these wires are instantaneously available to the recipient. With recent changes in the industry, the Fedwire has taken on more prominence. Until 1995, corporate and municipal trades were settled by next-day funds (funds usable by the recipient the day following receipt). In 1995, that was changed to same-day funds, which is, of course, what the Fedwire is set up to focus on. Therefore, just about all transactions between broker/dealers who are clearing and settling trades now settle the money portion of those trades over the Fedwire.

VI-H *OPTION SETTLEMENT*

As listed options trade in a certificateless environment, there isn't a need for a depository. Through the trade processing function option, transactions are compared and reports are produced showing the new positions. This was explained in detail previously. However, there is a money balance due. Actually two money balances are involved. The first involves the actual transaction settlement. The second is the margin required at OCC for open positions.

VI-H-1 Daily Activity Settlement

Each day, as a result of the trade processing function, there is a net premium balance of all options bought versus all options sold for clients that day. This net difference between buy and sell is then appended to the current balance from previous days. Let's assume that, over time, SF&R's clients have purchased more options than they have sold. SF&R would have money on deposit at OCC. If today's settling trades have more buyers than sellers, dollarwise, then the difference between the two would be added to the previous total. If, however, today's trades resulted in the clients having sold more options than they bought, SF&R would receive money from OCC. If, on the other hand, over time SF&R clients have sold more options than they've purchased, then the balance in the OCC account is a credit balance to SF&R. If today's settlement trades have more buys than sells dollarwise, then that figure will be reduced. If, on the other hand, today's trades have more sells than buys (as in the past), then that money balance will increase and SF&R will have a larger credit balance. The money difference must be settled in the morning. There's one slight twist: if OCC owes SF&R money based on the trading balances, then that money is first applied to SF&R's margin requirement.

Note that OCC acts as a passthrough in the daily money balancing. The firms that are carrying larger net buy money balances have received payments from their clients for those purchases. The money is owed to the firms that are carrying larger net sell money balances with OCC. Those firms owe the money to those of their clients who make up the net seller difference.

Example: SF&R has clients that have purchased options at a total value $25,000 higher than the totals of their clients who have sold options. That means that SF&R has received $25,000 more from those clients that purchased options than it owes to those clients who sold. As we are operating in a compared and balanced environment, the $25,000 must be owed to a firm or firms that have clients that sold a higher dollar amount than they bought. Let's assume that Boyle and Fry (BF), another clearing member of OCC, has client sales $25,000 greater than their clients' option purchases. BF will take the money from the clients who bought and pay it to the clients who sold. To completely satisfy the obligations to the selling clients, they will need $25,000 more. This is the money they will receive from OCC.

Note that if the firm also trades options for its proprietary accounts, there will be separate money balancing with OCC. Some firms clear and settle trades for market-making firms and specialist firms that do not have the staff to perform this function themselves. The clearing firm then receives separate reports from OCC for each of these firms and settles the net differences between them with OCC.

VI-H-2 OCC Margin

There are two computations for SF&R's margin requirements at OCC. One concerns customers and the other concerns proprietary trading. Both margin requirements are based on exposure to potential market swings. In the case of customers' margins, customers' fully paid-for options are excluded from the computation. The reason is that those options belong to the customers as they have been fully paid for and offer no exposure to their firm or OCC. They cannot be used by OCC to offset losses in the case where a firm gets into distress. On the proprietary side, since the firm is responsible for all of the option positions, OCC includes every single option that SF&R has in its proprietary positions and is responsible for. The proprietary computation includes long and short, spread and straddle, regardless of the strategy as a cohesive unit; based on the exposure of that cohesive unit, margin is charged. SF&R must also satisfy the margin requirement in the morning. If it turns out that, as a result of both the settlement and the margin computations, OCC owes money to Stone, Forrest & Rivers, SF&R will "pull the money down" from its balances and use it in their other daily transactions or pay down their letter of credit. If they owe, they must deposit the funds immediately. This is usually a simple process by which OCC draws down money against SF&R's letter of credit. (As explained earlier, a letter of credit is a guaranty for a set sum, issued and backed by a financial institution, such as a commercial bank, and given on behalf of the requester to another entity.) In this instance, SF&R has requested that First Continental Trust give a letter of credit to OCC. For the line of credit SF&R pays a fee whether or not OCC ever pulls down any funds to cover SF&R's obligations. When OCC does pull down money, it constitutes a loan and SF&R must pay interest to First Continental Trust in addition to the fee. As discussed previously, exercises and assignments of equity options are settled through NSCC as part of normal settlement. In the case of exercise of cash settling options, such as index options, those monies are part of the settlement we are referring to here and the money balance that it represented.

VI-H-3 Expiration

An option is a contract with an expiration date. If options are not exercised by the evening of that day, they cease to exist. Most exercises occur at or near expiration. That is because the time value portion of the premium is at a minimum. However, in the case of listed options, most "in-the-money positions" are traded out. Customer positions that are $.25 or more in the money and proprietary positions that are $.15 or more in the money will automatically be exercised by OCC at expiration, unless they are notified to the contrary.

With the end of the option cycle behind us, OCC adjusts the balances on its activity and margin balances through each clearing firm. This includes the elimination of the expired option positions.

VI-I *INSTITUTIONAL SETTLEMENT*

VI-I-1 Trade Suite, OASYS, and Omgeo

As stated previously, institutional clients of SF&R settle their trades through the Trade Suite or OASYS or Omgeo system. For the purpose of this section we will net all three into one and call it the Unified Consolidated Institutional Transaction (UCIT). The entire process is an electronic data transmission and book entry settlement self-enclosed system. When an institution opens an account with SF&R they usually have a custodian bank representing them. That custodian bank, under Rule 387 of the New York Stock Exchange, must be a member or affiliated with a member of a national depository. That information becomes part of the client master database and is referenced when the institutional entity does transactions through SF&R. Most institutions are set up on a *delivery-versus-payment (DVP)* basis. That means that the institution does not pay for purchases until SF&R delivers the securities to the custodian bank, and does not pay for sales until the custodian bank delivers the securities to SF&R. Because the custodian bank is a member of DTC (as is Stone, Forrest & Rivers), the transfer of securities from the custodian's control to SF&R's control is done by bookkeeping entry.

Here's an example: Major Insurance Company, a client of SF&R, buys 500,000 shares of RAM at $60 per share. Its custodian bank is Brooklyn Bank & Trust Company. On trade date, SF&R sends notification of the trade to Major Insurance Company. Major Insurance Company or its designee affirms or DKs the trade. In this case, Major Insurance Company affirms the trade. Brooklyn Bank & Trust is notified of the transaction as well as the affirmation notification to Stone, Forrest & Rivers. On settlement date, SF&R delivers the securities to Brooklyn Bank & Trust. This is all done electronically through accounts at DTC. Upon receipt of the securities, Brooklyn Bank & Trust releases the client's funds to SF&R.

Let's assume that SF&R purchases the 500,000 shares of stock from Giant, Reckor & Crane, which is operating for another institution, the Milwaukee Hedge Fund Company. When the sale takes place, Giant, Reckor & Crane notifies the Milwaukee Hedge Fund Company, or its designee, of the terms of the transaction. Milwaukee Hedge Fund affirms the trade in the same manner as Major Insurance Company does, notifying its custodian bank of the pending settlement as well as notifying Giant, Reckor & Crane of the acceptance of the trade. On settlement date, the custodian bank for Milwaukee Hedge Fund delivers the securities to GRC, which delivers the securities to SF&R via DTC, which delivers the securities to Brooklyn Bank & Trust.

All of these entries are processed electronically through the DTC bookkeeping entry system; no physical stock moves. The monies involved with the trade become part of each entity's settlement for that particular day. Note that at the end of the day, all entities must balance out both their security movements as well as their money movements. In the case of DTC and NSCC, all of the monies that they are involved with from day to day also must balance out at the end of the evening. Every debit must have an offsetting credit, and the sum of all entries must be zero.

In the Trade Suite or OASYS system, when Stone, Forrest & Rivers notifies Major Insurance Company of the transaction to purchase 500,000 shares of RAM, should the institution not know of the trade, they are to respond with a DK to SF&R as soon as possible. In the current system (a trade day + 3 system), they will respond by trade day + 1. Upon notification of the DK, Stone, Forrest & Rivers' operation personnel will contact the stockbroker to determine what went awry. Either Major Insurance Company has not processed the trade correctly or the stockbroker has put an incorrect account number on the transaction. Either way, the problems are to be resolved before settlement date so that SF&R can make a smooth transition from the contra broker to the client without having to unnecessarily finance positions overnight. Remember, as securities move one way, cash is generally moving the other way, so if Stone, Forrest & Rivers receives the stock from the selling broker/dealer but cannot deliver it to the institution for whatever reason, then Stone, Forrest & Rivers must pay the delivering broker and not get paid from the institution until the stock is delivered to them. If they are unable to deliver the stock on the same day that they receive it from the selling firm, they must finance it at a bank. That interest cost (the cost of borrowing money from the bank) cannot be recouped by SF&R.

As we are dealing with large quantities of stock, which, in turn, reflect large quantities of money, the Trade Suite and the OASYS system go a long way in assisting the institutional customers, their custodians, and broker/dealers in the resolution and settlement of transactions. If all goes smoothly and the institution affirms the trade, then on settlement date the trade will settle electronically.

Another service offered jointly by Thomson Financial and Depository Trust Company is called Omgeo. Omgeo takes the concept of Trade Suite and OASYS one step further by placing a third party between the broker/dealer and the institution. This third party—known as a *central matching unit (CMU)*—monitors the activity.

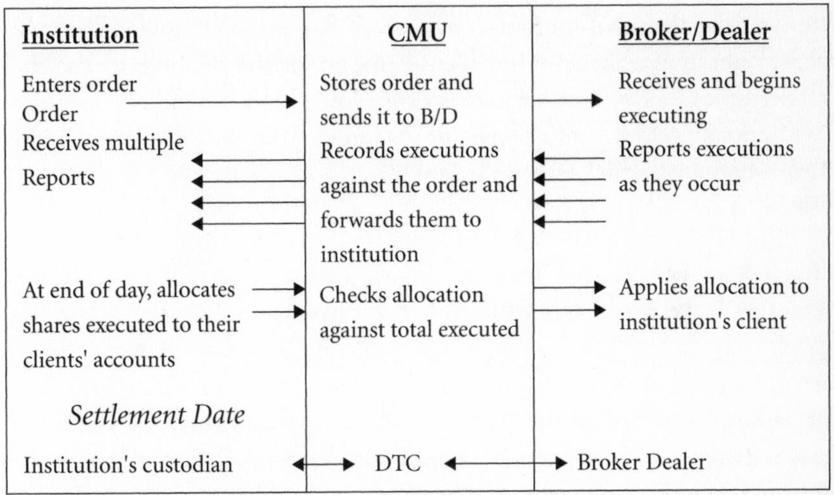

The value of the CMU is that there cannot be any mistake in the quantity or identity of the security being traded, nor can there be any miscounting of the amount to be allocated. The VMU runs checks and balances all through the process.

VI-I-2 Alert and SID

One of the newer innovations in the industry is to have the institutional accounts' standing instructions resident at either Depository Trust Company or Thomson Financial. Thomson Financial's service is called *Alert*; DTC's service is called *Standard Industry Database (SID)*. There are plans underway to merge these two systems into one cohesive database. The advantage of a database of this nature is that most institutions maintain accounts at multiple broker/dealers. Any changes to the delivery instructions must be permeated through all the broker/dealers that they do business with. This is error prone. Since we are dealing with institutions, we can safely assume we are dealing with large volumes of securities, which translates into large dollar amounts. Any mistake in the standing instructions can be very costly to either the institution or the broker/dealer. By having one central location where the institutions' standing instructions reside, and that one central location being able to be accessed by the broker/dealers it does business with, the possibility of a mistake is remote. Either all the transactions the institution does on a given day will be wrong or they will all be right. It also makes it much easier for an institution to verify the correct setup of a new standing instruction. Now it only goes to one location. Institutions no longer must wait for responses from 8 to 10 different broker/dealers with which they do business.

VI-J *MUTUAL FUND SETTLEMENT*

Let us begin with the fact that there are more mutual funds being offered to the public than there are stocks listed on the New York Stock Exchange. Add to this the number of pension plans, 401(K)s, IRAs, and so on that use mutual funds as investment vehicles. Then to this, add all of the individuals who have invested in these funds as part of their investment portfolios, and one can begin to imagine the number of daily transactions in this segment of the industry.

Before we discuss clearance and settlement, let us review the product that we are examining. There are two basic types of mutual funds: open end and closed end. Open-end funds make a continuous offering of their shares whenever a shareholder wants to buy, and they stand ready to reacquire those shares when the shareholder wants to sell. A closed-end fund makes an initial offering of its shares; the fund then closes and shares trade among the public similar to the way common stocks trade.

VI-J-1 Clearance

VI-J-1-a *Closed-End Fund Transaction Clearance*

Because the number of shares outstanding is set, closed-end mutual funds can be listed for trading on an exchange. The share price is determined by supply and demand. Trades in these funds settle through clearing corporations, such as National Securities Clearing Corporation, and settle at Depository Trust Company or a similar institution. From trade date to settlement date, there are three business days. They follow the path of equity securities.

VI-J-1-b *Open-End Fund Transaction Clearance*

Open-end mutual funds make a continuous offering of their shares. Therefore, per share price is determined by net asset value. This computation is comprised of the value of the portfolio, plus cash awaiting investment, less operating expenses, divided by the number of shares outstanding:

$$\frac{\text{Portfolio value} + \text{Cash} - \text{Expenses}}{\text{Number of shares outstanding}} = \text{Net asset value}$$

The fund shares are "traded" between the investors and the fund. Therefore, the shares do not trade on exchanges, nor do they trade in the over-the-counter market. Settlement of these fund shares is accomplished between the investor and the fund.

VI-J-2 Acquiring Fund Shares

Ms. Nicole Erin wants to invest in the Cutlass Fund. She obtains an application, completes it, and sends it along with a check to the Cutlass Fund. The fund will sell shares to her based on the share price set late in the afternoon on the day the check and application arrive. In this case, the fund will carry Ms. Erin's account on their books and all communications will be directly between Nicole and the fund.

Let us suppose that Ms. Erin uses the services of a Stone, Forrest & Rivers broker to select the Cutlass Growth Fund and to process the application and check. The SF&R broker will assist Nicole in completing the application. She can pay for the purchase by writing a check or having the funds subtracted from her brokerage account balance. The instructions and funds are forwarded to the mutual fund operation section of SF&R. The paperwork is checked and prepared for the next step in the process.

The mutual fund operations section processes instructions received from SF&R clients. These include purchase or sale of fund shares, exchanges between various funds offered by a particular fund group, as well as adjustments to clients' balances for dividend and capital gains reinvestments. Nicole's transaction, along with all the other fund transactions involving SF&R's clients and involving many different funds, are transmitted from SF&R on a daily basis. Add to this all of the other fund transactions being transmitted from other financial institutions to many different funds, and we can picture the paper nightmare that would evolve. This, in turn, would develop into a labor-intensive, paper-laden, and error-prone process.

Fortunately, systems have been set up to streamline the process. Let's look at FundServ, Mutual Fund Profile Service, and Automated Customer Account Transfer System.

VI-J-2-a *FundServ*

To facilitate the movement of data, National Securities Clearing Corporation offers FundServ, which acts as a conduit between the financial institutions and the mutual funds.

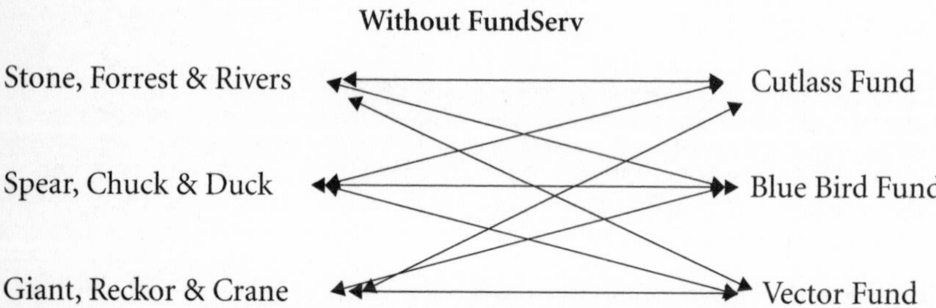

Add to the above mix many more financial institutions and many more funds, and the entangled mess grows geometrically. Participants in FundServ are financial institutions and the funds themselves. Instead of each financial institution communicating with each fund it conducts business with, the financial institutions transmit their transaction data to FundServ. The service then re-sorts this data in fund order and forwards the transaction data to each fund in an orderly fashion. The financial institutions and funds communicate through this one centralized conduit.

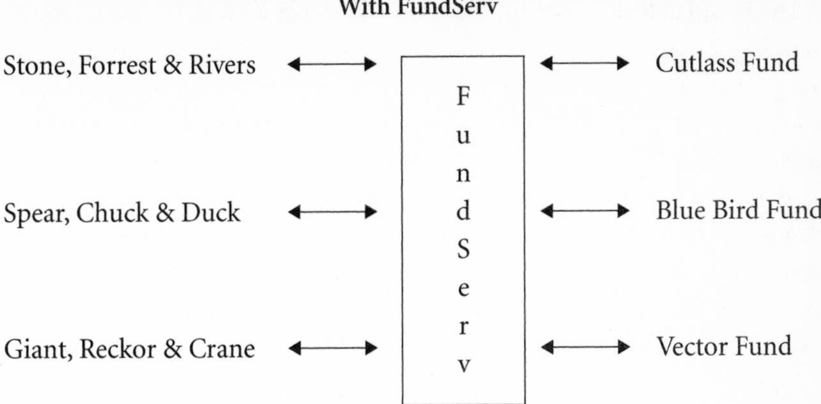

Another big benefit of FundServ is that each participant's account is debited or credited the amount involved with each transaction, and at the end of the recycle, the entries are netted so that each participant is owed money, owes money, or is even. This is settled by one money transfer being made for an entire day's business between the financial institution and NSCC on one side and the mutual fund and NSCC on the other. The time-consuming entry-by-entry settlement procedure between financial institutions and mutual funds has been eliminated.

Among the types of orders FundServ will accept are the usual buy and sell orders as well as exchange orders. The latter is used when a shareholder wants to switch from one fund to another fund within the same family of funds.

Example: The Cutlass Fund has a Cutlass Growth Fund, Cutlass European Fund, Cutlass Asian Fund, and Cutlass Africa Fund. A client who owns the Cutlass Growth Fund can use the exchange order to switch to another Cutlass fund. The exchange order cannot be used to switch from, let's say, the Cutlass Growth Fund to one of the Marquis funds, as they represent two different families of funds.

Participants in FundServ can transmit data via interactive communication, using a single batch each day or several batch transmissions per day. In addition, FundServ can accommodate as many different settlement cycles as required by the fund.

VI-J-2-b *Mutual Fund Profile Service (MFPS)*

NSCC maintains the Mutual Fund Profile Service (MFPS) to assist participants in keeping abreast of balances, dividends, and capital gains in their client funds. NSCC maintains a file per fund, which includes:

- The security ID number, symbol, and name
- Type of fund (load, no load), purpose, and focus
- FundServ settlement cycles
- Break point schedules
- Blue sky eligibility—being cleared for sale in the various states

Through this vehicle, brokers and other financial institutions receive the latest available information about the thousands of mutual funds being offered. By utilizing this service, broker/dealers and other financial institutions are able to adjust their clients' account and proprietary account positions in an accurate and timely way. In addition, as most mutual fund owners reinvest the funds' dividend/interest and capital gains payouts, the updating of customer balances is accomplished by the brokerage firm, in this case SF&R, "reading" these updates into its mutual fund system and adjusting the clients' balances.

As Stone, Forrest & Rivers is a participant in FundServ, it can respond to clients' mutual fund needs. This covers Ms. Nicole Erin's personal account as well as her 401(K). Ms. Jenna Rose has a wrap account with SF&R. A *wrap account* is one in which the client's financial assets are managed and maintained by the firm. The stockbroker is paid a fee based on the dollar amount of assets under management instead of commission on each transaction. Jenna's account has several types of funds that are managed, along with the rest of her assets, by Karl E. Beth, her broker.

VI-J-2-c *ACATS/FundServ*

Ms. Jenna Rose previously maintained her account with another firm. In her account were shares of common stock, bonds, and mutual funds. As the stocks and bonds clear through National Securities Clearing Corporation and settle at Depository Trust Company, the transfer of these positions is accomplished through Automated Customer Account Transfer System (ACATS). The mutual fund shares that we are discussing do not reside at DTC but instead are maintained by the individual funds in nominee name of the other broker/dealer, in this case Giant, Reckor & Crane, or the name of the actual owner (Jenna Rose care of GRC). When Jenna Rose wanted to transfer her account to SF&R, the fund made adjustments to their records to reflect the registration change so that dividends, capital gains, and so on would be paid to the correct firm. This process is accomplished through ACATS/FundServ.

ACATS/FundServ offers the best of the ACATS and the FundServ systems. ACATS moves positions between participating firms electronically, thereby negating the need to physically transport securities. FundServ notifies the issuing mutual funds of changes in ownership registration.

The SF&R investment adviser has Jenna Rose complete the appropriate forms and then submits them to NSCC, which, in turn, submits them to GRC. The positions that appear on the ACATS forms are verified and, if correct, are sent back to NSCC. Stock and bond positions are changed at DTC. Fund shares are reregistered at the fund to Ms. Rose's broker/dealer.

VI-J-3 Defined Contribution

As stated earlier, Nicole has her 401(K) account at SF&R. In her 401(K) account are several mutual funds from different families of funds. Nicole's current portfolio balance is:

30%	Cutlass Equity Fund
15%	Century Mid Cap Stock Fund
10%	Blue Bird Asian Equity Fund
10%	Vector European Growth Fund
20%	Regal Corporate Bond Fund
15%	Victoria Money Market Fund
100%	

As Nicole makes her periodic investments to her 401(K) retirement plan, the contributions must be distributed among the funds in the manner that Nicole has chosen. As SF&R carries the account, the operations staff is responsible for the allocation of contributions and the issuance of orders and checks to the individual funds. Nicole is just one of many clients that maintain their retirement accounts at SF&R. Each of these clients has its investments in funds that it has selected and with the weightings that it is comfortable with. As each client makes its contribution, SF&R goes through the allocation, order entry, and check process.

To alleviate this labor-intensive process, NSCC developed Defined Contribution Clearance and Settlement. Each client's allocation choice is maintained by the institution—in this case, Stone, Forrest & Rivers.

SF&R's Mutual Fund Operations Staff receives updated information from National Securities Clearing Corporation's Mutual Fund Profiling on mutual funds that participate in FundServ. It uses this information to apportion Nicole's 401(K) contribution among the funds that Nicole owns in the percentages she has chosen. Orders are then prepared electronically and transmitted to NSCC's FundServ, which in turn routes the orders to the respective fund along with all of the other orders being submitted by FundServ participants.

The funds either accept or reject the orders and report the disposition to NSCC, which, in turn, relays this information to the participating financial institutions. Rejected orders received by SF&R's Mutual Fund Operations are researched to determine the cause. Once the problem is discovered, the orders are corrected and re-sent to FundServ as part of the next cycle.

Orders that are executed are reported to NSCC's FundServ, which, in turn, routes the reports to the submitting entity. When SF&R's Mutual Fund Operations receives the electronic reports, Nicole's accounts are adjusted systemically to reflect the new balances.

National Securities Clearing Corporation and Stone, Forrest & Rivers monitor the daily transactions to determine the amount of money that must be paid or received at the end of the process. This function is carried out in SF&R's settlement area, which is responsible for the security and money settlement of all SF&R's transactions. On the morning after trade date (T + 1), NSCC notifies SF&R of money that is due or to be paid. NSCC then makes the appropriate debit or credit entry to SF&R's account.

CHAPTER VII

Custodial Services

As the majority of the instruments that we trade are maintained by broker/dealers or custodial banks, the institutions must service those positions. When a corporation pays a dividend, for example, they pay it to the registered holder, which is the nominee name of the custodian. In the case of dividends, the nominee is most likely Depository Trust Company Division of DTCC. They, in turn, credit the broker/dealers or custodian banks that they are holding the securities for, which, in turn, credit their clients. This chapter focuses on the services performed to ensure that clients receive what they are entitled to, and receive it when they are entitled to it.

VII-A *AUTOMATED CUSTOMER ACCOUNT TRANSFER SYSTEM (ACATS)*

Stockbrokers sometimes leave broker/dealer firms to go to other firms for a multitude of reasons, including better research and payout schedules. Clients change stockbrokers for a multitude of reasons. Perhaps they can get a better commission rate. Perhaps they feel that they are not getting the attention that they should. Maybe they lost money with a particular broker. The transfer of clients' accounts from one firm to another is generally processed through an Automated Customer Account Transfer System (ACATS). The ACATS form is filled out by the client and given to the receiving firm along with a copy of the customer's last statement. The form is then forwarded to the delivering firm with instructions on what the delivering firm is to do.

The delivering firm will execute the instructions and has 72 hours to respond to the receiving firm as to whether the information it has received is complete and accurate. The account will be delivered through DTC by adjusting the two participating firms' positions in the various securities that the client owns.

SF&R is about to get a new client. His name is Woodrow Oaks. Mr. Oaks currently has an account at Knune & Knight. Mr. Oaks has just moved from the town in which Knune & Knight has an office to a different state and now lives in a town where Knune & Knight has no presence. Therefore, based on recommendations of some new neighbors and other people that he has met, he wants to transfer his account from Knune & Knight to Stone, Forrest & Rivers.

Mr. Oaks contacts SF&R and, after speaking to one of their registered reps, opens a new account. This is standard practice and we will assume that the account that Woody opens is a cash and margin type of account. The SF&R representative sends Woody the new account forms to be completed and signed as well as an ACATS form, which gives Woody several alternatives.

1. Woody can transfer his entire account to Stone, Forrest & Rivers.
2. He can have his old firm liquidate his position and send a check to Stone, Forrest & Rivers.
3. He can do a partial delivery, keeping some of the securities and/or money at the old firm.

Woody elects to have the entire account transferred. One of the requirements is that Woody enclose a copy of his latest statement from the previous firm. Upon its receipt at SF&R, the paper processing is verified for completion and then forwarded to the previous firm. In the normal process, the old firm will instruct DTC to take securities out of their positions representing what Woody owns and transfer them electronically to Stone, Forrest & Rivers' positions. Notification of this is received by SF&R's operations personnel and forwarded to the stockbroker. Woody also receives a statement showing the receipt of securities and money. Woody checks this against what he believes should have been received and if there are no problems, the account now operates as if it were opened some time ago. If there is a problem, such as a wrong security or the quantity delivered, Woody will contact the SF&R stockbroker, who will then investigate the problem via SF&R's operations personnel.

ACATS performs a very important function in our broker's community as it allows customers to move their accounts in an efficient and inexpensive manner. Most movements are done electronically so the customer does not see or get involved with any of its physical aspects. After the forms are filled out, the industry does the rest.

VII-B *TRANSFERS*

While some elements of physical certificates still exist in the industry, the majority of certificates is now kept in an electronic form at a depository or other repository. Stocks that are maintained in physical form (securities that the clients insist on receiving and maintaining themselves) are issued through the auspices of the corporate transfer agent. Different entities perform these functions for different types of securities. However, certain securities are only issued in bookkeeping form—U.S. Treasuries and listed options, to name but a few. It is the industry's goal to eventually get to the point where physical securities no longer exist. However, until that point is reached, we will still be dealing with transfer agents and the reregistering of certificates from the former party's name to the name of the new owner or their nominee.

Most physical certificates today are maintained in the beneficial owner's name. Stock that is maintained at SF&R in customer name (beneficial owner's name) is only permitted in cash accounts and the process is known as *safekeeping.*

The majority of shares of stock, bonds, and so on are maintained at repositories, in electronic form, and registered in nominee name. This allows the broker/dealers to use these securities to finance customers' margin debit balances, to make deliveries, and to meet other needs as they arise. Customers who want securities registered in their names have the choice of keeping the stocks at SF&R or a custodial facility or home. Once the securities are shipped to the customer, SF&R is no longer responsible for the maintenance and support of the product. Dividends, interest, proxy information, and other correspondence will go directly from the dividend-dispersing agent or issuer's agent to the customer. The corporation's end-of-year statement goes directly to the customer. SF&R is not involved. If the customer loses the certificates, he must go through a rather extensive process, which includes being bonded, and completing and filing a multitude of forms. As SF&R is not involved with this, SF&R cannot lend support.

Stocks that the customers maintain and are registered in their names and held at SF&R are segregated from the regular cash accounts. In SF&R, as stated earlier, type 1 is cash, type 2 is margin, type 3 is short positions, and type 4 is dividends. SF&R uses type 5 for securities registered in customer's name (securities in safekeeping).

Since the stock in a type 5 account is nonnegotiable, SF&R does not want to mistakenly pay the customer on a sale of a stock until that stock is made negotiable through the use of a signed stock power. Therefore, it segregates the securities in a type 5 account. When the customer sells the stock, the system books the sale to a type 1 account, leaving the customer with a long (type 5) position and a short (type 1) position. This keeps the firm from accidentally paying the customer while they are still holding nonnegotiable paper.

A nonnegotiable security is not even worth the paper it is written on as it cannot be used for any purpose. Upon sale of such a security the branch office or the settlement area of the firm will send the customer a stock/bond power. This document replicates the back of the stock or bond certificate and can be used as a substitute for endorsement purposes. The customer completes the form, signs it, and mails it back to SF&R. SF&R personnel then obtain the certificate and affix the stock/bond power to the back of it. This renders the security negotiable. It is then sent to a transfer agent and reregistered in the firm's street name. Once the security is in negotiable form, SF&R can use other securities that it has in nominee name to effect delivery against a customer sale.

There are actually three types of transfers: stock going into the firm's name or into DTC's name (which is known as street name), stock being transferred into the name of the client, and stock coming in to transfer that requires special handling, known as legal transfer.

The majority of the securities maintained by the industry are in street name. Since Depository Trust Company is the major repository for securities, the securities are registered in their nominee name, CEDE. DTC, therefore, as far as registered owners are concerned, is the largest security owner in the United States and perhaps the entire world. However, they do not own one share or one bond of these securities; they are all registered to their nominee name. DTC is holding the securities in various forms for their members, which include custodian banks and broker/dealers, who, in turn, are carrying these positions for their customers, the you and me of the world. Stock transferred into either the firm's nominee name or into DTC's name is said to be transferred into street name.

When a customer requests that stocks be registered in their name, instructions are sent to the agent either by the broker/dealer (SF&R) or through DTC's Fast Automated Stock Transfer (FAST) system to the transfer agent. The majority of stock that DTC is holding is maintained at the transfer agent, normally a commercial bank that is the representative of the issuer, in bookkeeping form. DTC maintains on its premises a working supply of the necessary securities. When a client decides to have stock registered in their name, SF&R will send the instruction to DTC. DTC will electronically notify the transfer agent and the transfer agent will *cut* a new certificate. That new certificate will be the standard paper certificate that we have had for generations upon generations. It will carry the customer's name and address, issuer's name, class or type of security, the date of issuance and the CUSIP number, and a unique certificate number along with legal wording, as required. The transfer agent will send the certificate to DTC, which will send it to Stone, Forrest & Rivers, which, in turn, will mail it to the client. This is known as *customer transfer*. Many agents charge the requesting party a fee for this service.

Legal transfer affects the security when it's going into transfer, not when it comes out of transfer. This means that special documentation is needed before the transfer agent will remove the registered owner's name from its records and replace it with a new owner's name. This occurs, for example, when stock registered in an individual's name is sent to transfer to be reregistered because the registered owner has died. Copies of the death certificate, affidavit of domicile, tax waivers, and more are necessary to effect transfer. Stock registered in a corporation's name also requires special documentation to effect transfer. An interesting aspect of this part of the transfer process is that if the trustee of an account is a human being, he can be transferred out of the trust name by a nonlegal type of transfer. If, however, the trustee is an entity such as a commercial bank or other type of agent, a legal transfer requires special documentation. If stock is registered in the name of a custodian or under the Uniform Gift to Minors Act, before that stock can be transferred to the individual who became of legal age, a copy of the birth certificate is required, as is a letter from the custodian or the guardian releasing the obligation of the Uniform Gift to Minors Act.

Much of the above also applies in cases where the securities are maintained in street name. When a customer dies, her account is immediately marked "deceased" and becomes frozen until SF&R receives legal notification to act. That legal notification is either a copy of the will, which gives instructions as to how the account is to be allocated, or, in absence of a will, whoever the court appointed as administrator. A court-appointed administrator, in the case where there is no will, can only liquidate securities. However, SF&R must still get copies of the death certificate, tax waivers, affidavit of domicile, and the rest of the legal documentation that may be required to liquidate the account. That liquidation may be in the form of moving securities to beneficiaries or liquidating the securities themselves into a cash position and distributing the cash. Again, SF&R must wait for legal notification and cannot take orders from any kin or person in another relationship with the deceased person until such time as the required documentation is complete.

Joint tenants with rights of survivorship (JTROS) accounts are a special case. They are usually opened by married couples. Upon the death of one of the two people, the entire account reverts to the survivor and is not frozen in any way, shape, size, or form. However, getting the positions from the joint account to the survivor's new single account requires legal documentation, including:

- A copy of the death certificate
- Affidavit of domicile
- Medallion stamp

In the case of tenants in common (JT TEN), which is comprised of two principals, 50% of the account is frozen upon one's death. Unless there is a recently dated letter signed by both parties, there is an automatic 50/50 split. Fifty percent of the account will remain frozen until legal notification is received and an executor of the will steps forward, or the court appoints an administrator, at which time the instructions they receive, from either the will or the court, will be carried out. There is much more to this aspect of legal transfer than we will go into here.

A pilot is under way to expedite legal transfer. Through the use of a medallion stamp, the broker/dealer, bank, or other fiduciary claims that they have all the legal documentation necessary to effect transfer. Based on their word, the transfer agent will start the registration process.

VII-C *STANDING INSTRUCTIONS*

Within the client master database there reside the customer's standing instructions. These instructions tell SF&R how to process various aspects of the customer's accounts. For example, when SF&R credits the customer's accounts with dividends on their stocks or bond interest from their debt instruments, what does the client want to happen to the payments? Should they be sent to the customer on a monthly or weekly basis or held in the account and deposited into a money fund? When the customer sells securities, should the proceeds be mailed to the customer or held in the account and placed in a money fund? As for securities that SF&R is maintaining for the customer, should they be registered in street name (nominee name) or customer name (safekeeping)? Does the customer want the securities that they purchased held by SF&R or transferred into their name and shipped? All of these are part of customers' standing instructions. In the case of institutions, the standing instructions also contain the name of the custodian bank maintaining positions for the institution. Thomson Financials' ALERT System and DTC's SID (Standing Instruction Data Base System) have been set up to facilitate institutional delivery instructions. These facilities provide a central place for institutions to update their standing instructions. Prior to the advent of these facilities, the institution would have to contact every broker/dealer it did business with and tell them which accounts are undergoing some sort of standing instruction change. Remember, an institution may have 10, 12, or more accounts in a particular brokerage firm as well as having 5, 8, or 10 different brokerage firms servicing them. The possibility of all changes being made correctly the first time wasn't great. Whatever standing instruction was supposed to be changed and wasn't would negate the possibility of a transaction completing the entire trade cycle.

VII-D *DIVIDENDS AND BOND INTEREST*

Stocks pay dividends; bonds pay interest. Stocks never pay interest, and bonds never pay dividends. When a corporation is going to pay a dividend to its stockholders, it announces three dates: the *declaration date*, the *record date*, and the *payable date*.

The declaration date is the date the amount of the dividend is announced. The evening of record date is the date one must be legal owner to be entitled to the dividend. The payable date is the date the actual payment is made.

Here's an example: Loster Motor Corp. announces a $.50 per share dividend on May 1 (declaration date) that will be paid to shareholders of record of May 15 (record date); it will be paid on June 1 (payable date). On the night of May 15, SF&R's system produces a "takeoff" from the summary stock record. The dividend personnel then look for *as-of* trades (trades not processed on their day of execution) or other adjustments that may affect customers' accounts as of the evening of record. Next, a dividend control account is set up for the receipt and disbursement of money from the payment. After allocation and receipt of the dividend, the control account should go to a zero balance.

Example of a takeoff:

Name: Loster Motor Corp.
Sym LMC
CUSIP 345786107 — **RecDte 5-15** — **PayDte 6-1**
Rate .50

ACCT#	LONG	SHORT	Dr	Cr
T2E4500000	5000			2500
1BA0002362	500			250
1BA0045731	1000			500
1BS0083453		1000	500	
2NY0103565	800			
2NY0137652	300			150
2NK0004431	10000			5000
3DC0056731	100			50
DIV3457860				
DTC5000000		10100	5050	
NBL1000000		800	400	
NSL2035600		5000	2500	
NYV1000000		800		

The takeoff is in balance. SF&R will be crediting the clients' accounts that are long the security and charging the clients' accounts that are short. The exception is account 2NY0103565, which has a security in their name for safekeeping. Note that their account ends with a type 5 and the security is in the New York office's vault (NYV100000). That client will receive the dividend directly from the company's paying agent. As the money is received from those street-side accounts and other accounts that owe it, it is booked against the dividend control account. When the money is disbursed to the accounts that are owed, it is also booked against the dividend control account. The result should be the dividend control account balancing out to zero.

If the record date is May 15, then the last day the stock can be purchased for regular-way settlement, so that the owner will be entitled to the dividend, is May 12. May 12 trade date settles on May 15. Someone buying the stock on May 13 for regular-way settlement will settle the business day after the record date and will therefore not be entitled to the dividend. The first day a buyer is not entitled to receive the dividend is known as the *ex-dividend date.*

After the close of trading on the last day before the ex-dividend date, the market on which the security trades reduces the closing price to reflect the dividend that will be paid out. The stock opens for trading on the "ex" date against an adjusted closing price. This means that if Loster Motor Corp. common shares closed on May 12 at a price of $60 per share, the market price on which it trades would adjust the closing price to $59.50 to reflect the $.50 dividend. If the stock, let's say, opened on the ex-dividend day at $59.75, the net change would be +.25, not –.25, as the official closing price the night before was $60. Any time the net change of a stock that you are following looks incorrect, it is telling you that some type of corporate action occurred.

Stock splits are handled in a similar fashion to cash dividends. The one big exception is that the ex date is moved to the day after the payable date and is known as the *ex-distribution date.* The reason is that the price adjustment reflecting the split would be too drastic and cause many problems. For example, Ms. Blaire Ittout owns 100 shares of RIP at $90. The stock announces a 3 for 1 split. This means that Blaire's 100 shares (presently worth $90 per share) would be become 300 shares at $30 per share. Let us assume that Blaire had a margin account and the 100 shares were properly margined:

100 shares of RIP @ $90 per share:

$9,000 CMV
–4,500 Eq
$4,500 Dr

If the ex-dividend date was maintained as two business days before record date, Blair's account would have the following balance that morning:

100 shares of RIP @ \$30 per share:

\$ 3,000 CMV
+1,500 Eq
\$+4,500 Dr

Remember, the additional shares are not issued until payable date. Blair would have a negative equity and would be on call for additional collateral. In addition, with the stock trading at the "split" price with the additional shares not being issued, there would be a shortage of stock available to settle trades.

With the ex-distribution date falling the day after payable date, here are the balances in Blaire's account at the close of business on the payable date:

100 shares of RIP @ \$90 per share:

\$9,000 CMV
−4,500 Eq
\$4,500 Dr

But the balances open on the ex-distribution date as:

300 shares of RIP @ \$30 per share:

\$9,000 CMV
−4,500 Eq
\$4,500 Dr

Sometimes a corporation will issue stock dividends instead of cash dividends. If the stock dividends are less than 25%, the process followed is the same as for a cash dividend. If the distribution is more than 25%, the process used is the same as for a stock split.

VII-E CORPORATE ACTIONS (AKA REORGANIZATIONS)

Corporations merge, acquire other corporations, spin off subsidiaries of their corporation, make tender offers for other corporations, and do other types of nondaily business arrangements. The area of SF&R that processes these types of events is the Corporate Actions Department, formerly known as REORG.

VII-E-1 Mergers

In a merger, Company A and Company B merge into Company C. As a result of the merger, neither Company A nor Company B continue to exist. One of their names may, but the actual structure of the company changes. Mergers are very seldom on a share-for-share basis. Therefore, based on the evaluation of the two companies .09624 shares of Company A may entitle you to receive one share of Company C, whereas 1.272 shares of Company B will allow you to receive one share of Company C. It is the responsibility of SF&R's Corporate Actions Department to acquire sufficient shares to satisfy their customers and proprietary demands in a merger situation. They must surrender to the agent representing the merging factions the proper number of shares so that they receive back the proper number of shares of the newly formed company.

The Corporate Actions Department accesses the stock record and freezes a position "takeoff" for all the accounts that maintain positions in the shares of stock of the companies involved in the merger on the announced record date of the merger. They also look for "as-of" trades that may have missed the record date but should have been settled on that date. As the merger is mandatory, the department doesn't have to contact the clients to determine if they want to participate or not. Once they receive the "takeoff," they review the location positions to make sure they have sufficient shares to surrender to the agent for their clients' and the firm's proprietary accounts. The process becomes more difficult because the industry stopped using script (fractional shares) years ago. Instead, fractional share amounts are settled in *cash in lieu of script (cash)*.

SF&R programs determine the amount of cash instead of shares they will need to satisfy their clients. The Corporate Actions personnel inform

DTC of their need to satisfy their clients. This is an important step as DTC knows SF&R's total position and not the quantities per account making up that total.

When the allocation is made, SF&R computer systems allocate the securities and cash in accordance with what their clients are entitled to. Clients that have short positions owe SF&R the new shares so their accounts are charged. The entire process is handled through the use of a control account set up for this particular merger. At the end of the process, the account should be flat.

VII-E-2 Acquisitions

In an acquisition, Company A acquires Company B and Company A continues to exist. Again, this is very seldom on a share-for-share basis. The ratio used is determined by the share values of the two companies. For example, the shareholders of Company B could receive one share of Company A for every 2.7 shares of Company B they own. The difference, resulting in fractional shares, would be paid in cash. Again, the Corporate Actions Department accesses the online stock record to freeze the position on record date. The required shares are turned over to the agent through DTC, and the new shares are received into SF&R's account at DTC and allocated to the clients' accounts on SF&R's books.

The figures used in these examples are made up to show you some of the difficulties facing the Corporate Actions Department.

VII-E-3 Tender Offers

Sometimes a company will make a tender offer of cash or securities for the shares of another company. This is because either they want to have a controlling interest in the company or they want to make a substantial investment in that company. For example, they may be willing pay $30 per share for every share of Company A that is tendered. Company A is currently trading at $25 per share. Therefore, they are willing to pay a $5 premium to get control of the company or the targeted number of shares. Generally, in a tender situation the company making the tender is willing to pay a premium to get the shares. The company that the shares are being tendered for may send out notices advising their clients not to accept the tender because they do not want to lose control of the company. The tender itself may be for a fixed number of shares, which can be troublesome for the Corporate Actions Department.

Let's say the tender is for 1,000,000 shares of the company. A tender is normally voiced in such a way that the first 1,000,000 shares submitted are accepted. Therefore, the firms try to get their notices to DTC as soon as possible. In SF&R, the stockbrokers are notified of the tender offer and begin to alert clients who own the stock, asking whether or not they want to tender their securities. They explain to the customers that the tender might not be totally accepted. The Corporate Actions Department surrenders their stock and finds that of, say, 500,000 shares that SF&R submitted, only 300,000 were accepted because the total amount that various broker/dealers tendered to the agent reached 1,000,000 shares. Therefore, SF&R must go back to their clients and explain to them that all of their shares were not accepted. As these tender offers are usually made at a premium, the clients may become very disappointed and think that SF&R is not doing a good job in submitting their shares. Actually, all of the firms who submitted shares were prorated by DTC once the 1,000,000 shares were obtained by the agent. The agent will tell DTC what percentage has been accepted. DTC then prorates the tender among the firms participating in the offer. SF&R's Corporate Actions Department must now make adjustments to the customers' accounts, putting back in the stock that was not accepted in the tender and making the corresponding money adjustments.

VII-E-4 Stock Splits

When a company is doing very well, the stock rises in price, and, if its products are in the hands of the public, it will usually split the stock. Splitting stock accomplishes two things: It puts more of its shares into the public's hands and it does so at a lower price.

Let's suppose that Loster Motor Corp. stock has risen to $150 per share. As Loster makes automobiles, trucks, and other vehicles for the public, it wants the public to participate in its stock because if the public owns its stock, it will also probably buy its products and vice versa. But the public feels that the price ($150 per share) is to high to buy a round line so Loster's board of directors votes for a three-for-one split. This is carried out through

Loster's transfer agent, First National Bank and Trust Company of Dairy Falls, Minnesota. The transfer agent allocates the shares based on the registered holders. As DTC is the registered holder for stocks being held for SF&R, DTC will receive the additional shares for SF&R and all of the other members it is holding stock for. DTC will then allocate the additional shares to its members. SF&R's Corporation Department must make sure the amount of shares received equals what SF&R records show as owed.

People who own the stock will receive an additional two shares for every one share held. At the same time, the price of Loster Motor Corp. will become $50 per share. While there is no apparent monetary gain through the split, the shares become tradable at $50 per share, so a greater range of the public can now afford them.

VII-E-5 Reverse Stock Splits

Many times, a company whose stock is not doing well will do a *reverse split* of the stock to make its price seem more attractive. For example, Hosenphepher Mines stock is currently trading at $.10 a share. This is considered a penny stock and, therefore, quite risky. Its board of directors decides on a 100-to-1 reverse split, so for every 100 shares you have at $.10 per share, you will now have one share at $10 per share. By doing this Hosenphepher Mines looks like a going, financially strong concern as the stock is trading at $10 per share.

The Corporate Actions Department's responsibilities are to gather all of the shares that are on the books of SF&R, submit them through DTC, and make the corresponding adjustment to the accounts of clients that own or owe the stock. These shares will not pose a potential problem to SF&R. The potential problem is that clients who have the stock away from the industry (in their vaults, for example) may come into the firm five years later and want to sell the stock. They ask the stockbroker what Hosenphepher Mines is selling for. Let's assume it is selling for the same price as at the reverse split, $10 per share. They say, "Wow, I have 1,000 shares of that stock that's worth $10,000. Please sell it for me." The stockbroker sells the stock and on settlement date the customer walks in and submits the 1,000 shares of stock. When it goes into transfer to be reregistered into street name, it comes back as 10 shares due to the 100-to-1 reverse split. In the meantime, the customer is walking around with $10,000 of SF&R's money that, chances are, SF&R will not be able to recoup because the customer knew what he was doing when he brought in the stock certificate. It is called a scam. As we get further and further away from physical certificates, this problem will become nonexistent.

The last part of Corporate Actions' functions is in the case of a corporate spinoff.

VII-E-6 Spinoffs

As a company grows, it may find itself going into businesses that at first fit the corporate culture but later do not. In addition, as firms merge or acquire one another, there could be divisions of the new firms that do not fit the goal of the current management. Therefore, the management may vote to spin off the unwanted company as a standalone separate corporation. One of the most famous of all spinoffs had nothing to do with either goal. The U.S. Department of Justice believed that American Telephone and Telegraph had gotten too large and, therefore, made it spin off its seven subdivisions, such as Verizon. This was perhaps the greatest of all spinoffs of corporations that the world has ever seen. Since that time, many of the corporations that were spun off have merged so it seems to be in a cycle.

In the case of a spinoff, shares of the new companies are given to the shareholders of the former company. In other words, if you owned American Telephone and Telegraph at the time of the spinoff of the "Baby Bells," you received at no charge shares of all seven Baby Bells. You could, if you wished, sell the shares and retrieve money. When the company does a spinoff, the value of the remaining company affects the price of its shares. In other words, when AT&T did the spinoff, the price of AT&T stock dropped considerably. But thanks to the value of their new Baby Bell shares, AT&T stockholders didn't suffer.

This is not always true, however. Many times, when a company spins off another company, the company that is being jettisoned was dragging down the company that remains. Therefore, when investors learn of the spinoff, share prices of the remaining company (called the parent company) actually rise.

In the case of a spinoff, it is the Corporate Actions Department's responsibility to make sure that the existing shareholders as of a certain date, the record date, receive the shares of the spunoff company that they are entitled to. This is usually done in a very swift and clean manner. In the case of fractional shares, there will be a price determined, and the shareholders who are to receive the fractional shares instead receive cash in lieu of script. (*Script* is defined as less than one share of stock.)

Years ago the shareholder would receive script. However, this was a very cumbersome way of doing business, so script has been replaced by cash. As of a certain date, a market price is established and holders of a fractional share get a proportion of that market price.

The process is conducted by DTC. SF&R's Corporation Department has prepared control accounts that contain the number of spun-off shares they are expecting to receive. When DTC delivers the shares, the department reconciles them against their positions.

VII-E-7 Processing Corporate Actions

SF&R's Corporation Action Department is responsible for the accurate and timely processing of these corporate actions. They are first alerted of an action via industry venders, other internal departments (such as research) or by DTC.

They request a stock record takeoff at the close of business of the record date. This takeoff contains all of the accounts involved in the corporate action that SF&R is responsible for. The takeoff must be in balance so that the department can proceed with good information. If the record is not in balance, they must contact the Stock Record Department (discussed in Chapter XI) and determine what corrective action is being taken.

With a good stock record, the department begins to ascertain the changes that must occur in these accounts to satisfy the corporate action requirements. In the case of a merger of two companies, accounts will lose the old security positions and receive the new security positions. Some will receive securities and cash. The corporate action department must make sure that this is planned for in their instructions to DTC.

Accounts that are short over the record date owe SF&R the new securities. These accounts include the accounts of clients with short positions and stock loans. SF&R Corporate Action personnel must make sure that the proper quantity of the new shares is received.

On the effective date of the merger or acquisition, SF&R's Corporation Action personnel again balance the takeoff by making sure that they are in control of their control accounts and that they are resolving any differences remaining in the control account.

When the corporation action process is complete the control account should be flat.

CHAPTER VIII

Role of the Banks

A book on brokerage operations would not be complete without a discussion of the role that banks play in the brokerage industry. The services they provide run the gamut from client of the broker/dealer to financing broker/dealer activity or, to put it another way, from a broker/dealer's asset to a broker/dealer's liability. Many banks have broker/dealer divisions themselves, but still use the services of other broker/dealers, the same way a broker/dealer uses the services of several banks. Therefore, we must distinguish between the role of banks as competitors of brokerage firms and their role as service providers to the brokerage industry. This chapter focuses on the latter.

VIII-A *CUSTODIAN*

One of the primary functions of a bank is that of custodian. While most securities maintained by broker/dealers are on deposit at DTCC, certain securities are maintained at commercial banks for expeditious reasons. For example, SF&R maintains a large repo/reverse repo business. The most efficient and safest process for repos is known as a tri-party repo. Under this process, the bank acts as a third party, moving the security from the account of the borrower into their "hold" account, while at the same time moving the money from the lender's account into their hold account. If all is in order, the bank then moves the securities to the account of the lender and cash to the account of the borrower. This is all performed electronically so that the parties to the repo are assured (1) that the counterparty has fulfilled their obligation at the time the repo was executed, and (2) that nothing can get lost in transit as nothing moves out of the bank.

The role of custodian is also prevalent in the institutional client arena. Most institutions maintain their securities at commercial banks, which service the positions. Rule 387 of the New York Stock Exchange mandates that any bank offering custodial services must be a participant of DTCC or be affiliated with a bank that is. This means that the stocks the bank is holding for its institutional clients are not at the bank but at DTCC.

As we saw earlier, the settlement of institutional transactions, as well as those for approved high-net-worth individuals, is accomplished electronically. The institution sends the order to the broker/dealer, which executes it in the marketplace and reports back the terms of the trade. The institution notifies its custodian bank of the trade and, on settlement date, the bank and the broker/dealer exchange assets via DTCC to settle the transaction.

The role of custodian becomes dynamic as the institution invests in foreign markets. Here an international bank uses its foreign branches to execute the transactions and keep the main office advised of the foreign corporations' corporate actions.

The custodian function is usually performed by banks that are trust companies.

VIII B *FINANCING*

VIII B-1 Collateralized Loans and Hypothecation

Broker/dealers use banks' lending capabilities in several ways. They finance the trading inventory as well as the debit balances in clients' margin accounts by pledging the securities against the loan. In the case of clients' securities, the process is known as *rehypothecation* or simply *hypothecation*. SF&R's primary bank is First Continental Bank and Trust. As the stock in SF&R's trading and investment accounts are owned by the firm, SF&R can pledge entire positions at First Continental. However, SF&R must be careful with client accounts as Regulation T of the Federal Reserve permits the firm to use up to 140% of the clients' debit balance to secure funding. These loans must be marked to the market every day (brought to their current market value) and adjustments made so that the loan is adequately secured at the bank and SF&R has not used more collateral than it is allowed to.

VIII-B-2 Letters of Credit

To facilitate daily loan requirements that usually apply to such industry entities as clearing corporations, SF&R borrows against a letter of credit issued by First Continental. Industry entities are willing to accept the letter of credit as it is backed by the creditworthiness of the issuing bank and not the entity that is using it. Therefore, even though SF&R does not have any financial trouble, the firm uses letters of credit as part of its daily business. The firm pays a fee for the amount guaranteed by the bank, but only pays interest on the amount borrowed.

Each day when SF&R balances their cash position with the particular entity, such as NSCC or OCC, either the amount needed is pulled down against the letter of credit or the amount outstanding is reduced. This saves SF&R the trouble of having to arrange for and negotiate a new overnight loan each day. It also assures the industry entity that funds will be there as they are needed.

VIII-B-3 Lines of Credit

First Continental has also given SF&R an unsecured line of credit based on SF&R's creditworthiness. This unsecured line permits SF&R to borrow funds without the need to pledge collateral. The funds are used in the daily operation of the firm. For all intents and purposes, this operates in the same way as your personal credit cards.

VIII-C *TRANSFER AGENT*

Besides loaning funds, First Continental is also the transfer agent for corporations. First Continental is the agent for all of the security classes that the

Zappa Corporation has issued. As the transfer agent, First Continental maintains books of the registered holder of Zappa securities. From the names on these lists, First Continental determines to whom dividends, interest, proxies, and other corporate notices are sent. Besides the registered owner's name, the bank maintains its address and tax ID number.

Securities of some companies are not DTC-eligible. These securities must be maintained in physical form and require transfer when they are traded.

As transfer agent, First Continental maintains information on the registered holder of the security. In most cases, the registration is in nominee name and not that of the actual (beneficial) owner. For example, Mr. Marshal Law owns 1,000 shares of Uptite Tenshin Corp. The stock is maintained in his account, #3MI005672-2, at SF&R. The firm, in turn, maintains the securities at DTCC, which has the stock registered in their street name, CEDE. First Continental knows DTCC as the registered owner of the securities. DTCC, in turn, knows SF&R as owner, and SF&R knows Marshal Law as owner. CEDE is the nominee name that the securities are registered in. Marshal Law is the beneficial owner.

VIII-D *REGISTRAR*

The purpose of the registrar is to monitor and audit the transfer agents to make certain that:

1. The transfer agents' registration books are up to date.
2. The transfer agents' records are accurate.
3. The issuer has issued the quantity of securities authorized and reported in various financial and regulatory statements.

All three functions are very important as they reflect on the integrity of the issuing company. If the transfer agent's books are not up to date or accurate, then the wrong people will be receiving corporate information, dividends, or bond interest. In the case of item 3 above, where the amount of securities issued must be accurately reflected on financial statements, incorrect amounts could affect the corporate issue's ratings as being an investment vehicle.

VIII-E *PAYING AGENT*

When a corporation or other such entity wants to distribute a payment to owners of one of its issues, it uses the services of a paying agent. This agent is sometimes referred to as the dividend disbursing agent (DDA).

Loster Motor Corp. wants to pay their common stockholders their quarterly dividend of $.50 per share. The corporation instructs its dividend-disbursing agent to pay the dividend on June 1 to the registered holders on the night of May 15. Loster Motors uses Metropolis Bank and Trust as their DDA. Metropolis Bank and Trust obtains the list of registered holders as of the night of May 15 from its transfer agent, First Continental Bank and Trust. On June 1, Metropolis Bank and Trust issues payment to the registered owners.

Besides paying dividends on the equities that Loster Motors has issued, Metropolis Bank and Trust makes interest payments on Loster Motors' outstanding debt instruments.

VIII-F *PRODUCT ISSUER*

VIII-F-1 Commercial Paper

The bank is an issuer of Loster Motor Corp.'s credit division's commercial paper. The paper is either *bank placed* or *dealer sold.* As for bank-placed paper, Metropolis Bank and Trust, as well as other banks, such as First Continental Bank and Trust, has clients that want to invest in short-term instruments, such as commercial paper. The banks, knowing the amount of money their clients want to invest, "shop" the issuers of short-term debt to get the best value available. Once that best value is identified, the bank acquires the commercial paper on behalf of their investing clients.

Broker/dealers, such as Stone, Forrest & Rivers, buy commercial paper for their clients as well as for nondealer broker/dealers. In this case, the broker/dealer buys the commercial paper first and then sells it to their clients and to other broker/dealers as part of the normal trading function. The commercial paper transactions during the day are settled at DTCC in a manner similar to other security settlements. The major difference is that commercial paper, as are other money market instruments, is a same-day settler.

VIII-F-2 Certificates of Deposit

Another major component of the money market instrument market is the certificate of deposit. These short-term instruments are issued in various sizes and durations. The smaller ones (the ones that most people are familiar with) are not fungible and therefore not tradable. The "jumbo" certificates of deposit do trade in the marketplace.

VIII-F-3 Bankers' Acceptances

As stated earlier, bankers' acceptances are issued by some U.S. banks and generally represent loans made by foreign correspondent banks or foreign branches of the U.S. banks to finance international commerce. They are issued by the banks into the marketplace and are retired at the bank at maturity.

VIII-F-4 Asset-Backed and Mortgage-Backed Securities and Whole loans

Banks pool their clients' loans and issue securities against the pools. These are called *securitized products*. Boat loans, car loans, and credit card loans, for example, are pooled and become asset-backed securities. Real estate mortgages are pooled and securitized, and mortgaged-backed securities are issued against the pool. One advantage offered by these pooled securities is that an investor owns an interest in several loans or mortgages at one time, thereby homogenizing the risk.

Whole loans are sold by banks to institutions. This is primarily an illiquid market supported by very specialized entities. In these situations, the banks and the entity acquiring the debt go through an exchange of legal documents before the loan is transferred.

This completes the section on bank-issued securities. Remember that banks also issue the usual stocks and bonds on themselves that are traded on exchanges and NASDAQ and over-the-counter markets.

VIII-G *FOREIGN EXCHANGE*

An increasingly important role that banks play in the finance industry is that of foreign exchange. Broker/dealers have a need to exchange one currency for another as the financial world goes more global. SF&R, with its offices, subsidiaries, and correspondent firms around the world, is constantly converting cash. For example, something as simple as paying employees working offshore in their native currency requires foreign exchange. As SF&R is a U.S. broker/dealer, it must work and report its financials in U.S. dollars. However, SF&R Ltd. is a British entity under the supervision of Financial Services Authority (FSA—formerly the SFA), which is a British regulator, so its books and records are maintained in British pounds.

Many of the business transactions that SF&R enters into require quick access and conversion of cash. Grazie, Gracias and Danke is a European company that is about to offer a global initial public offering (IPO). SF&R is part of the underwriting group and plans to offer the securities through its offices at home and overseas. The securities it sells domestically will be settled in dollars, whereas the securities it sells to its clients abroad could settle in any major currency or a client's country's domestic currency. No matter what currency is used, SF&R is a U.S.-based firm so all currencies are eventually converted into dollars in its records. Banks perform a very important role in the conversion process.

VIII-H *CLIENT*

In addition to all of the above relationships, banks are clients of SF&R. They represent trust accounts, estate accounts, and money management services for their clients. Banks invest their proprietary money in securities. They also use SF&R for mergers, acquisitions, and other corporate activities.

In the case of trust accounts, the bank assigns unique identifiers to their accounts so as to keep confidential the identity of the client. For example, First Continental Bank has an account for the Nicojencar Foundation at 1 Oaking St. in Centerville, CA. When they enter orders for securities at SF&R, their computer system converts the account ID to 343108. When SF&R receives the order, they know that First Continental Bank account 343108 is 7SF400462. But SF&R does not know the name behind the account. All of First Continental Bank's customers' accounts that have been opened on SF&R's books are DVP accounts.

First Continental Bank and Trust also uses SF&R to represent it in mergers and acquisitions. About a year ago, First Continental management heard that Red Oak Bank and Trust may be interested in selling or merging with another bank. To disguise its interest, First Continental hired SF&R to investigate the company: Who are they? Who is their management? Who's their clientele? What's their main business? SF&R's Research Department analyzed the bank's historical record and future potential and gave its report to First Continental. After reading the report, the bank was interested in the possibility of buying Red Oak so it hired SF&R's Merger and Acquisition personnel to represent them and evaluate what would be a fair price. After negotiations with Red Oak's representatives, a price was agreed upon and the acquisition was completed.

Here are the terms of the acquisition: For each 2.5 shares of Red Oak Bank common stock, the shareholders were entitled to receive 1 share of First Continental Bank and Trust. Deep Valley National Bank was hired to manage and execute the exchange of stock. SF&R's Corporate Actions section took care of the conversion for the clients that maintained positions in Red Oak Bank common stock at SF&R.

CHAPTER IX

Cash Accounting

To understand brokerage accounting, you must first understand accounting in general. While most of us are trained to make entries affecting securities or futures products, what escapes our attention is that the cash, or the money side, of the entry drives the security entry and determines whether it is a debit or credit. Therefore, the reader must realize that most of the time, as securities move one way, cash is moving in the opposite direction. For example, the "clean up" of a fail to receive necessitates two entries: the receipt of security and the payment of cash.

The reality of accounting is further disguised by the simple fact that, whenever we see an "accounting" of our own finances, we are actually seeing it through the "eyes" of someone else. For example, when we deposit money into our checking account, the bank credits our accounts. The bank does so because "our" accounts are a liability to the bank; they owe us that money. Actually, "our" bank account is not "ours" at all. It is the bank's account, which it has assigned to us to use. It is their account, presented in the format of their account number structure, to which our name and other information are affixed. This is no different than your firm's clients' accounts. It is your firm's account number to which the client's name, address, and so on are assigned.

To prove this, when you call your bank or any other entity that you have an account with, you usually give your name, after which they ask, "And what is your account number?" That question serves two purposes: First, it gets them away from the embarrassment of not knowing who you are; second, it is easier for you to know the account number than it is for them to research it.

IX-A *THE ACCOUNTING PROCESS*

Accounting serves two main purposes: One is presentation. The other is control. Presentation is accomplished in a rigid format that is understood by all those involved in accounting. All balance sheets and profit and loss statements follow the same format. Once you know how to read one statement, then you can read a similar statement issued by any domestic entity.

Control, simply put, is to identify what happened, when, and what it affected. To put it another way, control involves the accurate and timely posting of entries to accounts, in the time period that they occurred. Control is maintained through the use of accounts, which are usually identified by account numbers. Your checking account and the various bills that you receive carry the unique account numbers assigned by the issuing entity.

To give an example of control, let's assume a company buys a truck in year 1 and uses the truck for a total of five years. It would be incorrect to take the expense (cost) of the truck in the year of purchase, apply it against the earnings for that year, and charge nothing for the next four years. Good accounting would dictate that the expense of the truck should be spread over the five years it will be used. This gives a truer picture of the company's yearly profits. The truck cost would be carried in its own account; depreciation and depreciation expense would be represented by their accounts. Through these accounts the firm would "control" the truck expense for the five-year period.

To depict this, let us look at two examples. In the first example the expense of the truck is applied only to the year of purchase. Let us assume that the truck cost $50,000 and the company earned $100,000 each year for five years. Again, the company planned to use the truck over a five-year period. Therefore, the use of the truck contributed to the firm's ability to earn the $100,000 per year.

Example 1:

	Year 1	Year 2	Year 3	Year 4	Year 5
Earnings	$100,000	$100,000	$100,000	$100,000	$100,000
Truck	–50,000	0	0	0	0
Gross profit	$ 50,000	$100,000	$100,000	$100,000	$100,000

With the same monetary assumptions as in Example 1, let us spread the expense of the truck over its expected use of five years.

Example 2:

	Year 1	Year 2	Year 3	Year 4	Year 5
Earnings	$100,000	$100,000	$100,000	$100,000	$100,000
Truck	–10,000	–10,000	–10,000	–10,000	–10,000
Gross profit	$ 90,000	$ 90,000	$ 90,000	$ 90,000	$ 90,000

Which one is a more accurate portrayal of the company's annual earnings? Suppose you wanted to buy the company today and only checked back three years. Did the company really earn $100,000 as depicted in Example 1? And what condition would you expect the truck to be in? Obviously, the second example is more accurate and would be the one that is used in setting the price to buy the company.

IX-B ACCOUNT CATEGORIES

All accounts fall into one of five categories: assets, liabilities, revenue, expense, or net worth. Entries are made to adjust the respective accounts to reflect movements among these five categories:

Assets: Something that is owned by or owed to the entity.

Liabilities: Something that the entity owes.

Revenue: Any form of income.

Expense: What is used up to earn revenue.

Net worth: The net value of all the above. (Net worth in a corporation is known as *stockholders' equity.*)

We can apply these concepts to our everyday activities:

Salary. Salary is income, and income is revenue.

Income taxes paid. Income taxes paid is an expense because it occurred from the income earned.

Credit card balance. Credit card balance is a liability because it represents something owed.

Savings account. A savings account is an asset because it is something belonging to us or that we own.

Automobile (owned). A car is an asset as it belongs to us.

Automobile loan. This is a liability as it represents money owed to a lending institution.

Loan interest. This is an expense because it is a cost involved in borrowing money.

IX-C *DEBITS AND CREDITS*

To understand the mechanics of accounting, remember that all accounting movements in a company are recorded by entries and that every entry has two equal and offsetting sides: a debit side and a credit side. The debit and credit sides of an entry must always be, in total, equal. To be complete, each entry must, therefore, have equal and offsetting debits and credits.

For the accounting system to work, a starting point is needed to which all agree and adhere, and against which all other entries are determined. Many years ago, it was determined that the entity's cash is an asset and that all asset accounts are to have debit balances. Asset accounts could have just as easily been credits and the accounting methodology would still be applicable but everything would be backwards—what we now know as debits would be credits and what we know as credits would be debits. However, the determination was made that asset accounts with correct balances were to be debits and so we have our current form of accounting. It was also decided that debit entries are to be posted on the left side of the entry page and credits entries are on the right. These two assumptions are the foundation for accounting as we know it and form a major part of control.

If cash is an asset, and if asset accounts are always debits, then regardless of the entry, if you can figure out the effect it would have on cash, you can figure out the entry.

Example: Lee Nolium begins a new job. At the end of the first week, she is paid a salary of $500. Since cash is an asset, assets are debits; we know that one side of the entry must be a debit to a cash account of $500. The other entry must account for where it came from: Salary is revenue, and therefore must be a credit account balance. Lee deposits her paycheck into "her" bank account. The bank credits "her" account, which is a liability to them, since they owe Lee the money, and they debit their asset account called cash. To the bank, Lee's bank account is an accounts payable, a liability. (Accounts payable is the bank's account that was assigned to Lee.)

Lee's accounting entries

Debit	*Credit*
Asset—Cash $500	Revenue—Salary $500

Bank's accounting entries

Debit	*Credit*
Asset—Cash account $500	Liability—Client's account $500

Following this through, if an asset account has a money balance, it must have a debit balance. If a liability account has a money balance, it must be a credit balance. In the above example, the bank has an asset (cash) of $500, which is shown as a debit, and has a liability, the money it owes to Lee, reflected as a credit.

Expenses and revenue accounts follow a similar pattern. In the above example, Lee received $500 cash representing salary. As cash is an asset and assets are debits, then Lee's cash account on her own books would be debited $500 and have a $500 debit balance (Dr). The source of this cash would have to be credited. In this case, the source is salary, a revenue account of Lee's. Therefore, all of Lee's revenue (income) accounts must be credit accounts and, if they have money balances, those balances must be credits (Cr).

Let us assume that Lee buys $25 worth of gasoline for her automobile. The entries made on Lee's books would be:

Account	Opening balance	Debt	Credit	Closing balance
Cash	$500 Dr		$25	$475 Dr
Fuel	$ 0 Dr	$25		$ 25 Dr

Lee now has two assets. She "owns" cash and she "owns" gasoline.

Let us now assume that Lee uses the automobile to drive back and forth to work. At the end of the week the car has used all of its fuel—$25 worth of fuel has been used up. Lee has incurred an expense of $25. (*Expense:* What is used up to earn revenue.) To properly "account" for this, the entry to Lee's books would be:

Account	Opening balance	Debt	Credit	Closing balance
Fuel expense	$ 0	$25		$25 Dr
Fuel	$25 Dr		$25	$ 0

Based on the above, we have established that if asset accounts have a money balance, that balance is debit balance. To add to the balance, one would debit the account. To reduce the balance, one would credit the account.

Type of account	Money balance	To increase	To decrease
Asset	Debit	Debit	Credit
Liability	Credit	Credit	Debit
Expense	Debit	Debit	Credit
Revenue	Credit	Credit	Debit

The last type of account is the net worth account or, in the case of a corporation, the stockholders' equity account. This should have a credit balance because, to be profitable, revenue (Cr) must exceed expense (Dr). Revenues minus expenses equal profit (if revenues are the larger figure) or loss (if expenses are the larger figure). In addition, the difference between assets and liabilities is the value that belongs to the owners (known as owner's equity). This is portrayed on a report known as a *balance sheet* as

Assets (Dr) = Liabilities (Cr) + Owner's Equity (Cr).

In this example, one would want owner's equity to be a credit balance also. This is explained in more detail in the next pages.

IX-D *JOURNAL AND LEDGER*

We will now follow Lee's monetary activity for a month. First we record the entries as they happen to a journal and then *post* the journal entries in the individual accounts in the ledger.

IX-D-1 Journal Entries

A *journal* is a book of original entry. For the month of January, assuming the same events occur each week, Lee would have made the following journal entries:

Journal Entries

Date	*Entry*	*Debit*	*Credit*	*Ledger entry*
1/5	Cash (checking account)	$500		①
	Salary		$500	①
	To record salary received			
1/5	Food expense	75		②
	Cash (checking account)		75	②
	Bought food, check #1001			
1/5	Tax expense	125		③
	Cash (checking account)		125	③
	Paid income taxes, check #1002			
1/5	Transportation expense	25		④
	Cash (checking account)		25	④
	Bought weekly fuel for car, check #1003			
1/12	Cash (checking account)	$500		⑤
	Salary		$500	⑤
	To record salary received			
1/12	Food expense	75		⑥
	Cash		75	⑥
	Bought food, check #1004			
1/12	Tax expense	125		⑦

(*continued*)

Date	*Entry*	*Debit*	*Credit*	*Ledger Entry*
	Cash		125	⑦
	Paid taxes, check #1005			
1/12	Transportation expense	25		⑧
	Cash		25	⑧
	Bought fuel for car, check #1006			
1/19	Cash (checking account)	$500		⑨
	Salary		$500	⑨
	To record salary received			
1/19	Food expense	75		⑩
	Cash (checking account)		75	⑩
	Bought food, check #1007			
1/19	Tax expense	125		⑪
	Cash (checking account)		125	⑪
	Paid income taxes, check #1008			
1/19	Transportation expense	25		⑫
	Cash (checking account)		25	⑫
	Bought fuel for car, check #1009			
1/26	Cash	$500		⑬
	Salary		$500	⑬
	To record salary received			
1/26	Food expense	75		⑭
	Cash		75	⑭
	Bought food, check #1010			
1/26	Tax expense	125		⑮
	Cash		125	⑮
	Paid taxes, check #1011			
1/26	Transportation expense	25		⑯
	Cash		25	⑯
	Bought fuel for car, check #1012			
1/26	Utilities expense	250		⑰
	Cash		250	⑰
	Paid utility bill, check #1013			
1/26	Rent expense	600		⑱
	Cash		600	⑱
	Paid rent, check #1014			

All of Lee's financial entries for January are recorded in the journal. Note that each entry affected an account and was offset by an equal and opposite entry.

IX-D-2 Ledger Account

The next step is to post the journal entries to their respective ledger accounts (which will be displayed as T accounts). In T accounts, entries to the left are debits; entries to the right are credits.

Ledger Accounts

Cash

	Debit	Credit	
①	500	75	②
		125	③
		25	④
⑤	500	75	⑥
		125	⑦
		25	⑧
⑨	500	25	⑩
		125	⑪
		25	⑫
⑬	500	75	⑭
		125	⑮
		25	⑯
		250	⑰
		600	⑱

Salary

	Debit	Credit	
		500	①
		500	⑤
		500	⑨
		500	⑬

Rent expense

	Debit	Credit
⑱	600	

Food expense

	Debit	Credit
②	75	
⑥	75	
⑩	75	
⑭	75	

Tax expense

	Debit	Credit
③	125	
⑦	125	
⑪	125	
⑮	125	

Transportation expense

	Debit	Credit
④	25	
⑧	25	
⑫	25	
⑯	25	

Utility expense

	Debit	Credit
⑰	250	

Net worth

Debit	Credit

The next step is to close or balance out each account. For example, here's the cash account:

Cash

Debit	Credit
500	
	75
	125
	25
500	
	75
	125
	25
500	
	75
	125
	25
500	
	75
	125
	25
	250
	600
2,000	1,750
−1,750	
250	Debit

When each of the individual accounts is totaled, their balances are brought forward. If each debit entry had an equal and offsetting credit, then the results of the preceding entries should be in balance.

IX-D-3 Trial Balance

The last step is commonly known as a *trial balance,* which tests whether all posted entries are in balance

Debit			Credit	
Cash account	$ 250		Salary account	$2,000
Rent account	600			
Food account	300			
Tax account	500			
Transportation account	100			
Utilities account	250			
	$2,000	=		$2,000

From the trial balance, we can now extract the profit and loss statement and balance sheet, presented earlier.

IX-D-4 Profit and Loss Statement and Balance Sheet

The *profit and loss statement* takes into account all of the revenue received and all of the expenses incurred during that period to earn that revenue.

Example: At the end of the month, which contained four pay periods (some months contain five), Lee Nolium received a total salary of $2,000. She paid rent of $600, taxes of $500, and utilities of $250. Transportation to and from work came to $100; $300 went for food and meals. From an accounting standpoint Lee had the following profit and loss profile:

Lee's Profit and Loss Statement for period ending January 31, 20XX

Revenue: Salary		$2,000
Expenses:		
Rent	600	
Taxes	500	
Utilities	250	
Transportation	100	
Food	300	
Total expenses		1,750
Net profit		$ 250

Since Lee deposited her pay into her checking account and paid each bill as it came in, she should have $250 remaining in her checking account. The remaining $250 in cash is offset by the $250 net profit. It would be appropriate to move the result of the operations, the $250 profit, into the net worth section of the balance sheet.

The *balance sheet* reflects the balances remaining in all assets, liabilities, and net worth accounts. As asset accounts are to have debit balances and liability accounts are to have credit balances, then her net worth account has to have a credit balance for Lee to avoid financial problems. We always want assets (debits) to be greater than liabilities (credits): Assets − Liabilities = Net Worth. Therefore, if we placed liabilities on the other side of the equal sign, we would have Assets = Liabilities + Net Worth, which is the formula for the balance sheet presentation.

Lee's Balance Sheet as of January 31, 20XX

Debit		**Credit**	
Asset: Cash	$250	Liability	0
		Net Worth	250
	$250		$250

Based on what we know, Lee has a net worth of $250.

We have explored the initial steps in accounting. Naturally, accounting practice goes much deeper than has been portrayed here. There are accepted methods for evaluating inventory, managing depreciation, expensing an item, and so on. Decisions about these methods are made in discussions between the company and its outside accounting/auditing firm. The results of these discussions affect the company's financials and must be considered when analyzing one company against another.

A corporation uses the same accounting practices. They have stock and bondholders that invest cash:

Debit: Cash Credit: Stockholders

Debit: Cash Credit: Bondholders

They may purchase inventory by paying part in cash and owing the remainder:

Debit: Inventory Credit: Cash

Credit: Accounts Payable

They can take some of the inventory and place it into production:

Debit: Inventory expense Credit: Inventory

General accounts fall into the following categories:

Assets	Liabilities	Expenses	Revenue	Stockholders' equity
Cash	Accounts payable	Inventory used	Sales	Preferred stock
Account receivables	Notes payable	Salary paid	Services	Common stock
Notes receivables	Taxes payable	Utilities paid	Interest income	Retained earnings
Securities owned	Utilities payable	Interest paid	Dividend income	Reserve accounts
Inventory	Salary payable	Taxes paid		
Real estate	Mortgage	Rent paid		
Furniture and fixtures	Bank loans			
Goodwill	Bonds			
Trademarks				

CHAPTER X

Brokerage Accounting

Like all other industries, the security brokerage industry uses accepted accounting practices. While operations personnel process the firms' transactions using terminology unique to the industry, the methodology and classifications of accounts still follow accounting practices.

Example: Al Luminum, a client of SF&R, buys 100 ZAP at $47 for a total cost of $4,770, including commission. Al's confirmation reads:

First money, $4,700; commission, $70; net money $4,770

First Money		Commission		Net Money
$4,700	+	$70	=	$4,770

X-A *CASH MOVES THE SECURITY*

Because SF&R acted as a broker in the transaction, it purchased the security from another firm. It owes that firm $4,700 when the stock is received. If the stock is not received by settlement date, the position will become a fail to receive.

In essence, a fail to receive is an accounts payable. This is part of brokerage accounting that becomes confusing. While we are trained to focus on the particular security, in name and account position, it is the value of the issue, both present and future, that is of concern.

For booking purposes, even though the contra firm owes SF&R stock, the entry is booked from the money standpoint. SF&R owes the contra firm

$4,700 so it is booked as an account payable, a liability, a credit. Likewise, while SF&R owes Al stock, Al owes SF&R $4,770, so the entry is posted as a debit, an asset, an account receivable. The $70 difference is the commission charged. Commission is revenue, and revenue accounts are to have credit balances. Therefore, $4,700 (liability/credit) + $70 (revenue/credit) = $4,770 (asset/debit). To understand brokerage accounting, you must understand the money side of the entry.

Account	Shares		Money	
	Dr	Cr	Dr	Cr
Al Luminum	100		$4770	
Fail to receive		100		$4,700
Commission				$ 70
	100	100	$4,770	$4,770

Example: Client Sandy Beech buys 1,000 Water Logs, Inc. shares at $16 per share. The trade is an agency transaction, since SF&R bought the stock for Sandy from Meadows & Pond, another broker/dealer. Beech's account would reflect the following position (commission and taxes are omitted):

Account	Security		Description	Money		
	Debit	*Credit*		*Debit*	*Credit*	Balance
S. Beech	1,000		Water Logs, Inc.	16,000		$16,000 Dr

If the stock is not received from Meadows & Pond, a fail to receive will be set up. It will look like this:

Account	Security		Description	Money		
	Debit	*Credit*		*Debit*	*Credit*	*Balance*
Fail/Receive		1,000	Water Logs, Inc.		16,000	16,000 Cr

Note: Entries 1 and 2 are equal and opposite.

Beech pays for the purchase:
Beech's account on SF&R's books.

Account	Security		Description	Money		
	Debit	*Credit*		*Debit*	*Credit*	*Balance*
S. Beech			Check received		16,000	0

Cash account on SF&R's books:

Account	Security		Description	Money		
	Debit	*Credit*		*Debit*	*Credit*	*Balance*
Cash			Check vs. Beech	16,000		$16,000 Dr

Naturally, SF&R's cash account balance would be greater than $16,000 as it is a going business. The example shows the $16,000 debit would be added to the balance. In other words, the cash portion of the accounts receivable (AKA Beech's account) was "cleaned up." The firm's cash account was debited and now reflects the balance.

As to the street side, Meadows & Pond delivers the 1,000 shares and SF&R pays them $16,000. The entries are as follows:

Account	Security		Description	Money	
	Debit	*Credit*		*Debit*	*Credit*
Fail/Receive	1,000		Water Logs, Inc.	16,000	
(Clean up fail to receive)					
DTC A/C		1,000	Water Logs, Inc.		
(Entry putting security in the depository)					
Cash Account			Cash		16,000

All of these entries would occur in the respective accounts:

Sandy Beech: 3L0004321

Fail to receive: NFR500000

Depository:	DTC100000
Cash:	666USD666

The first set of entries places the trade in the client's account and offsets it with a fail to receive. The second set of entries reflects the client paying for the purchase. The final set represents the clean-up of the fail to receive.

If you review the entries, you will notice that the fail to receive account and cash account balance out to zero. However, account CHKVS3LO004321 is long 1,000 shares (Dr) versus SF&R's account at Depository Trust Company, DTC100000, which is short 1,000 shares (Cr). If we deliver the stock to the client, these two accounts go flat also.

When a client or the firm's trading account first buys a security, the account is debited. The term used is *long*—they are long the issue. Since the purchase requires payment, the cash, or money, side of the transaction is debited, since it is an account receivable to the firm, which is an asset. The firm's traders as well as their clients must pay for their purchases. While the clients pay by check or wire transfer, the traders are charged interest on the firm's money they are using. In either case, the purchase is carried as an account receivable by the firm.

When the stock becomes part of the firm's possessions, the location account, where the position is maintained, is credited to offset the long position.

X-B *LOCATION ACCOUNTS*

The account, which is the location account for the client's or trading account's long position (debit), is a credit. Where is security maintained? It is maintained in:

1. Vault
2. Transfer
3. Stock loan
4. Depository
5. Custodial bank
6. Bank loan

Stock going into any of these six positions is posted as a credit. Therefore, these position accounts either have credit balances or are flat (have no balance).

Account #	Security				Money		
	Debit (Long)	Credit (Short)	Balance	Description	Debit	Credit	Balance
3L0004321	1,000		1,000 Dr	Water Logs, Inc.	$16,000		16,000 Dr
NFR500000		1,000	1,000 Cr	Water Logs, Inc.		$16,000	16,000 Cr
666USD666				CHKVS3LO004321	$16,000		16,000 Dr
3L0004321				Check Received		$16,000	0
NFR500000	1,000		0	Water Logs, Inc.	$16,000		0
666USD666				Cash paid		16,000	0
DTC100000		1,000	1,000 Cr	Water Logs, Inc.			

X-C OFFSET TO SHORT SALES

When a client or the trading account first sells, the account is credited. The client or trading account is said to be *short*. The money position is also credited, because money is owed the client or the trading account by the firm. The sale represents an account payable, therefore a liability, and therefore a credit. If the short position is a bona fide short sale, as opposed to a sale where the client hasn't delivered the owned stock by settlement date of the trade, the security sold must be borrowed. Since the security's short sale position is a credit, the offset (that is, the account from which the security was borrowed) must be debited. Therefore, stock can be borrowed from the following accounts:

Stock borrowed

Client

Proprietary (trading)

Client Mandy Post (account 4CG013421) wants to sell 100 shares of POP short in her account for $5,000. SF&R borrows the stock from Giant, Reckor & Crane, clearing broker/dealer 243, and delivers the stock against Mandy's sale. The entries would be:

Debit Account				Credit Account			
Account	*Shares*	*Security*	*Money*	*Account*	*Shares*	*Security*	*Money*
NSB-500243	100	POP	$5,000	DTC100000	100	POP	
				666USD666			$5,000

First, the stock borrow is set up by debiting the stock borrow account both shares and money. The stock is placed in the depository and SF&R pays Giant, Reckor & Crain $5,000 as collateral against the borrowed stock.

Then:

Debit Account				Credit Account			
Account	*Shares*	*Security*	*Money*	*Account*	*Shares*	*Security*	*Money*
DTC500000	100	POP		4CG-013421	100	POP	$5,000
666USD666			$5,000				

Mandy Post sells the stock short; SF&R delivers it from the depository account to the purchasing firm and gets paid.

X-D *CHART OF BROKERAGE ACCOUNTS*

The brokerage side of the business has its own unique set of accounts. They can be placed into three categories:

- Proprietary
- Client
- Location (street side)

Under the category of proprietary accounts, one finds:

- Trading
- Investment

Under client accounts, one finds:

- Retail
- Institutional
- Employee

Accounts in the above two categories may have long/debit or short/credit positions or may be flat.

In the location category one finds:

- Those with a long/debit or flat position:
    - Stock borrowed
    - Fail to deliver
- Those with a short/credit or flat position:
    - Vault
    - Depository
    - Custodial bank
    - Stock loan
    - Fail to receive
    - Bank loan
    - Transfer
- Those that may have either long or short positions:
    - Suspense/error
    - Corporate action control
    - Dividend control

It is important to understand the positions that these accounts can have as they have a direct impact on processing. The experts that work with these accounts are able to identify erroneous positions quickly. For example, if the stock record reflected a long (debit) position in the DTC account DTC100000, they would know that it is a bad position because securities going into the DTC account are a credit entry and therefore the account can have a credit (short) position or be flat. A debit (long) position would mean that more securities were taken out of DTC than deposited. Therefore, something would be wrong. Anytime an account reflects a position that cannot ever be correct, we refer to it as an *illogical position.*

CHAPTER XI

Stock Record

Every brokerage firm maintains two sets of records that comprise the backbone of the organization from a regulatory and control standpoint. These two sets of documents together are known as books and records of the firm. One set is called the *stock record;* the other is called the *general ledger*. Their names may vary from one firm to another. However, their contents remain the same throughout the industry. These reports reflect each and every daily movement of securities and cash within the firm as well as the balances that the multitude of accounts have. In this chapter, we will explain the stock record function.

During the day in a typical brokerage firm:

- Customers buy and sell securities over the Web or through registered representatives.
- Most institutional accounts are maintained on a delivery-versus-payment basis (DVP). Securities are received and delivered against payment for most institutional customers via their custodian banks through depositories. The movements are made electronically.
- Most retail clients maintain their security positions at their broker/dealer. However, there are cases where customers still want to see the physical certificates so that in the typical brokerage firm, some customers are still delivering stocks when they sell and receiving stocks when they buy.
- The central office receives securities from its branches as well as delivers securities to the branch offices' clients. The central office also receives securities from other firms, through clearing corporations, from transfer agents, from loan accounts, and from allocation of new issues. Most of these entries are made electronically without the movement of

physical securities. However, each and every one must be "booked" to the proper account and appear on the stock record.

- The central office also services securities owned by the firm's clients, by sending them to depositories, using them as collateral for clients' loans, sending them to the transfer agents, and handling other client-initiated activities. Actions initiated by the issuer, such as a corporation, must be applied to accounts maintaining position in those issues that appear on the firm's records. These actions include stock splits, mergers, and acquisitions.

The firm must record all of these movements and many others on the stock record. These include all equity products, all debt instruments, mutual funds, options, exchange-traded funds (ETFs), and other derivatives—the exception being futures and most forwards, which are accounted for on their own record.

To properly record the movement of securities, the stock record must balance debits versus credits (longs versus shorts). That is, for every debit entry, there must be an offsetting credit and vice versa. Sometimes the debit entries are called long and the credit entries are called short. Those are just terms to distinguish the different types of entries. There are long entries that are not truly "long entries" and there are short entries that are not truly short entries. However, that is the lingo used in the industry instead of saying *debit and credit.*

Example: When a security is purchased for a client, the client's account is debited or made "long," and the firm's depository account is credited with the security entry when the trade settles. If the street side doesn't deliver the stock, the offset to the client's purchase would be a fail to receive, which is a credit (short). Sometimes the expression is used to make the entry short although locations, like the fail to receive account and depository account, are not truly short positions but are, in fact, credit positions or offset accounts. When settlement occurs, entries will be made, moving the security position from the firm's fail to receive account to the central depository, for example. The fail to receive account will appear on the stock record as being debited and the depository account will appear as being credited to reflect the movements. The net result is that the client is long (debit) and the depository is short (credit). Another way of saying what the entry does is that the client's account has been debited the stock the firm is carrying for the client, and the depository has been credited the position that the firm is carrying on its accounts.

Account	Long [Debit]	Short [Credit]	New Psn.
Customer	100		100 Dr
Fail to Receive		100	100 Cr
Fail to Receive	100		0
Depository		100	100 Cr

X1-A *TYPES OF STOCK RECORDS*

There are two versions of the stock record: the activity stock record and the summary stock record.

XI-A-1 Activity Stock Record

The *activity stock record* or *daily stock record* reflects all movements in each security on a particular day. It is maintained in security order and, within a security, by account number. The only accounts appearing on the activity record are those that have had movements on the particular day.

The other version of the stock record, which is a snapshot of all the accounts that maintain security positions that the firm is responsible for, is called the *summary stock record*. It too is maintained in security order and, within a security, by account.

The activity stock record contains:

- Security name
- Symbol
- CUSIP number and/or ISIN number
- Internal identifying codes
- CNS/DTC eligibility or Clearing Corp/depositary
- Last recorded market price
- Primary market

- Whether or not the security is marginable
- Only accounts having a position movement on that day:
    * Proprietary accounts: having a position movement
        - Previous position
        - Previous activity date
        - Account number and type
        - Movement that occurred on the particular day
        - Resulting new position
        - Other internal codes
        - Account's short name
    * Customer accounts:
        - Previous position
        - Previous activity date
        - Account number and type
        - Movement that occurred on the particular day
        - Resulting new position
        - Seg lockup
        - Other internal codes
        - Account's short name
    * Street side or location:
        - Date of last activity
        - Previous security position
        - Account number and type
        - Security movement
        - New position
        - Account's short name
    * Break Account
        - Only the new break account (if one exists)

Because every debit must have a corresponding credit, or every long must have a corresponding short, the activity stock record must balance. If there should be more debit entries than there are credit entries in a particular security or vice versa, then a systemic break account will be created. Stone, Forrest & Rivers maintains break accounts by having the date of the break as the first four digits of the account number, followed by five number nines (e.g., 042199999 indicates a break that occurred on April 21). Therefore, staff in the Stock Record Department can identify the break account and know on which date it occurred because of the numbering functions that are used.

Activity Stock Record

ZAPPA CORPORATION Sym: ZAP CUSIP 876432107 PX 47.40

EXCH: NYSE CCD: CNSDTC: Mgn: Y

Prior position	Previous date	Account	Activity	Debit	Credit	Closing position
	00000	1BS007862-1	BOT	1000		1000
500	0914XX	2NY014353-2	SLD		100	400
	000000	2DC000546-1	REC	200		200
	000000	3MI065612-1	BOT	1500	1500	
100	0521XX	3MI156423-1	JNL		100	0
	000000	3MI156423-2	JNL	100		100
–25786	0921XX	DTC10000-0			2400	–28186
	000000	042199999-9			200	–200

The activity stock record of 04/21 shows a break of 200 shares credit. There were 2,500 shares purchased and 100 shares sold. These trades netted to 2,400 shares, which appear to have been deposited into DTC. The journal entry is in balance. The only entry without an offset is the "Receive" at the Washington, DC, office. The normal method of operation is that a security received at a branch office is first wired to the home office as *stock over the wire (SOW)*; then the physical stock is sent overnight to the home office. The entry missing is the transit account, TNS500000. The stock record specialist, after verifying that the stock was actually forwarded to the central office, will make a journal entry debiting account 042199999-9 and crediting account TNS500000 for 200 shares.

XI-A-2 Summary Stock Record

The other stock record—the *summary stock record,* sometimes referred to as the *main stock record* or the *weekly stock record*—reflects all accounts for which positions exist on a given day. It is the stock record's balance sheet. It contains all of the positions in all of the accounts in all of the securities for which Stone, Forrest & Rivers is responsible. Not only does it contain all of the accounts within a given security, it also contains any break accounts that might be open from that particular security.

The typical summary stock record contains:

- Security name
- Symbol
- CUSIP number and/or ISIN number
- Internal codes, including CNS/DTC eligibility
- Last recorded market price
- Primary market
- Marginability
- Clearing Corp/depositary eligibility
- All of the accounts having a position in that security:
    - Client accounts:
        - Date of last activity
        - Account number and type
        - Security position
        - Seg position
        - Client's short name
        - Nonnegotiable security, in-transfer, and legal item codes
    - Street side or location accounts:
        - Date of last activity
        - Account number and type
        - Security position
        - Account's short name
    - Break accounts:
        - Date of last activity
        - Account number and type
        - Security position

The stock record serves other functions in the brokerage firm. The summary stock record contains all of the accounts that maintain positions in a particular security. It is, therefore, accessed when an issuing company pays a dividend on its shares of stock or when an issuer is making payment of interest on its debt instruments (bonds, notes, etc.). As the summary stock record has all of the accounts within a position, SF&R's personnel can determine to which account it owes a payment and which accounts owe the firm the payment.

For example, Giant, Reckor & Crane (GRC), another clearing broker/dealer, borrowed stock from SF&R to complete a delivery. GRC's

SUMMARY STOCK RECORD

		SFR: 3564				
		Desc: Loster Motor Corporation	SYM: LMC	CUR: USD	CL: EQUITY	
	MKT: NYSE	MGN: Y	CNSDTC: Y	DIV/NT: Y	PX: 45.20	
SSR A/O 09/26/XX	MAT:	CALL: N	COUPON:	POOL #:	FACTOR: 1	
Sec#510435107				SEG	NNEG	
04/15XX	1BA0002211	500		500		1N03746569877
01/24/XX	1BS0034562	2300		300		1N04150000565
09/26/XX	1BS0048765	700		700		1N01240000004
06/16/XX	1HT9000151	5000		5000		1N09261389614
06/13XX	1HT9000172	200				3P06160134306
04/30/XX	2NY0016572	300				1N06136784843
09/15/XX	2NY0002495	1200		1200	1200	1N04306838226
07/11/XX	2NY0030961	2000		2000		REC0915000007
05/27/XX	2NY0074652	15000		4500		1N07110008471
06/23/XX	3AT0094563		300			1N05270034619
11/18/XX	3MI1004542	400		100		1N06231056376
09/26/XX	3MI0005672	800		400		1N11182627986
09/19/XX	4CG0003452	1000		1000		1N09260052654
05/25/XX	4DT0000341	600		600		1N09194006532
10/23/XX	4DT0000382	500				1N05250037134

(*continued*)

SUMMARY STOCK RECORD

	SFR: 3564					
	Desc: Loster Motor Corporation			SYM: LMC	CUR: USD	CL: EQUITY
	MKT: NYSE	MGN: Y		CNSDTC: Y	DIV/NT: Y	PX: 45.20
SSR A/O 09/26/XX	MAT:	CALL: N		COUPON:	POOL #:	FACTOR: 1
Sec#510435107					SEG	NNEG
09/26/XX	4DT0001011	7000			7000	1N10230000034
08/04/XX	5DL0095633		1000			1N09260048621
07/14/XX	6PO0000451	3000			3000	1N08040000354
05/23/XX	7SF0012432	600				1N07140065278
08/23/XX	8LA0034522	4000				1N05230011345
09/26/XX	8SD0000131	5000			5000	ACAT09262344
09/26/XX	CNS5000000		2300			
09/26/XX	DTC1000000		32200		26800-	
09/26/XX	NBL1000030		13400			
08/04/XX	NSB3005900	1300				
09/22/XX	NSL4000120		1000			
06/23/XX	NYV5000030		1200			1200-

clearing number at DTCC is 026. The security position remained in SF&R stock loan (NSL500026) account over the record date for a dividend payment. As GRC used the borrowed stock to make a delivery, SF&R will not get paid the dividend from the dividend disbursing agent (DDA). Instead, whomever GRC delivered the stock to will get the dividend (assuming it was reregistered into the new owner's name or that of its nominee. It is most possible that the security never moved at all and that DTC made position entries against the various accounts involved. Still, GRC owes SF&R the dividend. Therefore, GRC has incurred an out-of-pocket expense insofar as it owes the dividend to SF&R. SF&R will claim the dividend from GRC. On the dividend-payable date, GRC will pay SF&R the dividend owed. (In all likelihood, the party that was supposed to deliver the security to GRC will be charged the dividend by GRC in the same manner as SF&R is claiming the dividend from GRC.) Interindustry charges are settled as part of the firms' settlement figures with DTCC, thereby negating the need for individual checks between firms.

Another use of the summary stock record is the issuance of proxy. At least once a year, a company issues proxy notices to its common stockholders apprising them of major issues before their board of directors as well the proposed board of directors for the next period. The common stockholders vote on those issues. The summary stock record reveals who owned the stock on the record date for proxy purposes as well as the number of shares they owned. This, in turn, tells SF&R staff the number of votes each shareholder can receive.

As part of their ongoing surveillance, the Securities and Exchange Commission and the various SROs send out questionnaires to obtain information on the holdings of certain securities as of a given date. SF&R's personnel will access a backdated stock record from their workstations and provide the required information.

As stated earlier, Securities and Exchange Commission's Regulation T requires the firm to lock up securities in clients' cash accounts and a portion in their margin accounts. The lockup is referred to as segregation, or seg. The firm (here, SF&R) must have possession or control of those securities at all times. Clients with cash accounts must have 100% of their stock locked up, whereas margin accounts require the amount over 140% of the client's debit balance to be locked up. The remaining securities in the margin account may be used to finance the client's loan.

Example: Client Marshal Law (account 2NY231962-1) in New York owns 1,000 shares of Erin Rose Cosmetics in a cash (type 1) account. Client Millie Terry (account 6PO017932-2) owns 1,000 shares of Erin Rose Cosmetics in her margin account. To buy the 1,000 shares of stock, which is selling at $30 per share, the Portland, Oregon client (6PO) borrows $15,000 from SF&R. The firm can use up to 140% of the debit balance to finance the loan. The seg requirements on those two accounts are:

2NY231962-1	1,000 shares
6PO017932-2	300 shares
	1,300 total

(140% × $15,000 = $21,000; $21,000 ÷ $30 per share = 700 shares; 1,000 shares − 700 shares = 300 shares). The seg position would show on the stock record as follows: On the same line as 2NY231962-1, "long 1,000 shares" would be a memo field showing 1,000 in seg. On the same line as 6PO017932-2, "long 1,000 shares" would be a memo field showing 300 shares. Elsewhere in this security position on the stock record summary would be the "offset" account that would contain the 1,300-share credit in a memo field.

XI-A-3 Trade Date Stock Record

When Stone, Forrest & Rivers opened online services to its clients, it developed a trade date mini stock record. This real time stock record adjusts clients' positions on trade date, thereby giving the client, the registered representative, the margin personnel, and others the data on the client's account. This is especially important as SF&R has set limits on the type of business the client can enter into and the amount of money or credit it will allow the client to trade in one day. This mini stock record is in account order and security order within the account.

It contains each clients':

- Short name
- Account number and assigned registered representative number
- Settled security position
- Trades pending settlement position

- Money balances on a trade date basis
- Available trading limit

Example: A client, Ms. Rhoda Broome, wants to sell 300 shares of PIP Inc. Rhoda's position on the stock record shows a settled position of 300 shares. Therefore, the sale is permitted and the funds involved with the sale are added to the amount SF&R allows Rhoda to trade in one day. Later, Ms. Broome enters another order to sell 300 shares of PIP Inc. Is this a duplicate? Is Rhoda day trading and had she bought 300 shares earlier in the day? Does Rhoda want to sell a different security? Does she have another 300-share lot? Does Rhoda want to sell PIP Inc. short? Does she have the stock somewhere else?

With a real time trade date stock record, all of the above questions except one will be summarized when Ms. Broome is contacted by the registered representative, who asks what she is trying to do. Had Broome bought 300 shares earlier in the day, the transaction would have hit the stock record and the trade date position would reflect her new 300 shares long. Therefore, had the new purchase occurred, the sale of the second lot of 300 would have been permitted without intervention by the stockbroker.

Example: Another client, Mort Tishen, wants to buy 1,000 shares of ZOW at $30 per share. His trading limit is $25,000. When the order enters the order management system, it is directed to Mort's client management representative. The rep checks the account, the client history file, and the financials that appear in the client master database. A determination is made to permit the trade to occur.

It is common knowledge that the longer an error or problem goes undetected, the greater the risk and financial exposure. The trade date stock record is a valuable tool in detecting problems early.

XI-B *BREAKS AND ILLOGICAL POSITIONS*

Each day the Stock Record Department inspects the activity stock record looking for breaks and "illogicals." *Breaks* occur when debits and credits do not equal. *Illogicals* require a better understanding of the stock record since they appear on the surface to be valid entries but are incorrect. For example, an entry is made that reflects taking stock out of the firm's Chicago vault that was never deposited there. The other side of the entry is the transit account. The entry balances a debit to the Chicago vault and a credit to the transit account, but there is a bad position (illogical) on the stock record for the Chicago vault. A stock record specialist will have to research the error and make correcting entries.

A report is produced listing all of the securities that have break account positions. As stated earlier, breaks occur when the debits (longs) and credits (shorts) are not equal. The stock record department will track down the missing entry and make the correction. In a well-run operation, stock record breaks should not be open for more than 24 hours without the cause being identified. The stock record department keeps the record divided alphabetically among the personnel. Looking at their workstations, the personnel pull up the stock record and review it on their respective screens. They also access a break account run, which gives them all of the securities that have breaks. They then focus on those security positions, analyze and research the entries, and make the necessary corrections. The ability to understand SF&R account numbering methodology expedites the correction process.

XI-C *ACCOUNT NOMENCLATURE*

An intelligent numbering scheme enables the stock record department to easily read the stock record. To anyone outside the department the record looks like a long numbering system.

Before we discuss Stone, Forrest & Rivers' numbering system, let's focus on this concept. Like many firms, SF&R uses a system that consists of four categories of numbers: proprietary, client, location, and general business.

1. Proprietary accounts include such accounts as the firm's trading accounts and investment accounts. At SF&R these are identified by the first and third digits being letters or alpha symbols and the second being a numeric. These are followed by six numeric digits. For example, T2E1000000 is an equity trading account operating out of New York (T=trading, 2=second division, E=equity). Further, the firm has established a numbering scheme for the fourth, fifth, and sixth positions. If 100 appears, it is the primary or main common stock trading

account. T2C100000 is the main corporate debt trading account in New York; T2C120000 is for long-term debt; T2C130000 is for corporate intermediate debt. T4M100000 is the primary or main municipal trading account number in Chicago (T=trading, 4=fourth division, M=municipal debt).

2. On the client side, unique numbers identify the client's account number, the division the account is maintained in, as well as the branch servicing the account. The first digit, a numeric, identifies the division. The next two are alpha, designating the branch. The remaining six are numeric, representing the account number. Account numbers are set aside for employees, DVP accounts, principals of the firm, and others. Account 7SF000454 belongs to the San Francisco office (7=seventh division).

3. For the street side or location side, alpha digits in the first three locations of an account number are used to record the movement of securities through various locations, such as the vault, the depositories, transfer, fail to receive, and fail to deliver. DTC100000, for example, is the firm's account number for securities maintained at Depository Trust.

4. The fourth set of account numbers is used for general business. The first three digits in the account number are numeric, signifying a cash-only account. The second three are alpha numeric. The last three are numeric.

5. The fifth set of accounts are problem accounts. They include break accounts and suspense accounts. We mentioned break accounts when we spoke of the stock record. This type of account is also used when SF&R checks its internal account against external accounts. For example, on a quarterly basis, it must check its DTC position account against what DTC claims it is holding for SF&R. Any difference is placed in a special break account and researched.

Suspense accounts are different from break accounts. A suspense account is used when SF&R has received funds or securities and doesn't know to whom they belong or where they came from.

Both accounts should have the positions temporarily and be "cleaned up" within a day or two

On the customer side, SF&R identifies each branch location by an abbreviation as well as the division in which that branch operates. The Boston office symbol is BN, whereas Detroit is signified by DT, San Francisco by SF, and so on. As Boston is in the first division, it will be 1BN. As Detroit is in the fourth division, it will be 4DT. As San Francisco is in the seventh division, it will be 7SF.

The account itself is identified by a unique six-digit number. An account in the Boston branch might be numbered 1BN004566. The first digit before the branch code signifies the division that the branch belongs to. SF&R has several sales divisions. The digit 1 preceding the branch code signifies a branch in the New England division; 2 designates a branch in the Mid-Atlantic; 3, the Southern Atlantic offices; 4, the Northern Midwest; 5, the Southern Midwest; 6, the Northern Pacific; 7, the Central Pacific divisions; and 8, the Southern Pacific Division. They also use 9 for branches in Canada and employ 0 for branches in Mexico. SF&R uses an alpha code in the first and fourth place and a numeric code in the second and third positions for branches that are not in North America. Because Boston belongs to the New England group, its account numbers always begin with 1BN, whereas Chicago always gets 4CG and Los Angeles gets 8LA.

For its street-side operations, SF&R's division- and branch-level cashiering areas have a second numbering system. The vault in New York is NYV500000, whereas the vault in Chicago is CGV500000. New York's account for reregistering of securities into the firm's nominee name is numbered NYT100000; the account for reregistering of securities into client's name is numbered NYT200000. Note that the first two digits in the street-side range indicate location, not the sales division.

Finally, trading accounts and proprietary accounts are identified by their locations. T represents trading; the next digit is the location, such as 2 for New York. The next digit is the type of security being traded. E is for common stock, C is for corporate debt and so on.

With this stock account system, SF&R's Stock Record Department can easily read the records.

Example: The firm buys 50,000 Chicago High School District FA8%-2025 for its Chicago inventory trading account. The trading desk quickly resells 5,000 of them to a Chicago client. On settlement date, the bonds are received into SF&R's account at DTC in New York from the selling firm. The stock record shows the following entries under the heading "Chicago High School District's FA8%-2025-CUSIP#936454210."

Account	Price or entry	Debit (long)	Credit (short)	Position
4CG013122	97.5	5,000		5,000
T4M140000	97.0	50,000		
T4M140000	97.5		5,000	45,000
DTC100000	REC		50,000	50,000 Cr

To the stock record personnel as well as those familiar with the stock record, each entry is a sentence and the sentences becomes a paragraph and the paragraphs become stories. Some of these stories tell the employee the probable solution to a problem or break.

Example: ZAP stock movement for yesterday is recorded as follows:

Account Number	Activity	Debit	Credit
2DC103163	BOT	100	
2DC096237	BOT	100	
7SF806023	JNL	200	
7SF901027	JNL		200
8LA042963	REC	200	
DTC100000	REC		200
042199999			200

Can you figure out which entry is possibly missing?

Stock purchases were done by the Washington, DC office's accounts and appear to have settled in DTC100000. All the security movements affecting the SF accounts seem to be offset against each other. But what happened to the LA security movement? The stock record employee would immediately look for an "in-vault" entry for a LAV500000 account or transit account TRN800000 that wasn't processed.

Because many securities have very similar name, the LAV500000 or TRN800000 entry may have been erroneously processed to another security. If so, that security position would have a debit break. The employee will correct both breaks at the same time.

To minimize these types of breaks, SF&R has their employees batch and balance all entries before being transmitted. Therefore, in this particular case the LA data entry personnel—while the shares must have balanced in this particular entry—should have caught the discrepancy in the security's name. SF&R's system will not accept a batch that is not balanced and rejects the batch when it is transmitted erroneously.

Any breaks can and should be corrected as soon as possible. The ledgers of the firm must be up to date and accurate at all times.

With the stock record in hand, an employee of this department looks for entries that do not balance. Due to the vast number of entries hitting the stock record from many different sources, it is possible for one side of an entry to appear while the other side does not. SF&R's stock record personnel must track down each and every out-of-balance condition and make the appropriate correcting entries.

In addition, a good stock record professional can "see" illogical entries when reading the record. An illogical entry or position is one that either appears incorrect or cannot happen. For example, the stock record reflects the following set of entries:

Account	Price or entry	Debit (long)	Credit (short)	Position
1BS286741-1	REC	1,000		1,000
SFV500000-0	REC		1,000	1,000 Cr

It is very unlikely that a client of the Boston, MA, office brought a security into the firm's San Francisco office. This is one form of illogical movement. Both entries would be verified.

Another form of illogicals is an illogical position:

Account	Price or entry	Debit (long)	Credit (short)	Position
2NY034545-1	Del		500	0
DTC100000-0		500		500 Dr

A debit position at the depository (DTC) means that SF&R removed stock that according to the record was not booked as a deposit. Either it is the wrong security that is being delivered or the original deposit was booked to the wrong security.

To the novice, the record is just a set of numbers signifying security movements. To a stock record professional, however, each series of numbers tells us a story. The story can be read and corrective action taken even though an out-of-balance position may not exist.

CHAPTER XII

General Ledger

SF&R's General Ledger Department is a multifaceted group whose responsibilities extend to many areas. First, it must reconcile the daily cash positions. Second, it must receive and issue checks for services rendered and received. Third, it is required to complete regulatory and financial reports. Fourth, it must monitor the firm's trading activity positions.

Though not part of operations, the general ledger plays an integral part in the daily operations of a broker/dealer. Whereas the stock record carries three categories of accounts (clients, proprietary, and street side or location), the general ledger carries four:

1. Clients
2. Proprietary
3. Street side or location
4. General business

General business includes those accounts that all businesses have, whether or not they are in the financial industry. Accounts such as employee payroll, telephone, and travel expenses are found in that category. In addition, the accounts roll down to more specific categories and are referred to as subledgers or even subsubledgers. For example, in the accounting section of this book, we used the term *cash account.* The firm may have several cash accounts located in one or several banks. The issue then becomes "need to know." At a high level of management, the amount of cash available is important; where it is located isn't. So the highest-level account will be *cash in banks.* Those who are responsible for making sure that cash is where it has to be when it is needed will know the location of the cash. They will know accounts by their location (e.g., First Continental Bank,

National Bank & Trust). Those responsible for balancing the bank's records versus the firm's records or for the actual movement of cash will know which account at which bank is involved with the reconcilement.

First Continental Bank's main ledger account number at SF&R is 666FCB000. The several accounts SF&R carries at the bank are 666FCB001, 666FCB002, 666FCB003, and so on, representing the different purposes of accounts SF&R has at First Continental. These accounts roll up to 666FCB000, which contains the total money on deposit at First Continental Bank. In turn, 666FCB000 rolls up with all of the other banks that SF&R maintains accounts at to the main cash account, 666USD666.

The number of accounts and subaccounts that SF&R has is determined by need and by control purposes. For example, each employee has an account number. That number rolls up to the location where the employee works, which in turn rolls up to the office.

The general ledger's three other account categories (proprietary, clients, and street side) are accessed by different departments for different purposes. For example, SF&R employs analysts that monitor the firm's trading position to assess risk and to make sure that traders do not go over their trading limits. This is monitored on a real time basis. There is a group involved in reviewing the total margin debits and allocating part of the interest charged to clients to the appropriate sales offices. Still another area is responsible for the allocation of registered representatives' commissions and, of course, the profitability of each revenue-producing area after the allocation of applicable expenses.

As with all businesses, there is an accounts payable department and an accounts receivable department. The accounts payable department is responsible for verifying the accuracy of vendor bills and paying them in accordance with firm policy. They also review all travel and expense (T&E) reports submitted by employees before reimbursing them. Let's not forget the most important department of all to us, the payroll department.

The component departments that make up and/or feed the general ledger are widespread in purpose and differ extensively in function. We are concerned with the cash-side operations.

XII-A *DAILY CASH REPORT*

All the cash movement in the firm is captured on the *daily cash report*. It is the money side of the activity stock record. Unlike the activity stock record that is produced in security order and then by account within each security, the daily cash report, as are all general ledger reports, is produced in strict account number order. This is another reason why the intelligence going into the number scheme is so important.

In reconciling the firm's daily cash balances, the personnel work with all of the money-moving areas of SF&R. To manage this data, control numbers are assigned to each area. This gives the accounting personnel a way to locate out-of-balance conditions. In theory, each area responsible for the movement of money should have their entries balanced before submission. However, mistakes happen—especially when the entries are made across departments. While the software used by SF&R validates the entries before they are processed, there are certain entries that are offset by entries entered from elsewhere in the firm. These are the areas where out-of-balance entries could occur.

For example, SF&R's Detroit office wires New York that it received 15 checks from clients totaling $75,892.67. The respective clients' accounts are credited to reflect the receipt. The branch deposits the checks at the bank the Detroit branch office uses. When the bank reconciliation department runs the reconciliation program, it finds an exception. When the bank's reported position, which is received electronically, is checked against SF&R internal bank account records, it is discovered that only $73,925.84 was deposited. There is a difference of $1,966.83 between these two sources of data. The cash reconciliation area will review the entries to determine where the error is. Because of this out-of-balance condition, the entire firm cannot have its total cash position in balance. There could be a check missing from the deposit, perhaps a check was accounted for twice; or maybe the bank is wrong. Through the use of control numbers, the exception report highlights the probable data input points at which to begin the search.

Please keep in mind that here we identified the problem first and filtered up to the exception report. In the real world, it works the opposite way. First, SFR's accounting personnel receive the exception report and then they unravel the problem.

The accounts reflected on the daily cash report are either the main accounts or the actual accounts that had the money movements. What appears depends on the size of the firm, in terms of both geographical size and infrastructure complexity. The larger firms, like SF&R, produce the main daily cash that contains the primary account numbers and daily cash reports of the subaccounts. For the most part, people who work in the areas reflected by the subaccounts are responsible for balancing their own work. The adjustments and corrections when added to or subtracted out of the balance position of the main daily cash report should negate the money difference. The balancing, which is systematized, between the main daily cash report and the subledgers' daily cash reports, serves as a double check on the balancing process.

Individuals who correct stock record books work very closely with the individuals who balance the brokerage side of the daily cash. A mistake on one side could easily cause a problem on the other.

As with the stock record, it is imperative that the daily cash report be balanced every day.

XII-B General Business

As with all other businesses, Stone, Forrest & Rivers maintains a general accounting area. As SF&R is a multinational firm, it has general accounting areas in all of its major centers. These areas are responsible for the financial running of the firm. Departments include:

- Accounts payable
- Accounts receivable
- Travel and entertainment (T&E)
- Payroll
- Bank reconciliation
- Credit analysis (whom we do business with)
- Market risk analysis (what positions our traders are carrying)

XII-C *TRIAL BALANCE*

The general ledger is the other part of the firm's books and records. The main accounts, such as "cash at banks" (666USD000), become part of the trial balance. The *trial balance* is the cash equivalent of the summary stock record.

It contains the primary accounts of all the account groups and their combined balance reflected in one total. For example, the debit balances in all of the margin accounts of SF&R clients appear as one figure. Likewise, all of the credit balances in clients' accounts appear as one figure on the trial balance.

It is from this record that the profit and loss statement and the balance sheet are developed. Besides the apparent difference between the summary stock record and the trial balance, there is one that is not obvious. The stock record contains the actual accounts that maintain positions, whereas the trial balance contains only the major or main accounts.

From the general ledger and the stock record, the firm produces the regulatory required Focus Report (Rule 15c3-1 of the 1934 Act) and Customer Protection Report (Rule 15c3-3 of the 1934 Act).

XII-D *PROFIT AND LOSS STATEMENT*

The *profit and loss statement*, also known as the *income statement*, takes all of the revenue and expense accounts from the trial balance and totals them. Then the total expenses are subtracted from total revenue to determine if the entity was profitable or not.

Here's an example of a profit and loss statement:

STONE, FORREST & RIVERS
Profit and Loss Statement
For Period Ending December 31, 20XX

Revenue:

- Commission
- Interest income
- Trading profits
- Underwriting fees
- Management fees
- Service and misc. fees

Total revenue: $ X, XXX, XXX.XX

(Continued)

Expenses

- Sales compensation
- Traders' compensation
- Employees' salaries
- Bonuses
- Insurance
- Heath and welfare
- Travel and entertainment
- Interest
- Dividends
- Mortgage
- Rent and leases
- Memberships
- Clearing
- Utilities
- Furniture
- Equipment
- Office supplies
- Miscellaneous

Less total expenses:	X, XXX,XXX.XX
Gross profit:	$ XXX,XXX.XX
Less taxes:	XXX,XXX.XX
Net profit:	$ XXX,XXX.XX

Profit and loss statements always cover a specific period of time. They are a running record of the firm's operations from period A to period B. That is why the heading reads "For Period Ending . . ."

XII-E BALANCE SHEET

The *balance sheet* is a snapshot of the firm's financial position at a given point in time. It always carries the phrase *as of* and the date. It contains the "running" accounts of the firm—namely, assets, liabilities, and stockholders' equity (net worth). The presentation for the balance sheet is Assets = Liabilities + Stockholders' Equity. For example:

STONE, FORREST & RIVERS
Balance Sheet
As of December 31, 20XX

Assets	**Liabilities**
Cash	Customer credit balances
Customer reserve account	Fail to receive
Customer debit balances	Stock loan
Traders' inventory	Bank loan
Firm investments	Accounts payable
Fail to deliver	Mortgage payable
Stock borrowed	Bonds payable
Accounts receivable	Subordinated loans
Notes receivable	Stockholders' equity
Exchange and other memberships	Preferred stock
Plant and equipment	Common stock
Prepaid subscriptions	Retained earnings
Goodwill	
$XX,XXX,XXX.XX	$XX,XXX,XXX.XX

Note that one of the last entries takes the net profit or loss from the profit and loss statement and journals it against retained earnings in the balance sheet. Remember, every entry must have equal debit and credit amounts. But the accounts affected may not be from the group in question. For example, cash (asset) is used to pay employees' salaries (expense). Asset accounts belong to the balance sheet; expense accounts belong in the profit and loss statement. Netting down the income and expense accounts to a single difference figure should yield an amount equal and opposite to the difference figure found in the balance sheet when the total liabilities and stockholders' equity are subtracted from total assets. That last entry balances out the balance sheet while netting out all of the revenue and expense accounts so that they start the new period with a zero balance.

XII-F *STATEMENT OF CASH FLOW*

The *statement of cash flow*'s purpose is to determine how effectively the firm used cash. The report reverses all entries that didn't really use cash, such as depreciation and amortization. It then looks at the result of three areas of the firm.

The accounts that comprise revenue, those belonging to operations, and those involving investments are reviewed. Revenue should be a positive number. Expense should be a negative number, and the revenue number should be greater than the operations number. If not, what happened? Or should the amount by which the revenue number exceeded the operations number be greater? In the income figure is positive, it means the firm spent money on investments. If it is negative, it means the firm had to borrow money. If it's negative, why?

CHAPTER XIII

Regulatory Reporting

XIII-A NET CAPITAL AND AGGREGATE INDEBTEDNESS (RULE 15c3–1 OF THE 1934 SECURITIES AND EXCHANGE ACT)

Like other brokerage firms, SF&R has to file certain information with the government and self-regulatory bodies. Perhaps the most familiar of such reports is the *Financial and Operational Combined Uniform Single (FOCUS) Report*. The report obtains some of its calculations from the computation of net capital and aggregate indebtedness that is found in the Code of Federal Regulations of the 1934 Securities and Exchange Act, which most commonly known as 15c3–1. Depending on the type of business the broker/dealer is involved with, another federal regulation affecting the FOCUS report is 15c3–3, the Customer Protection Report of the 1934 Securities and Exchange Act. Finally, information required to complete the FOCUS is obtained from the firm's financial reports and from the stock record. The FOCUS report demonstrates the firm's financial ability to carry on its business.

The net capital rule (15c3–1) creates an accounting barometer indicating the financial strength of the broker/dealer. Of primary concern is the firm's ability to pay off its debts promptly if it must. Therefore, any assets that cannot be readily turned into cash, regardless of how valuable they are, are ignored. The report discounts all nonliquid assets by 100% (it ignores their value completely). In this category are real estate, memberships in exchanges, and furniture and fixtures, to name but a few. The rule then instructs the broker/dealer to reduce the value of other assets according to the amount of market risk that they prudently represent. This adjustment is known as *haircuts.* A more formal way of saying it is the value a broker/dealer could expect to receive if it had to dispose of its assets in a hurry. The rule says, for example, that a prudent calculation of the value of the broker/dealer's common stock positions, in case they had to be liquidated quickly, would be 85% of the current market value. The 15% haircut is deducted when the stock in question is traded on an exchange or there are three or more market makers in the over-the-counter market. If either of these two criteria is not met, a greater amount is charged. In addition, if the particular security position comprises more than 25% of the firm's total equity trading position, an additional 15% haircut is taken. There are similar rules for other security products. These haircuts apply to assets in the firm's proprietary positions and not to clients' accounts that the firm is maintaining.

On the client side, we previously discussed margin and talked about an account being *on maintenance.* The purpose of SRO-imposed maintenance rules is to ensure that firms have adequate collateral to cover the client's debit (loan) balance. What would happen if the company, represented by the security in the client's margin account, goes bankrupt and there is a debit balance in the client's account? The security of the company would be virtually worthless, yet when the company was a going concern, the stock had value and therefore the client acquired it on margin. Now it is worthless and the client still owes the firm money for the amount of the loan. This could be an example of an unsecured debit balance and the client's deficit would be charged against the firm's capital until the client brought in the necessary collateral.

The firm's liabilities are carried at full exposure except for those that are 100% covered by the firm's own assets as defined by federal regulators, which are excluded. After deducting the latter, the remaining liabilities are divided by the adjusted liquid assets to arrive at the net capital ratio. The ratio resulting from this test dramatizes the firm's strength in the face of adversity. Under this rigid test, liabilities usually exceed assets. Ratios of 4 to 1 (that is, $4 of liabilities to $1 of assets) to 8 to 1 are normal. Various self-regulatory organizations monitor firms and grow suspicious of those whose ratios reach 10 to 1 or 12 to 1.

In the computation of the ratio, should it be $10 of liabilities to $1 of assets, the firm is not permitted to expand its business and at $12 of liabilities to $1 of assets it must condense its business. The rule is that a firm's ratio may not exceed 15 to 1. At this point, a firm usually goes out of business. While these ratios may look frightening, bear in mind that all nonliquid assets have been removed and the remaining liquid assets have been discounted (given a haircut), which leaves a small portion of the firm's assets with which to work the formula.

XIII-A-1 The Broker/Dealer's Capital

The firm's capital is made up of the stockholders' equity and can include subordinated loans and secured demand notes. While the latter two are debts, the lenders have subjugated the loans to all other debts of the company and therefore the loans are considered capital.

XIII A-2 Computation of Net Capital

In computing net capital, the firm's stockholders' equity must be calculated first. This is found in the firm's balance sheet and adjusted for any profit or losses occurring from the time the balance sheet was prepared to the current time. Then the subordinated debt is added. Because subordinated debt, both subordinated loans and secured demand notes, are junior to all other debt, it is considered part of the firm's capital. The two together give SF&R their total available capital.

From this figure nonallowable assets are subtracted. Nonallowable assets are generally defined as nonliquid assets, such as fixed assets (e.g., real estate, and furniture and fixtures) and nonsalable assets (e.g., prepaid expenses). After that step, haircuts on the firm's inventory positions are calculated and subtracted to arrive at net capital. Here's an example:

PUSHIN ANPULLOUT CO.
Trial Balance
A/O 12/31/20XX

Account	Debit	Credit
Cash	$ 600,000	
Cash (special reserve account)	125,000	
Client debit balances	3,950,000	
Accounts receivable (clients)	650,000	
Accounts receivable (broker/dealers)	2,550,000	

(*Continued*)

Stock borrowed (firm)	2,000,000	
Stock borrowed (customer)	500,000	
Inventory	4,500,000	
Prepaid expenses	25,000	
Exchange memberships	3,000,000	
Fixed assets	4,000,000	
Client credit balances		$ 1,320,000
Accounts payable (clients)		100,000
Accounts payable (broker/dealers)		1,525,000
Accounts payable (vendors)		150,000
Stock loans (firm)		3,500,000
Stock loans (customer)		3,680,000
Bank loans (firm)		1,000,000
Bank loans (customer)		1,850,000
Mortgage payables		350,000
Subordinated debt		2,000,000
Stockholders' equity (beginning of year)		6,025,000
Commission income		4,500,000
Interest income		500,000
Compensation expense	1,000,000	
Benefits expense	300,000	
Administrative expense	1,500,000	
Depreciation expense	500,000	
Interest expense (client and inventory)	300,000	
	$25,500,000	$25,500,000

Now we solve for net capital. First, we calculate the trial balance.

Stockholders' equity (beginning of the year)			$ 6,025,000
Profit or loss:			
Income:			
Commission income		$ 4,500,000	
Interest income		500,000	
Total income:		$ 5,000,000	
Less expenses:			
Compensation expense	$ 1,000,000		
Benefits expense	300,000		
Administrative expense	1,500,000		

Depreciation expense	500,000		
Interest expense	300,000		
Total expenses:		$ 3,600,000	
Income			+ 1,400,000
Adjusted stockholders' equity			$ 7,425,000
Subordinated debt			+ 2,000,000
Total available capital			$ 9,425,000
Nonallowable assets:			
Less:			
Prepaid expenses		$ 25,000	
Exchange memberships		3,000,000	
Fixed assets		4,000,000	
Total nonallowable assets			7,025,000
Capital before inventory adjustments			$ 2,400,000
Inventory adjustments:			
Less:			
Haircuts on inventory			
.15 × $2,500,000 =			675,000
Net capital			$, 1,725,000

Aggregate indebtedness includes all of the firm's liabilities with two exceptions: any liability secured by the firm's assets and subordinated debt. We will assume that the liabilities are not secured by the firm's assets.

Client credit balances	$ 1,320,000
Accounts payable (clients)	100,000
Accounts payable (broker/dealers)	1,525,000
Accounts payable (vendors)	150,000
Stock loans (customer)	3,680,000
Bank loans (customer)	1,850,000
Total	$ 8,625,000

$8,625,000/$1,725,000 = 5 to 1

The firm is operating at a ratio of 5 to 1, which is indicative of a financially sound firm.

XIII-B CUSTOMER PROTECTION—RESERVES AND CUSTODY OF SECURITIES (RULE 15C3-3 OF THE 1934 SECURITIES AND EXCHANGE ACT)

Customer Protection—Reserves and Custody of Securities, rule 15c3–3 of the 1934 Securities and Exchange Act, protects customers by isolating all clients' exposure to the firm and vice versa. The firm applies certain tests on accounts that could affect the financial safety of clients' accounts. If the test fails, then the monetary value by which the test failed must be set aside for the benefit of the client. For example, if a DVP was made and the funds had not been received for seven days, that money is set aside for the client. If stock has been in transfer for more than 41 days and not confirmed by the agent, the value is set aside for the benefit of the client and said to belong to the client.

To calculate the reserve requirement, the firm first totals all of the credit cash balances and all of the debit cash balances in the clients' accounts. After adjustments for potential exposure (such as unsecured or not collectable debits, suspense items, and positions that exceed certain allowable time limits), if total customers' credit balances exceed their debit balances after the debit figure has been reduced by 1%, SF&R has to deposit the difference into a special bank account set aside for this exclusive reason. If total customer debit exceeds credit, after the debits are haircut by 1%, the deposit is not necessary. To protect themselves against potential error, SF&R always deposits an additional sum to cover the time when a mistake may have been made in the calculation.

Retail firms have clients with margin accounts. These margin debits can easily be greater that client credit balances.

The following general classes of accounts are used:

- Client owes broker/dealer:
    - Debit balances in client's account
    - Failing to deliver client's securities
    - Stock borrowed for client short sales
- Broker/dealer owes client:
    - Credit balance in client's account
    - Failing to receive client's securities

- Stock loaned from client's account
- Firm loans made with client's securities
- Firm's inventory selling short to client
- Market value of security difference over 30 days old

As for fail accounts, the reason why SF&R is failing to deliver securities to the client is that they owe the firm money (a receivable). The reason why the fail to receive is in the "broker/dealer owes client" column is that the firm is holding the client's proceeds of sale until the security is received from the client.

XIII-C *FOCUS*

Financial and Operational Combined Uniform Single (FOCUS) is a federally required series of reports that must be filed by broker/dealers.

FOCUS Part I must be completed monthly and filed by the 10th business day of the following month. It contains a series of questions as to the financials and operational efficiency of the firm. Most of the information required is obtained from the net capital and aggregate indebtedness computations described previously in this section.

FOCUS Part II is filed quarterly by broker/dealers that clear or carry customer accounts. Part II must be filed by the 17th business day of each quarter as well as 17 days after the filing of the firm's annual audit if the audit does not fall on one of the company's fiscal quarters.

FOCUS Part II is similar to FOCUS Part I but delves deeper into the financials of the firm. Some of the questions can only be answered by reviewing the firm's balance sheet and profit and loss statement, and even utilizing the firm's trial balance, subledgers, and stock record.

FOCUS Part IIA is completed by firms that do not clear or carry customer accounts. It too must be filed by the 17th business day of each quarter as well as 17 days after the filing of the firm's annual audit if the audit does not fall on one of the company's fiscal quarters.

CHAPTER XIV

Conclusion

The intent of this book was not only to give the reader an introduction to the processing side of a broker/dealer's security business but also to include those areas that affect and interact with the processing cycle. Some of these industry utilities affect the processing cycle directly, others more indirectly. Still others promulgate and enforce those rules and regulations that guide the industry day to day. Discussion of intrafirm departments that are not directly involved with the processing cycle were included so that the reader could get a better understanding of how a broker/dealer operates.

In addition, the reader has been introduced to the major products that are offered. These have ranged from equity products through the many types of debt instruments and the multitude of derivatives. Not only have the products been introduced, but their characteristics and trading patterns have been explored.

The book has also examined different processes used to bring a trade from execution to settlement. The various processes accommodate the idiosyncrasies of the products and the marketplace that serves them. Some of these processes seem state of the art; others have a way to go.

Finally, the book has attempted to show how important the accurate and efficient processing of transactions is to the bottom line—the profitability of the firm.

I trust you found the book informative and helpful in understanding how the industry functions and will refer to it throughout your career.

Thank you.

Glossary

A

ABS. See *Asset-Backed Security* and *Automated-Bond System.*

ACATS. See *Automated Customer Account Transfer System.*

accounting. A financial method of tracking financial events affecting an entity. It focuses on recording what happened, when, and what did it effect?

accrued interest. The amount of interest that the buyer owes the seller on transactions involving fixed-income securities, such as most bonds and notes.

ACES. See *Advanced Computerized Execution System.*

ACT. See *automated confirmed trade.*

active seg. Refers to a system that permits securities to be released from a seg position on a real time or multibatch system. It is a valuable tool in inventory management.

Activity Stock Record. A record displaying all the security movements on a particular day in accounts that the firm is responsible for. It is produced in security order and account order within each security. Also known as the daily stock record.

ADF. See *Alternate Display Facility.*

ADR. See *American Depositary Receipt.*

Advanced Computerized Execution System (ACES). A NASD system that routes an order to the market maker as if it were being received from a branch office of the market maker's firm.

advisory processing. Procedure by which the opposing firm's version of a trade is accepted by the named firm. Advisory notices accompany regular-way contract reports received from NSCC.

agency transaction. A trade in which the firm operates as a broker; that is, it executes trades as an agent and charges a commission for the service.

ALERT. A product of Thomson Financial Services. It is an institutional name-and-address database that is a central point for access by broker/dealers. It is currently called Omgeo Alert. See *Omgeo.*

all or none. A phrase used in certain underwritings and on some orders. In an underwriting, it is an instruction from a corporation to a standby underwriter to take all of the forthcoming issue or none. On large-quantity orders, it is an instruction to fill all of the order or none of the order over a preset time period.

allocation. A term used in mortgage- and asset-backed securities to explain the formation and distribution of pools to buyers. It is also used in the institutional segment when the results of a day's trading are shared among the accounts of the institution.

alternate display facility. A quotation service offered by NASDAQ that permits the quotation and other data from several markets in the same security to be displayed on one screen.

American Depositary Receipt (ADR). A share of the stock that is issued by an American bank and backed by foreign securities on deposit at the bank.

American Stock Exchange (AMEX). A major stock and option exchange located at 86 Trinity Place, New York, NY.

AMEX Option Switch (AMOS). An electronic order-routing and -reporting system used to transport option transactions to and from the American Stock Exchange.

amortization. An accounting term indicating the apportionment of an incurred expense over the life of an asset. For example, if a three-year magazine subscription (an expense) is paid in year one, it should be amortized (spread out) over the three-year life of the subscription (the asset).

AMOS. See *AMEX Option Switch.*

annual report. A statement produced by a company that contains information about the company, its management, products, accomplishments over the year, and plans for the future as well as its financials.

arbitrage. Comes in two varieties: risk and riskless. A risk arbitrage exists when professional traders, known as arbitrageurs, take on two positions, expecting some event to occur, such as a merger. A riskless arbitrage occurs when there is an aberration in the price of two issues, one of which is exchangable into the other. For example, RAP preferred is convertible into five shares of common; the common is trading at $15.05 per share and the preferred is trading at $75 per share. The arbitrageur would buy the preferred share @ $75, convert to five times the number of common, and sell the equivalent number of common at $15.05 × 5 = $75.25, locking in $.25 per preferred share converted.

as of. A term used to describe any trade processed not on the actual trade date, but "as of " the actual trade date.

asked. The offer side of a quote or the selling price. A quote represents the highest bid and lowest asked (offer) available in the marketplace at a given point in time.

asset. Any item of value owned by or owed to the corporation.

Asset-Backed Security. A passthrough security that pays principal and interest on a periodic basis and is backed by pool of various types of loans such as car loans and credit card loans.

at the opening. A type of order that is to be executed "at the opening" of trading on a given day. If for whatever reason the order is not eligible to be included in the first trade of the day, it is canceled.

automated bond system (ABS). The automated bond system is owned and operated by the New York Stock Exchange. Is it a screen-based quotation service of over 2,000 bonds. Subscribers to this service quote or accept bids or offers.

Automated Confirmed Trade (ACT). A NASDAQ-developed system used to compare trades between executing broker/dealers before they are sent to National Security Clearing Corporation.

Automated Customer Account Transfer System (ACATS). A DTCC service by which clients' accounts or parts thereof are transferred from one broker/dealer to another. This practice usually occurs when clients change the stockbroker that they do business with.

average. Also known as an *index*, it is a mathematical computation that indicates the value of a number of securities as a group. Three of the more popular averages are the Dow Jones Industrial Average (DJI), Standard & Poor's (S&P) 500, and the New York Stock Exchange Composite. A security-based average, which may be market weighted, share weighted, or price weighted, indicates performance.

B

backwardation. A term used in the futures market when the near-term value of a future product contract is higher than the longer-term contract on the same commodity.

balance sheet. An accounting statement reflecting the firm's financial condition in terms of assets, liabilities, and net worth (ownership). In a balance sheet, Assets = Liabilities + Net Worth.

BAN. See *Bond Anticipation Note.*

banker's acceptance. A discounted debt instrument used in international trade to expedite payment of goods in transit between exporting and importing countries.

basis price. A method of pricing municipal bonds, T-bills, and certain other instruments. It is an expression of yield to maturity.

bear. Someone who thinks that the value of the market or of a security will fall.

bear market. A market in which prices are generally declining.

bearer form. Unrecorded security ownership. The individual bearing the instrument is assumed to be the owner.

bearer instrument. Any instrument (security) that is not registered in anyone's name.

beneficial owner. The owner of a security who is entitled to all the benefits associated with ownership; customers' securities are often registered not in the name of the customer, but rather in the name of the brokerage firm or the central depository. Even so, the customer remains the real or beneficial owner.

best-efforts underwriting. An offering of new stock in which the underwriter makes a best effort to place the issue but is not responsible for unsold portions.

best execution. SEC rule 19(b)(7) requires broker/dealers to seek out the best possible price for their client orders.

bid. The buy side of a quote. A quote is comprised of the highest bid (price at which someone is willing to buy) and offer (the price at which someone is willing to sell).

big board. A popular name for the New York Stock Exchange.

blocks. Orders to transact large quantities of securities are considered *block orders.* Generally, orders of 10,000 shares or more or that represent a minimum value of $200,000 are considered block orders.

blotter. Another name for a listing used in operations. A blotter usually carries trades and customer account numbers, segregated by point of execution.

blotter code. A system by which trades are identified by type and place of execution. The code enables firms to balance customer to street-side trades.

blue chip. A term used to describe the common stocks of corporations with the strongest reputations. (In poker, the blue chip is usually assigned the highest money value.)

blue sky rules. Security rules of the various states. A new issue being sold must be registered and approved for sale in every state in which it is being offered. The process is known as "blue skying" the issue.

bond. A debt instrument; a security that represents the debt of a corporation, a municipality, the federal government, or any other entity. A bond is usually long term in nature: 10 to 30 years.

Bond Anticipation Note (BAN). A short-term municipal debt instrument issued in the expectation to issue long-term debt in the near future that will pay off the notes.

bond hub. One of several bond trading screens where dealers post their inventory and quotes so that others can trade against these positions for themselves or their clients.

book value. A value computed by subtracting the total liabilities from the value of all assets on the balance sheet, then dividing by the number of common shares. This is an accounting term that has no relation to the securities' market value.

books and records. A term used for the major documents required to be maintained by a broker/dealer. Among these are the stock record and general ledger.

booth support system (BSS). An order-routing system that transmits orders electronically from the broker/dealer's office to a preselected booth on the NYSE trading floor.

Boston Stock Exchange (BSE). An equities exchange in Boston, Massachusetts.

bounce. An operating term referring to the nonacceptance and return of an erroneously received security.

box. (1) Another name for *vault*; the place where securities are maintained at the firm.

(2) The electronic option exchange operated by the Boston Stock Exchange.

break. A term used when there is disagreement between two sides of a position that are supposed to agree. For example, in the working of the stock record, the long-side entries should equal the short-side entries per security position per day. If they do not, the position is said to break.

break account. A temporary account that is used to place imbalances in positions.

breakpoint. A purchase of shares in an open-end investment company mutual fund that is large enough to entitle the buyer to a lower sales charge. A series of breakpoints is established by the fund, at each of which the charge is reduced.

British pound sterling. Currency of Great Britain. AKA *GBP.*

broker. (1) An individual who buys or sells securities for customers (a stockbroker). (2) On an exchange, one who executes public orders on an agency basis (a floor broker or commission house broker). (3) As a slang term, a firm that executes orders for others (a brokerage firm).

broker's call rate. The rate that banks charge brokerage firms for the financing of margin accounts and inventory positions.

brokerage firm. A partnership or corporation that is in business to provide security services for a general marketplace.

BSE. See *Boston Stock Exchange.*

bull. Someone who thinks that the value of the market or of a security will rise.

bull market. A market in which prices are generally rising.

busted trade. A trade that is entered into by one party in error and that the contra party is willing to walk away from. As no profit or loss is incurred directly from both parties agreeing to negate the terms of the trade, the trade is said to be *busted.*

buy close. An option transaction that reduces or eliminates a written position.

buy open. An option transaction that establishes or increases a holder's (owner's) position.

buying power. In a margin account, the maximum dollar amount of securities that the client can purchase or sell short without having to deposit additional funds.

C

CAES. See *Computer Assisted Execution System.*

call (option). An option that permits the owner to buy a contracted amount of underlying security at a set price (strike or exercise price) for a predetermined period of time (up to the expiration date).

callable. A security's feature that allows the issuer to retire an issue ahead of the expected termination date, as stated in the security description. Should the issue be called, the issuer usually pays a premium.

capital gain. A trading profit. Trading gains that occur in one year or less are short-term capital gains; those that occur in periods longer than one year are long-term capital gains. Short-term and long-term capital gains are treated differently for tax purposes.

capital loss. A trading loss. Losses are long or short term as are gains. See *capital gain.*

capital stock. The common and preferred stock of a company.

capitalization. The total dollar value of all common stock, preferred stock, other net worth accounts, and bonds issued by a corporation.

cash account. A customer account in which all securities purchased should be paid for in full by the third business day, but no later than the fifth business day after trade. The security must be delivered into the client's accounts within 10 calendar days after settlement date.

cash dividend. A form of dividend that corporations pay, on a per-share basis, to stockholders from their earnings.

cash over the wire (COW). The process in which branch offices or subdivisions of a firm notify the main office that money has been received and deposited in a local bank. The deposit is posted to the bank's account by the main office and is then directed to a needed location once the funds have cleared.

cash sale. A trade that settles on trade date and that is used primarily in equities at the end of the year for tax purposes.

CBOE. See *Chicago Board Option Exchange.*

CBOEdirectHYTS. The CBOE's hybrid trading system, combining electronic order routing, execution, and reporting systems with floor-derived open outcry trading.

CBOT. See *Chicago Board of Trade.*

CCA. See *Clearing Cash Adjustment.*

CD. Canadian dollar; the currency of Canada.

CD. See *certificate of deposit.*

certificate. The physical document evidencing ownership (a share of stock) or debt (a bond).

certificate of deposit (CD). A short-term debt instrument issued by banks. CDs of large denominations are negotiable and can be traded in the secondary market.

CFTC. See *Commodities Future Trading Commission.*

Chicago Board of Trade (CBOT). A major commodity exchange located at 141 East Jackson Boulevard, Chicago, IL.

Chicago Board Option Exchange (CBOE). Listed option trading was originated by this marketplace on April 26, 1973.

Chicago Mercantile Exchange. A major commodity exchange in Chicago, IL.

Chicago Stock Exchange. Located in Chicago, IL, it offers trading in equity securities. Called the Midwest Stock Exchange until 1993.

Clearing Cash Adjustment (CCA). A method used by National Securities Clearing Corporation to homogenize the difference in prices per security per day so that netting of trades between clearing firms is possible.

clearing corporation. A central receiving and distribution center operated for its members, which are various brokerage firms. Many offer automated systems that expedite comparison procedures. Among these are NSCC (National Securities Clearing Corp. Division of Depository Trust and Clearing Corporation) and OCC (Options Clearing Corporation).

clearing member trade assignment (CMTA). A process by which an option trade executed by one member of an option clearing corporation is settled by another member.

client master database. An electronic database that contains relevant personal information regarding the firm's clients.

closed-end fund. A fund whose offering of shares is closed. That is, once the initial offering is completed, the fund stops offering and acquiring its shares. The value of the shares is then determined by supply and demand, rather than by calculation of net asset value.

CME. See *Chicago Mercantile Exchange.*

CMO. See *collateralized mortgage obligation.*

CMS. See *common message switch.*

CMTA. See *clearing member trade assignment.*

CNS. See *continuous net settlement.*

CNS deposit. A deposit of securities into the broker/dealer's account at Depository Trust Company that is to be used to "clean up" a pending delivery.

collateral. An asset pledged to support a loan.

collateral trust bond. A debt instrument issued by one corporation and backed by the securities of another corporation.

collateralized mortgage obligation (CMO). A form of asset-backed security that is securitized and issued in time sequences or tranches.

combination order. In listed options trading, an order to simultaneously buy or sell a put and a call with the same underlying security but different series designations.

COMEX. A commodity exchange located in New York, NY.

commercial paper. A short-term debt instrument issued by corporations. Its rate of interest is set at issuance and can be realized only if held to maturity.

commission. (1) The amount charged by a firm on an agency transaction. (2) The method by which account executives are compensated.

commission house broker. A floor broker who is employed by a brokerage house to execute orders on the exchange floor for the firm and its customers.

commodities house broker. A floor broker who is employed by a brokerage house to execute orders on a future exchange's floor for the firm and its customers (now known as house broker).

Commodities Future Trading Commission (CFTC). An agency responsible for the enforcement of rules and regulations of the futures industry.

commodity swap. An exchange of assets between two parties, usually involving a future contract for a physical commodity.

common message switch (CMS). A system owned by the NYSE and AMEX that directs orders from member firms to selected locations on the respective trading floor.

common stock. A security, issued in shares, that represents ownership of a corporation. Common stockholders may vote for the management and receive dividends when declared by the corporation's board of directors.

comparison. The process by which two contra brokerage firms in a trade agree to the terms of the transaction. Comparison can occur at the point of execution, through a clearing corporation, or on a trade-for-trade basis (that is, ex the clearing corporation).

Computer Assisted Execution System (CAES). An intermarket system that seeks out the best price available in the various marketplaces.

confirmation. A trade invoice, issued to customers of brokerage firms, that serves as written notice of the trade, giving price, security description, settlement money, trade and settlement dates, plus other pertinent information.

continuous net settlement (CNS). The process by which a broker/dealer's previous day's unsettled position in a security is merged into the next day's settling transactions.

contract sheet. Report received from clearing corporations by a clearing firm that shows the status of their trades that are pending settlement in the comparison process.

convertible issue (bond). A feature in some security issues that permits the issue's owner to exchange the issue into another issue, usually common stock. This privilege can be used only once. The preferred stock, or bond, owner can convert from that issue to another, but not back.

cooling-off period. The period, usually 20 days, between the filing of the registration statement on a new issue with the SEC and the effective date of the offering.

corporate action. A corporate happening (such as a merger or stock split) affecting the owners of or lenders to the corporation.

corporate bond. A long-term debt instrument issued by a corporation. It is usually fixed income, that is, it carries a fixed rate of interest. A corporate bond may offer many features, ranging from floating rate to callable to convertible. From issuance, the life of a bond may be from 10 to 30 years.

corporate note. An intermediate-term debt instrument issued by a corporation. It is usually issued at a fixed interest rate, though it can also be issued in floating-rate form. From issuance, the life of a note may be from 1 to 10 years.

correspondent clearing firm. A broker/dealer that uses the services of another broker/dealer to clear and settle their client and/or proprietary trades.

COW. See *cash over the wire.*

credit balance. The funds available to a client in a cash or margin account. In a short sale, this balance in the client's short account represents the customer's liability.

CRM. See *customer relationship manager.*

cumulative preferred. A preferred stock feature that entitles the holder to the later payment of dividends that were not paid when due. The dividends are, in this sense, cumulative. The dividends accumulate and must be paid (along with present dividends) before common stockholders may receive any dividends.

Curb Exchange. An archaic name for the *American Stock Exchange (AMEX).*

currency swap. The exchange of currencies between two parties. This is usually accomplished through borrowing by respective parties in their respective homelands and then swapping loans.

CUSIP (*Committee on Uniform Security Identification Procedure*). An interindustry security coding service. Each security issue has its own unique CUSIP number.

custodian bank. A bank that services its clients' financial assets, such as security portfolios. In addition to warehousing securities, the bank collects dividends and/or interest as well as actively pursuing other corporate actions that may affect their clients' portfolios.

customer protection. Rule 15c3–3 under the Securities and Exchange Act of 1934 mandates that a firm set aside certain clients' funds in a special bank account expressly set up for the benefit of the client.

customer relationship manager. An employee (usually registered) of a broker/dealer that responds to questions or problems that could arise from clients using online trading services, such as trying to trade amounts higher than their allowable limits.

D

daily cash report. A listing of all accounts that had cash movements on a given day.

daily stock record. See *Activity Stock Record.*

dated date. The first day that interest starts to accrue on newly issued bonds.

day order. An order that, if not executed on the day it is entered, expires at the close of that day's trading.

day trade. The buying and selling of the same security on the same day.

day trader. See *Pattern Day Trader.*

DBO. See *delivery balance order.*

dealer. A firm that functions as a market maker and that, as such, positions the security to buy and sell versus the public and/or brokerage community.

debenture bond. A debt that is issued by a corporation and backed or secured by nothing but the good name of the issuing company.

debit balance. (1) The amount of a loan in a margin account. (2) A way of posting assets and expenses in accounting.

declaration date. The date that a corporate action is announced. In the case of a dividend, it is the date that the amount of the dividend, the record date, and the payable date are announced.

deed of trust. See *indenture.*

defined contribution. A service of FundServ used when a broker/dealer's client invests in several mutual funds using a predetermined allocation. This is most commonly found in an IRA account where investments are made simultaneously to several funds on a periodic basis.

delete of compared. A form, as well as a process, used to delete trades that were compared by mistake through NSCC.

delivery balance order (DBO). An order issued by the clearing corporation to any firm that, after the day's trades are netted, has a delivery or sale position remaining. The order defines what is to be delivered and to whom.

depository. A central location for keeping securities on deposit.

Depository Trust Company (DTC). A corporation, owned by banks and brokerage firms, that holds securities, arranges for their receipt and delivery, and arranges for the payments in settlement. It is now part of Depository Trust and Clearing Corporation.

Depository Trust and Clearing Corporation—Parent company to Depository Trust Company, National Securities Clearing Corporation and Fixed Income Clearing Corporation

depreciation account. An account in which a firm writes off the declining value of machinery and equipment over the earning life of the equipment.

derivative product. A derivative product is one whose value is based on the value of another product. The market values of options, forwards, and futures, for example, are based on the current market value of the security, issue, or commodity underlying it.

Designated Order Turnaround (DOT). An order-routing and -execution reporting system of the NYSE. Variations that appeal to different segments of the market are known as Super DOT and Anonymous Super DOT.

designated primary market maker (DPM). A market maker that operates on the floor of the Chicago Board Option Exchange (CBOE) and is responsible for maintaining an orderly market by trading for their own account when required. This differs from the other market makers on the trading floor, who trade for their own accounts when they want to.

director. A corporate board member elected by the stockholders. A title given to individuals at various levels of management.

discretionary account. A client account in which the account executive is permitted to buy and sell securities for the client without the client's prior permission. The opening of such an account requires the special permission of the firm's management.

discretionary order. An order entered by the account executive for a discretionary account. The account executive decides on the security, quantity, and price.

display book. The terminal used by specialists on the New York Stock Exchange to track orders in their assigned securities that are transmitted over Super DOT (DOT) or entered by other means.

dividend. A portion of a corporation's earnings paid to stockholders on a per-share basis. Preferred stock is supposed to pay a regular and prescribed dividend amount. Common stock pays varying amounts when declared.

DK. See *don't know.*

DNI. See *Do Not Increase.*

DNR. See *Do Not Reduce.*

dollar cost averaging. An investment method used in mutual funds by which clients invest the same dollar amount periodically. Because mutual funds permit the buying of fractional shares, all of the investor's payment is used in the acquisition of fund shares.

do not increase (DNI). An instruction that informs order-handling personnel not to increase the quantity of shares specified on the order in the event of a stock dividend. DNI is placed on buy limit, sell stop, and stop limit GTC orders.

do not reduce (DNR). An instruction that informs the order-handling personnel not to reduce the price of the order by the amount of dividends, if and when paid by the corporation. DNR is placed on buy limit, sell stop, and sell stop limit GTC orders.

don't know (DK). A term used throughout the industry meaning "unknown item." On the AMEX, the term applies to equity transactions that cannot be compared by the morning of trade date plus three business days. It is also used over the counter for comparison purposes.

DOT. See *designated order turnaround.*

double taxation. Corporations pay taxes on revenue before paying dividends. The dividends, in the hands of the stockholder, are taxed again as ordinary income—hence, double taxation.

downstairs trader. A trader who operates on the floor of an exchange and who "trades" positions against the public market. Also see *upstairs trader.*

downtick. A listed equity trade whose price is lower that that of the equity's previous sale.

DPM. See *Designated Primary Market maker.*

DTC. See *Depository Trust Company.*

DTCC. See *Depository Trust and Clearing Corporation.*

due bill. An IOU used primarily in the settlement of trades involved in dividend and stock split situations, when the new shares are unavailable for delivery.

due diligence meeting. The last meeting between corporate officials and underwriters prior to the issuance of the security. At the meeting, the content of the prospectus is discussed, and relevant parts of the underwriting are put into place.

E

earnings report. A corporate financial statement that reports and nets out all earnings and expenses to a profit or loss. It is therefore sometimes referred to as the *profit and loss (P&L) statement.*

effective date. The first date, after the cooling-off period, of a new issue that the security can be offered.

electronic pool notification. The process by which members of the Mortgage Backed Securities Division of Fixed Income Clearing Corporation notify their counterparties of the pool(s) of mortgages being delivered in settlement of TBA trades.

EPN. See *Electronic Pool Notification.*

equipment trust bonds. Debt instruments that are issued by some corporations and backed by "rolling stock" (such as airplanes or locomotives and freight cars) of the issuer.

equity. The portion in an account that reflects the customer's ownership interest. A term reflecting ownership of a company.

escrow receipt. A guarantee of delivery issued by a qualified bank to a clearing corporation, such as OCC, on behalf of the bank's customer. The member brokerage firm acts as a conduit for this document.

euro. The currency of the European Union.

ex by ex. A process by which in-the-money options about to expire are automatically exercised unless instructions are received to the contrary.

Exchange Traded Funds (ETF). A trust composed of equivalent shares of an index that is traded on exchanges. The components can be accumulated to make the ETF or the ETF can be taken apart.

ex-distribution date. Usually the day after payable date when the issue trades at a price based on the previous night's adjusted closing price that accommodates the stock split or stock dividend of an amount greater than 25%. In a two-for-one stock split, 100 shares of stock trading at $40 per share will become 200 shares trading at $20 per share on the ex-distribution date.

ex-dividend date. The first day on which the purchaser of the security is not entitled to the dividend. It is also the day that reflects the adjustment of the previous night's closing price to reflect the dividend amount.

exemption. A method used by members of the Depository Trust Company to control and manage their security positions on deposit there.

exercise price. See *Strike Price.*

expense. Costs incurred in trying to obtain revenue.

expiration month. The month in which an option or futures contract ceases to exist (expires).

extension. Term used for the process of extending the time a client has to meet a trade obligation. The request must be approved and filed with NASDR.

F

face value. The debt (or loan) amount that appears on the face of the certificate and that the issuer must pay at maturity.

facilitation order. An order entered to assist in the execution of large orders. The entering firm stands ready to absorb any part of the order that is not taken through normal trading mechanisms.

factor table. A table used to compute the outstanding principal on passthroughs (Ginnie Maes, Fredddie Macs, and Fannie Maes).

fail. A transaction that is not settled on the appropriate day.

Fail to Deliver. An unfulfilled commitment by a selling firm to deliver a security that was traded and not settled on settlement date.

Fail to Receive. An unfulfilled commitment by a purchasing firm to receive a security that was traded but is unable to settle on the settlement date.

fast automatic stock transfer (FAST). A service offered by DTC.

Fed fund rate. The rate charged by the Federal Reserve Bank on money it lends to banks to meet their reserve requirements or other needs. The rate is used when one bank lends funds to another bank. It is also the rate against which interest on other short-term loans are based.

Fed funds. Same-day money transfers between member banks of the Federal Reserve System by means of the Fedwire. These transfers are drawdowns and immediately available loans of reserve deposits.

Fedwire. Method used to settle agency and Treasury transactions at the Fed as well as the delivery vehicle for cash settlement between industry utilities, broker/dealers, and custodian banks.

FICC. See *Fixed Income Clearing Corporation.*

figuration. The computation of the monies involved in trades, performed in a purchase and sale department or in trade processing systems.

Fill or Kill (FOK). An order that requires execution of the entire quantity immediately. If it's not filled, the order is canceled.

Financial and Operational Combined Uniform Single (FOCUS) system. A series of financial reports filed by broker/dealers with the Securities and Exchange Commission and their self-regulatory organizations.

fiscal year. The 12-month period during which a business maintains its financial records. Since this cycle does not have to coincide with the calendar year, it is known as the fiscal year.

FITS. The system formerly used by NSCC to compare and process corporate and municipal bond trades.

Fixed Income Clearing Corporation. Agency created by a merger of the Mortgage Backed Securities Clearing Corporation (MBSCC) and Government Securities Clearing Corporation (GSCC). MBSCC clears TBA trades of government agencies, while GSCC clears U.S. Treasury and debt instruments of Ginnie Mac, Fannie Mae, and Freddie Mac.

flat. A bond trading without accrued interest is said to be trading flat.

floor broker. An exchange member who is permitted to conduct business on the exchange floor.

FOCUS. See *Financial and Operational Combined Uniform Single* system.

FOK. See *fill or kill.*

foreign exchange. A term referring to the trading of different countries' currencies against one another.

FOREX. See *foreign exchange.*

forward. Basically an over-the-counter traded future. Whereas a future product has fixed terms and trades on an exchange, a forward generally has negotiated terms and trades over the counter.

fourth market. An electronic market in which institutions trade large-quantity orders among each other.

free stock. Loanable securities; that is, securities that can be used for loan or hypothecation. The securities are firm-owned shares of stock in a margin account that represents the debit balance (amount of loan).

FundServ. A clearing service offered by NSCC, a division of DTCC, that facilitates mutual fund transactions between its members and the mutual funds.

future. A contract that sets the price, at the time of the transaction, at which a delivery will be made at a later date. The terms of the contract are set by the exchange on which it trades.

futures contract. A long-term contract on the underlying instrument, such as a grain, precious metal, index, or interest rate instrument, by which the buyer and seller lock in a price for later delivery.

FX. See *FOREX.*

G

General Obligation (GO) Bond. A muni bond whose issuer's ability to pay back principal and interest is based only on its full taxing power.

GNMA. See *Government National Mortgage Association.*

GO. See *general obligation bond.*

good till . . . A time period during which an order to buy or sell securities remains in force. The order is either executed during its life or canceled at the end of the time period—for example, good through month (GTM).

good-till order. An instruction on an order stating that it should be cancelled if not executed. GTC means good till cancelled. GTM means good through month.

Government National Mortgage Association (GNMA). A division of Housing and Urban Development (HUD) primarily involved with issuance of government-insured or -guaranteed mortgages.

growth stock. Stock of a company in an existing emerging industry.

H

haircut. An industry term that is applied to the value of an asset. Depending on its liquidity, the value is reduced by what amount could be expected if the asset had to be liquidated in a hurry.

hedge fund. A pooling of money by a partnership that has an almost unrestricted range of investments to choose from.

hedger. A type of trader—on future exchanges, for example—who offsets physical positions with the use of futures contracts.

house broker. See commission house broker.

house call. A call for additional collateral sent to a margin client when the equity in the account falls below the broker/dealer's (house) minimum equity requirement.

house excess. The amount of the special memorandum account that a client can use without triggering a maintenance call.

hypothecation. A brokerage firm's pledging of margin securities at a bank to secure the funds necessary to carry a client account's debit balance.

I

ID system. See *institutional delivery system* and *trade suite.*

IDCE. See *Intraday Comparison System for Equities.*

illogical position. An account's balance position that appears in the stock record and/or general ledger that can never be correct, such as an account that can only have a credit balance or be flat, appearing as a debit balance.

Immediate or Cancel (IOC). An instruction on an order that requires as many lots as can be filled immediately and the rest of the order canceled.

Income Bonds. Bonds issued when the ability of the issuing company to pay interest is questioned. They are speculative instruments that are to pay high rates of interest if and when the company emerges from its financial difficulty.

indenture. The terms of a corporate bond. Also known as *deed of trust*, it appears on the face of the bond certificate.

Industrial Revenue (ID revenue, ID revs, or industrial rev) Bond. A form of muni bond whose issue's ability to pay interest and principal is based on revenue earned from an industrial complex.

industry utility. A clearing corporation-, depository-, or vendor-supplied service used by industry participants to facilitate operations.

initial public offering (IPO). A security issue brought to market for sale to the public for the first time. This is also referred to as a *primary offering.* When the initial purchasers of the security sell the stock, they sell it in the secondary market.

institution. A entity such as a corporation, mutual fund, pension fund, or trust organization that manages investments.

institutional account. An account belonging to an entity created by law, such as a corporation or mutual fund. This type of account generally operates through a broker/dealer on a delivery-versus-payment (DVP) basis, using the facility of a custodian bank to house its investments.

institutional delivery system. A service by Depository Trust Company (DTC) by which broker/dealers confirm and settle trades electronically. (See *trade suite.*)

interest rate swaps. An exchange of interest rate payments between two parties—for example, fixed-payment loan responsibilities exchange for floating-rate responsibilities.

internal audit. A department or area within the broker/dealer that is responsible for verifying that money and securities positions are maintained on a timely and accurate basis. In addition, they review client accounts and sales practices to ensure that the clients' objectives and goals are being adhered to.

International Security Exchange (ISE). The newest option exchange, it encompasses the use of high-level technology. The ISE is an electronic exchange and does not operate with a physical trading floor.

International Security Identification Number (ISIN). A unique 12-digit number assigned to each security issue. The use of the number in interfirm, interagency, and international transactions removes all doubt or confusion as to what issue is being received or delivered.

Intraday Comparison System for Equities (IDSCE). System used by the AMEX to compare equity transactions entered into by its member firms. This system supercedes the comparison process formerly accomplished at NSCC.

introducing broker. See *correspondent clearing firm.*

inventory management. A term used to describe the use of securities in a firm's various position accounts. By applying securities to the most efficient purposes, it reduces costs and thereby increases profits.

investment banker. A financial institution, such as a broker/dealer, that assists corporations in raising capital through either private means or public offerings.

IPO. See *initial public offering.*

ISE. See *International Security Exchange.*

ISIN. See *International Security Identification Number.*

issue. (1) The process by which a new security is brought to market. (2) Any security.

J

journal. (1) Known as the book of original entry, it is generally the first step in recording a financial transaction to the entity's books. (2) The name of a form that moves security and/or cash positions from one account to another.

junior bond. A bond whose standing in the company is behind other bonds in the collection of interest and, in the case of insolvency, behind the claims of more senior debt instruments.

K

Keogh Plan. One of several tax-deferred retirement plans.

L

ledger. A book of accounts, maintained by an entity, into which financial activity is posted and retained. All financial statements are drawn from the ledger.

legal transfer. A type of security ownership registration transfer that requires legal documentation in addition to the usual forms. Usually, a security registered in the name of a deceased person requires legal transfer.

Letter of Credit. A loan instrument issued and backed by a bank stating an amount of funds that they are willing to lend on behalf of a borrower. The letter is deposited with a third party, such as a clearing corporation, which draws down money as needed to cover net settlement obligations.

liability. Any claim against the corporation's or entity's assets. Accounts payable, salaries payable, and bonds are considered liabilities.

Limit Order. An order that sets the highest price the customer is willing to pay for a security or the lowest price acceptable for a sale. Buy orders may be executed at or below the limit price, but never higher. Sell orders may be executed at or above the limit price, but never lower.

limited tax bond. A muni bond whose ability to pay back principal and interest is based on a special tax.

liquidation. (1) Closing out a position. (2) An action taken by the margin department when a client hasn't lived up to a requirement.

liquidity. The characteristic of a market that enables investors to buy and sell securities easily.

listed stock. Stock that has qualified for trading on an exchange.

load. The sales charge on the purchase of the shares of some open-end mutual funds.

Loan Value. The amount of money, expressed as a percentage of market value, that is part of an amount a customer may borrow from the firm.

long position. (1) In a customer's account, securities that are either fully paid for (a cash account) or partially paid for (a margin account). (2) Any position on the firm's security records that has a debit balance.

M

mainline. The name of the daytime settlement cycle at Depository Trust and Clearing Corporation.

Maintenance Margin. The term used in many products signifying the point at which more collateral is required to be deposited by the client in their account.

management company. The group of individuals responsible for managing a mutual fund's portfolio.

margin. The use of securities in a client account to borrow money against.

margin account. An account in which the firm lends the customer money on purchases or securities on short sales. Customers must have enough equity in the account to pay for purchases by the third business day after trade or meet obligations that may be incurred immediately.

margin department. The operations department responsible for ensuring that customers' accounts are maintained in accordance with margin rules and regulations.

margin excess. See *Reg T excess* and *house excess.*

marginable securities. Securities owned by a broker/dealer's clients on which they can lend funds to their clients. These securities must be approved for margin by the Federal Reserve.

markdown. The charge that is subtracted by a firm, acting as principal, from the price on a sell transaction.

mark-to-market. The process by which the value of a security position is adjusted to reflect its current market value. This is applicable to the value of securities in margin accounts as well as the firm's own proprietary accounts.

Market Order. An order to be executed at the current market price. Buy market orders accept the current offer, and sell market orders accept the current bid.

maturity. The date on which a loan becomes due and payable; when bonds and other debt instruments must be repaid.

MBSD. See *Mortgage Backed Security Division.*

member. An individual who owns a membership (a seat) on an exchange.

member firm. A partnership or corporation that owns a membership on an exchange.

memo seg. A record reflecting the quantity of a certain security required to be locked up in seg. This record informs DTC of which stocks in a firm's position the firm can use to clean up trades and which they cannot because of the firm's seg requirement.

merger. The combination of two or more companies into one through the exchange of stock.

minimum maintenance. Established by the exchanges or other regulatory entity, the level to which the equity in a margin account may fall to before the client must deposit additional equity (money or securities). It is expressed as a percentage relationship between debit balance and equity or between market value and equity.

money market fund. A mutual fund that specializes in securities of the money market, such as T-bills and commercial paper.

money market instruments. Short-term debt instruments (such as U.S. Treasury bills, commercial paper, and bankers' acceptances) that reflect interest rates and that, because of their short life, do not respond to interest rate changes as longer-term instruments do.

Mortgage Backed Securities Clearing Corp. Former name of *Mortgage Backed Securities Division.*

Mortgage Backed Securities Division (MSBD). The part of Fixed Income Clearing Corporation (FICC) responsible for comparing and clearing forward and TBA trades in Mortgage-Backed Securities.

mortgage banker. An agent that facilitates the development of mortgage money by selling either whole mortgages or pooled mortgages into the marketplace.

mortgage bond. A debt instrument issued by a corporation and secured by real estate (such as factories or office buildings) owned by the corporation.

MSRB. See *Municipal Securities Rule Making Board.*

muni. Slang for *municipal bond.*

municipal bond (muni). A long-term debt instrument issued by a state or local government. It usually carries a fixed rate of interest, which is paid semiannually.

municipal note. A short-term debt instrument of a state or local government. Most popular are revenue, bond, and tax anticipation notes.

Municipal Securities Rule Making Board (MSRB). Establishes rules and regulations to be followed in the trading, dealing, and customer relationships involved in municipal securities.

mutual fund. A pooling of many investors' money for specific investment purposes. The fund is managed by a management company, which is responsible for adhering to the purpose of the fund.

Mutual Fund Profile Service. A service offered under the FundServ umbrella by NSCC that updates participants as to the price, dividend distributions, and other information on funds that their clients own.

N

name and address over the wire (NAOW). The electronic process by which new account and client update information is sent from the point of entry (a branch office, for example) to the Client Master Database.

NAOW. See *name and address over the wire.*

NASD. See *National Association of Securities Dealers.*

NASDAQ. See *National Association of Securities Dealers Automated Quotation Service.*

National Association of Securities Dealers (NASD). A self-regulating authority whose jurisdiction includes over-the-counter securities.

National Association of Securities Dealers Automated Quotation Service (NASDAQ). A communication network used to store and access quotations for qualified over-the-counter securities. It is also the electronic trading facility for qualified over-the-counter securities.

National Securities Clearing Corporation (NSCC). A major clearing corporation offering many services to the brokerage community, including comparison and netting of NYSE, AMEX, and over-the-counter transactions. NSCC recently merged with Depository Trust Company (DTC) to form Depository Trust and Clearing Corporation (DTCC).

needs analysis report. A report used by the settlement area of the broker/dealer that prioritizes deliveries to maximize cash flow and minimize interest expense.

negative interest. A process by which the seller pays the buyer interest that will accrue to the buyer by the record date. The process is employed in some countries to account for interest when a bond nears its payment period.

negotiable. A feature of a security that enables the owner to transfer ownership or title. A nonnegotiable instrument has no value.

net asset value (NAV). The dollar value of an open-end fund divided by the number of outstanding fund shares. In an open-end fund quote, the NAV is the bid side; the offer side includes the sales charges.

net worth. Part of the balance sheet presentation. Assets − Liabilities = Net Worth. It is what belongs to the entity after the liabilities are subtracted from assets.

New York Stock Exchange (NYSE). Located at 11 Wall Street, New York, NY, a primary market for buying and selling the securities of major corporations.

1933 Act. See *Truth in Securities Act.*

1934 Act. See *Securities and Exchange Act.*

no-load fund. An open-end fund that does not impose a sales charge on customers who buy their shares.

not held (NH). An indication on an order that the execution does not depend on time; the broker or trader should take whatever time is necessary to ensure good execution.

notional. The amount of principal involved in a swap.

O

OASYS. A communication network between institutional clients and broker/dealers through which orders are entered and broker/dealers report back executions.

OATS. See *order audit trail system.*

OBO. See *order book official.*

OCC. See *Options Clearing Corporation.*

OCO. See *one cancels the other.*

OCS. See *on-line comparison system.*

odd lot. A quantity of a security that is smaller that the standard unit of trading.

Omgeo. A joint venture between Depository Trust and Clearing Corp. and Thomson Financial used in the processing of trades between institutions and their broker/dealers.

on-line comparison system (OCS). The New York Stock Exchange comparison and correction system. It ensures that all transactions entered into between members are compared before they are sent to NSCC for settlement processing.

on the close. A type of order that is to be executed on the last trade of the day.

One Cancels the Other (OCO). An order strategy that is used in certain derivative markets by which the individual attempting to execute the order is given a choice of outcomes. Whichever one occurs first negates the need for the other, so it is canceled.

open-end fund. A mutual fund that makes a continuous offering of its shares and stands ready to buy its shares upon surrender by the shareholders. The share value is determined by net asset value of the fund.

OPRA. See *Option Price Reporting Authority.*

option. A contract that entitles the buyer to buy (call) or sell (put) a predetermined quantity of an underlying security for a specific period of time at a preestablished price.

option class. The group of options, put or call, with the same underlying security.

Option Price Reporting Authority (OPRA). All listed option exchanges report option executions to the Option Price Reporting Authority, which, in turn, disseminates the prices to the public. When you retrieve a quote of an option series from a pricing vendor, it has obtained the information from OPRA.

option series. The group of options having the same strike price, expiration date, and unit of trading on the same underlying stock.

Options Clearing Corporation (OCC). A clearing corporation owned jointly by the exchanges dealing in listed options. OCC is the central or main clearing corporation for the listed options. Options traded on any SEC-regulated exchange can be settled through OCC.

order audit trail system (OATS). An order entry and report monitoring system managed by NASD to ensure that orders are entered and executions are reported on a timely basis.

Order Book Official (OBO). An employee of certain exchanges who executes limit orders on behalf of the membership.

order room. An operations department responsible for monitoring pending orders, recording executions, maintaining customers' GTC orders, and resolving uncompared trades.

order management system. A series of programs that takes an order to buy or sell instruments from the point of entry to the point of execution and back again while entering the results of the trade into the broker/dealer's trade processing system.

order match. Part of an order management system responsible for verifying that the order being entered contains the necessary information to satisfy the broker/dealer's information requirements. It routes the order to the point of execution and locks the execution report to the order, creating one data stream.

ordinary shares. In most other countries, the term for common stock.

OTC. See *over-the-counter market.*

OTCBB. See *Over-the-Counter Bulletin Board.*

Over-the-Counter Bulletin Board. A trading market for equity securities that are not traded on NASDAQ or on exchanges.

over-the-counter market. A network of telephone and telecommunication systems over which unlisted securities and other issues trade. It is primarily a dealers' market.

P

Pacific Exchange (PSX). An exchange located in San Francisco and Los Angeles.

p&s department. See *purchase and sales department.*

par. The value of an instrument equals its face value. A $1,000 bond trading for $1,000 is said to be trading at par.

par value. A value that a corporation assigns to its security for bookkeeping purposes.

participating preferred. Preferred stock whose holders may "participate" with the common stockholders in any dividends paid over and above those normally paid to common and preferred stockholders.

passthrough security. Instrument representing an interest in a pool of mortgages or other types of loans. Passthroughs pay interest and principal on a periodic basis. Unlike conventional bonds that pay back their principal at maturity, these instruments pay back their principal over the life of the instrument.

pattern day trader. An individual who enters into and closes out positions within the confines of a day on a regular basis. They are covered by a different set of margin rules than regular margin accounts.

payable date. The day on which a distribution is made by an issuer's agent to those who owned the security on the date of record.

paying agent. Usually a bank that is acting for a corporation or other such entity and is responsible for the distribution of cash or securities to the entity's issues' owners as part of a corporate action.

PDQ (pretty darn quick). The nighttime settlement process employed by DTCC on the evening of T+2.

penalty bid. A syndicate manager's bid to buy back newly issued securities from the underwriting participant's clients before the syndicate has broken. The underwriting participant loses its selling concession.

penny stock. Extremely low-priced security that trades over the counter.

PER. See *Post Execution Reporting.*

Philadelphia Stock Exchange (PHLX). An equities and options exchange located in Philadelphia.

PHLX. See *Philadelphia Stock Exchange.*

PMM. See *primary market maker.*

point. A unit of measure of price movement. For example, a stock rises one point when its price goes from $23 to $24 per share.

portfolio. The different securities owned in an account of a client. The more that different securities are in the account, the more diversified the portfolio.

post-execution reporting (PER). An electronic order-routing and -reporting system for equity orders entered at the American Stock Exchange (AMEX).

preemptive right. A right, sometimes required by the issuer's corporate charter, by which current owners must be given the opportunity to maintain their percentage ownership if additional shares of the same class are issued. Additional shares of the soon-to-be issued security are offered to current owners in proportion to their holdings before the issue can be offered to others. Usually one right is issued for each outstanding share. The rights and a predetermined cash amount are used to subscribe to the additional shares.

preferred stock. Stock that represents ownership in the issuing corporation and that has prior claim on dividends and, in the case of insolvency, a prior claim on assets ahead of the common stockholder. The expected dividend payment is part of the issue's description.

preliminary prospectus. See *Red Herring.*

primary market. (1) The initial offering of certain debt issues. (2) The main exchanges for equity trading.

primary market maker (PMM). A member of the International Security Exchange (ISE), it is responsible for the fair and orderly trading of assigned options.

prime brokerage. A method by which institutions can execute transactions through several broker/dealers but have the settled transactions reside at one broker/dealer. That broker/dealer provides trade confirmations and monthly statements that reflect all of the institution's activity and positions so that the institution doesn't receive statements from all the broker/dealers with whom they conduct business.

principal. A brokerage firm when it acts as a dealer (principal) and marks up a purchase price or marks down a sale price when reporting the execution. The broker/dealer owns the issue being traded.

priority. A term used to establish an order of events that are about to occur. For example, clearing firms set their preference of when they want to receive stocks as part of their settlement process.

projection report. An electronic report, distributed by National Securities Clearing Corporation, that depicts the firm's current, next-day and the day-after positions due for settlement.

prospectus. A document that explains the terms of a new security offering: the officers, the outside public accounting firms, the legal opinion, and so on. It must be given to any customer who purchases new corporate and certain municipal issues.

proxy. A form and a process for voting via the mail, permitting stockholders to vote on key corporate issues without having to attend an actual meeting.

proxy fight. An attempt by a dissident group to take over the management of a corporation. The group sends proxies that can elect them to the board; the current management sends proxies favoring themselves. The shareholders cast their votes by selecting one proxy or the other.

PSX. See *Pacific Exchange.*

public offering date. The first day a new issue is offered to the public, on or shortly after the effective date.

purchase and sale department. Part of trade processing. Involved with figuration, confirmation and comparison.

put. An option that permits the owner to sell a standard amount of an underlying security at a set price for a predetermined period.

Q

questionable trade (QT). A form used when an NYSE-originated trade cannot be compared by the morning of the trade date plus one.

quote. The highest bid and lowest offer on a given security at a particular time.

R

RAN. See *Revenue Anticipation Note.*

RBO. See *Receive Balance Order.*

real time trade match (RTTM). A real time trade comparison system used by the clearing corporations of Depository Trust & Clearing Corporation (DTCC).

receive balance order (RBO). An order issued by the clearing corporation to any firm with a long (or buy) position remaining after the day's compared trades have been netted. It states what will be received, what must be paid, and who is to deliver.

Receiver's Certificate. A certificate issued when a company is in financial trouble. Its purpose is to provide the company with funds to complete processing cycles so that more money can be obtained through its liquidation.

reclamation. An operations term referring to the erroneous delivery of a security, whereby the sending party recalls (reclaims) the security.

record date. The day that an individual or entity must be owner of record to be entitled to an upcoming dividend, interest payment, or other distribution.

red herring. The preliminary prospectus. The name comes from the advisory that is printed on the face of the prospectus in red ink.

redemption. The retiring of a debt instrument by paying cash.

refunding. The retiring of a debt instrument by issuing a new debt instrument.

Reg T Excess. In a margin account, the amount by which the loan value exceeds the debit balance, or the equity in the account exceeds the margin rate. (See *Regulation T.*)

registered form. The recording of a security's ownership on the issuer's central ledger. The registration may be in the name of the actual owner (beneficial owner) or a legally recognized surrogate (nominee name).

registered trader. A member of an exchange who is responsible for adding liquidity to the marketplace by purchasing or selling assigned securities from his or her inventory. Also known as *competitive market maker* and *option principal member.*

registrar. A commercial bank or trust company that controls and monitors the issuance of securities.

registration statement. Document filed with the Securities and Exchange Commission (SEC) explaining an impending issue and pertinent data about the issuer. Based on the information provided, the SEC either permits or prevents the issue from being offered.

Regular-Way Contract. The first contract sheet received from NSCC that contains compared, uncompared, and advisory data.

regular-way delivery. A type of settlement calling for delivery on the third business day after trade dates for stocks, corporate bonds, and municipals. For government bonds and options, delivery is the first business day after trade.

Regulation A. A regulation governing the issuance of new securities.

Regulation T (Reg T). A federal regulation that governs the lending of money by brokerage firms to their customers.

Regulation U (Reg U). A federal regulation that governs the lending of money on securities by banks to their customers.

Rejected Option Trade Notice (ROTN). A procedure and form by which an uncompared listed option trade on the CBOE is returned to the broker who executed it for reconcilement.

Repurchase Agreement (Repo). (1) An agreement used to finance certain government and money market inventory positions. The brokerage firm sells securities to the financing organization, with the agreement that the firm will repurchase them in the short term. (2) An action similar to stock loan, where securities are lent to borrowers who need the security to satisfy a delivery or other obligation.

restricted account. As defined by Regulation T, a margin account in which the equity balance is below the margin rate but has not decreased to the point where the client must deposit additional collateral.

restricted stock. Stock that is not allowed to be publicly traded because of some failure to meet required standards—for example, shares that have not been registered with the Securities and Exchange Commission.

revenue. Income earned or received by the entity.

Revenue Anticipation Note (RAN). A short-term debt instrument that is issued by municipalities and that is to be paid off by future (anticipated) revenue.

revenue bond. A muni bond whose issuer's ability to pay interest and principal is based on revenue earned from a specific project.

right. See *preemptive right.*

risk arbitrage. The simultaneous purchase and sale of different securities in anticipation of some sort of corporate action.

round lot. A standard trading unit. In common stocks, 100 shares make up a round lot. A round lot of bonds in the over-the-counter market is five bonds.

RTTM. See *real time trade match.*

Rule 144 stock. Stock issued to insiders of a company or an affiliate that cannot be sold for a period of at least one year and, after that, can be sold in accordance with a quantity formula.

Rule 144A stock. Stock that is not fully registered with the SEC but can be sold to and among qualified institutional buyers and high-net-worth individuals.

Rule 145 stock. Stock that was issued as part of a Rule 144 holding that must follow the same procedures as the 144 security. Generally, 145 stock is issued when the issuer of stock being held under Rule 144 declares a distribution, spinoff, or similar type of corporate action.

Rule SHO. This rule is experimenting with doing away with the "tick" rules on short sales. Stocks in the Russell 1000 Index can be sold short without an uptick after the close of business, as can select stocks in the Russell 3000 during the trading day.

Russell indexes. The Russell 3000 index is comprised of two subindexes: the Russell 1000 and the Russell 2000. The index consists of investment-grade securities held by institutions. There are other Russell indexes besides these.

S

SBO. See *Settlement Balance Order.*

scalper. A local trader that operates on the trading floor of the future exchanges. Scalpers trade for their own account and risk addition, and add liquidity to the marketplace.

SEC fee. See *Securities and Exchange Commission (SEC) fee.*

secondary market. The market in which securities are traded after the initial (or primary) offering. Gauged by the number of issues traded, the over-the-counter market is the largest secondary market.

Secured Demand Note. A loan to a company that it can demand payment or if funds are needed. The note issuer has last claim on assets in case of financial difficulties.

Securities and Exchange Act (the 1934 Act). The act governs the lending of money by brokerage firms (Reg T), and includes the short-sale (uptick) rule and requirements regarding trading by insiders or control persons.

Securities and Exchange Commission (SEC). The federal agency responsible for the enforcement of laws governing the securities industry.

Securities and Exchange Commission (SEC) fee. A fee charged on the dollar amount of sell trades executed on national exchanges and NASDAQ.

Securities Industry Automated Corporation (SIAC). The computer facility and trade processing company for NYSE, AMEX, NASDAQ, and NSCC.

security master database. An electronic database containing all the information needed for processing transactions and servicing security positions.

seg. See *segregation.*

Seg Report. An electronic or paper report used by several areas of the cashier or settlement section. It reflects customer securities that are available for use by the firm and those that they cannot touch (those locked up in seg).

segregation. The isolation of securities that the firm may not use for hypothecation or loan. The securities, which must be "locked up" by the firm, represent fully paid-for securities or the portion of a margin account in excess of loanable securities.

sell close. An option transaction that reduces or eliminates a holder's position.

sell open. An option transaction that establishes or increases a writer's position.

selling against the box. A short sale in which the client is also long the security. The tactic is used to "box" a profit or loss for application at another time.

selling concession. A fee paid to a broker/dealer that participates in a security offering.

serial bonds. An issue of bonds that has component parts that mature over a period of years.

settled inventory. The portion of a trader's position that the firm has paid for and maintains. This is the portion that must be financed.

Settlement Balance Order (SBO). An instruction issued between two parties, usually by a clearing corporation, giving details of settlement requirements.

settlement date. The day when a transaction is to be completed. On this day, the buyer is to pay and the seller is to deliver.

settlement date inventory. The total of all positions in a security on settlement date, including vault, transfer, fails, and others.

SFP. See *Stock Futures Product.*

short account. Account in which the customer has sold securities that it does not own or does not intend to deliver against sale. Before a customer may sell short, a margin account must be opened.

short exempt. A phrase used to describe a short sale that is exempt from the short sale rules—for example, buying a convertible preferred, submitting conversion instructions, or selling the common stock before the stock is received.

short position. (1) A position in a customer's account in which the customer either owes the firm securities or has some other obligation to meet. (2) Any position on the firm's stock record having a credit balance.

short sale. The sale of securities that are not owned or that are not intended for delivery. The short seller "borrows" the stock to make delivery with the intent to buy it back at a later date at a lower price.

SIAC. See *Securities Industry Automated Corporation.*

SID. See *standing instruction database.*

side. The opposing, or contra, firm's side of trades. For example, customer agency transactions consummated on an exchange must be offset and balanced against the "opposing firm" or street-side reports.

size. The number of shares available in a quote. For example, if the quote and size on a stock is 9.25–.35 30×50, it means that the bid is $9.25 per share, the offer is $9.35 per share, 3,000 shares are bid, and 5,000 shares are offered. As the trading lot is 100 shares, two zeros are dropped when reporting the size (e.g., 30=30×100=3,000).

SMA. See *special memorandum account.*

Small Order Execution System (SOES). Electronic order-routing, -execution, and -reporting system used by NASDAQ. It accepts orders up to 9,999 shares. It is also known as Super SOES.

SOES. See *Small Order Execution System.*

SOW. See *Stock Over the Wire.*

Special Memorandum Account (SMA). A memorandum field that tracks certain events that could affect a margin account. For example, it stores margin excess that is not used by the client or proceeds of sales if they're not withdrawn by the client.

specialist. A member of certain SEC-regulated exchanges who must make a market in assigned securities. Specialists also act as two-dollar brokers in executing orders entrusted to them.

spread. (1) A long and short option position in either puts or calls on the same underlying stock but in different series. (2) The difference between the bid and offer sides of a quote. (3) In underwriting, the difference between what the issuer received from the underwriter and what the underwriter sells the security for to the public on the offering.

standard margin. A term used in futures products to specify the minimum amount a client must deposit per contract bought or sold.

Standing Instruction Database (SID). An institutional name and address database developed by Depository Trust Company that acts as a central information source for broker/dealers. It currently is known as Omgeo SID.

stock. A security that represents ownership in a corporation and that is issued in shares.

stock/bond power. A form used as a substitute for endorsement of a certificate. The security can be processed for delivery or transfer.

Stock Borrow. See *Stock Loan/Borrow.*

stock dividend. A dividend paid by corporations from retained earnings in the form of stock. The corporation declares the dividend as a percentage of shares outstanding.

stock futures product. A contract setting the price and date for which common stock or another security product is to be delivered at a later date. Unlike an option, where the holder (owner) can decide whether to exercise the privilege, the owner of the future will receive the underlying security from the seller and must pay the seller the contracted price.

stock loan/borrow. Part of the settlement function, this operation's department is responsible for lending excess seg stock and firms' proprietary securities, as well as obtaining securities when needed by the firm. The primary purpose of this activity is to expedite settlement.

stock over the wire. A method by which branch offices, subsidiaries, and so on notify the main office that securities have been received. The main office may then use these issues as part of their inventory management.

stock record. A ledger on which all security movements and positions are recorded. The record is usually in two formats: one showing movements of the security the previous day, and the other showing all current security positions.

stock split. The exchange of existing shares of stock for more newly issued shares from the same corporation. Since the number of shares outstanding increases, the price per share goes down. Splits do not increase or decrease the capitalization of the company; they just redistribute it over more shares. The effect is the adjustment to the trading price.

stop limit order. The order is similar to a stop order, but it becomes a limit order instead of a market order. Buy stop limit orders are entered above the current market; sell stops are entered below it.

Stop Order. A memorandum order that becomes a market order when the price is reached or passed. Buy stops are entered above the current market price; sell stops are entered below it.

STP. See *straight-through processing.*

straddle. Simultaneous long or short positions of puts and calls having the same underlying security and same series designation.

straight-through processing. A processing system that takes an order from the point of entry through execution and settlement in a seamless manner.

street name. A form of registration in which securities are registered in the name of a brokerage firm, bank, or depository, that is acceptable as good delivery.

strike (exercise) price. The price at which an option can be exercised. For example, the owner of a call ZAP April 40 can call in (buy) 100 shares of ZAP at 40; the strike price is $40.

Subordinated Loan. The lending of cash or collateral to a broker/dealer for use in the company. The lender has last claim on assets in case of financial difficulties.

Summary Stock Record. A record displaying all of the accounts carrying security positions for which the firm is responsible. It is produced in order by security and then by account within each security.

Super DOT. See *Designated Order Turnaround.*

super montage. NASDAQ's multimarket screen bringing quotes and other information from several markets, including ECNs, to one location. It is an important step in assisting dealers in their efforts to obtain best execution.

Super SOES. See *Small Order Execution System.*

Supplement Contract. A contract issued by clearing corporations that includes totals from the regular-way contract as well as adjustments and additions.

suspense account. An account that is used temporarily to house securities and/or cash when the true account is unknown.

swaps. The exchange between two parties of currency, interest payments, or commodities.

syndicate. The group formed to conduct an underwriting. It includes the underwriting manager and other underwriters.

synthetic position. A position that results from using derivative products to achieve a false position. A position of sold (short) call options and bought (long) put options is set in anticipation of the underlying security losing market value. This position is said to be a "synthetic short."

T

takeover. The acquisition of control over a corporation by another company, which normally ousts the current management. The takeover can occur by means of a proxy fight or the acquisition of a controlling quantity of common stock.

TAN. See *tax anticipation note.*

tape. A broadcasting facility that disseminates listed trades in order of their occurrence.

Tax Anticipation Note (TAN). A municipal note issued in anticipation of revenues from a future tax.

tax-exempt bonds. Municipal securities or other securities whose interest distribution is free from federal income tax.

TBA. See *to be announced.*

TBS. See *Trade Processing System.*

tender offer. The offer made by one company or individual for shares of another company. The offer may be in the form of cash or securities.

third market. The third market is part of the over-the-counter market. Orders for large quantities of securities are placed with third-market firms that position the security and offer the trades to other large institutions or broker/dealers that specialize in dealing with institutions. The quantity to be bought or sold is generally too large for the usual market to absorb.

to be announced (TBA). A term applied to forward trading of to-be-issued Government National Mortgage Association (GNMA) mortgage-backed securities. It refers to the unique number that GNMA will assign to that specific pool.

trade date. The day a trade occurs.

tombstone ad. An advertisement placed in a newspaper or other periodical listing the underwriters and basic terms of a new issue or secondary offering.

TRACE. See *Trade Reporting and Compliance Engine.*

TRACS. See *Trade Comparison and Reporting Service.*

Trade Comparison and Reporting Service (TRACS). A NASDAQ comparison system used for trades executed via their Alternate Display Facility.

trade date inventory. A term used by trading departments to mean the total of all positions of a security at the start of the trading day.

trade-for-trade settlement. A form of settlement in which the buying clearing firm settles a trade directly with the selling firm. It excludes the use of any netting, CNS, or clearing system.

trade processing system (TPS). An automated system that takes a trade from the point of execution into the settlement process.

Trade Reporting and Compliance Engine (TRACE). All members of the NASD that trade OTC bonds are expected to report their executions to TRACE.

Trade Suite. A set of services offered by Depository Trust Company (DTC) to streamline the trade processing between broker/dealers and their institutional clients.

tranche. Part of a CMO issue with a fixed maturity date. A pool of debt is sectioned and sold with different maturities. Each maturity is a tranche.

transfer. The process by which securities are reregistered to new owners. The old securities are canceled and new ones are issued to the new registrants.

transfer agent. A commercial bank that retains the names and addresses of registered securities owners and that reregisters traded securities to the names of the new owners.

transfer-on-death account. An account whose assets transfer to the beneficiary upon the death of the account's principal.

trial balance. An accounting procedure whereby all cash balances are brought forward to determine that all cash entries were properly posted.

Truth in Security Act (1933 Act). A federal regulation governing the issuance of new corporate securities. The act also covers certain municipal securities and mutual funds.

two-dollar broker. An exchange member who executes orders from other member firms and charges a fee for each execution.

T+. Refers to the settlement cycle of the particular trade. For example, T+3 = means that a trade settles three business days after the trade date.

U

underlying. (1) The security behind an option. (2) The commodity underlying a future contract.

underwriter (investment banker). In a municipal underwriting, a brokerage firm or bank that acts as a conduit by taking the new issue from the municipality and reselling it. In a corporate offering, the underwriter must be a brokerage firm.

underwriting. The process by which investment brokers bring new issues to the market.

underwriting manager. (1) In a negotiated underwriting, the investment banker whose client is the corporation wanting to bring out a new issue. (2) In a competitive underwriting, the lead firm in a group that is competing with other group(s) for a new issue.

Uniform Practice Code. Part of the NASD rules that govern firms' dealings with each other.

unit. At issuance, a package of securities, such as a bond and warrant, that becomes separable at a later date.

USA Patriot Act. A federal act aimed at preventing and curtailing terrorism. It includes anti-money-laundering rules and reporting actions.

U.S. Treasury bill (T-bill). The shortest-term instrument issued by the federal government. The maturities of these discounted issues do not exceed one year at issuance, with three-month (90-day) or six-month (180-day) paper being very common.

U.S. Treasury bond (T-bond). The longest-term debt of the federal government, issued in coupon or interest rate form and usually for 1 to 10 years.

U.S. Treasury note (T-note). An intermediate debt instrument of the federal government, issued in coupon or interest rate form and usually for 1 to 10 years.

unsecured loan. A loan that is supported by nothing but the good name and creditworthiness of the borrower.

uptick. A listed equity trade at a price that is higher than that of the last sale.

V

variation margin. Daily mark to the market on clients' future contract positions.

W

warrant. A security that allows the owner to purchase the issuing corporation's stock for a certain price over a stated period. That period could be 10 or 20 years, and the price of the conversion is much higher than the current price of stock issue. A warrant is usually issued with another security, such as one warranty plus one bond, both of which form one unit.

weekly stock record. See *summary stock record.*

when issued (WI). A phrase applied to securities that are about to be issued and whose settlement date is not set. Usually common stock issued under a rights offering trade WI. Also, government bills that are auctioned on Tuesday but settled on Thursday trade for the days in between as "when issued."

Y

yen. The currency of Japan.

yield. The rate of return on an investment. There are as many computations as there are yields, such as current yield and yield to maturity.

Z

Z tranche (zero tranche). An investment level of a CMO that does not pay interest. It is discounted and resembles a zero-coupon bond.

Index